# EMBRACING MIXED HEALTH SYSTEMS

## Navigating the Development Trap

## World Scientific Series in Health Investment and Financing

**Print ISSN: 2591-7315**
**Online ISSN: 2591-7323**

**Series Editor:** Alexander S. Preker *(Columbia University, USA and Health Investment & Financing Corp, USA)*

---

Most western developed countries offer universal access to healthcare through mechanisms that provide financial protection against its high cost, either through insurance or government subsidy programs.

In most middle- and low-income countries, financing is often at the center of reforms in the healthcare sector. Success or failure of these reforms can have major impact on the political survival of governments that get involved, and major implications for the dynamics of the healthcare industry and overall economy.

With this series, World Scientific will contribute knowledge about a policy area which is still poorly-understood. The series merges policy and practice, exploring the economic underpinnings of real trends in health investment and financing.

The series will appeal and be accessible to investors, the health insurance industry, healthcare actuaries, business schools with healthcare tracts, healthcare management programs, researchers, graduate students, policy makers and practitioners working in the health sector worldwide.

Vol. 7 *Embracing Mixed Health Systems: Navigating the Development Trap*
by April L. Harding and Dominic Montagu

Vol. 6 *Global Health in Practice: Investing Amidst Pandemics, Denial of Evidence, and Neo-dependency*
by Olusoji Adeyi

Vol. 5 *Sustainability: Business and Investment Implications*
edited by Diane-Charlotte Simon, Alexander S. Preker and Susan C. Hulton

Vol. 4 *Health Microinsurance: Implementing Universal Health Coverage in the Informal Sector*
by David M. Dror

Vol. 3 *Financing the Education of Health Workers: Gaining A Competitive Edge*
edited by Alexander S. Preker, Hortenzia Beciu and Eric L. Keuffel

Vol. 2 *Financing Micro Health Insurance: Theory, Methods and Evidence*
by David M. Dror

More information on this series can also be found at https://www.worldscientific.com/series/wsshif

*(Continued at end of book)*

World Scientific Series in Health Investment and Financing – Vol. 7

# EMBRACING MIXED HEALTH SYSTEMS

## Navigating the Development Trap

April L. Harding
Health Investment & Financing Corporation, USA

Dominic Montagu
University of California, San Francisco, USA

World Scientific

EW JERSEY • LONDON • SINGAPORE • BEIJING • SHANGHAI • HONG KONG • TAIPEI • CHENNAI • TOKYO

*Published by*

World Scientific Publishing Co. Pte. Ltd.
5 Toh Tuck Link, Singapore 596224
*USA office:* 27 Warren Street, Suite 401-402, Hackensack, NJ 07601
*UK office:* 57 Shelton Street, Covent Garden, London WC2H 9HE

**Library of Congress Cataloging-in-Publication Data**
Names: Montagu, Dominic, author. | Harding, April, 1964– author.
Title: Embracing mixed health systems : navigating the development trap / author, Dominic Montagu, April Harding.
Other titles: World scientific series in health investment and financing ; v. 7. 2591-7315
Description: New Jersey : World Scientific, [2025] | Series: World scientific series in health investment and financing, 2591-7315 ; volume 7 | Includes bibliographical references and index.
Identifiers: LCCN 2024017565 | ISBN 9789811291845 (hardcover) | ISBN 9789811291852 (ebook for institutions) | ISBN 9789811291869 (ebook for individuals)
Subjects: MESH: Health Care Sector | Public-Private Sector Partnerships
Classification: LCC RA418 | NLM W 74.1 | DDC 362.1--dc23/eng/20240516
LC record available at https://lccn.loc.gov/2024017565

**British Library Cataloguing-in-Publication Data**
A catalogue record for this book is available from the British Library.



For any available supplementary material, please visit
https://www.worldscientific.com/worldscibooks/10.1142/13803#t=suppl

Desk Editors: Aanand Jayaraman/Yulin Jiang

Typeset by Stallion Press
Email: enquiries@stallionpress.com

# Preface

Political debate about healthcare financing and delivery of care continues to present many "false dichotomies" between different approaches: public vs private ownership and service delivery; government vs non-governmental funding; civil service vs contractual employment; planning vs competitive markets; public health vs patient-centered care, etc. The list is long.

In reality, most low- and middle-income countries have "mixed" healthcare systems that reflect various degrees of public and private roles. Likewise, the healthcare systems of OECD countries span a complex range of approaches. This evolution is the result of a recognition that there are no silver bullets in the financing and provision of healthcare. Each approach has its own strengths and weaknesses. No single approach is sufficient on its own. The final balance is the outcome of a "strife of interests" over time.

Although each health system is different, some common patterns have emerged. Most healthcare provided by Ministries of Health, especially in low- and middle-income countries, rely heavily on a centralized national health service model of public funding and delivery of health services. These health systems depend heavily on strategic planning, regulations, benchmarking, and management approaches to both funding and providing care. Policymakers, managers, and providers "tell" patients why they are sick and what to do, relying mostly on "low-powered" incentives like "trust" and "loyalty" to influence patient behavior. Patients either play the game and comply with the rules or are deprived of care with no alternatives. Increasingly, it is recognized that this model of care is bureaucratic and non-responsive to patient's perceived needs, disempowering them from involvement in their own care.

As a result, many of these health systems have tried giving patients a greater "voice" by allowing for feedback through client satisfaction surveys, complaint procedures and lawsuits to address grievances. Although there is a range of "medium-powered" incentives that make funding and healthcare delivery somewhat more responsive to patient needs and expectations, the resulting imbalances between supply and demand almost always lead to long waiting lists, poor quality of care and patient dissatisfaction.

Despite these efforts, such health systems remain bureaucratic and non-responsive, especially when organized in a national and centralized manner. As a result, over the past 30–40 years, many policymakers have begun departing from the national health service model of care by introducing "high-powered" incentives, allowing patients to express their choice more directly through some form of "money-follow-the-patient" mechanism. This empowers patients to "vote with their feet" by "exiting" when they are not satisfied. Funders and providers quickly learn that it hurts their "bottom line" when they are unresponsive to their patients who end up going elsewhere for their care. The funders and providers that survive are those that can deliver "patient-centered care".

The opposite trend is equally true in countries that are at an earlier stage in the development of their health systems. In many low- and middle-income countries that have not yet introduced some form of risk-sharing mechanisms such as health insurance and where public subsidies for healthcare are so low that the range and quality of services provided through the state system is rudimentary and inadequate, patients must rely mostly on direct out-of-pocket payments to providers. Although these health systems rely mostly on "high-powered" incentives and patients can "vote with their feet", such systems leave individuals and families with no financial protection against the high cost of catastrophic illness or expensive care. They are also vulnerable to unscrupulous behavior, profit-seeking providers, and a wider range of known market failures. These healthcare systems are progressing toward more policy, regulatory or quality oversight.

There is no single perfect system. Not surprisingly, in recent decades, there has been a convergence across income levels and regions of the world toward mixed healthcare systems that combine all three incentive regimes: low-, medium- and high-powered.

The authors of this book paint a vivid picture of how, in many countries, the functions of policymaking, planning, monitoring, surveillance, and core medical education are dominated by the public sector, whereas activities in the manufacturing sectors, such as pharmaceuticals, medical technology, health IT and a wide range of other inputs to healthcare, are dominated by the private sector. Everything else is somewhere in between. This includes management, provision of services, diagnostics, financing and allied healthcare activities that are needed to make the health system function.

During normal times, this "organic" evolution and convergence toward "mixed" health systems is in dynamic flux — not static — responding over time to political and ideological pressures on the one hand and market forces on the other hand. As indicated by the contributing authors, over the past few years, population dynamics (aging of the population and epidemiological shifts) as well as fiscal pressures have exacerbated limitations in both funding and delivery of services by the public sector. This has led to an increase in reliance on private funding and private healthcare providers as individuals seek better care outside of government facilities, especially in the case of care for chronic diseases. Patients have a greater awareness about health issues due to easy access to information through the internet and higher expectations about what to expect when seeking care.

This trend ended abruptly with turmoil in healthcare that was brought on by the COVID-19 epidemic. The impending global disaster with millions of anticipated deaths led to a global panic. With a few exceptions, like Sweden, most governments in the OECD reintroduced draconian "command and control" approaches from an earlier era to influence individual behavior and how healthcare providers would respond to the epidemic in a planned and more controlled way than what would be expected from a *laissez-faire* public–private mix.

This return to heavy-handed government intervention in financing, policymaking, management, and service delivery had two major negative effects on the previous evolution of mixed health systems. Both demand for and supply of healthcare for all non-urgent conditions not related to COVID-19 were dramatically reduced by an "executive order" from the public health community to ringfence dedicated capacity to treat and care for an anticipated wave of COVID-19 patients. This was more significant in OECD countries than in emerging economies, but also affected health services in middle- and low-income countries that were overwhelmed by patient demand during the peak of the epidemic. In most healthcare systems that have some form of activity-based reimbursement, this reduction in normal clinical activities (especially higher-paying elective surgery and procedures) affected funding in a dramatic way for healthcare providers, especially in the private sector.

Just as countries started recovering from the negative effects of what in retrospect was probably massive government overreach in response to the COVID-19 epidemic, healthcare providers — especially in the private sector — were once again faced with a new crisis caused by inflation and higher production costs (cost of labor, pharmaceuticals, medical technology, medical supplies, food and energy).

Whereas the epidemic response and dealing with inflation was an opportunity to become more efficient, fix previous weaknesses, build resilience against future shocks like epidemics or climate change, and evolve into something better than they had before, most countries were left struggling with survival. For example, staff were depleted, and those who remained exhausted. There was no money to deal with the backlog that had built up for months. As a result, most healthcare systems in both high-income countries of the OECD and middle- to lower-income countries ended up weaker rather than stronger than before.

In addition, the perceived mishandling of the epidemic by some segments of society has caused a broad backlash against what was perceived by many as an abuse of power by public health agencies and a loss of trust in the public sector.

Now comes the hard task of regaining lost ground by rebuilding capacity, resilience, and trust in mixed healthcare systems. These are among the exciting topics dealt with in detail by the editors and contributing authors of this book.

**Alexander S. Preker**
*Series Editor-in-Chief,*
*World Scientific Series in Health Investment and Financing*

# Acknowledgments

This book is the culmination of nearly a decade of work by the authors and well over two decades of inspiration from friends and colleagues interested in the complexities of mixed health systems around the world. I am particularly grateful to the following individuals: Kara Hanson, for her early work as a graduate student, trying to make some of the first measurements of the scale of private healthcare provision in low- and middle-income countries; April L. Harding, Alexander S. Preker , and Ben Loevensohn, for their leadership in writing on this subject at the World Bank; Anne Mills, Catherine Goodman, Sarah Bennett, and Barbara McPake, who inspired me at LSTHM; Abdo Yazbeck, who was brilliant and approachable on the topic of contracting at the 2001 International Health Economics Association (iHEA) Conference; Birger Forsberg, for inspiring the creation of a social network for those exploring private care during the 2007 iHEA Conference, which eventually grew into a working group and then a network and association affiliated first with iHEA and now with Health Systems Global; Tim Evans and Phyllida Travis, who hired and guided me at WHO in an effort to create a private sector working group; Mukund Uplekar, Mario Raviglione, Knut Lonnroth, Dale Huntington, Henrik Axelson, and Leopold Blanc, who were unstintingly generous with their ideas, friendship, and support while I was in Geneva; David Clarke, who picked up that mantle and created that group a decade later; Ben Bellows, Nirali Chakraborty, Kim Longfield, Steven Chapman, Dana Hovig, Nicki Charman, Guy Stallworthy, Ruth Berg, Kenzo Fry,

Nel Druce, Ruairi Brugha, Lizzie Smith, Gopi Gopalakrishnan, Khama Rogo, and Billy Stewart, who were co-travelers on the path to better understand how private sector engagement could advance and improve health care access and quality — they were not afraid to try, measure, and share with full transparency both successes and failures so as to improve everyone's results; Roger England, who writes with an ease and fluidity that others can only dream of; Ariel Pablos-Mendez, Stefan Nachuk, and Gijs Elzinga, who saw potential in me and supported my early efforts to create private provider networks addressing TB care and HIV; and Cynthia Eldridge and my dear departed friend John Darrah, for their collaboration in that effort.

I am also grateful to the colleagues with whom I have taught and from whom I have learned about private health issues and policy during long and short courses around the world: Pandu Harimurti, Aparaa Somanathan, Malabika Sarker, Shita Listya Dewi, Siripen Supakankunti, Chantal Herberholz, Laksono Trisnantoro, Bill Hsiao, Winnie Yip, Eduardo (Dodo) Banzon, Gerry La Forgia, E.K. Yeoh, Jack Langenbrunner, David Peters, and many others. I also wish to extend my thanks to the following individuals: Chialing Yang and Chiaki Yamamoto; Peter Berman, who was always infuriating for not preparing but still being so charming and eloquent that students loved him best; Bill Savedoff and Jishnu Das, for their inspiring intellectual depth of knowledge, interest, and excitement; Malcolm Potts and Julia Walsh, for encouraging my oddball interest in the private sector during graduate school; George Rutherford and Richard Feachem, who supported my private sector research studies and academic efforts at UCSF; and Heather Kinlaw, Adam Visconti, Andrea Sprockett, May Sudhinaraset, Nadia Diamond-Smith, Amy Penn, Sarah Downs, and Gavin Yamey, who were wickedly fun and brilliant friends and colleagues there.

My thanks to my wife and children, who put up with the many weeks and months I was away doing research and writing for this book, only occasionally making snide comments about how much fun we all seemed to have in the group photos. To paraphrase Robert Frost, in the most fortunate of cases, one's avocation and one's vocation can be one. I have been fortunate in this.

# Contents

# List of Figures

## Chapter 2



## Chapter 3

**Chapter 4**



**Chapter 5**



**Chapter 6**



**Chapter 8**



**Chapter 9**



**Chapter 12**

# List of Tables

**Chapter 12**

# List of Acronyms

| | |
|---|---|
| ACT | Atemisinin-based Combination Therapy (for treatment of Malaria) |
| AFRO | African Regional Office (of the WHO) |
| AIDS | Acquired Immunodeficiency Syndrome |
| AMFm | Affordable Medicines Facility — malaria |
| ARI | Acute Respiratory Infection |
| CCMs | Country Coordinating Mechanisms (of the Global Fund) |
| CSM | Commodity Social Marketing |
| DfID | Department for International Development (of the UK) |
| DHS | Demographic and Health Survey |
| EMRO | European and Middle East Regional Office (of the WHO) |
| FBO | Faith-Based Organization |
| FP | Family Planning |
| GAVI | Global Alliance for Vaccines |
| GCD | Growing Commercial Delivery |
| GFATM | Global Fund for AIDS, TB and Malaria |
| GPOBA | Global Program for Output-Based Aid |
| HBC | High Burden Country (for tuberculosis) |
| HIV | Human Immunodeficiency Virus |
| IMCI | Integrated Management of Childhood Illnesses |
| IPT | Intermittent Presumptive Treatment (of malaria) |
| ITN | Insecticide-Treated Net |

| | |
|---|---|
| KfW | Kreditanstalt Für Wiederaufbau (German Investment and Development Bank) |
| LAPM | Long-Acting and Permanent Methods (of contraception) |
| LLIN | Long-Lasting Insecticide-impregnated Nets |
| LMIC | Low- and Middle-Income Country |
| MDR-TB | Multi-Drug-Resistant Tuberculosis |
| MERG | Monitoring and Evaluation Reference Group (of Roll Back Malaria) |
| MFL | Master Facility List |
| MICS | Multiple Indicator Cluster Survey |
| NGO | Non-Governmental Organization |
| OECD | Organization for Economic Co-operation and Development |
| OOP | Out-of-Pocket Expenditure |
| ORS | Oral Rehydration Solution *or* Oral Rehydration Salts |
| PAHO | Pan-American Health Organization (a regional office of the WHO) |
| PHC | Primary Health Care |
| PMI | President's Malaria Initiative |
| PPMV | Private Patient Medicine Vendor |
| RBM | Roll Back Malaria |
| RCT | Randomized Controlled Trial |
| SEARO | South-East Asian Regional Office (of the WHO) |
| SIDA | Swedish International Development Agency |
| STI | Sexually Transmitted Infection |
| TB | Tuberculosis |
| TSM | Traditional Social Marketing |
| UHC | Universal Health Coverage |
| USAID | United States Agency for International Development |
| WB | World Bank |
| WHO | World Health Organization |
| WPRO | Western-Pacific Regional Office (of the WHO) |

# About the Authors

**April L. Harding**, senior associate with Health Investment and Financing, is an economist and international healthcare policy expert based in Washington, DC, USA. She is a recognized expert on governance arrangements and policy processes in mixed health systems, as well as on public–private partnerships, health system assessment, and health development assistance. She has worked in more than 25 countries, helping governments and project teams undertake health system diagnostics and formulate strategies to address identified problems, typically with the support of the World Bank and other development agencies. With the Center for Global Development, she has conducted research on the delivery of health development assistance and its influence on recipient countries' policy approaches and implementation. In addition to her operational and advisory work, Harding has developed curricula and delivered health policy courses for policy practitioners from developed and developing countries, including a global online course on "Managing Markets for Health" with the University of Edinburgh.

She has published articles on these topics in a range of journals, including *Health Affairs*, *The Lancet*, and the *Bulletin of the World Health Organization*. She has also published co-authored books, such as *Private Participation in Health Services*, with A Preker (2003), and *Innovations in Health Service Delivery: The Corporatization of Public Hospitals*, with A Preker (2003). She was a contributing editor at *Health Affairs* (2007–2009), where she helped the journal increase the range and depth of their international coverage.

Harding received her doctorate in economics from the University of Pennsylvania, USA, and a dual bachelor's degree in Russian and economics from the University of Kentucky, USA.

**Dominic Montagu** is a professor emeritus of epidemiology and biostatistics at the University of California, San Francisco, and the founding CEO of the data-science NGO, Metrics for Management. His research is focused on the private delivery of health services in developing countries and on market functions for health services and health commodities. He has worked extensively in Africa and Asia and has taught on the private sector in developing countries, comparative health systems and health financing, and on regulation of private hospitals and public–private partnerships at UCSF, UC Berkeley, and on behalf of the World Bank, UK, and US development agencies, and others.

**Ruth Berg** is a former managing partner at Palladium. As part of a four-person partnership, she was responsible for business growth, project excellence, strategic partnerships, and client relations. She also oversaw Palladium's International Health Practice, its US health portfolio, and its role as implementation manager of the Utkrisht Development Impact Bond, the world's first maternal health impact bond. Prior to this, she served as Palladium's Vice President of the Center for Private Markets and Vice President of International Health. Before joining Palladium, she held a number of senior roles at Abt Associates, including co-director of Abt's Evaluation Center, project director of USAID's flagship Sustaining Health

Outcomes through the Private Sector (SHOPS) project, and project director of USAID's global Private Sector Partnership-*One* project. Ruth holds an MA and PhD in sociology and demography from the University of Texas at Austin and a BA in economics and international relations from the University of California at Davis.

**Peter Berman** (MSc, PhD) is a health economist with 50 years of experience in research, policy analysis and development, and training and education in global health. He became professor emeritus of population and public health at the School of Population and Public Health, University of British Columbia in Vancouver, Canada, in January 2023, where he had been professor and director. He is also adjunct professor of global health at the Harvard T. H. Chan School of Public Health, where he was previously a professor until 2019. His recent research focuses on government decision-making in response to public health crises. He has also been engaged in health systems research in Ethiopia since 2012. Prior to this recent engagement, Prof. Berman has long been involved in collaborations in India, where he holds an adjunct professorship at the Public Health Foundation of India (PHFI) in New Delhi. He was the founding faculty director of Harvard Chan's Doctor of Public Health degree. He is the editor in chief of the World Scientific publications series on *Global Health Economics and Public Policy* (see https://www.worldscientific.com/series/wssghepp) and the author or editor of six books on global health economics and policy and more than 60 academic papers in his field. A few of his contributions include: co-author of *Getting Health Reform Right: A Guide to Improving Performance and Equity* (Roberts *et al.*, 2018); co-author and editor with Hong Wang of *Tracking Resources for Primary Health Care: A Framework and Practices in Low- and Middle-Income Countries* (World Scientific, 2020); co-editor of the *Guide to the Production of National Health Accounts* (World Bank, World Health Organization, and USAID, 2003); and co-editor of *Paying for India's Health Care* (Berman and Khan, 1993).

**Flavia Bustreo** is a leading physician, public health professional, and advocate for the health and human rights of women, children, adolescents, and the elderly. She is known for taking action on the social and environmental determinants of health.

She is currently the interim chair of Fondation Botnar, chair of the Governance and Ethics Committee at the Partnership of Maternal, Newborn and Child Health (PMNCH), and co-chair of the Lancet Commission on Gender-Based Violence and Maltreatment of Young People. Dr. Bustreo is a member of several boards, including chairing the United Nations University's International Institute for Global Health, and advises several governmental and non-governmental entities, such as the Global Future Council on Health and Healthcare of the World Economic Forum.

Dr. Bustreo was Assistant Director-General for Family, Women's and Children's Health at the World Health Organization (WHO) from 2010 to 2017 and also served as vice-chair of the Board of Gavi, the Vaccine Alliance, from 2015 to 2017. At WHO, she led the organization's work in reproductive, maternal, child, and adolescent health; climate change; aging; vaccinations; health and human rights; and health and gender equity. Previously, she was the executive director of PMNCH and served in a variety of roles at WHO and UNICEF. Dr. Bustreo also worked for seven years at the World Bank, where she managed the WHO–World Bank partnership concerning child health. This included formulating policy, influencing the allocation of resources at the country level through lending instruments, and producing joint publications.

Dr. Bustreo is the author of more than 100 peer-reviewed articles and book chapters in leading medical journals such as *The Lancet* and the *British Medical Journal.* She is also a frequent commentator in the media on public health issues and international issues concerning women and children. For her scholarly work on the right to health, she received an honorary degree from Essex University, UK. She has been the keynote speaker at several academic conferences and has lectured at Cambridge

University and the London School of Hygiene and Tropical Medicine in the UK, the Harvard School of Public Health in the US, the Sapienza University of Rome and Padua University in Italy, the University of Makeni in Sierra Leone, and many other universities.

**Nirali Chakraborty** is the chief strategy officer for Metrics for Management (M4M) and the managing partner of Insight Metrics. At M4M, she is part of the team working to create evidence-based, standardized, and simple performance measures for health services in low- and middle-income countries. Prior to her work at M4M, Dr. Chakraborty oversaw the quality and dissemination of Population Services International's reproductive health-related research internationally. Nirali also previously worked as a consultant for the World Bank and Broad Branch Associates, specializing in health systems and performance-based financing, and has expertise in quantitative research methods. Dr. Chakraborty has conducted research and published articles on social franchising, health equity, health workforce performance, reproductive health, and maternal health. Nirali received her PhD in international health, with a concentration in health systems, from the Johns Hopkins Bloomberg School of Public Health.

**Catherine Goodman** is a professor in health economics and policy at the London School of Hygiene and Tropical Medicine, UK. She has over 25 years of experience in applied health systems research in low- and middle-income settings, including extended periods based in Kenya and Tanzania. Her work focuses on understanding private sector engagement in healthcare provision and evaluating interventions to improve this, such as regulation, accreditation, social franchising, social marketing, and quality improvement.

**Albert Kilian**, now retired, is a malaria expert with 28 years of experience in all aspects of malaria control, from strategy and policy development and implementation at district, national, and international levels to epidemiological and operations research to surveillance, monitoring and evaluation, and learning. He has worked for a variety of organizations, including the German Technical Cooperation (GTZ), the US Centers for Disease Control and Prevention, the Malaria Consortium, and Tropical Health — a consultancy firm he co-founded and where he served as technical director. One of his special interests has been the prevention of malaria with insecticide-treated mosquito nets (ITNs), and in this context, he has worked intensively with the private sector, internationally through the Roll Back Malaria Partnership activities, but also in many African countries. This included public–private partnership projects to promote the ITN retail market in Uganda and Mozambique, supporting social marketing and voucher schemes in Uganda, Tanzania, and Nigeria, comprehensive ITN market analysis and the development of action plans to incorporate the private sector into the national malaria elimination strategy in Tanzania and Nigeria, and detailed retail market analyses in several African countries.

**Christine Oduor** is the global head of program management — digital health at Population Services International (PSI). She happily refers to herself as the "voice of the digital consumer," working closely with other insight teams across the organization to provide consumer digital insight leadership and help narrate a unified, cohesive, and actionable story, committed to ensuring that all business and user needs are met in the digital experience.

Christine has over 12 years' experience in project management and social and market research in public health. She has a background in population studies and a bachelor's in education from the University of Nairobi.

When not on the job, this Kenyan native can be found on the nature trails, hiking, camping, or working her culinary magic!

**Amy Penn** is a primary care physician at Kaiser Permanente in the US' Northern California region. Prior to her medical education at the University of California, San Francisco, and internal medicine residency at Kaiser in the US, she was a research assistant and educator at UCSF Global Health Sciences, where she also obtained her master in science degree. Her research interests cover various domains, including HIV medication adherence and "lost to follow-up," social franchising, and obstetric emergencies in developing countries.

Professor **Alexander S. Preker** is a globally recognized expert on financing, capital investment, private sector development, and market-based solutions to public policy challenges. He is the President and CEO of the Health Investment & Financing Corporation and a member of the board of several companies and organizations, including the USA HealthCare Alliance (USAHA) that works closely with the US Department of Commerce and the Export–Import Bank of the USA (EXIM).

Prior to his current work, Professor Preker had a distinguished career, working at different times for the World Bank Group (WBG), including the International Bank of Reconstruction and Development (IBRD), the International Development Association (IDA), and the International Finance Corporation (IFC). At various times, he was on external assignments with the World Health Organization (WHO) and the International Labour Organization (ILO). From 2007 to 2012, Professor Preker was the Head of the Health Industry Group and Investment Policy for the Investment Climate Department of the World Bank/IFC. The department was a leader in investing in new solutions to the threats of climate change, infrastructure, public–private partnerships, health and education, e-Government solutions, and competition. He and his team set up a US$1 billion Investment facility to improve the market environment for private sector participation and expand small and medium-sized businesses in the Africa Region and did the preparatory work to set up a similar facility for Asia.

Professor Preker has published extensively, having written many scientific articles and authored over 20 books. He is the Editor-in-Chief of the *World Scientific Series on Health Investment and Financing*.

Previously, Professor Preker was the Chair of the Editorial Board for the *World Hospitals and Health Services* journal of the International Hospital Federation (IHF) and is now an Honorary Member of the Governing Council of the Federation. During his tenure at the World Bank, he was a member of the Editorial Board for the World Bank's External Operations Publication Department and Editor-in-Chief of the Bank's *Health, Nutrition, and Population Series*.

Professor Preker holds several academic appointments. He is an Adjunct Associate Professor of Health Policy and Management at Columbia University, an Executive Scholar at the Icahn School of Medicine at Mount Sinai in New York and a Lecturer with the joint Ecole des Hautes Etudes commerciales de Paris (HEC)–Weill Cornell Medicine-Qatar Leadership Program. His education includes a PhD in Economics from the London School of Economics and Political Science, an MD from the University of British Columbia/McGill, and a Diploma in Medical Law and Ethics from Kings College, London.

**Mukund Uplekar** recently retired as a senior medical officer from the policy, strategy, and innovations unit of the Global TB Programme at the World Health Organization (WHO) in Geneva. Prior to his tenure at WHO, he was in private medical practice in Mumbai, India, while also working with voluntary organizations in Mumbai and Pune engaged in community health research. During his tenure at WHO, spanning nearly two decades, Dr. Uplekar coordinated the development and drafting of WHO's expanded DOTS strategy in 2002, the Stop TB Strategy in 2006, and the current End TB Strategy endorsed by the World Health Assembly in May 2014. In parallel, Dr. Uplekar was instrumental in formulating, experimenting, and promoting global policies and strategies for engaging private care providers in TB response through "public–private mix" (PPM) approaches. Since its inception, he led the WHO-based Secretariat of the Stop TB

Partnership's global Working Group on PPM for TB care and prevention. Currently, Dr. Uplekar resides in Pune, India, where he is an honorary professor at Pune University's School of Health Sciences.

**Adam Visconti** is a family medicine-trained physician and assistant professor at the Georgetown University School of Medicine Department of Family Medicine, US. He completed training in public health at UC Berkeley and medicine at UC San Francisco, both in the US. He has published on numerous topics, including primary care for people who inject drugs, economic analysis for hepatitis C treatment, comparative health systems, and HIV prevention. Beyond his medical and research activities, Dr. Visconti recently served as chief medical officer for the District of Columbia Department of Health's HIV/AIDS, Hepatitis, Tuberculosis, and Sexually Transmitted Infections Administration.

**Joyce Wanderi** is a public health leader with two decades of experience in the design and implementation of public health programs in Africa. She has spearheaded several initiatives on private sector engagement in health, including social franchising for health, access to affordable credit, and health financing to improve access and quality of health services. She is very passionate about improving the plight of women and girls; what began as a career has become a true purpose for her: making a difference in women's lives.

# Summary of Chapter Abstracts

## Part 1 Overview

### Chapter 1. The Private Sector and Public Health

*Dominic Montagu*

This chapter provides an introduction to the book and an overview of the types of private providers of healthcare and health services in low- and middle-income countries (LMICs).

In most countries, healthcare services are delivered by a combination of both public and private providers – pharmacies, clinics, hospitals, and everything in between. While governments are responsible for the overall management of healthcare, including the education of health professionals, the provision of medical supplies, disease outbreak surveillance, and assuring the quality of care, they are not responsible for all provision of care and seldom pretend to that role.

During the past decades, population growth and limited tax revenues have, in some countries, exacerbated inadequate governmental health financing and therefore increased the importance of, and reliance on, private provision as citizens seek care outside of government facilities. Aging populations, the epidemiological shift toward long-term management of non-communicable diseases, growing private investment, ease of access to information, and greater awareness and higher expectations among patients have all contributed to the increasing importance of private healthcare provision in many LMICs.

The private sector represents a significant part of healthcare services in nearly all countries, sometimes the dominant part. Despite this, data collection, effective integration into referral and reporting systems, and guarantees of quality and cost limits are all weak in most LMICs. This needs to change, and it seems likely to. There is a growing recognition that improving the reach, quality, and equity of health systems will be possible only if the public and private sectors work together and that no government can afford to ignore the role of the private sector in its health system. If properly engaged and regulated, the private sector can positively contribute to the population's healthcare needs and strengthen the overall health system of the country.

## Part 2 Size, Scale, and Context

### Chapter 2. The Provision of Private Healthcare Services in European Countries: Recent Data and Lessons for Universal Health Coverage in Other Settings

*Dominic Montagu*

In this chapter Dominic Montagu uses the well-documented experiences of countries in Europe to show what is and isn't possible to accomplish through a health system that encompasses well-regulated and centrally funded private health providers. These lessons are given as examples to understand the potential for LMICs in addressing system integration in subsequent chapters.

Universal Health Coverage (UHC) exists in all of the countries in Europe, despite variation in the ownership structure of healthcare delivery systems. As countries around the world seek to advance UHC and manage the private sector within their health systems, the European experiences can offer useful insights. We found four different models for the provision of healthcare, with the private sector predominant in some countries but of minimal importance in others. The European experiences indicate that UHC can be effectively provided with or without large-scale private sector provision in hospitals, and specialty, and primary care services, and that, moreover, it can be provided with high levels of patient satisfaction.

These findings offer regulatory models for countries in other regions to review as they advance UHC. Better regulation of the private sector is a key requirement for more efficient and effective management of mixed public and private systems, as described in the rest of the book.

## Chapter 3. Standard Survey Data: Insights into Private Sector Utilization

*Dominic Montagu and Nirali Chakraborty*

Authors Dominic Montagu and Nirali Chakraborty explore who uses the private sector and for what in this chapter. Universal health coverage in LMICs is increasingly expanding through the incorporation of private clinics, pharmacies, and hospitals into an overall health system funded in whole or in part through government-managed health insurance. This underscores the importance of policies on health provision, which apply across the whole delivery system regardless of ownership status. In this chapter, we summarize current knowledge on the scale and scope of private provision in LMICs. To accomplish this, we have analyzed data on the source of inpatient and outpatient care from 65 countries. While past studies have conducted similar analyses, ours advances the field in two ways. First, we limit our analysis to data sets from 2010 to 2019, making our study more up-to-date than past studies, while changing health-seeking patterns for maternal health since 2010 means that our data set is more representative of overall inpatient care. Second, while past multi-country analyses of public–private ownership have been based on the Demographic Health Surveys, we have added to this data from the Multiple Indicator Cluster Surveys, significantly increasing the number of countries in our analysis.

Key findings from our analysis, according to the World Health Organization regions, are as follows: outside of the EURO region, where the private sector delivers just 4% of all healthcare services, the private sector remains significant and, in many countries, represents more than half of all care. The private sector provides nearly 40% of all healthcare in PAHO, AFRO, and WPRO regions, 57% in SEARO, and 62% in EMRO. While specific countries with two recent surveys show variation in the scale of both inpatient and outpatient private provision, we did not find regional or global trends toward or away from private care within LMICs. Private inpatient care is most important for the wealthy in many countries; public versus private care varies less, by wealth, for outpatient services.

## Chapter 4. Who Serves the Poor? An Equity Analysis of Public and Private Providers of Family Planning and Child Health Services in Kenya

*Nirali Chakraborty, Dominic Montagu,*
*Joyce Wanderi, and Christine Oduor*

This chapter further explores clients of the private sector, focusing on equity. Authors Nirali Chakraborty, Dominic Montagu, Joyce Wanderi, and Christine Odour assess differences in the wealth status of clients of family planning and child health services by health sector. It also describes the reasons for facility choice, the cost of services, and the proportion of additional clients of these services and assesses if there are any differences by health sector.

A cross-sectional survey of 2,173 clients from 96 health facilities in urban areas of six counties in Kenya was conducted, stratified by health facility type. The four strata were public, faith-based, private for-profit, and social franchise. Client wealth was benchmarked against the national and urban population of the 2014 Kenya DHS and assessed using EquityTool.

There were significant differences in client wealth distribution between facility types, and public sector facilities served a significantly higher proportion of poor clients than other types of facilities. In all three non-public facility types, more than 25% of clients were from the poorest two wealth quintiles, without significant differences between facility types. No facility type stands out as expanding access to health services more than another.

Results show that social franchises do better at reaching out to the poor than earlier studies have indicated, though not as well as faith-based and public facilities. The findings suggest that private providers remain important within the larger health system, more so for family planning than childhood illness management. In urban areas with significant facility choice, this study quantifies differences in client wealth across four health sectors. Incorporating these findings into policy and programmatic interventions can improve equity in access to and use of quality health services.

## Chapter 5. Prohibit, Constrain, Encourage, or Purchase: How Should We Engage with the Private Health-Care Sector?

*Dominic Montagu and Catherine Goodman*

This chapter, originally published in *The Lancet* sets out a framework for understanding how governments and donor agencies can, and should, work with or regulate the private sector. Authors Dominic Montagu and Catherine Goodman set out the context of the private for-profit sector's prominence in healthcare delivery, concerns about its failures to deliver social benefit, and the resulting search for interventions to improve the sector's functioning. From that starting point, the chapter reviews the evidence for the effectiveness and limitations of such private sector interventions in LMICs and sets out a framework for defining the focus of different interventions.

While few robust assessments are available, some conclusions are possible. Prohibiting the private sector is very unlikely to succeed, and regulatory approaches face persistent challenges in many LMICs. Attention is therefore turning to interventions that encourage private providers to improve quality and coverage (while advancing their financial interests), such as social marketing, social franchising, vouchers, and contracting.

Evidence about the effect on clinical quality, coverage, equity, and cost-effectiveness is inadequate for generalizations. While interventions have been effective in many instances, for example, in addressing a number of specific, focused problems related to cost, access, efficiency, and quality on a restricted scale, challenges remain concerning scalability and scope, indicating the limitations of such interventions as a basis for universal health coverage.

## Chapter 6. Recent Trends in Working with the Private Sector to Improve Basic Healthcare – A Review of Evidence and Interventions

*Dominic Montagu, Catherine Goodman, Peter Berman, Amy Penn, and Adam Visconti*

Building on the framework from Chapter 5, Dominic Montagu and Catherine Goodman, along with Peter Berman, Amy Penn, and Adam Visconti, use this chapter to look at the evidence and practice that exists for a set of key private-sector engagement interventions.

A number of interventions in LMICs have, for many years, applied different models of subsidy, support, and engagement to address social and efficiency failures in private healthcare markets. This chapter reports on a review of these models and the evidence in supporting them to better understand what interventions are currently common, and to what extent practice is based on evidence. Using the typology from Chapter 5, we examined five models of intervention with private markets for care: commodity social marketing, social franchising, contracting, accreditation, and vouchers.

To bring together the evidence for this evaluation, we conducted a systematic review of both published and gray literature, identifying programs large enough to be cited in publications and studies of the listed intervention types. A total of 343 studies were included in the review, including both published and gray literature. We identified 380 programs, the earliest having begun operation in 1955. Commodity social marketing programs were the most common intervention type, with 110 documented programs operating for condoms alone at the highest period. Existing evidence shows that these models can improve access, utilization, and, possibly, quality; however, for all program types, the overall evidence base remains weak, with practice in private sector engagement consistently moving in advance of evidence. Future research should address key questions concerning the impact of interventions on the market as a whole, the distribution of benefits by socioeconomic status, the potential for scale-up and sustainability, cost-effectiveness compared to relevant alternatives, and the risk of unintended consequences. Alongside better data, a stronger conceptual basis linking program design and outcomes to context is needed.

# Part 3 Lessons from the Field

## Chapter 7. Private Patients Prelude: The Poor Health of Health Programs

*April L. Harding*

This chapter shifts from the larger "systems" perspective to a focus on healthcare delivery, the programs which focus on specific services, and the beneficiaries of those programs. Data, however well collated, cleverly analyzed, and thoughtfully interpreted, can only provide a skeleton on which to hang our understanding of private healthcare delivery in LMICs: how the private sector is viewed by clients; what it means for providers, both those working full time in the private sector and those employed both in the public and private sectors; and how governments and international development agencies think about and react to the private sector.

This chapter provides an introduction to the views and priorities of patients in selecting care for themselves or their loved ones, what factors matter, and when and how real people deal with difficult choices.

## Chapter 8. Private Sector: Here, and Here to Stay

*Dominic Montagu*

In this chapter, Dominic Montagu provides the opposite context: exploring what is known about the providers who deliver services in LMICs. As the chapter title states, "Private Sector: Here, and Here to Stay." Private sector healthcare providers, in all but the most dysfunctional failed states, function within a health system that is measured, regulated, and policed. This chapter sets out, in brief, the ways in which governments think about the private sector, categorize the different parts of it, and regulate it (well or badly). This is, in turn, influenced by clear trends in market functioning, which drive how different components of the private sector function.

There are a few rules of thumb which hold true in nearly all countries. Products – medicines, self-administered test kits, and beauty products – are all more likely to be sold by private providers than public providers. These might be shops, drug vendors, patent-medicine sellers, chemists, or pharmacies, depending on the product and the country, but the source will almost invariably be private.

Ambulatory care is more likely to be private than public. That's particularly the case with dentists and non-clinical specialists (psychiatrists, optometrists, etc.), but it is also true for primary care doctors. In most LMICs, most primary care doctors work in solo practices, and while they might have a "day job" in a government facility, most of their time is spent in their private clinics, and most of their income comes from that after-hours private practice.

Hospitals, by contrast, are likely to be public in most countries – subsided by governments, absorbing a large portion of the national health budget, and being a visible indicator of public healthcare assurance. Uncertain regulations and duplicative or complex subsidies (i.e. paying for facility infrastructure from one budget, provider salaries from a second, and consumables used during care from a third) make public services likely to be continued even when questions about their comparative advantages over the private sector exist.

In financing and in oversight, government attitudes toward the private sector influence what services are delivered where, to whom, and by whom. The framing of this chapter sets the scene for the following case studies.

## Chapter 9. The Private Sector and Malaria

*Albert Kilian*

Albert Kilian describes the complexities of diagnosis, treatment, and prevention in this chapter. Malaria is a major killer in the developing world. In 2012, approximately 207 million episodes of clinical malaria occurred, leading to the deaths of an estimated 627,000 people – mostly African, mostly children, and mostly poor. Programs to reduce malaria mortality focus on prevention, often mosquito abatement or the use of nets to prevent mosquito bites at night, or treatment, increasingly with effective combinations of effective medicines.

This chapter examines the experience with malaria programs and private sector engagement to shed light on when and how the private sector can contribute to delivering malaria interventions. We examine how the habits and operating norms of the agencies and people involved in the global malaria effort have influenced the consideration and deployment of such strategies.

Through a series of case studies, we argue that while malaria programs have achieved remarkable increases in net ownership and use deployment, they have faced rather more difficulty increasing treatment coverage. This is at least, in part, because national malaria programs' focus on speed, product procurement, and distribution has discouraged the development of strategies to mobilize private drug sellers, net producers, distributors, and retailers. Program managers and donors, in many countries, need to shift to diversifying their strategies, adding private sector channels, so that programs can achieve broader goals.

## Chapter 10. The Private Sector in TB Programs

*Mukund Uplekar*

This chapter by Mukund Uplekar describes drawing on his many years leading the World Health Organization's work to guide private sector engagement with national TB programs around the world. Developing country governments and global agencies have responded to TB's resurgence as a serious health threat with stepped-up resources and attention to control programs. Initially, donor-supported TB programs sought to reach patients primarily through public facilities. Where most TB sufferers were seeking private care, the results were disappointing.

Based on considerable evidence that private engagement can accelerate TB control, global health organizations now advocate engaging private practitioners, and some countries have taken important steps in this direction. Programs which pursue engagement frequently succeed, for example, in improving private providers' practices. Still, the magnitude of the effort falls short of the private sector's potential contribution to TB control. A number of countries with a high TB burden are unlikely to achieve the desired reductions in TB cases without expanding the engagement of private providers. Donors and technical agencies may accelerate progress by refining this dimension of TB program strategy in countries where private providers play a large role in the healthcare provision system.

## Chapter 11. Family Planning and the Role of the Private Sector

*Ruth Berg and April L. Harding*

Ruth Berg and April L. Harding draw on years of experience with program design and management in this chapter on "Family Planning and the Role of the Private Sector." Like many health innovations, access to and use of contraceptives in the developing world initially lagged far behind that in wealthier countries. In the 1960s, several aid agencies and philanthropies mobilized to address this gap via support for developing countries' family planning (FP) programs. From the mid-1960s to the mid-1990s, average fertility in the developing world fell from six to three children per woman. Some estimates attribute 43% of the decline in world fertility during this period to FP programs.

Today, the local private sector contributes considerably to FP efforts in many developing countries. In addition to large numbers of unaffiliated providers and retailers, private non-profit organizations contribute to FP through a range of strategies, including social marketing, social franchising, and vouchers, as well as through more systemic mechanisms, such as insurance coverage and contracting. Private distributors, pharmacies, and retail outlets make it easy for people to pick up condoms, pills, spermicides, and other products. Many social insurance organizations cover FP services provided by public and private providers. In some countries, health agencies contract with private providers for a service package which includes FP. Private organizations perform critical stewardship activities too. Under social marketing, they often manage health communication activities and coordinate private distributors' and retailers' efforts. Under social franchising, they accredit and monitor providers. Under social insurance and voucher schemes, they verify whether services have been provided and manage reimbursements.

## Chapter 12. Child Health

*Flavia Bustreo*

This chapter by Flavia Bustreo looks at the experience of programs and policy initiatives related to child health and tries to understand why these problems occur. In particular, it aims to understand why these programs tend to be implemented without engaging the private sector and what impact this has. Our research indicated that ignoring private provision is undermining program impact in many countries, and our analysis yielded some suggestions about program design and policy changes at the country level.

In this chapter, we examine how donor support is developed and implemented and how these processes influence the problems we observe.

From this analysis, we suggest changes that donors can make in their development assistance for child health. We indicate where these changes are needed to improve program impact, especially where the context makes it likely that the private health sector will need to be brought into programs to help them achieve their goals.

Programs should, as a priority, scrutinize existing health system data from household, provider, and retailer surveys. They should aim to identify the most critical gaps between the populations they target to reach and the best available evidence on where those people are obtaining their services and products. Where private actors are playing a significant role, local consultation is necessary to identify where there is both capacity and willingness to engage in public–private collaborations. Program managers should seek opportunities for collaboration around the manufacture and distribution of products (e.g. fortified foods and oral rehydration salts). Where provider networks are substantially private, officials should consider contracting, either by public or social insurance agencies; "lighter touch" collaboration with private providers to expand coverage of priority interventions should also be considered (e.g. for immunization).

To achieve all of this, it is vital that political will and commitment exist at the global, national, and local levels to expand private sector participation, as well as coordination and communication among the multiple stakeholders.

## Afterword

*Alexander S. Preker and April L. Harding*

The authors of the Afterword, Alexander S. Preker and April L. Harding, review the institutional economics and the organizational underpinnings of mixed healthcare systems. They initially trace the historical context of healthcare systems as they have evolved over time. Then, they review the theoretical underpinnings of mixed healthcare systems from the perspective of both neo-classical microeconomics and organizational theory rooted in new institutional economics. This is followed by a detailed analysis of both market failure in private healthcare markets and government failure observed in large state-run national healthcare systems that are typical of government health services run by Ministries of Health at all country income levels. Following that, the authors look at a range of instruments available to governments in addressing market failure — from least to most intrusive. These include doing nothing, requiring information disclosure, introducing regulations, contracting for services through prepayments, direct payments, subsidies through reimbursements, mandates, guaranteeing universal access, and public production. This is followed by a discussion on recent trends in the reform of mixed healthcare systems and what policymakers can do to take decisions about when to "make or buy" healthcare goods and services "in-house" or "contract out" to non-governmental and private funders and providers of healthcare. The final section of the chapter looks at how to get from "here to there" in terms of creating high-performing mixed healthcare systems. The authors conclude that policymakers could significantly improve the performance of their healthcare systems by empowering patients to get more involved in their own care by giving them a greater voice in their care and giving them an "exit" — "voting with their feet". Such reform would require policymakers to depart from their historical dependence on loyalty and trust by patients in underperforming healthcare, which is seen in so many countries, and secure a strong policy framework and high performance of mixed health systems. These topics are central to understanding mixed health systems.

# Part 1

# Overview

# Chapter 1

# The Private Sector and Public Health

**Dominic Montagu**


## Abstract

This chapter provides an introduction to the book and an overview of the types of private providers of healthcare and health services in low- and middle-income countries (LMICs).

In most countries, healthcare services are delivered by a combination of both public and private providers – pharmacies, clinics, hospitals, and everything in between. While governments are responsible for the overall management of healthcare, including the education of health professionals, the provision of medical supplies, disease outbreak surveillance, and assuring the quality of care, they are not responsible for all provision of care and seldom pretend to that role.

During the past decades, population growth and limited tax revenues have, in some countries, exacerbated inadequate governmental health financing and therefore increased the importance of, and reliance on, private provision as citizens seek care outside of government facilities. Aging populations, the epidemiological shift toward long-term management of non-communicable diseases, growing private investment, ease of access to information, and greater awareness and higher expectations among patients have all contributed to the increasing importance of private healthcare provision in many LMICs.

The private sector represents a significant part of healthcare services in nearly all countries, sometimes the dominant part. Despite this, data collection, effective integration into referral and reporting systems, and guarantees of quality and cost limits are all weak in most LMICs. This needs to change, and it seems likely to. There is a growing recognition that improving the reach, quality, and equity of health systems will be possible only if the public and private sectors work together and that no government can afford to ignore the role of the private sector in its health system. If properly engaged and regulated, the private sector can positively contribute to the population's healthcare needs and strengthen the overall health system of the country.

## 1. Introduction

In most countries, healthcare services are delivered by a combination of both public and private providers – pharmacies, clinics, hospitals, and everything in between. This is true despite the persistent widespread perception in many LMICs that both financing and delivery of health services are the responsibility of the government, with care delivered by government facilities, either free at the point of care or at a highly subsidized rate. Healthcare provided by the public sector is seen both as a public entitlement and a societal safety net. Governments are indeed responsible for the overall management of healthcare, including the education of health professionals, the provision of medical supplies, disease outbreak surveillance, and assuring the quality of care, wherever provided (Lagomarsino *et al.*, 2009; World Health Organization, 2020; World Bank, 2011). They are, indubitably, not responsible for all provision of care and seldom pretend to that role.

During the past decades, population growth and limited tax revenues have, in some countries, exacerbated inadequate governmental health financing and therefore increased the importance of, and reliance on, private provision as citizens seek care outside of government facilities (Hooda, 2017; Davalbhakta *et al.*, 2020). In countries with rapidly expanding economies, these challenges are lower; however, in some instances, growing middle classes have led to an increase in demand for healthcare, outstripping the capacity of government facilities and, again, leading to the expansion of private provision (Hort and Annear, 2012). Aging populations, the epidemiological shift toward long-term management of non-communicable diseases, growing private investment, ease of access to information, and greater awareness and higher expectations among patients have all contributed to the increasing importance of private healthcare provision in many LMICs (Mackintosh *et al.*, 2016).

## 2. Private Health Sector and Private Healthcare Sector

The private sector ranges from informal caregivers using traditional or indigenous systems of medicine to the Western system of medicine. It includes both "for-profit" and "non-profit" groups. Polyclinics, nursing homes, specialty hospitals, and hospitals affiliated with medical colleges constitute various forms of private sector facilities. Further differentiation within the private sector exists according to the primary funding source (user fees, donations, government contracts, or insurance) and level of quality assurance (accredited or not, and by whom). While most private sector providers and facilities are autonomous, in a number of middle-income countries, the proportion of "corporate" hospitals and hospital chains, while still small, is growing (Morgan and Ensor, 2016).

The most significant sub-division within the private sector is according to ownership and motivation. Not-for-profit providers are typically health facilities funded or managed by philanthropic, religious, or charitable trusts and, in some countries, by external donors and are termed *non-governmental organizations* (NGOs). Although there are a small number of countries where religious hospitals provide up to one-quarter of facilities and care (notably the Philippines, Indonesia, Tanzania, and Benin), in most countries the private sector is overwhelmingly for-profit (Montagu and Chakraborty, 2021; Kagawa *et al.*, 2012). This is particularly true for dispensing and outpatient diagnostic services, which are nearly always both private and for-profit. Examples include pharmacies, drug sellers, and laboratories for routine tests (Babar, 2021).

## 3. Characteristics and Attributes of the Private Healthcare Sector

### 3.1 *Evolution and growth of private healthcare providers*

Healthcare services originated, in most countries, from for-profit private practitioners and charitable clinics and hospitals. In Sub-Saharan Africa, the backbone of health services before 1960 was mission hospitals and clinics (McPake, 2009). In Latin America, it was the same, and early hospitals were established by the Catholic Church (León-Cortés *et al.*, 2019). Government prominence in care provision took over in many countries, but with only a few exceptions, made space for private care to exist in parallel (León-Cortés *et al.*, 2019). In Vietnam, Cambodia, and Laos, the government started allowing private medical services in the early 1990s, and they have been growing rapidly since then (Hort and Annear, 2012; Witter, 1996; Chuc and Tomson, 1999).

The growth of private provision in recent decades has been rapid in many countries, particularly those, such as China, Vietnam, Kazakhstan, and Tanzania, which have transitioned from planned to market-based economies. However, health systems are slow to change, and the global data do not support a universally shared trend toward private sector growth. Two analyses of global household survey data in the past 15 years agree that private sector care provision is growing in some countries, shrinking in others, and overall largely static as a proportion of all care provided (Montagu and Chakraborty, 2021; Grépin, 2016). There are, nevertheless, some clear global commonalities: charitable care is less important now than 50 years ago, and for-profit care is more significant. In nearly all countries, private provision is much more predominant in urban settings, where patients are numerous and incomes are higher. Population density and greater wealth, for obvious reasons, make the business of healthcare – whether in a pharmacy or a hospital – more attractive to providers, investors, and entrepreneurs.

## 3.2 *Responsiveness of private healthcare providers*

For patients, private providers are often popular because they are easy to access, have longer working hours, and have shorter waiting times, which are critical to the working poor who cannot afford a day off from work to wait for medical treatment. Private providers are also seen to be responsive to the spoken and unspoken demands or expectations of patients, even when contrary to medical best practices. Antibiotics are available over the counter in most LMICs and are widely overprescribed. In fact, many low-level providers make the bulk of their income from medicine sales (Siddiqi *et al.*, 2002). Studies have shown that patients in all countries are more satisfied when they leave with some kind of treatment, even when that treatment, such as antibiotics for a viral infection, may not be warranted (Trivedi and Jagani, 2018; Young *et al.*, 2000). Private providers may be more or less skilled than their public counterparts; however, they are frequently more responsive to the preferences of their paying clients (Khattak *et al.*, 2012).

### 3.3 *Increase in utilization of the private healthcare sector*

The healthcare delivery component of the private sector and the corresponding service provision by the public health sector are the most visible aspects of the overall health system and absorb the largest amount of financing, specialized staffing, oversight, and attention. Patients rightly think first of "care" when thinking about health systems. If care is affordable and good, the overall health system is working well. If it is not, then something is wrong, and interventions are needed.

Household surveys across 70 LMICs suggest that 67% of diarrhea and 63% of fever cases among children are attended to by private providers (Chakraborty and Sprockett, 2018; Grépin, 2016). While there is variation among the six regions of the World Health Organization, the private sector is important in all. It provides nearly 40% of all healthcare in the Pan-American, African, and Western Pacific Regions, 57% in the Southeast Asian Region, and 62% in the Eastern Mediterranean Region (EMR). In countries in the EMR, 81% of the poorest quintile seek services from the private sector (Montagu and Chakraborty, 2021). In Egypt, Pakistan, and India, more than two-thirds of all outpatient care is privately provided, while within hospitals and clinics in Egypt, Pakistan, and Bangladesh, more than two-thirds of all deliveries are privately provided (Montagu and Chakraborty, 2021; National Institute of Population Studies (NIPS), 2019).

### 3.4 *Informality in the private healthcare sector*

Informality defines much of care at the lower end of the spectrum. A high proportion of people in both rural areas and urban slums in LMICs depend on the "services" rendered by unqualified providers categorized as "quacks," informal practitioners, and "faith-healers," all working for pay, albeit outside of the regulatory and quality assurance systems of government oversight (Shah *et al.*, 2011; Sudhinaraset *et al.*, 2013). At the same time, informality does not imply a clear differentiation from services of formal care. The overlap exists clearly in a few areas of clinical care, notably in support for delivery services, and is widespread in the sale of medicines. Drug sellers serving lower-income communities are common, whether wholly unlicensed or licensed only for over-the-counter medicines, and these sellers frequently sell a wide range of Western medicines, which are nominally prescription medicines and should only be sold by trained and licensed pharmacists. In some countries, especially in Asia, a significant proportion of private care providers are licensed practitioners of indigenous health systems of medicine (e.g. *Ayurveda, Tibb, Unani*, and Homeopathy) and are not to be considered part of the informal sector. In many countries in Africa, drug sellers (*duka la dawa baridi (DLBD)*, private patent medicine vendors (PPMVs), etc.) are licensed to sell a mix of traditional and Western medicines and bridge the informal and formal sectors.

Apart from medicine sales and clinical care, a wide range of clinical-support service providers, such as laboratories, diagnostic centers, blood banks, pharmacies, and ambulance operators, exist predominantly in the private sector. In India and a few other countries, the majority of medical education and training institutions are run by the private sector (Solanki and Kashyap, 2014; Mahal and Mohanan, 2006). The private sector also dominates pharmaceuticals, biomedical equipment and devices, and clinical and non-clinical supplies.

## 4. Harnessing the Private Healthcare Sector Toward Public Sector Goals

### 4.1 *Regulation of the private healthcare sector*

Private providers, both non-profit and for-profit, are driven by many motivations, including the desire to cure, to assure community betterment, to serve the needy, to achieve the highest possible level of quality, and to generate income and profit. Like their public-sector counterparts, private providers respond to incentives, both positive and negative. They seek to make money, to assure and enhance their personal and institutional reputation, to adhere to the tenets of science and rationality, to be efficient, and more.

The regulation of private providers by governments seeks to encourage the best aspects of private care (entrepreneurial innovation and investment; responsiveness to the priorities of patients and clients; and experimentation with new business models, opening hours, locations, and technologies) and deter the worst (conflict of interest as providers diagnose, treat, and sell medicines to patients; prioritizing the wealthy over the poor; over-treatment; or the focus on quality of "hotel services" rather than quality of "clinical services," the latter being frequently less visible to paying clients).

Regulations are ultimately the practical embodiment of national policies and legislation, as the latter are inherently more generic and broader. Some countries, such as the Philippines, Thailand, and South Africa, have encouraged and incentivized the growth of the private sector as a policy, whereas in other countries, private provision of care has grown indiscriminately without regulatory supervision of physical standards, quality, tariffs, or staffing norms (Pakistan, Egypt, Sudan, and Nigeria). In most LMICs, regulatory oversight is limited in scope and effectiveness. Often, this is due in part to the complexity of regulatory issues, a lack of local staffing, a lack of clarity regarding oversight authority and guidance for enforcement, conflicting authorities between different branches or levels of government, and frequent challenges of corruption and weak management. Even where regulations are clear, the relatively low funding of governmental oversight systems inherently limits regulatory capacity. While many aspects of governance in other sectors are highly visible and thus influenced by public opinion – air transport safety, for instance – most dimensions of healthcare are difficult for the public to assess, and so weak regulation of private providers often can and does endure.

The lack of regulation is problematic for two reasons: quality and cost. Healthcare services are highly idiosyncratic, meaning they are dependent on the needs and desires of the patient, which can vary greatly from person to person depending on age, sex, genetic makeup, personal, cultural, or religious preferences, co-morbidities, the ability to pay for care, or other factors. Healthcare services also stand out for the high level of differential information between the provider and the patient – a differential that exists in brain surgery or in treatment for pediatric fever. Many studies have shown that patients are extremely poor judges of clinical quality (Trivedi and Jagani, 2018; Rannan-Eliya *et al.*, 2015; McFarland *et al.*, 2017; Fayyaz *et al.*, 2020; Aujla *et al.*, 2021), and the obvious challenges with comparison shopping for clinical care (imagine trying to compare hospitals when seeking treatment for an urgent medical issue) leave patients at a disadvantage when trying to assure both the quality of care and the appropriateness of costs.

Where governance systems are strong, regulators step in to assure quality and often set rules on pricing transparency. Where purchasers of care are large, well organized, and properly incentivized – whether governments, social health insurance systems, or large private health insurance companies – they can negotiate strongly on the basis of large patient volumes and demand standardized pricing, thorough documentation, and predictability of both quality and cost. Unfortunately, neither strong governance nor organized large purchasers are the norm in most LMICs. The result is a wide variation in quality and cost among private providers. The resulting risks of poor treatment or family impoverishment due to medical costs fall most heavily on the poor (Yadav *et al.*, 2021; Barasa *et al.*, 2017; Khan *et al.*, 2017).

## 4.2 *Public–private engagement: First and foremost*

Government commitments to achieve universal health coverage (UHC) in recent years have led to growing attention to, and interest in active engagement with, private providers in many LMICs. This is needed: in a country where a third or a half of all health services are provided by private hospitals, clinics, providers, and pharmacies, there is no way to UHC without engaging this component of the overall health system.

What that engagement looks like naturally varies. There are four key approaches to engagement depending on governmental priorities, regulator and fiscal capacity, the organization and quality of private provision, and health-seeking preferences of the population (Harding and Montagu, 2009). These approaches include prohibition, constraint, encouragement, or purchase, each responding to one or more identified market failures, which are expanded on in Chapter 5 (Montagu and Goodman, 2016). *Prohibition* of the private sector is seldom effective: it requires strong governance and enforcement systems and implies the existence of public alternatives. Both are rare, and so effective prohibition is seldom appropriate or attempted. *Encouragement* and *constraint* are effectively two sides of the same coin: policy strategies toward the private sector, effected by a mix of regulatory methods, including strengthening or weakening the enforcement of licensure, registration, employment, oversight, and quality assessment rules, along with related regulations on access to finance, data reporting standards, and referrals or other interactions with the public sector.

The strongest engagement method, providing the most scope for assuring quality and appropriate pricing and influencing public health-related benefits, is the fourth method noted above: *purchase*. The widespread adoption of UHC as a goal in many countries has led to an unprecedented expansion of government contracting and both direct and indirect purchasing of privately delivered healthcare from private providers. In some instances, such as Ghana, Mexico, and Lesotho, this has been accomplished through direct government contracts to providers. More common has been the creation or expansion of national or social health insurance agencies that collect and disburse money quasi-independently from the government and are therefore more easily able to maintain independent standards for pricing, provision, quality, and related norms and to enforce these as a condition of payment eligibility among both private and public institutions. In Kenya, the Philippines, South Africa, and many other countries, the expansion of social health insurance systems is facilitating private sector engagement, particularly for hospitals, nursing homes, and, to a lesser extent, clinics. This expansion is leading to increased facility-level quality accreditation and use of care by the poor and other previously excluded populations.

The experiences of OECD countries, summarized in Chapter 2, make clear that assuring these benefits in the future will require investments in oversight, accounting and claims reviews, and enforcement (Montagu, 2021). A similar engagement on a smaller scale has happened in many countries to support service- or disease-specific services. TB care, family planning, malaria testing and treatment, and some maternity services are often subsidized in the private sector, with free or low-cost medicines supplied to providers in order to increase access to goods and services critical to public health (Randive *et al.*, 2013; Tougher *et al.*,

2012; Lönnroth *et al.*, 2004). Distributing subsidized medicines and diagnostics holds less risk and requires less oversight than supporting the provision of wide-ranging clinical treatments. Experience with these less complex support programs is important in building positive relations between public and private actors and in giving government regulators experience in engagement, which can provide a foundation for the more intensive work needed to purchase general services (McPake and Hanson, 2016). By the same token contracting for deliveries, HIV/AIDS care, pediatrics, or a broad range of healthcare serving all ages, while more complex and expensive, can also provide more scope for purchasers to set and enforce conditions (Lagarde and Palmer, 2009). These conditions for payment can be set to complement regulatory goals and assure that private actors meet quality and public benefit criteria. Examples could include requiring third-party quality accreditation for hospitals or cold chains for drug storage, sterilization standards, opening hours, patent records and privacy, and a host of other norms important for ensuring healthcare quality, building patient confidence, and increasing early health-seeking practices.

The government cannot be a passive participant in health provision, even when, perhaps especially when, provision is significantly undertaken by private providers and organizations. Engagement by policymakers and regulators cannot be limited to expanded financing alone. Engagement is a key precondition for governance and ensuring the safe and beneficial activities of the private healthcare sector within the larger health system. When coupled with effective regulation – with clear rules on licensure, quality, transparency, staff qualification, equipment standards, and a host of other issues – engagement through dialogue and financial support can make the formal components of the private sector effective partners to advance UHC. Engagement and regulation are combined in the national health policies of some LMIC countries.

## 4.3 *Data sharing and information compliance*

The precondition for developing or refining strategies and policies toward the private sector must begin with accurate estimates of the number of private providers at different levels of care, their geographic distribution, and the range and volume of services they provide. In many LMICs, this first hurdle is still a bottleneck to good policies because accurate master facility lists do not exist. When that is the case, getting the count right must be a priority.

The informal private sector, by definition, is not compliant with licensure and registration standards and does not report data to government purchasers, regulators, or the broader public sector health information system (Sudhinaraset *et al.*, 2013). For this reason, engagement must always prioritize formal private sector providers. Regulation and financial engagement are both predicated on good information: what services were provided, using what diagnostics, equipment, and medicines; how often, to whom, and with what outcome. While a system of reporting from government clinics and hospitals exists in most LMICs and is reasonably well functioning in many (required, and minimal penalties associated with service provision), reporting from private providers at all levels is widely agreed to be poor. There are many reasons for this: reporting is onerous; it brings few or no benefits; and it opens providers to risks such as greater attention, accusations of providing unlicensed services, and demands for taxes or unofficial payments by government agents at all levels. In a growing number of LMICs, national data information systems have made data reporting more standardized, faster, and easier (Karara *et al.*, 2015). This has not yet expanded to private providers.

It is clear that ensuring better data reporting will require the introduction of either new rules and enforcement or new incentives. Health systems academics are currently hoping that expanding purchase agreements, either directly from governments or indirectly through social health insurance agencies, will provide enough incentive to overcome the real and perceived risks (World Health Organization, 2005). In the meantime, governments need to assure that registration of local businesses is in place for clinics, push for more effective clinical licensure verification, and advance dialogues with and self-regulation by private representative bodies (private hospital associations, private clinical specialist associations, etc.). These representative organizations are a key vehicle to increase awareness and adoption of electronic health information system reporting by private facilities and assure the most accurate picture possible of where services are provided and by whom. Nationally representative surveys, such as the

USAID-supported Demographic Health Surveys (DHSs), which are conducted every five years in over 40 countries around the world, can also provide some basic information to estimate the importance of the private sector. This is only indicative, and encouraging better data sharing – through ease of engagement, assuring non-punitive uses, and financial incentives – is the key first step to effective governance.

## 4.4 *Cost of private healthcare*

Privately delivered healthcare exists at the highest end of care in many LMICs, including quite often the very best hospitals measured by clinical excellence, staff training and comprehensiveness of modern equipment and methods, patient–staff ratios, waiting times, and what are broadly characterized as "hotel services," meaning the comfort of patients before, during, and after care. These facilities charge rates in accordance with their standards and are highly priced by local, and sometimes international, norms. Private healthcare also, as noted above, dominates the lowest end of the healthcare spectrum and provides near-to-patient drug sales, diagnostics, outpatient services of all kinds, formal and informal clinical care, and more. These services range from very low-cost to highly overpriced, which is a challenge for patients because of the unpredictability of costs inherent to most medical care and the difficulty of estimating the appropriateness of charges.

Higher-end hospitals, in particular, offer treatments which include high-end technology and highly paid specialists not available in public facilities. This can both explain and appropriately justify the high costs of care. At all cost levels, private payment creates dangerous incentives for providers to conduct costly diagnostics or treatments in order to assure the use of expensive technologies that in turn require patients to pay fee-based charges. In LMICs, an unregulated private sector escalates healthcare costs and negatively affects quality, patient safety, equity, access, and health system priorities. In countries where the private sector is a major service provider and where private out-of-pocket (OOP) payment is the mode of financing for accessing services, the economic consequences for poor households could be devastating. The share of OOP expenditure as a percentage of total health expenditure is estimated to be 78% in Afghanistan, 77% in Iraq, 67% in Pakistan, 63% in Sudan, and more than 63% in India.

### 4.5 *Dual employment*

In many instances, the public and private clinicians are the same (Das *et al.*, 2012). While numbers are hard to come by, studies in Angola, Indonesia, Peru, and elsewhere have reported dual public–private practice among clinicians to be "ubiquitous and unregulated" (Báez-Montiel *et al.*, 2014; Macaia and Lapão, 2017). While this raises concerns for many reasons, not least self-referrals, as public doctors advise patients to visit their private clinic after hours, there is some evidence that the same provider, operating in both public and private clinics, gives better clinical care in private – due largely to spending more time with patients and asking more questions about their illness (Das *et al.*, 2012; Das and Hammer, 2007). The incentives to be responsive to patients can lead to positive outcomes as well.

## Conclusion

The private sector represents a significant part of healthcare services in nearly all countries, sometimes the dominant part. Despite this, data collection, effective integration into referrals and reporting systems, and guarantees of quality and cost limits are all weak in most LMICs. This needs to change, and it seems likely to. There is a growing recognition that improving the reach, quality, and equity of health systems will be possible only if the public and private sectors work together and that no government can afford to ignore the role of the private sector in its health system. If properly engaged and regulated, the private sector can positively contribute to the population's healthcare needs and strengthen the overall health system of the country.

Regulation of private providers is a large part of the work of health departments and ministries in these countries. Private provision is not disappearing anywhere in the world, and so to assure effective governance, the private sector will need to become prioritized in LMICs, and a significant level of effort and investment in oversight and regulation needs to be made by ministries of health in these countries.

## References

N. Aujla, Y. F. Chen, Y. Samarakoon, *et al.* (2021). Comparing the use of direct observation, standardized patients and exit interviews in low-and middle-income countries: A systematic review of methods of assessing quality of primary care. *Health Policy and Planning* **36**(3): 341–356.

Z. U. Babar. (2021). Ten recommendations to improve pharmacy practice in low and middle-income countries (LMICs). *Journal of Pharmaceutical Policy and Practice* **14**(1): 6.

B. B. Báez-Montiel, E. Gutiérrez-Islas, M. Bolaños-Maldonado, *et al.* (2014). The odysseys of Ulysses. A study of tales in a normal working day of the family doctor in Paraguay, Mexico, Peru, and Spain. *Atención Primaria* **46**(2): 68–76. (Spanish).

E. W. Barasa, T. Maina and N. Ravishankar. (2017). Assessing the impoverishing effects, and factors associated with the incidence of catastrophic healthcare payments in Kenya. *International Journal for Equity in Health* **16**(1): 31.

N. M. Chakraborty, A. Sprockett. (2018). Use of family planning and child health services in the private sector: An equity analysis of 12 DHS surveys. *International Journal for Equity in Health* **17**(1): 50.

N. T. Chuc and G. Tomson. (1999). "Doi moi" and private pharmacies: A case study on dispensing and financial issues in Hanoi, Vietnam. *European Journal of Clinical Pharmacology* **55**(4): 325–332.

J. Das, A. Holla, V. Das, *et al.* (2012). In urban and rural India, a standardized patient study showed low levels of provider training and huge quality gaps. *Health Affairs (Millwood)* **31**(12): 2774–2784.

J. Das and J. Hammer. (2007). Money for nothing: The dire straits of medical practice in Delhi, India. *Journal of Development Economics* **83**(1): 1–36.

S. Davalbhakta, S. Sharma, S. Gupta, *et al.* (2020). Private health sector in India-ready and willing, yet underutilized in the Covid-19 pandemic: A cross-sectional study. *Frontiers in Public Health* **8**: 571419.

R. Fayyaz, F. A. Ahmed, A. Abid, *et al.* (2020). The quality of patient care in oncology departments in Karachi, Pakistan: Patients' perceptions. *International Journal of Health Care Quality Assurance*. **34**(1): 52–69.

K. A. Grépin. (2016). Private sector an important but not dominant provider of key health services in low- and middle-income countries. *Health Affairs (Millwood)* **35**(7): 1214–1221.

A. Harding and D. Montagu. (2009). Role of the private sector in health-care financing and provision. In: B. Carrin and Q. Heggenhougen (eds.), *Health Systems Policy, Finance, and Organization.* Geneva: Elsevier.

S. K. Hooda. (2017). Growth of formal and informal private healthcare providers in India: Structural changes and implications. *Journal of Healthcare Finance* **44**(2).

K. Hort and P. Annear. (2012). The growth of non-state hospitals in Indonesia and Vietnam: Market reforms and mixed commercialised health systems. http://www.ssrn.com/abstract=2069757. (Accessed November 5, 2021).

R. C. Kagawa, A. Anglemyer and D. Montagu. (2012). The scale of faith based organization participation in health service delivery in developing countries: Systematic [corrected] review and meta-analysis. *PLoS One* **7**(11): e48457.

G. Karara, F. Verbeke and M. Nyssen. (2015). The role of hospital information systems in Universal Health Coverage monitoring in Rwanda. *Studies in Health Technology and Informatics* **216**: 193–197.

J. A. M. Khan, S. Ahmed and T. G. Evans. (2017). Catastrophic healthcare expenditure and poverty related to out-of-pocket payments for healthcare in Bangladesh — An estimation of financial risk protection of universal health coverage. *Health Policy and Planning* **32**(8): 1102–1110.

A. Khattak, M. I. Alvi, M. A. Yousaf, *et al.* (2012). Patient satisfaction — A comparison between public & private hospitals of Peshawar. *IJCRIMPH* **4**(5): 713–722.

M. Lagarde and N. Palmer. (2009). The impact of contracting out on health outcomes and use of health services in low and middle-income countries. *Cochrane Database of Systematic Reviews* **4**: CD008133.

G. Lagomarsino, D. de Ferranti, A. Pablos-Mendez, *et al.* (2009). Public stewardship of mixed health systems. *Lancet* **374**(9701): 1577–1578.

J. L. León-Cortés, G. Leal Fernández and H. J. Sánchez-Pérez. (2019). Health reform in Mexico: Governance and potential outcomes. *International Journal for Equity in Health* **18**(1): 30.

K. Lönnroth, M. Uplekar, V. K. Arora, *et al.* (2004). Public-private mix for DOTS implementation: What makes it work? *Bulletin of the World Health Organization* **82**: 580–586.

D. Macaia and L. V. Lapão. (2017). The current situation of human resources for health in the province of Cabinda in Angola: Is it a limitation to provide universal access to healthcare? *Human Resources for Health,* **15**(1): 88.

M. Mackintosh, A. Channon, A. Karan, *et al.* (2016). What is the private sector? Understanding private provision in the health systems of low-income and middle-income countries. *Lancet* **388**(10044): 596–605.

A. Mahal and M. Mohanan. (2006). Growth of private medical education in India. *Medical Education* **40**(10): 1009–1011.

D. C. McFarland, M. J. Shen, P. Parker, *et al.* (2017). Does hospital size affect patient satisfaction? *Quality Management in Healthcare* **26**(4): 205–209.

B. McPake. (2009). Hospital policy in sub-Saharan Africa and post-colonial development impasse. *Soc Hist Med*; **22**(2): 341–360.

B. McPake and K. Hanson. (2016). Managing the public-private mix to achieve universal health coverage. *Lancet* **388**(10044): 622–630.

D. Montagu. (2021). The provision of private healthcare services in European countries: Recent data and lessons for Universal Health Coverage in other settings. *Frontiers in Public Health* **9**: 636750.

D. Montagu and N. Chakraborty. (2021). Standard survey data: Insights into private sector utilization. *Front Med (Lausanne)* **8**: 624285.

D. Montagu and C. Goodman. (2016). Prohibit, constrain, encourage, or purchase: How should we engage with the private health-care sector? *Lancet* **388**(10044): 613–621.

R. Morgan and T. Ensor. (2016). The regulation of private hospitals in Asia. *International Journal of Health Planning and Management* **31**(1): 49–64.

National Institute of Population Studies (NIPS). (2019). Pakistan demographic and health survey, 2017–2018. https://dhsprogram.com/pubs/pdf/FR354/FR354.pdf. (Accessed November 19, 2021).

B. Randive, V. Diwan and A. De Costa. (2013). India's conditional cash transfer programme (the JSY) to promote institutional birth: Is there an association between institutional birth proportion and maternal mortality? *PLoS One* **8**(6): e67452.

R. P. Rannan-Eliya, N. Wijemanne, I. K. Liyanage IK, *et al.* (2015). The quality of outpatient primary care in public and private sectors in Sri Lanka — How well do patient perceptions match reality and what are the implications?. *Health Policy and Planning* **30**(suppl_1): i59–i74.

N. M. Shah, W. R. Brieger and D. H. Peters. (2011). Can interventions improve health services from informal private providers in low and middle-income countries? A comprehensive review of the literature. *Health Policy and Planning* **26**(4): 275–287.

S. Siddiqi, S. Hamid, G. Rafique, *et al.* (2002). Prescription practices of public and private healthcare providers in Attock District of Pakistan. *International Journal of Health Planning and Management* **17**(1): 3–40.

A. Solanki and S. Kashyap. (2014). Medical education in India: Current challenges and the way forward. *Medical Teacher* **36**(12): 1027–1031.

M. Sudhinaraset, M. Ingram, H. K. Lofthouse, *et al.* (2013). What is the role of informal healthcare providers in developing countries? A systematic review. *PLoS One* **8** (2): e54978.

S. Tougher, Y. Ye, J. H. Amuasi, *et al.* (2012). Effect of the affordable medicines facility — Malaria (AMFm) on the availability, price, and market share of quality-assured artemisinin-based combination therapies in seven countries: A before-and-after analysis of outlet survey data. *Lancet* **380**(9857): 1916–1826.

R. Trivedi and K. Jagani. (2018). Perceived service quality, repeat use of healthcare services and inpatient satisfaction in emerging economy: Empirical evidences from India. *International Journal of Pharmaceutical and Healthcare Marketing*.

S. Witter. (1996). 'Doi Moi'and health: The effect of economic reforms on the health system in Vietnam. *International Journal of Health Planning* **11**(2): 159–172.

World Bank. (2011). Healthy partnerships: How governments can engage the private sector to improve health in Africa. https://openknowledge.worldbank.org/handle/10986/2304. (Accessed November 8, 2021).

World Health Organization. (2005). Social health insurance: Sustainable health financing, universal coverage and social health insurance: Report by the Secretariat. https://apps.who.int/iris/handle/10665/20302. (Accessed November 18, 2021).

World Health Organization. (2020). Engaging the private health service delivery sector through governance in mixed health systems. https://www.who.int/docs/default-source/health-system-governance/strategy-report-engaging-the-private-health-service-delivery-sector-through-governance-in-mixed-health-systems.pdf?sfvrsn=3e870582_1. (Accessed November 6, 2021).

J. Yadav, G. R. Menon and D. John. (2021). Disease-specific out-of-pocket payments, catastrophic health expenditure and impoverishment effects in India: An analysis of national health survey data. *Applied Health Economics and Health* **Policy** 19: 769–782.

G. J. Young, M. Meterko, and K. R. Desai. (2000). Patient satisfaction with hospital care: Effects of demographic and institutional characteristics. *Medical Care* **38**(3): 325–334.

# Part 2

# Size, Scale, and Context

The five chapters which make up Part 2 of this book are all drawn from previously published papers. Each addresses the context in which private providers – hospitals, drug sellers, clinics, dentists, pharmacists, and every other kind of medical service institution or individual – work as an often-unacknowledged part of the much larger health system.

Many people confuse the public financing of healthcare with direct public provision. Chapter 2 uses data from Europe, where public financing is very much the norm, and looks at the wide variations in public and private delivery of care across the continent. The quality of healthcare, measured by national satisfaction surveys in terms of health outcomes, wait times, and other indices, varies according to national health system design, but not by ownership. There are distinct typologies, with pharmacies and dentists nearly always privately operated and financing nearly always either government managed or very strictly regulated so as to assure universal coverage. But ownership models are less important to coverage and quality than policies, funding, and regulatory enforcement. Chapter 3 uses data from nationally representative surveys in LMICs to explore the same issues: How large is the private sector around the world?

What does that mean in practice (for hospitals, clinics, etc.)? And who chooses to use private providers rather than public where such choices exist?

Chapter 4 uses data from family planning providers in Kenya to look at who goes to public or private providers. It confirms earlier studies that many low-income households use private outlets, which cost more than public facilities because of time constraints and limited public opening hours, but also shows that costs for preventative care do deter usage by the poor, and advancing access must involve public, free, or low-cost service availability. Markets alone will leave out at-risk groups, even with subsidies, close proximity, long opening hours, and other benefits they may bring.

In Chapter 5, we explore the implications of the prior chapters: if the private sector exists, is large, and serves the poor but imperfectly, what should national policy and the approaches of donors, NGOs, and aid agencies be? The chapter proposes a set of four policy options and assesses when and how each should be applied.

Chapter 6 summarizes the experiences of bypassing policies and using direct interventions to leverage private infrastructure to expand public health goals.

Taken together, these chapters set out the importance, goals, and policy and programmatic issues which are the context for considering the private sector in health systems around the world.

# Chapter 2

# The Provision of Private Healthcare Services in European Countries: Recent Data and Lessons for Universal Health Coverage in Other Settings*

**Dominic Montagu**

## Abstract

In this chapter, Dominic Montagu uses the well-documented experiences of countries in Europe to show what is and isn't possible to accomplish through a health system that encompasses well-regulated and centrally funded private health providers. These lessons are given as examples to understand the potential for LMICs in addressing system integration in subsequent chapters.

Universal Health Coverage (UHC) exists in all of the countries in Europe, despite variation in the ownership structure of healthcare delivery systems. As countries around the world seek to advance UHC and manage the private sector within their health systems, the European experiences can offer useful insights. We found four different models for the provision of healthcare, with the private sector predominant in some countries but

*This chapter was originally published in "Montagu, D. Frontiers in Public Health, Vol. 9 (2021) 636750".

of minimal importance in others. The European experiences indicate that UHC can be effectively provided with or without large-scale private sector provision in hospitals, specialty, and primary care services, and that, moreover, it can be provided with high levels of patient satisfaction.

These findings offer regulatory models for countries in other regions to review as they advance UHC. Better regulation of the private sector is a key requirement for more efficient and effective management of mixed public and private systems, as described in the rest of the book.

## 1. Background

There is a global movement to make healthcare accessible for those in need, assuring Universal Health Coverage in all countries by 2030. While pursuing this, many LMICs continue to struggle with how and how much to integrate private providers into the formal government regulated and funded health system. This is a very immediate question in countries, such as Nigeria, India, and Myanmar where well over 50% of all services provided are private and quality assurance is a challenge, but also relevant to countries, such as Ethiopia or Vietnam where private care is below 25% and policy makers must wonder if higher levels would accelerate investments in coverage and care availability (1–3).

Ministerial level platforms like the Joint Learning Network use case studies to provide examples for health officials on key policies related to financing and governance which can advance Universal Health Coverage (4,5). Case studies on health reforms have been used to demonstrate important lessons on regulatory changes and the system and health outcomes that result (6). Researchers hope to understand how the divisions in public–private service ownership affect critical health system indicators, such as efficiency, morbidity, mortality, and equity. This descriptive paper seeks to establish a categorization of systems and provide a foundational first step for future research in both OECD and LMIC settings. Healthcare services in Europe are effective, appreciated by their citizens, and delivered with many different models and degrees of private involvement (7,8).

In the push for UHC, Europe can provide insights into differing experiences with private provision in the context of nationally managed systems. This study provides an up-to-date review of private provision across different sectors in countries across Europe. The experiences are relevant to many settings.

## 2. Financing Context

Provision of healthcare functions independently of financing and there is more competition, more variance, and more change within the ownership, incentives, and regulation of care provision than is the case with financing. Nevertheless, financing sets the context for ownership, together with policy and regulatory guidance, directly or indirectly determining what ownership mix can develop.

Universal Health Coverage (UHC) exists in all of the European countries we studied. Unlike LMICs, healthcare financing in Europe is almost universally government managed, either directly through taxation revenue (as in the UK) or semi-directly through mandated, managed, and government subsidized Social Health Insurance (as in Germany). Across Europe, government and social health insurance provide a healthcare safety net for nearly all citizens as shown by data from the OECD health system survey (Figure 1, blue bars). While the form of insurance varies between countries, and supplemental private insurance (orange bars) is common in some (Belgium, Holland, Slovenia) but not others (France, Norway), the most important implication for service provision, is that where they exist, private providers in most countries are paid either by national health insurance systems or by tightly regulated social health insurance schemes that coordinate purchasing (4–6). Out of pocket payments for healthcare are consistently low across all European countries surveyed, totaling <0.5% of spending on preventative care and <20% of Total Health Expenditure in 2018 (9,10). The lesson for other countries is that government purchasing and regulation are neither a guarantee of, nor a barrier to a large private market for healthcare provision.

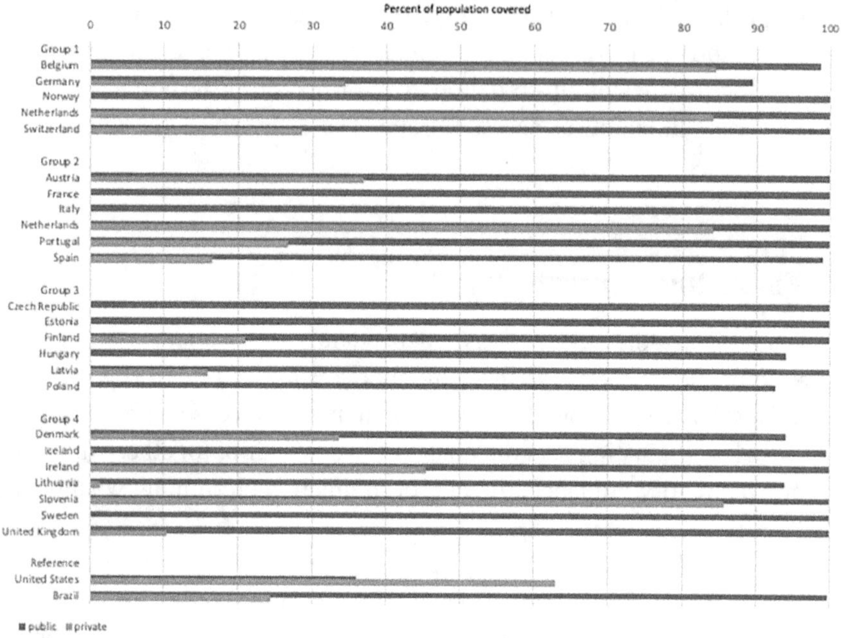


Figure 1. (Color available online) Public and private insurance coverage. Blue bars show population covered by public insurance. Orange bars show population with private insurance*.

*Note*: *Private insurance is supplemental to public in all countries except the US, where private coverage is often a substitute for public insurance. Countries showing zero private insurance coverage did not report any to the OECD in 2018. (*Source*: https://stats.oecd.org/).

# 3. Methods

## 3.1 *Scope and focus*

We restricted our analysis to European countries which are members of the OECD. We excluded EU members which were not also OECD members, and OECD countries outside of Europe. Turkey is an OECD country and partially on the European continent, however 97% of the landmass is in Asia and we made a decision to exclude it from this analysis for that reason. In this paper, for the sake of simplicity, we refer to the selected countries as "Europe."

## 3.2 *Data sources*

We reviewed all publications on the included countries' health systems from the OECD and WHO European websites. For each country we also searched for journal publications in English through PubMed and Google Scholar, and where data was contradictory or lacking we conducted subject specific Google Scholar searches by country (e.g., "dentist Luxembourg") for additional sources from white papers. Where all of these sources failed, we contacted experts within WHO and personal connections within academic institutions in the countries with information gaps for supplemental sources in other languages.

When calculating the scale of the private sector role within each country we relied heavily on the Health System in Transition (HSiT) national reports from the European Observatory on Health Systems and Policies. These ranged in date-produced from 2003 (Iceland) to 2019 (Latvia) (11,12). If country-specific reports use pre-2008 data, regardless of when they were published, we set them aside, and instead used data from the 2008/9 OECD health system survey (8). When journal publications or national reports had credible national data which was more recent than either the 2008/9 Survey or the national HSiT report, we used that source. The year of data used for each country is shown in a Supplementary Material.

We applied the healthcare service categories used by the OECD to look separately at inpatient services, specialist services, primary care, and pharmacies (8,13). We use hospitals as a proxy for inpatient services, this reflecting the majority of providers and care delivered in hospitals across all countries surveyed (14). Outpatient Specialist services and dentistry are treated together. Primary Care could be either general practitioners (UK) or primary care centers (Sweden). And pharmacies here refer only to community pharmacies and so exclude hospital- based pharmacies.

### 3.3 *Patient and public involvement*

This study used publicly available data to look at health-systems behaviors. No patients were involved, and no direct data collection was undertaken which would have prompted public involvement.

## 4. Results and Discussion

We evaluated each country on hospital ownership data and then reviewed for consistency against other aspects of care provision. From this we

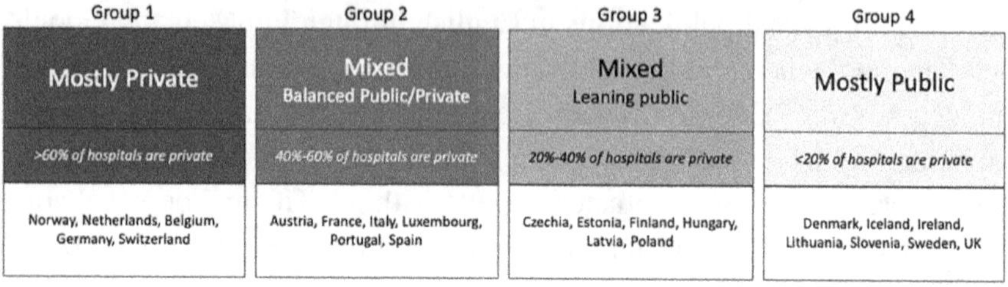


Figure 2. Hospital ownership models within European health systems. Data not available for: Greece and Slovakia.

grouped the health systems in Europe into four types (Figure 2), based on how reliant the overall system is on private provision. This grouping was informed by analyses of the interaction between regulatory and purchasing agencies of government and privately owned providers of care across health service domains (15–17). Health systems are highly path-dependent (18,19) and the four types, or Groups, reflect the continued influence of the financing and ownership models which created current structures. In Germany, the influence of the Bismarkian model of social insurance and privately contracted delivery remains evident (20). In the UK, the influence of Beveridge's vision for the National Health System continues to resonate in current days (21). Nevertheless, as Kutzin argued convincingly a decade ago already, the distinctions between European health systems are becoming less important as financing models align, driven by aging populations and growing expectations for care so that government funding fills more and more gaps in traditional social health insurance, while competition is increasingly common in national health insurance systems to manage costs (22–24).

## 4.1 *Hospitals*

Hospitals are in transition across Europe as outpatient services shift outside of medical facilities and most countries push for increased efficiency as measured by shorter average stays and higher bed usage rates (14, 15). Our findings from countries with more recent data showed little change from the ownership status summarized in a 2008/2009 survey among OECD countries (8). Across all European countries the role, and

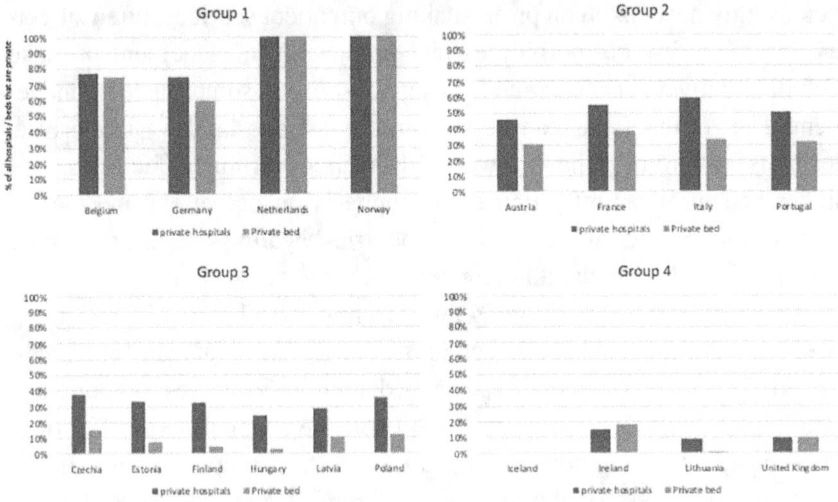


Figure 3. (Color available online) Percent of all hospitals that are private and percent of all hospital beds that are private. Where private beds are much smaller than hospitals, hospitals focus on outpatient care. Data not available for: Denmark, Greece, Luxembourg, Slovenia, Slovakia, Spain, Sweden, and Switzerland.

importance, of private hospitals within the larger health system fall into four distinct categories (Figure 2).

The behavior of private hospitals differs between the four groups, as can be seen in how private hospitals contribute to available inpatient bed within each group (Figure 3). In some countries private hospitals provide inpatient beds and services in proportion to their importance within the overall system; in other countries private hospitals have very few beds, focusing instead on outpatient care only. In Group 1, the private hospitals beds roughly match the private hospital numbers: this is where most inpatient care of all kinds is offered. Where public and private hospitals exist in parallel, as in Germany, the differences in services offered, bed numbers, bed-stay duration, and patient experiences between public and private hospitals are minimal: to the consumer and the social health insurance payer, public and private facilities are functionally equivalent. These countries' health systems are based on Bismarck's model of care and financing.

In Group 2, this equivalence exists for some services, or in some regions, but is not universal. In these countries private facilities increasingly have taken on profit-making outpatient services, often surgeries that have few co-morbidities and predictable management but also including delivery services and (among non-profits) some cancer management. The result of this can be seen in the average facility size: private hospitals in Group 2 have fewer beds than government facilities, and higher bed turnover reflecting their emphasis on outpatient and clearly defined, lower risk, care (25). These countries' health systems are heavily influenced by the Bismarckian model.

In Group 3 this same leaning away from comprehensive inpatient services and toward a narrower set of short-stay areas of care continues. Facilities are smaller and more specialized; non-profits are less predominant within the overall mix of facilities. While private hospitals exist, they offer fewer inpatient stay opportunities and take on fewer inpatient, chronic, or emergency services. Health systems in Group 3 countries have, largely, derived from the Semashko model which influenced much of Eastern European social services during the 20th century (Box 1) (26,27).

**Box 1. Countries in Transition: Group 3 Hospitals (26)**

A decade ago, the countries in Group 3 would have been called "economies in transition" from planned economies, organized around government provision of social services, including health, to market economies. It may be, then, that Group 3 will shift, or has already shifted, in ways not reflected in our data from 4 or 5 years ago, towards or away from Group 2.

The Group 4 countries are all countries with a strong national emphasis on social services. This group also includes many of Europe's small and isolated countries. For these, centralized management of a limited number of facilities is practical and competition unlikely to be an effective complement to government purchasing. In all Group 4 countries private hospitals either don't exist at all (Iceland), or exist as a small minority of facilities, principally serving only private patients for services not covered by national insurance (eg: cosmetic surgery) or outpatient services for patients who are willing to pay to avoid the wait times for government care. Health systems based upon Beveridge.

The differing role of private hospitals can be seen in the different ratio of beds-per-hospital shown in Figure 3, using the most recent data from each country. Ireland appears to be an anomaly; the only country where the private sector has more beds/facility than the public, although as elsewhere these beds are primarily for short-term services (28,29). The very low percentage of private beds in all Group 3 countries indicates that in all of these countries private hospitals exist, but largely to provide outpatient surgeries and consultations.

## 4.2 *Dentists*

Nearly all dentists in Europe work privately either in solo or group practices. In France 91% of the country's dentists are self-employed private practitioners (25). In Czechia the rate is 95%, in Austria 80%. Other than a few within hospitals, nearly 100% of dentists are private practitioners in Iceland, Italy, Lithuania, Luxembourg, Netherlands, Portugal, Greece, Germany, Spain, and the UK (10,11,30–37). The exceptions are few. In Finland private practitioners represent just more than half of all dentists and provide approximately one half of all dental care (38,39). While there is some concern within the dental profession regarding how the growth in third- party payments will affect practices, most dental services across Europe continue to be funded by a mix of direct patient payment and government subsidy (40). Dental services for children up to 18 are government funded in all European countries (41). In Italy and Greece, dental services are nominally free within the government sector, but long wait times leads many patients to seek care from private offices (41). In the UK, dental care has been included in National Health Service (NHS) funding since 1948, however as in other countries, since 1951 adults have a co-payment required for non-acute services (41).

## 4.3 *Specialist services*

Data on specialist services (Table1) comes from the OECD health systems survey (8). It found that in more than half of surveyed European countries specialists operate in private practice, either as solo practitioners

Table 1. Principal mode of specialist and primary care provision.

| | Primary Care | Specialist Care |
|---|---|---|
| **Group 1** | | |
| Belgium | Private Solo Practice | Private Solo Practice |
| Germany | Private Solo Practice | Private Solo Practice |
| Netherlands | Private Group Practice | Private Group Practice |
| Norway | Private Solo Practice | Private Solo Practice |
| Switzerland | Private Solo Practice | Private Solo Practice |
| **Group 2** | | |
| Austria | Private Solo Practice | Private Solo Practice |
| France | Private Solo Practice | Private Solo Practice |
| Italy | Pubic Center | Public Hospital |
| Luxembourg | Private Solo Practice | Private Solo Practice |
| Portugal | Pubic Center | Public Hospital |
| Spain | Pubic Center | Public centers |
| **Group 3** | | |
| Czechia | Private Solo Practice | Public Hospital |
| Finland | Public Center | Public Hospital |
| Hungary | Private Solo Practice | Public Center |
| Poland | Pubic Center | Public Center |
| **Group 4** | | |
| Denmark | Private Group Practice | Private Solo Practice |
| Iceland | Pubic Center | Private Group Practice |
| Ireland | Private Solo Practice | Public Hospital |
| Sweden | Pubic Center | Public Hospital |
| United Kingdom | Private Group Practice | Pubic Hospital |

*Comparable data not available for: Estonia, Greece, Latvia, Lithuania, Slovenia, and Slovakia.*

(9/22 countries) or in groups (3/22). The countries where government specialist services dominate are all either in Group 2 (Italy, Spain, Portugal), Group 3 (Czechia, Finland, Hungary, Poland), or Group 4 (Ireland, Sweden, UK).

## 4.4 *Primary care*

The 2008/9 OECD health systems survey found that primary care services were predominantly provided in private settings in 15 of the 22 European countries, including almost all countries with social health insurance systems and five countries with national health systems: Denmark, Ireland, Norway, France, and the United Kingdom. In Finland, Iceland, Italy, Poland, Portugal, Spain, and Sweden primary care is mostly public (Table 1).

In Sweden, primary care is provided by health centers, comprised of a multidisciplinary workforce including general practitioners, nurses, specialist nurses with expertise in diabetes or other chronic illnesses, and often occupational therapists and psychologists. In 2019, 56.2% of Sweden's 496 primary care centers are public. The remaining 43.8% are private, operating under contracts with a region (42).

## 4.5 *Pharmacy*

Outside of hospitals, community pharmacies across Europe are all privately owned and operated. There remain country variations in ownership restrictions, with Spain, France, and other countries restricting ownership by corporate chains and franchise arrangements as a way to protect and encourage local ownership (43). Eighty-five percent of the 145,143 pharmacies in Europe are private. Of these private pharmacies, one in three are affiliated with a franchise or other shared brand and one in eight are part of a chain (44,45). The retail pharmaceutical component of the health system is sometimes inefficient, inequitable, unevenly distributed, and expensive. But it mostly works, and despite some shortcomings pharmacies function much like groceries, bakeries, or other commodity retailers. As a result most countries in Europe regulate pharmacies as a traditional, privately owned, market (46). The case study of Estonia, which liberalized its pharmacy market between 1993 and 1995 after gaining independence from the USSR, showed private ownership resulted in greater use, lower cost to the consumer, and greater client satisfaction (47). However, by 2014 regulation was needed to correct for market failures. Specifically, rural communities unserved by pharmacies were able to apply to the State which then mandated pharmacy chains meet certain size criteria to open a pharmacy in those regions (48).

In Sweden, a similar transition occurred. Until 2009 all pharmacies were government owned as part of the National Corporation of Swedish Pharmacies. From 2009, half of the government pharmacies were sold, and new private pharmacies were permitted. The total number of pharmacies increased by 20% in the following year and by 2011 there were 13 pharmacy operators in the country (49). The trend toward greater free-market structuring of pharmacies, and adaptive regulation to correct for market failings, has occurred across most countries of Europe, albeit at differing rates.

### 4.6 *Satisfaction*

Gallup Poll data from 2016 shows high levels of satisfaction with national health services in Group 1 countries with high levels of private hospitals, private primary care, and private specialist services; but equally high satisfaction numbers in some countries within Groups 2 and 4 (Table 2) (50). Past studies have concluded that what European patients value most is choice and low out-of-pocket costs, and these are determined more by financing policies than service ownership arrangements (51).

## 5. Conclusions

The delivery of healthcare in Europe, from hospitals to primary care to specialty services to pharmacies, demonstrates that while there have been and remain significant variations in how the private sector is engaged to provide healthcare within the larger health system, the variety can be taken to show that there are many ways to effectively deliver care. The private sector is neither necessary for the provision of national health care, nor is private sector service an impediment to a strong and effective national healthcare system. That can be said about hospitals, where the distinctions between ownership models are most stark and most clearly determined by national policy differences and changes. It can also be said for the provision of primary and specialty care, where the degree of private provision has historic roots, but both public and private models appear to deliver effective equity, access, and care (20).

Table 2. Citizen satisfaction with the health care system, 2016.

| | | |
|---|---|---|
| **Group 1** | **AVG** | **89.4%** |
| Belgium | | 91% |
| Germany | | 88% |
| Netherlands | | 86% |
| Norway | | 89% |
| Switzerland | | 93% |
| **Group 2** | **AVG** | **73.7%** |
| Austria | | 88% |
| France | | 78% |
| Italy | | 56% |
| Luxembourg | | 86% |
| Portugal | | 63% |
| Spain | | 71% |
| **Group 3** | **AVG** | **60.5%** |
| Czechia | | 72% |
| Finland | | 77% |
| Hungary | | 50% |
| Poland | | 43% |
| **Group 4** | **AVG** | **73.2%** |
| Denmark | | 85% |
| Iceland | | 67% |
| Ireland | | 60% |
| Sweden | | 78% |
| United Kingdom | | 76% |

*Source*: *Gallup World Poll, cited in OECD "Government at a Glance" (50) statlink* http// dx.doi.org/10.1787/888933533834.

At the same time, there is a near-universal accord within European health systems that the provision of community pharmacy and dental services are best served by private markets. These services and products are the most standard between providers, and hence the easiest for both purchasers and citizens to compare based on cost and accessibility. Among all healthcare goods and services, these behave the most like traditional market-based products and economists argue that private provision is the most efficient delivery option for this reason, something the European experience appears to confirm (52).

Case studies are critical for the many LMIC countries current expanding national and social health insurance, increasing investments, and revising regulatory systems to advance toward Universal Health Coverage in alignment with the Sustainable Development Goals. The European examples provide a critical insight for these governments: large scale privately provided medical services are neither necessary for achieving UHC nor a barrier to it. For any country now pursuing UHC, historical experiences and path dependency may dictate whether the private sector is an important provider of care. This was the case across the countries studied here. The varied models, and success, of Europe show that any extant delivery mix can be managed. Well-planned national policies and financing can assure effective universal coverage regardless of any inherited delivery structure.

This study offers a foundation on which further analysis should be conducted. We hope future efforts will assess the applicability of the system categories developed for Europe to countries in Asia, Africa, and Latin America.

## Funding

This work was funded under a contract with the World Health Organization, PO 202529299. WHO had no influence on the design, analysis, or interpretation of findings and policy implications in this work.

## Supplementary Material

The supplementary material for this article can be found online at: https://www.frontiersin.org/articles/10.3389/fpubh.2021.636750/full#supplementary-material.

## References

1. Grepin KA. Private Sector An Important But Not Dominant Provider Of Key Health Services In Low- And Middle-Income Countries. Health Aff (Millwood). 2016 Jul;35(7):1214–21.
2. Campbell OMR, Benova L, MacLeod D, Baggaley RF, Rodrigues LC, Hanson K, *et al.* Family planning, antenatal and delivery care: cross-sectional survey evidence on levels of coverage and inequalities by public and private sector in 57 low- and middle-income countries. Trop Med Int Health. 2016 Apr;21(4):486–503.
3. Mackintosh M, Channon A, Karan A, Selvaraj S, Zhao H, Cavagnero E. What is the private sector? Understanding private provision in the health systems of low-income and middle-income countries. LANCET. 2016 Aug 6;388(10044):596–605.
4. Thomas C, Makinen M, Blanchet N, Krusell N, editors. Engaging the Private Sector in Primary Health Care to Achieve Universal Health Coverage: Advice from Implementers, to Implementers. Joint Learning Network for Universal Health Coverage, PATH, Wipro Ltd.; 2016.
5. Joint Learning Network for Universal Health Coverage. Using Health Data to Improve Universal Health Coverage: Three Case Studies [Internet]. Thailand: PATH, Wipro Ltd.; 2018 p. 48. Available from: www.jointlearningnetwork.org.
6. Okma K, Paraje G, Chinitz D, Tenbensel T, Ashton T, Cheng TM, *et al.* Health Care Reforms across the World. Am Aff J. 2018;2(1):34.
7. Tchouaket ÉN, Lamarche PA, Goulet L, Contandriopoulos AP. Health care system performance of 27 OECD countries: HEALTH CARE SYSTEM PERFORMANCE OF 27 OECD COUNTRIES. Int J Health Plann Manage. 2012 Apr;27(2):104–29.
8. Paris V, Devaux M, Wei L. Health Systems Institutional Characteristics: A Survey of 29 OECD Countries [Internet]. 2010 Apr [cited 2017 Dec 18]. (OECD Health Working Papers). Report No.: 50. Available from: http://www.oecd-ilibrary.org/social-issues-migration-health/health-systems-institutional-characteristics_5kmfxfq9qbnr-en.
9. Orosz E, Morgan D. SHA-Based National Health Accounts in Thirteen OECD Countries: A Comparative Analysis. Paris: OECD; 2004 p. 148. Report No.: 16.
10. OECD.Stat [Internet]. [cited 2020 Jul 2]. OECD Statistics. Available from: https://stats.oecd.org/.
11. Halldorsson M. Health Care Systems in Transition - Iceland [Internet]. Copenhagen: European Observatory on Health Systems and Policies; 2003

[cited 2020 Jun 20]. 118 p. (Health Care Systems in Transition; vol. 5). Available from: http://www.euro.who.int/__data/assets/pdf_file/0006/80844/e82881.pdf?ua=1.

12. Behmane D, Dudele A, Villerusa A, Misins J, Kļaviņa K, Mozgis D, *et al.* Health Systems in Transition: Latvia Health Systems Review. 2019;21(4):196.
13. Saltman R, Busse R. Balancing regulation and entrepreneurialism in Europe's health sector: theory and practice. In: Regulating entrepreneurial behavior in European health care systems. Philadelphia: World Health Organization on behalf of the European Observatory on Health Systems and Policies; 2002. (European Observatory on Health Systems and Policies).
14. Rigaud M. Competition in Hospital Services. Geneva: OECD; 2012 p. 58. (Competition and Regulation). Report No.: 2.
15. Harding A, Montagu D. Role of the Private Sector in Health-Care Financing and Provision. In: Health Systems Policy, Finance, and Organization, Carrin, Buse, Heggenhougen, Quah editors. Geneva: Elsevier; 2009.
16. Harding A, Preker AS, editors. Private participation in health services. Washington, D.C: World Bank; 2003. 349 p. (Health, nutrition, and population series).
17. Montagu D, Goodman C. Prohibit, constrain, encourage, or purchase: how should we engage with the private health-care sector? The Lancet. 2016 Aug 6;388(10044):613–21.
18. Zelmer J. Path Dependence and Health Policy: Intersections between the Past and the Future. Healthc Policy Polit Santé. 2013 Aug 19;9(1):8–11.
19. Wilsford D. Path Dependency, or Why History Makes It Difficult but Not Impossible to Reform Health Care Systems in a Big Way. J Public Policy. 1994 Jul;14(3):251–83.
20. Moisidou DA. Beveridge, Bismarck and Southern European Health Care Systems: Can we decide which the Best in EU-15 is? A Statistical Analysis. 2017;5.
21. Whiteside N. The Beveridge Report and Its Implementation: a Revolutionary Project? Histoire@Politique. 2014;24(3):24.
22. van der Zee J, Kroneman MW. Bismarck or Beveridge: a beauty contest between dinosaurs. BMC Health Serv Res. 2007 Dec;7(1):94.
23. Kutzin J. Bismarck vs. Beveridge: is there increasing convergence between health financing systems? 2011;31.
24. Mossé P. Steering from bismarck to beveridge: the french experience. Rev Bras Em Promoção Saúde [Internet]. 2018 Dec 21 [cited 2021 Jan 31];31(4). Available from: http://periodicos.unifor.br/RBPS/article/view/8781.

25. Chevreul K, Brigham KB, Durand-Zaleski I, Hernandez-Quevedo C. Health Systems in Transition: France Health System Review. 2015;17(3). Available from: http://www.euro.who.int/__data/assets/pdf_file/0011/297938/France-HiT.pdf?ua=1.
26. McKee M, Healy J, European Observatory on Health Care Systems, editors. Hospitals in a changing Europe. Buckingham; Philadelphia: Open University Press; 2002. 295 p. (European Observatory on Health Care Systems series).
27. Põlluste K, Kasiulevičius V, Veide S, Kringos DS, Boerma W, Lember M. Primary care in Baltic countries: A comparison of progress and present systems. Health Policy. 2013 Feb;109(2):122–30.
28. Private Hospital Association [Internet]. [cited 2020 Jun 20]. Private Hospitals in Ireland. Available from: http://privatehospitals.ie/private-hospitals-in-ireland/.
29. McDaid D, Wiley M, Maresso A, Mossialos E. Health Systems in Transition: Ireland Health Systems Review. 2009;11(4):298.
30. Janulyte V, Aleksejuniene J, Puriene A, Peciuliene V, Benzian H. Current employment characteristics and career intentions of Lithuanian dentists. Hum Resour Health. 2014 Dec;12(1):74.
31. Busse R, Blümel M. Health Systems in Transition: Germany Health System Review. 2014;16(2):331.
32. Simões J de A, Augusto GF, Fronteira I, Hernandez-Quevedo. Health Systems in Transition: Portugal Health System Review [Internet]. Copenhagen: European Observatory on Health Systems and Policies; 2017 p. 211. (Health Systems in Transition). Report No.: Vol 19, No. 2. Available from: http://www.euro.who.int/__data/assets/pdf_file/0007/337471/HiT-Portugal.pdf?ua=1.
33. Ferré F, de Belvis AG, Valerio L, Longhi S, Lazzari A, Fattore G, *et al.* Health Systems in Transition: Italy Health System Review. 2014;16(4):200.
34. Luxembourg Country Health Profile 2017 [Internet]. Paris: OECD; 2017 [cited 2020 Jun 20] p. 20. (State of Health in the EU). Available from: http://dx.doi.org/10.1787/9789264283480-en.
35. Kroneman M, Boerma W, van den Berg M, Groenewegen P, de Jong J, van Ginneken E. Health Systems in Transition: Netherlands Health System Review. 2016;18(2).
36. Economou C, Kaitelidou D, Karanikolos M, Maresso A. Health Systems in Transition: Greece Health System Review. 2017;19(5):196.
37. UK Government Dental Contract Reform [Internet]. Available from: https://www.gov.uk/government/collections/dental-contract-reform-prototypes.

38. Vuorenkoski L, Mladovsky P, Mossialos E. Health Systems in Transition: Finland [Internet]. Copenhagen: European Observatory on Health Systems and Policies; 2008 p. 195. (Health System Review). Report No.: 10 (4). Available from: http://www.euro.who.int/__data/assets/pdf_file/0007/80692/E91937.pdf?ua=1.
39. Linden J, Widström E, Sinkkonen J. Adults' dental treatment in 2001–2013 in Finnish public dental service. BMC Oral Health. 2020 Dec;20(1):121.
40. Council of European Dentists. CED Resolution: Dental Practice and Third Parties in Europe [Internet]. CED; 2018 [cited 2020 Jun 15]. Available from: https://cedentists.eu/component/policy/policy/79-ced-resolution-dental-practice-and-third-parties-in-europe.html.
41. Biggs A. Dental reform: an overview of universal dental schemes [Internet]. Australia: Social Policy Section, Parliament of Australia; 2012 [cited 2020 Jul 15] p. 13. (Department of Parliamentary Services). Available from: http://parlinfo.aph.gov.au/parlInfo/download/library/prspub/1438909/upload_binary/1438909.pdf;fileType=application/pdf#search=%222010s%20background%20note%20(parliamentary%20library,%20australia)%22.
42. Holmstöm C. Ekonomiafacta. 2019 [cited 2020 Jun 10]. Varden i privat regi. Available from: https://www.ekonomifakta.se/Fakta/Valfarden-i-privat-regi/Vard-och-omsorg-i-privat-regi/Varden-i-privat-regi/.
43. Lowe RF, Montagu D. Legislation, regulation, and consolidation in the retail pharmacy sector in low-income countries. South Med Rev. 2009;2(2):35–44.
44. Panteli D, Arickx F, Cleemput I, Dedet G, Eckhardt H, Fogarty E, *et al.* Pharmaceuitical regulation in 15 European countries: Review. Health Syst Transit. 2016;18(5):1–118.
45. Dudley J. OTC Distribution in Europe - the 2016 edition - Facing the Challenges of the New Global Agenda. James Dudley International; 2016.
46. Massialos E, Mrazek M, Walley T. Regulating Pharmaceuticals in Europe: Striving for Efficiency, Equity and Quality. Qual Saf Health Care. 2005 Jun 1;14(3):227–8.
47. Volmer D, Bell JS, Janno R, Raal A, Hamilton DD, Airaksinen MS. Change in public satisfaction with community pharmacy services in Tartu, Estonia, between 1993 and 2005. Res Soc Adm Pharm. 2009 Dec;5(4):337–46.
48. Habicht T, Reinap M, KaseKamp K, Sikkut R, Aaben L, van Ginneken E. Health Systems in Transition: Estonia Health System Review. 2018;20(1):220.
49. Anell A, Glenngard A, Merkur S. Health Systems in Transition: Sweden Health System Review. OECD. 2012;14(5):1–159.

50. OECD. Government at a Glance 2017 [Internet]. Paris: OECD; 2017 [cited 2021 Jan 26]. 282 p. Available from: http://dx.doi.org/10.1787/gov_glance-2017-en.
51. Wendt C, Kohl J, Mischke M, Pfeifer M. How Do Europeans Perceive Their Healthcare System? Patterns of Satisfaction and Preference for State Involvement in the Field of Healthcare. Eur Sociol Rev. 2010 Apr 1;26(2):177–92.
52. Preker AS, Harding A, Travis P. "Make or buy" decisions in the production of health care goods and services: new insights from institutional economics and organizational theory. Bull World Health Organ. 2000;12.

# Chapter 3

# Standard Survey Data: Insights into Private Sector Utilization*

**Dominic Montagu and Nirali Chakraborty**

## Abstract

Authors Dominic Montagu and Nirali Chakraborty explore who uses the private sector and for what in this chapter. Universal health coverage in LMICs is increasingly expanding through the incorporation of private clinics, pharmacies, and hospitals into an overall health system funded in whole or in part through government-managed health insurance. This underscores the importance of policies on health provision, which apply across the whole delivery system regardless of ownership status. In this chapter, we summarize current knowledge on the scale and scope of private provision in LMICs. To accomplish this, we have analyzed data on the source of inpatient and outpatient care from 65 countries. While past studies have conducted similar analyses, ours advances the field in two ways. First, we limit our analysis to data sets from 2010 to 2019, making our study more up-to-date than past studies, while changing health-seeking patterns for maternal health since 2010 means that our data set is more representative of overall inpatient care. Second, while past multi-country analyses of public–private ownership have been based on the Demographic Health Surveys, we have added to this data from the

---

*This chapter was originally published in "Montagu, D, and Chakraborty, N. Frontiers in Medicine, Vol. 8 (2021) 624285".

Multiple Indicator Cluster Surveys, significantly increasing the number of countries in our analysis.

Key findings from our analysis, according to the World Health Organization regions, are as follows: outside of the EURO region, where the private sector delivers just 4% of all healthcare services, the private sector remains significant and, in many countries, represents more than half of all care. The private sector provides nearly 40% of all healthcare in PAHO, AFRO, and WPRO regions, 57% in SEARO, and 62% in EMRO. While specific countries with two recent surveys show variation in the scale of both inpatient and outpatient private provision, we did not find regional or global trends toward or away from private care within LMICs. Private inpatient care is most important for the wealthy in many countries; public versus private care varies less, by wealth, for outpatient services.

## Introduction

This study sets out to summarize the importance of private provision of inpatient and outpatient care within health systems of 65 countries in Latin America, Africa, Europe, and Asia. We expand on and update prior studies which have used similar data, and create regional summaries. The reason to undertake this analysis is the change in delivery patterns around the world which makes our data set of inpatient source of care a better proxy for overall inpatient care than was true in the past, and the expansion in recent years of both the system level goal of Universal Health Coverage (UHC) and of the use of Social Health Insurance (SHI) as a vehicle to advance it (1). SHI initiatives are increasingly engaging the private sector as a necessary way to achieve UHC in countries where a large part of the existing service provision infrastructure, providers, and care-seeking, is private.

The push toward UHC has thus underscored the need to assure common standards of care are applied to both public and private sector facilities and providers, and that all sources of healthcare are coordinated regardless of ownership status. Referrals between public and private providers, pharmacies, laboratories, blood banks, and hospitals must be seamless and efficient if care for patients is to take precedence over monopolies driven either by profit or ideology. Sharing of data, diagnosis, medicines, and information is often critical for public health. The experiences of tuberculosis and vaccines have shown the world that integration of care between public and private is possible, and that when done well it can greatly advance health goals (2). Advancing both integration and common standards requires adjustments, often significant adjustments, to regulatory systems designed to address only the public sector. These changes include policy, programmatic, and implementation challenges (3). Addressing them requires the awareness and attention of policy makers, and of global institutions which can provide guidance and examples of relevant best practices. The work of this study is intended to inform both of these constituencies, as well as providing information on where lessons applicable to any one country may best be drawn.

## Measuring the Private Sector

For nearly 20 years nationally representative surveys have been used to identify variations in access to health services by country and region as well as across wealth and geographic regions within countries. Using Demographic and Health Surveys (DHS) researchers have been able to inform policy and program decision-making with information on care-seeking for families with pediatric illnesses, maternity services, and family planning. This survey data can inform country comparisons. It matters, for example, for national governments, international agencies, and donors to know that 80% of pediatric care in Pakistan is sourced exclusively from the private sector, while in Ethiopia the percent of all pediatric care that is private is only 24% (4,5).

Payment data has the potential to offer an alternative measure of public–private health mix in many countries, however there are challenges. With some variation depending on the source data used, there is consistency in findings that 95% or more of all private expenditure on health is out-of-pocket (OOP) payment for care directly to providers, and that OOP payments are surprisingly stable, hovering around two percent of GDP. An important implication of this is that OOP decreases as a percent of total healthcare expenditures as countries become wealthier and government expenditures toward health increase (6). Domestic private expenditure makes up nearly 50% of current health expenditure in the WHO AFRO region, 61.4% in EMRO and 67.5% in SEARO (7). While private voluntary insurance and social health insurance expansion is changing this slowly, the effects of both are relatively small in LMICs (1, 8).

Expenditures are a strong measure of the risks of household impoverishment and of access challenges, but show poor correlation to source of care: payments are made to both public and private providers. As such, OOP payments are not a good measure of the importance of the private sector relative to overall healthcare service provision (6,9,10). Utilization of care, measured through mostly-standardized questions on large-scale household surveys around the world, provides a more stable and comparable — across times and countries — estimate of the private sector's importance overall. This in turn can inform the need for policy attention to focus specifically on privately owned pharmacies, clinics, and hospitals within the context of overall health systems regulation and guidance.

The importance of policy decisions specific to private healthcare provision has been underscored by recent analysis (10), and by the growing recognition that private healthcare, in many LMICs, is external to both the regulatory and financing systems which are expanding to assure Universal Health Coverage (3,11). Where regulatory and subsidy systems have included private providers, the results have been overall improvements in access and quality; better than when these same providers act externally to the national overall health regulatory structure (12). Evidence on the importance of private provision within overall national contexts is therefore important as policy makers consider how much attention to give to this issue. Informing this is knowledge of what other countries might have provider sectors of roughly equivalent scale and so provide models worth examining to inform national policies (13–16).

Past efforts to provide this evidence have relied primarily on the DHS as the sole source of nationally representative data on source of care (4,17–19). We have both updated the DHS data used from prior studies, and nearly doubled our data points by added in surveys from UNICEF's Multiple Indicator Cluster Surveys (20).

Our analysis examines 65 countries using DHS and MICS surveys, including more countries than previous studies by Campbell and Footman (21–23). Our work also utilizes data sets from 2010 to 2019, updating previous work that used data from time points between 1990 and 2014 (18,21–25). We have used a specific definition of the private sector to include private hospitals, NGO or faith-based hospitals, private clinic/doctor, private pharmacy, and other NGO or faith-based operations such as clinics, outreach services, or community health workers. Our specificity of the definition of the private sector, examination of changes over time, and use of recent data sources are novel.

## Methods

Using freely available standardized, nationally representative survey data, we estimate the relative use of the public and private sectors across a diverse set of LMICs. After reviewing available data sources, only the Demographic and Health Surveys (DHS) and the Multiple Indicator Cluster Surveys (MICS) provided comparable and comprehensive information on source of care for inpatient and outpatient conditions.

### *Data*

Parameters for inclusion were that a country has a nationally representative MICS or DHS survey between 2014 and 2019. A second survey, if present, needed to have been conducted between 2010 to within 3 years of the first survey, with preference given for the shortest time period within this if there are more than a single survey meeting these criteria. Surveys spanning 2 years (such as 2014–2015) are defined as having been conducted in the earlier year, which has implications for inclusion criteria in some instances. One hundred and twelve surveys met these criteria, however one survey was excluded because the data did not match the other datafiles (Guinea-Bissau MICS 2010). The total number of countries included in the analysis is 65.

The analysis uses information on care seeking for delivery as a proxy for inpatient care. Similarly, care seeking for childhood illnesses is a proxy for outpatient care. The analysis investigates proportion of care sought within the public vs. private sector. Surveys conducted between 2010 and 2019 cover DHS rounds 6 and 7, and MICS rounds 4–6. The surveys differ across rounds, in definition of illness, and populations for whom data is collected. For example, in DHS surveys, the analysis obtains information on the place of birth, for a woman's most recent birth in the past 5 years, while in MICS surveys, this may be in the past 2 or 3 years.

For childhood illnesses, the analysis categorizes the place of care sought, for an illness in the prior 2 weeks for the youngest child under age 5 in the household. Illnesses included in the study are diarrhea, or Acute Respiratory Infection (ARI)/Fever. Care seeking for ARI (suspected pneumonia) and fever are reported together in all of the surveys for which children with fever are asked about place of care sought.

## *Definitions*

The definition of ARI used is consistent with that used for each source survey, and the definitions differ across source surveys (DHS 6, DHS 7, MICS6, MICS 4, and 5).

### *Definitions of ARI*

#### DHS 6

Cough accompanied by short rapid breathing. Children with cough who do not meet definition of ARI were still asked about care-seeking. We have removed them from the denominator and only conducted analyses on those who meet definition of fever or ARI (suspected pneumonia) as defined by the survey.

#### DHS 7

Short rapid breathing which was chest-related, and/or difficult breathing which was chest related. Children with rapid breathing that is not chest related do not meet the definition of ARI, but were still asked about care-seeking. We have removed them from the denominator and only conducted analyses on those who meet definition of fever or ARI (suspected pneumonia) as defined by the survey.

#### MICS (4–6)

Definition of ARI is illness with a cough, accompanied by a rapid or difficult breathing and whose symptoms were due to a problem in the chest, or both a problem in the chest and a blocked nose. Children with rapid breathing that is not chest related do not meet the definition of ARI, but were still asked about care- seeking. We have removed them from the denominator and only conducted analyses on those who meet definition of fever or ARI (suspected pneumonia) as defined by the survey. In some MICS5 surveys, the question on whether the problem was in the chest is not asked. In MICS4 surveys, place of care-seeking for fever or diarrhea is not asked.

For each household with an included reason for care, the analytic dataset captures the country, year, household weight, household wealth quintile, reason for needed care (recent birth, diarrhea, fever or ARI) and source(s) of care for the illness. Additionally, we include the WHO region and sub-region, and country population for the year of the survey from the UN Population Division. For childhood illnesses, more than one source of care for an episode was possible. Source of care was manually recategorized into one of 9 mutually exclusive categories (**Box 1**). Each country's data extraction and log files were rechecked by a second analyst for quality control. Surveys from Cuba and Qatar did not include any wealth quintiles. Surveys from Columbia 2015, Serbia and Kazakhstan did not ask about childhood illness.

## BOX 1: Sources of care

1. **Public Sector**
   a. Hospital
      i. *Classify hospital/clinic as a hospital*
   b. Everything else
      i. *Clinic, CHW, PHC, etc*
2. **Private sector**
   a. Private Hospital
   b. NGO or FBO Hospital
   c. Private Clinic / doctor
   d. Private Pharmacy
   e. NGO or FBO other
      i. *NGO clinic, NGO outreach, NGO Community health worker, etc.*
   f. Shop, drug seller, other (classified as informal)
3. **No care sought outside of home**

If it was not clear what sector a source of care belongs to, then it is classified as "other." As a result, some care that is counted as informal may actually be provided by a trained health worker. An example of this is a code of "fieldworker," without any specification as to what sector the fieldworker belongs to. In some analyses, private sector care is subcategorized into (a) Private hospitals, clinics, doctors, and pharmacies; (b) NGO and FBO facilities; (c) Informal facilities.

## Regional Analyses

For the most recent survey for countries within each WHO region, data were weighted by country population size for the year of the survey. Wealth quintiles were kept as in the original country data, so the regional analyses by wealth represent the behavior of households in the same relative wealth groups.

## Assumptions and Limitations

We make a number of assumptions in summarizing and analyzing this data, and in particular in drawing conclusions about all inpatient, outpatient, and overall health system usage based on sources for only a few care-seeking practices. We do so primarily because these data provide more information with which to make system-level inferences than other sources. We use them not for their accuracy, but because they are less inaccurate than other options.

Specifically, in our analysis we assume that care seeking patterns for childbirth represent inpatient care seeking patterns. We assume that care seeking for routine childhood illnesses (ARI, Fever and Diarrhea) represent outpatient care seeking patterns. We recognize that these assumptions are weak, and that they are simply a result of lack of available data across countries for care sought for other reasons. Additionally, the data on childhood illness is with regard to illnesses in the 2 weeks prior to the survey, while for birth, the recall period ranges from 2 to 5 years, depending on the survey. No attempt was made to reconcile the time periods, when describing care-seeking patterns as the focus of this analysis is on ratios of care-seeking, not quantity of care-seeking. WHO analysis shows that of all spending on health within 46 LMIC for which there is data, 25% is spent on inpatient and day curative care, and 28% is spent on outpatient and home-based curative care(7). Using this ratio, we weight the data on source of care by reason, in order to derive an estimate of overall care-seeking patterns.

## Results

Of the 65 countries for which we have data, the majority are in the WHO African region(26), followed by the region of the Americas(11). There were 49 countries with MICS surveys meeting inclusion criteria, and 62 countries with DHS surveys. (See **Table 1** for list).

**TABLE 1.** Country and data sources included.

| | Survey type | |
|---|---|---|
| Country | MICS | DHS |
| Afghanistan | 1 | 1 |
| Albania | | 1 |
| Angola | | 1 |
| Armenia | | 2 |
| Bangladesh | | 2 |
| Belize | 2 | |
| Benin | 1 | 1 |
| Burundi | | 2 |
| Cambodia | | 2 |
| Cameroon | 1 | 1 |
| Chad | 1 | 1 |
| Colombia | | 2 |
| Congo | 1 | 1 |
| Cote d'Ivoire | 1 | 1 |
| Cuba | 2 | |
| Dominican Republic | 1 | |
| Egypt | | 1 |
| El Salvador | 1 | |

*(Continued)*

**TABLE 1.** (*Continued*)

| | Survey type | |
|---|---|---|
| Country | MICS | DHS |
| Eswatini | 2 | |
| Ethiopia | | 2 |
| Gambia | 1 | 1 |
| Ghana | 1 | 1 |
| Guatemala | | 1 |
| Guinea | | 2 |
| Guinea-Bissau | 1 | |
| Guyana | 1 | |
| Haiti | | 2 |
| India | | 1 |
| Indonesia | | 2 |
| Iraq | 2 | |
| Jordan | | 2 |
| Kazakhstan | 2 | |
| Kenya | | 1 |
| Kyrgyzstan | 2 | |
| Lao People's Democratic Republic | 2 | |
| Lesotho | | 1 |
| Malawi | | 2 |
| Maldives | | 1 |
| Mali | 1 | 1 |
| Mauritania | 2 | |
| Mexico | 1 | |
| Mongolia | 2 | |
| Myanmar | | 1 |
| Nepal | | 2 |

**TABLE 1.** (*Continued*)

| Country | Survey type | |
|---|---|---|
| | MICS | DHS |
| Nigeria | 1 | 1 |
| Pakistan | | 2 |
| Paraguay | 1 | |
| Philippines | | 2 |
| Rwanda | | 2 |
| Sao Tome and Principe | 1 | |
| Senegal* | | 2 |
| Serbia | 2 | |
| Sierra Leone | 1 | 1 |
| South Africa | | 1 |
| State of Palestine | 2 | |
| Sudan | 2 | |
| Suriname | 2 | |
| Tajikistan | | 2 |
| Tanzania | | 2 |
| Thailand | 2 | |
| Timor-Leste | | 1 |
| Tunisia | 2 | |
| Turkmenistan | 1 | |
| Uganda | | 2 |
| Zimbabwe | | 2 |
| **Total** | **49** | **62** |

**Senegal uses a continuous DHS survey.*

The region with the greatest reliance on the private sector is the Eastern Mediterranean region; weighted regional results from most recent surveys in each country indicate that 53% of inpatient and 66% of outpatient care takes place in the for-profit private sector (**Figure 1**). This data is heavily influenced by Egypt and Pakistan. Conversely, citizens in the WHO European region are the most reliant upon public sector services, as seen within the eastern European and Central Asian countries for which we have data (96% of care sought in public sector).

For outpatient care in Africa, 35% of those who seek care go to the for-profit private sector, while 17% seek care at shops, faith healers and other informal providers (**Figure 2**). Overall, 26% of care seeking is done in the private sector, with an additional 10% with informal providers.

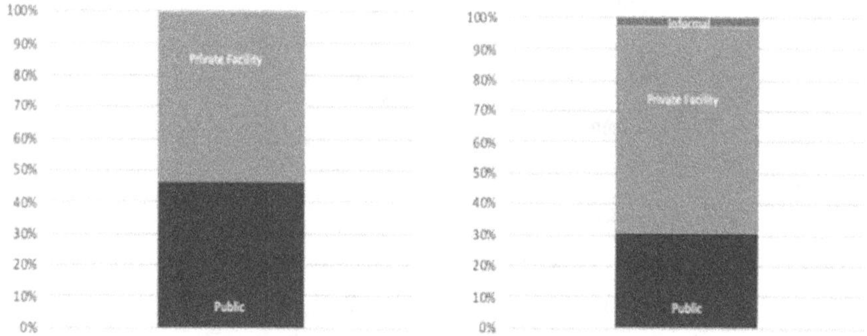


(a) (b)

**FIGURE 1.** (a) Public/Private inpatient distribution EMRO. (b) Public/Private outpatient distribution EMRO.

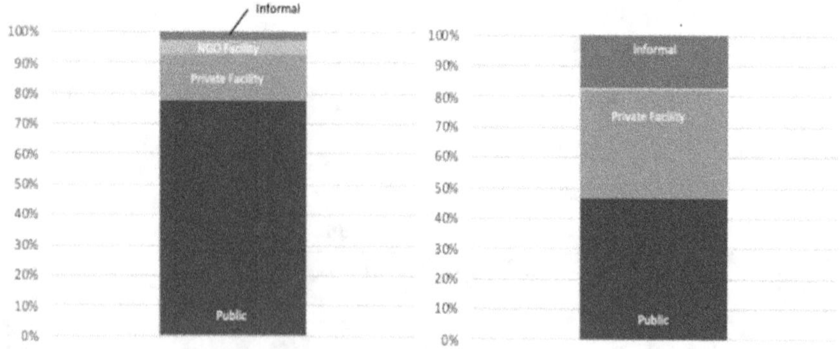


(a) (b)

**FIGURE 2.** (a) Public/Private inpatient distribution AFRO. (b) Public/Private outpatient distribution AFRO.

**TABLE 2.** Proportion of care provided by private sector medical providers — Top 3 countries per region.

| | | Private as a percent of all care | | |
|---|---|---|---|---|
| Region | Country | Total | Inpatient | Outpatient |
| African | Uganda | 40.2 | 21.4 | 56.9 |
| | Nigeria | 36.8 | 33 | 40.2 |
| | Swaziland | 29 | 31.6 | 26.7 |
| Americas | Mexico | 33 | 15.8 | 48.3 |
| | Suriname | 28.6 | 29.9 | 27.4 |
| | Dominican Republic | 28.3 | 29.7 | 27.1 |
| Eastern Med | Egypt | 75.2 | 71.2 | 78.8 |
| | Pakistan | 73.8 | 65.5 | 81.2 |
| | Jordan | 44.9 | 33.9 | 54.6 |
| European | Albania | 7.8 | 3.4 | 11.8 |
| | Kyrgyzstan | 7.1 | 1.5 | 12.1 |
| | Armenia | 4.5 | 3.8 | 5.4 |
| South-Fast Asia | Indonesia | 60 | 61 | 59.1 |
| | Bangladesh | 57.2 | 59.5 | 55.2 |
| | India | 52.6 | 34.3 | 68.8 |
| Western Pacific | Cambodia | 33 | 17.6 | 46.7 |
| | Philippines | 32.2 | 29.1 | 34.9 |
| | Laos | 14.6 | 2.5 | 25.3 |

The greatest proportion of private sector care seeking occurs in Nigeria (52%), while in Cameroon, Uganda and Benin, >40% of care is sought in the private sector. All figures are for those who choose to seek care for the conditions studied in this analysis.

**Table 2** lists the top three most privatized countries in each WHO region, and the overall, inpatient and outpatient proportion of care sought in for-profit private sector (excluding NGO or Informal). **Table 3** gives ownership proportions for each WHO region.

For those countries with more than one data set we have examined the changes in percent of care sourced from private providers (**Table 4**).

**TABLE 3.** Ownership ratio by WHO region.

| | | Inpatient (%) | Outpatient (%) |
|---|---|---|---|
| PAHO | Informal | 1 | 9 |
| | NGO | 0 | 0 |
| | Private | 31 | 37 |
| | Public | 68 | 54 |
| AFRO | Informal | 3 | 17 |
| | NGO | 4 | 1 |
| | Private | 15 | 35 |
| | Public | 78 | 47 |
| EMRO | Informal | 0 | 3 |
| | NGO | 0 | 0 |
| | Private | 53 | 66 |
| | Public | 46 | 31 |
| EURO | Informal | 0 | 1 |
| | NGO | 0 | 0 |
| | Private | 1 | 7 |
| | Public | 99 | 93 |
| SEARO | Informal | 0 | 7 |
| | NGO | 1 | 0 |
| | Private | 35 | 68 |
| | Public | 64 | 24 |
| WIPRO | Informal | 3 | 12 |
| | NGO | 0 | 0 |
| | Private | 27 | 36 |
| | Public | 70 | 51 |

*Weighted by country population from year of most recent DHS or MICS survey.*

While variations are clearly smaller for inpatient services than outpatient (reflecting perhaps the stability inherent to high-infrastructure investment costs), there are no clear global or regional trends toward overall increase or decrease of private care.

**TABLE 4.** Change in private sector percentage of service provision, most recent two surveys.

| Country | Inpatient (%) | Outpatient (%) |
|---|---|---|
| Afghanistan | 1 | –8 |
| Armenia | 0 | 0 |
| Bangladesh | 0 | –2 |
| Belize | 1 | 8 |
| Benin | 1 | –8 |
| Burundi | –2 | –2 |
| Cambodia | –1 | –1 |
| Cameroon | 0 | –18 |
| Chad | –2 | 9 |
| Colombia | 0 | 0 |
| Congo | 1 | 3 |
| CoteD'lvoire | 3 | –15 |
| Cuba | 0 | 0 |
| Ethiopia | 1 | 1 |
| Gambia | 1 | 1 |
| Ghana | –1 | –9 |
| Guinea | 0 | 10 |
| Haiti | 0 | –1 |
| Indonesia | 0 | 1 |
| Iraq | 0 | –1 |
| Jordan | 1 | 0 |
| Kazakhstan | 0 | 0 |
| Kyrgyzstan | 0 | –1 |
| Laos | –5 | 4 |
| Malawi | –2 | –4 |
| Mali | –1 | 5 |
| Mauritania | 0 | 13 |
| Mongolia | 0 | 0 |
| Nepal | –2 | –1 |

(*Continued*)

**TABLE 4.** (*Continued*)

| Country | Inpatient (%) | Outpatient (%) |
|---|---|---|
| Nigeria | 5 | 12 |
| Pakistan | 0 | –1 |
| Palestine | –1 | –16 |
| Philippines | 2 | 0 |
| Rwanda | –1 | –8 |
| Senegal | 2 | –5 |
| Serbia | 0 | 0 |
| Sierra Leone | 0 | 3 |
| Sudan | –6 | 10 |
| Suriname | 3 | –7 |
| Swaziland | –1 | 3 |
| Tajikistan | 0 | –1 |
| Tanzania | 0 | 2 |
| Thailand | 0 | 1 |
| Tunisia | 0 | –2 |
| Uganda | 0 | –3 |
| Zimbabwe | 1 | 2 |

# DISCUSSION

We are making inferences regarding overall public/private healthcare which have significant implications for policy attention to private providers, based upon a limited set of data. This is due to what data is available, rather than what data would be ideal, but we have no reason to believe there is a systematic bias to the conclusions we draw.

## Drawing Conclusions From Imperfect Data

Perhaps most notably, we use self-reported information on delivery location as a proxy for overall public–private inpatient care ratios. We do not make adjustments for potential differences in care seeking decision differences for delivery vs. other inpatient care seeking; nor do we adjust for differences in bed turnover rates between public and private facilities. We do not explore if delivery rates are reflective of staffing, costs, and health outcomes. These are all important areas for future exploration.

A comparison of OECD reported data and DHS data from Mexico shows that all-bed ratios and patient reported delivery site ratios are broadly aligned; 26% private for all-beds, vs. 16% private for deliveries (27). Data from Kenya suggests that private bed turnover ratios (the number of deliveries/bed) are roughly half that of public facilities, meaning that for every 10 women who report delivering in a private facility 20 will have delivered in a public facility of the same size (26). A study from Nepal suggests that bed occupancy rates in Maternity wards is not very different from overall hospital bed occupancy rates (91 vs. 74%) and, importantly for our study, that more than two fifths of all inpatients (41.86%) were admitted in the maternity ward (28). Facility deliveries have increased significantly in the past decade (24). With the exception of only the poorest quintiles in the AFRO region, the majority of the respondents included in our analysis delivered their last child in a healthcare facility. Based on all of this we believe that in the absence of better data it is appropriate to use place-of-delivery data as an unbiased proxy for overall inpatient care in LMICs around the world. A similar argument justifies the use of our pediatric data as a proxy for outpatient care sources.

## Conclusions

Our findings confirm earlier studies showing that the private sector remains dominant for outpatient care in many countries, particularly in AFRO, EMRO, and SEARO regions, and significant in inpatient care across the same parts of the world. Comparing our findings to earlier studies, and across repeated surveys within our timeframe, we do not find any clear trend to increasing or decreasing private provision as a component of LMIC health systems. This is perhaps not surprising: the evidence from health systems in OECD countries shows a wide range of ownership frameworks associated with country delivery models, no one clearly evident of better quality or efficiency than another (29,30). Indeed, in a number of countries the ratio of public to private ownership of care delivery have changed significantly within just a few years as policies have shifted: evidence of the political nature of ownership decisions, but not of the benefits of one ownership model over another which, if clear, would lead to a trend as countries advance in wealth or effectiveness of national governance (31,32). Rather than search for, plan for, or encourage a shift toward greater or smaller private participation in healthcare deliver, our findings show that mixed healthcare systems remain the norm in LMIC countries, across regions, and across wealth levels within countries.

The implications of this for UHC are important for regulation and policy, and the national planning bodies responsible for governance together with the global agencies that advise and support them: the management of mixed public and private healthcare systems will determine the success or failure to achieve UHC for many countries. Our analysis should provide countries with a path to identify nations with similar levels of public–private mix, with which to study and share experiences on quality assurance, reporting, referral integration, financing systems, and the many other aspects critical to good management in a complex delivery context.

Further work and examination of lessons specific to countries and regions will be needed to inform better policies in the future.

## Data Availability Statement

Publicly available datasets were analyzed in this study. This data can be found here: https://dhsprogram.com/; https://mics.unicef.org/.

## Author Contributions

DM and NC designed the study, agreed on interpretation, and analysis of results. NC extracted the data, led the analysis, and reviewed and edited the final draft. DM wrote the paper. Both authors contributed to the article and approved the submitted version.

## Funding

This work was supported by a contract from the World Health Organization PO 202382734. The funder was not involved in analysis or writing of this paper and had not influence on it's contents.

## References

1. Cotlear D, Nagpal S, Smith O, Tandon A, Cortez R. *Going Universal: How 24 Developing Countries are Implementing Universal Health Insurance Reforms from the Bottom Up*. Washington, D.C: World Bank; 2015.
2. World Health Organization. *Public–private mix for TB prevention and care: a roadmap*. Geneva: World Health Organization; 2018. Report No.: WHO/CDS/TB/2018.32.
3. Sieverding M, Onyango C, Suchman L. Private healthcare provider experiences with social health insurance schemes: Findings from a qualitative study in Ghana and Kenya. *PLoS ONE*. 2018 Feb 22; 13(2):e0192973.
4. Bradley SEK, Rosapep L, Shiras T. Sources for Sick Child Care in 24 USAID Priority Countries [Internet]. Bethesda, MD: Abt Associates; 2017 p. 12. (Sustaining Health Outcomes through the Private Sector Plus Project). Available from: https://www.privatesectorcounts.org/childhealth/prevalence.html.
5. ShopsPlusProject. Private Sector Counts. [cited 2021 Mar 8]. Private Sector Counts.org. Available from: https://www.privatesectorcounts.org/childhealth/prevalence.html.
6. Musgrove P, Zeramdini R, Carrin G. Basic patterns in national health expenditure. *Bull World Health Organ*. 2002;13.
7. World Health Organization. Global Spending on Health: a world in transition [Internet]. WHO; 2019. (WHO/HIS/HGF/HFWorkingPaper/19.4). Available from: https://www.who.int/health_financing/documents/health-expenditure-report-2019.pdf?ua=1.
8. Ly C, Eozenou P, Nandakumar A, Pablos-Mendez A, Evans T, Adeyi O. The economic transition of health in Africa: A call for progressive pragmatism to shape the future of health financing. *Health Syst Reform*. 2017 Oct 2; 3(4):290–300.
9. Mackintosh M, Channon A, Karan A, Selvaraj S, Cavagnero E, Zhao H. What is the private sector? Understanding private provision in the health systems of low-income and middle-income countries. *The Lancet*. 2016 Aug;388(10044):596–605.
10. McPake B, Hanson K. Managing the public–private mix to achieve universal health coverage. *The Lancet*. 2016 Aug;388(10044):622–30.
11. Suchman L, Hart E, Montagu D. Public–private partnerships in practice: collaborating to improve health finance policy in Ghana and Kenya. *Health Policy Plan*. 2018;0(0):9.

12. Malmborg R, Mann G, Squire S. A systematic assessment of the concept and practice of public-private mix for tuberculosis care and control. *Int J Equity Health*. 2011;10(1):49.
13. Berman P, Rose L. The role of private providers in maternal and child health and family planning services in developing countries. *Health Policy Plan*. 1996;11(2):142–55.
14. Newell J. The implications for TB control of the growth in numbers of private practitioners in developing countries. *Bull World Health Organ*. 2002;80(2):2.
15. Olorunsaiye CZ, Langhamer MS, Wallace AS, Watkins ML. Missed opportunities and barriers for vaccination: a descriptive analysis of private and public health facilities in four African countries. *Pan Afr Med J* [Internet]. 2017 [cited 2019 Dec 23];27. Available from: http://www.panafrican-med-journal.com/content/series/27/3/6/full/
16. Clarke D, Doerr S, Hunter M, Schmets G, Soucat A, Paviza A. The private sector and universal health coverage. *Bull World Health Organ*. 2019 Jun 1;97(6):434–5.
17. Montagu D, Visconti A. *Health Care Utilization Around the World* [Internet]. Presentation presented at; 2011 [cited 2021 Mar 8]; San Francisco, CA. Available from: https://www.shopsplusproject.org/resource-center/health-care-utilization-around-world
18. Grepin KA. Private sector an important but not dominant provider of key health services in low- and middle-income countries. *Health Aff* (Millwood). 2016 Jul;35(7):1214–21.
19. Montagu D, Goodman C. Prohibit, constrain, encourage, or purchase: How should we engage with the private health-care sector? *The Lancet*. 2016 Aug;388(10044):613–21.
20. UNICEF. Multiple Indicator Cluster Survey (MICS). 2019 [cited 2019 Nov 20]. Multiple Indicator Cluster Survey (MICS) _ Statistics and Monitoring _ UNICEF.htm. Available from: https://www.unicef.org/statistics/index_24302.html
21. Campbell OMR, Benova L, Macleod D, Goodman C, Footman K, Pereira AL, *et al*. Who, What, Where: an analysis of private sector family planning provision in 57 low- and middle-income countries. *Trop Med Int Health TM IH*. 2015 Dec;20(12):1639–56.
22. Campbell OMR, Cegolon L, Macleod D, Benova L. Length of stay after childbirth in 92 countries and associated factors in 30 low- and middle-income countries: Compilation of reported data and a cross-sectional analysis from nationally representative surveys. Myers JE, editor. *PLoS Med*. 2016 Mar 8;13(3):e1001972.

23. Footman K, Benova L, Goodman C, Macleod D, Lynch CA, Penn-Kekana L, *et al.* Using multi-country household surveys to understand who provides reproductive and maternal health services in low- and middle-income countries: a critical appraisal of the Demographic and Health Surveys. *Trop Med Int Health*. 2015 May;20(5):589–606.
24. Montagu D, Sudhinaraset M, Diamond-Smith N, Campbell O, Gabrysch S, Freedman L, *et al.* Where women go to deliver: Understanding the changing landscape of childbirth in Africa and Asia. *Health Policy Plan*. 2017 Oct 1;32(8):1146–52.
25. Chakraborty NM, Sprockett A. Use of family planning and child health services in the private sector: An equity analysis of 12 DHS surveys. *Int J Equity Health*. 2018 Dec;17(1):50.
26. Ayah R, Ongore D, Agwanda ATO. Measuring the effectiveness of maternal delivery services: A cross-sectional and qualitative study of perinatal mortality in six primary referral hospitals, Kenya. F1000Research. 2018 Jun 12;7:732.
27. Organization for Economic Co-operation and Development. OECD.Stat. 2019 [cited 2019 Dec 19]. OECD Statistics. Available from: https://stats.oecd.org/.
28. Paudel BP, Paudel, GS. Study on management efficiency of a tertiary level referral hospital in western Nepal. *MOJ Yoga Phys Ther*. 2018;3(4):102–5.
29. Atun RA, Menabde N, Saluvere K, Jesse M, Habicht J. Introducing a complex health innovation — Primary health care reforms in Estonia (multimethods evaluation). *Health Policy*. 2006 Nov;79(1):79–91.
30. Saltman RB. Structural patterns in Swedish health policy: A 30-year perspective. *Health Econ Policy Law*. 2015 Apr;10(2):195–215.
31. Volmer D, Bell JS, Janno R, Raal A, Hamilton DD, Airaksinen MS. Change in public satisfaction with community pharmacy services in Tartu, Estonia, between 1993 and 2005. *Res Soc Adm Pharm*. 2009 Dec;5(4):337–46.
32. Anell A. The public–private pendulum — patient choice and equity in Sweden. *N Engl J Med*. 2015 Jan 1;372(1):1–4.

# Chapter 4

# Who Serves the Poor? An Equity Analysis of Public and Private Providers of Family Planning and Child Health Services in Kenya*

**Nirali Chakraborty, Dominic Montagu, Joyce Wanderi, and Christine Oduor**

## Abstract

This chapter further explores clients of the private sector, focusing on equity. Authors Nirali Chakraborty, Dominic Montagu, Joyce Wanderi, and Christine Oduor assess differences in the wealth status of clients of family planning and child health services by health sector. It also describes the reasons for facility choice, the cost of services, and the proportion of additional clients of these services and assesses if there are any differences by health sector.

A cross-sectional survey of 2,173 clients from 96 health facilities in urban areas of six counties in Kenya was conducted, stratified by health facility type. The four strata were public, faith-based, private for-profit, and social franchise. Client wealth was benchmarked against the national and urban population of the 2014 Kenya DHS and assessed using EquityTool.

---

*This chapter was originally published in "Chakraborty, N. M., Montagu, D., Wanderi, J. and Oduor, C. Frontiers in Public Health, Vol. 6 (2019) 374".

There were significant differences in client wealth distribution between facility types, and public sector facilities served a significantly higher proportion of poor clients than other types of facilities. In all three non-public facility types, more than 25% of clients were from the poorest two wealth quintiles, without significant differences between facility types. No facility type stands out as expanding access to health services more than another.

Results show that social franchises do better at reaching out to the poor than earlier studies have indicated, though not as well as faith-based and public facilities. The findings suggest that private providers remain important within the larger health system, more so for family planning than childhood illness management. In urban areas with significant facility choice, this study quantifies differences in client wealth across four health sectors. Incorporating these findings into policy and programmatic interventions can improve equity in access to and use of quality health services.

## Introduction

Understanding where women and children seek care is an important first step in being able to provide affordable access to all and to ensure that the care being received is of high quality (1,2). Such knowledge can inform supply side interventions addressing availability and affordability, as well as demand side interventions addressing ability to seek, reach and pay for care, ultimately informing program planning (3).

A number of health financing and health system interventions to improve coverage of basic health services have been implemented throughout LMICs. These include removal or reduction of user fees in the public sector, targeted vouchers for poor clients, contracting out to the private sector, results-based financing initiatives to incentivize improving coverage of particular health services, quality improvement initiatives, and social franchising of private sector providers. Social franchising is an intervention which organizes independent private sector providers under a common brand, provides quality assurance and training, and demand generation services by the franchisor.

As social franchise organizations and other not-for-profit and for-profit service providers have begun to systematically assess equity by capturing the wealth profile of their clients, questions are emerging regarding what an optimal client wealth distribution should be, and how clients at one facility type compare to another facility type including public, private for profit, and not-for-profit institutions.

The Demographic and Health Surveys (DHS) provide an important source of information on the use of basic health services, with the ability to analyze data by various indicators of socio-economic status. These nationally representative surveys are conducted using a standard base questionnaire, and have occurred in over 90 countries, supported by the United States Agency for International Development (USAID). Surveys are often conducted every 5 years in collaboration with national government agencies. In 2004, Gwatkin and colleagues noted that the use of health services is regressive (with the rich using more services than the poor), even for basic and preventative health services such as immunization, medical treatment of childhood illnesses (fever, diarrhea and respiratory infection), and antenatal care (4). A recent multi-country analysis of DHS data also quantified the extent of socio- economic differences in use of health services by sector and country, generally showing that the public sector provides more services to those in the poorest wealth quintile than the private sector, with the poor more likely to forego care for common childhood illness (5). Yet, the private sector is much more heterogeneous than the public sector, comprising both formal and informal sources of care. Formal sources include clinics and pharmacies, while informal sources include drug shops and community-based distributors. The DHS do not allow for more refined distinctions between types of private sector facilities, differentiation between sizes, patient volume, locale, or whether or not private providers are affiliated with franchised networks or other system of support or quality assurance. DHS are not designed to provide sufficient estimates from each type of facility to be able to compare client characteristics, eliminating nuance between types of private sector facilities and detailed information on equity in service use. Thus, while the information provides a national perspective on use, DHS data cannot tell us what the mix of patients is at any one facility type.

## Context

Kenya, a lower-middle income country undergoing an epidemiologic transition, continues to have wealth-related disparities in use of and access to preventive and curative primary health services as well as differences in quality by service type (6–9) In Kenya, 53% of married women use modern methods of family planning (FP); however, there is significant difference in use between those in the wealthiest and poorest quintiles (57.7 vs. 29.2%) (10). The public sector provides 59.9% of all contraception, the remaining 40% is delivered by retail outlets, NGOs, faith-based organizations, social franchised providers, and for-profit clinics. Faith-based organizations are those run by or overseen by a religious entity.

In the 2 weeks preceding the most recent 2014 DHS survey, 8.5% of children had symptoms of acute respiratory infection (ARI), 24.4% had fever and 15.2% had diarrhea. For all illnesses, care was sought from a health facility or provider for more than 55% of cases, irrespective of wealth quintile (10). Source of treatment varies across wealth quintiles for FP and child health illnesses (5).

The private sector, and in particular social franchising, is well- developed in Kenya, and includes PSKenya's Tunza network and Marie Stopes' Amua network. 2014 surveys by Amua showed that 86% of their clients were from the top two wealth quintiles, when benchmarked against the 2008 Kenya DHS survey (KDHS) (11). Given that overall wealth in Kenya has likely increased between 2008 and 2014, these data may not accurately reflect the socio- economic status of franchised clients. It may also be that in the catchment areas served by social franchises, only the wealthy seek care, and public, faith-based, or private for-profit providers would all have equivalent client profiles. We cannot currently make these comparisons because similar data for other providers is not available.

The primary objective for this study is to assess whether there are differences in the wealth status of clients of FP and child health services by health sector. A secondary objective of the study is to describe the proportion of additional clients of FP and child health services, and assess if there are any differences by health sector. Understanding how sectors differ in proportion of additional users served indicates whether any one sector is superior in improving access to care for these services.

## METHODS

### Study Design and Sampling Strategy

An observational, cross-sectional design was employed for this study. The study was restricted to facilities in urban and peri-urban regions only, due to the higher concentration of private sector facilities in these areas. One county from each region except the Nairobi and North-Eastern Regions was selected. These two regions were excluded due to the highly skewed nature of their wealth distributions. The 2014 KDHS indicates that wealth in the other six regions is more equally distributed (10).

Counties without any franchised (Tunza or Amua) or faith based (FBO) facilities were excluded. One county from each region with the highest number of franchised facilities was purposively selected. Within the county, franchised facilities were listed and sorted by sub-county. One sub-county from each county with at least three franchised facilities and three FBO facilities was randomly selected, and a second was randomly selected as the back-up. The back-up was selected in case the facilities in the chosen sub-county did not meet inclusion criteria listed below, or an insufficient number agreed to participate in the study.

### Facility Inclusion Criteria

Facilities were identified from the lists provided by Tunza and Amua franchise managers, as well as the Kenya Master Facility List (MFL), providing details of facility by county, sub-county, facility type, and number of beds. All identified facilities were visited prior to data collection to gain permission to conduct the study, and to assess the facility's suitability for inclusion. Facility in-charge personnel were asked to answer a short questionnaire detailing the types of services offered, and the average number of FP and child health clients seen daily.

Facilities had to be uniquely identified as belonging to one of four categories: 1- public sector (government) health centers or dispensaries; 2- faith based, church, mission hospitals or clinics (FBO); 3- private for-profit hospitals or clinics; 4- private franchised facilities branded as Tunza or Amua. All facilities were located in urban or peri-urban areas, as defined by presence of a daily market and identifiable market center, and reported providing FP and child health services. Level 4 and Level 5 facilities (equivalent to a district or referral hospital) were excluded from the initial frame, because the focus of the study was on primary care services. Having more than 10 inpatient beds was originally included as an exclusion criteria, but not retained due to unreliable data on this factor from the MFL, although efforts were made to select non-hospital private facilities. Facilities that reported seeing on average less than one client per day were excluded.

## Facility Selection

Where possible, facilities were randomly selected after establishing a minimum daily volume of eligible clients required for each facility in that stratum. These minimum daily volumes ranged from three to six clients, depending on the facility type, and determined by the client flow recorded during the eligibility visits.

## Client Inclusion Criteria

Eligible respondents were women aged 18–49 who received a FP service, or guardians of children aged 0–5 who sought care for fever, cough/respiratory infection, or diarrhea (child health services).

## Sample Size

Sample size was calculated to estimate the proportion of clients seeking FP or child health services who are in the poorest 40% of the national population, stratified by facility type, with a desired precision of 5%, power of 80%, and at alpha = 0.05. Data from the 2014 Kenya DHS survey indicating the proportion of users in the bottom 2 wealth quintiles seeking FP services from the public, NGO, and private sector were used to estimate the proportion of users (P) and the maximum sample size require for each stratum. A design effect estimate of 1.8 — more conservative than the highest value provided by KDHS 2014 for each subpopulation — was applied to the resulting sample sizes. This sample was increased by 10% per stratum for non-response.

## Data Collection

Data collection occurred over 4 weeks in August and September 2016. Potential respondents were screened after services had been sought. Interviewers were instructed to approach any woman appearing to be in the eligible age range, as well as anyone exiting with a child who could be five or younger. If they met the inclusion criteria, they were asked to participate in the survey. There was no quota established for each client type. For each facility, interviewers were given a skip pattern to follow when approaching potentially eligible clients for consent in order to ensure clients representative of all times of the day were interviewed. The skip pattern was derived from estimates of daily client volume and a desire to interview at a given facility for at least 2 days. Consequently, at higher volume facilities, interviewers may have been instructed to skip several potentially eligible clients before approaching the next client, whereas in lower volume facilities they may have been instructed to approach several clients and then skip one client.

## Ethical Approval

Ethical review for this study was received from AMREF (ESRC P247/2016) and the Marie Stopes Ethical Review Board (016-16). Approval to conduct the study was also sought and received from the Kenya Ministry of Health, the Christian Health Association of Kenya, Marie Stopes Kenya, and Population Services Kenya.

## Analysis

Analyses described below are descriptive and were conducted using Stata13. The wealth index results were calculated using the Kenya EquityTool methodology, comparing respondents to both the national and urban wealth distributions (12). This methodology reduces the number of questions that need to be asked to assess relative wealth, and divides the Kenyan population into five quintiles of 20% each, defined by the most recent, 2014, DHS, which is nationally representative (10,13). Using such a measure ensures that these data are comparable to DHS surveys, and that differences in service utilization can be more easily compared across countries. An additional user was defined as someone who is an initiator of modern contraception (either someone who has never used modern contraception before or someone returning to modern contraceptive use) for FP, and — for child health services — as someone who has never used the formal health sector before for the illness in question, either because they did not previously have a need or because they sought care from an informal source. Variables were assessed for normality graphically, using quantile-normal plots. One outlier observation was removed in the analysis of cost of services. *T*- tests and ANOVA were used to compare continuous variables between and across the four strata, while chi-squared tests were used to compare results for wealth quintile and other categorical variables from the four strata. Results were adjusted for clustering by facility where noted, using the **svy** functions in Stata. Given the multiple comparisons (between each pair within the four strata) in the main study outcomes, statistical significance is determined only after applying the Holm-Bonferroni correction (14).

## RESULTS

### Facility and Respondent Characteristics

Of 248 facilities that were visited, 209 were eligible for study inclusion. County level permission was required to visit public sector facilities, and was obtained without concern in 5 of 6 counties. In Mombasa county, numerous attempts to receive permission were unsuccessful. Given that two ethical review boards and the National Ministry of Health had already reviewed the proposed sample and given permission to conduct the study in the 6 selected counties, it was not considered an option to replace Mombasa county with another county. The allocated public sample from Mombasa was reallocated to the other 5 counties. The FBO sample in

Mombasa also had to be reallocated because there were no eligible facilities in the primary or back-up sub-counties. In the other counties, four facilities revoked their permission to conduct the study after the initial visit, and the allocated sample for those facilities was also reallocated to facilities in the same stratum and county, if a replacement facility could not be found. Among those eligible, 96 facilities were chosen to be a part of the study, distributed across 6 counties and four strata.

Three thousand four hundred and fifty-nine individuals were approached to participate in the study, and 3,407 (98.5%) agreed to participate. 63.8% of those who consented to participate were eligible for the study. A total of 2,173 individuals were interviewed, across 96 chosen facilities. **Table 1** illustrates the distribution of study facilities and respondents by county and stratum.

**TABLE 1.** Distribution of facilities by county and stratum.

| | | | Number of respondents interviews per facility | | | |
|---|---|---|---|---|---|---|
| County | Stratum | Facilities | Minimum | Median | Maximum | Total |
| Nakuru | Public | 6 | 22 | 24 | 24 | 141 |
| | FBO | 6 | 11 | 30 | 31 | 160 |
| | Private | 4 | 13 | 23 | 24 | 83 |
| | Franchise | 5 | 12 | 20 | 20 | 92 |
| Mombasa | Pubic | 0 | — | — | — | 0 |
| | FBO | 0 | — | — | — | 0 |
| | Private | 5 | 0 | 19 | 21 | 71 |
| | Franchise | 6 | 4 | 19 | 21 | 98 |
| Machakos | Pubic | 5 | 26 | 30 | 31 | 145 |
| | FBO | 3 | 16 | 30 | 42 | 88 |
| | Private | 4 | 1 | 19 | 25 | 64 |
| | Franchise | 6 | 0 | 18 | 28 | 88 |
| Kakamega | Public | 5 | 10 | 27 | 28 | 103 |
| | FBO | 2 | 6 | 15 | 24 | 30 |
| | Private | 4 | 15 | 22 | 26 | 85 |
| | Franchise | 5 | 2 | 19 | 20 | 79 |

(*Continued*)

**TABLE 1.** (*Continued*)

| | | | Number of respondents interviews per facility | | | |
|---|---|---|---|---|---|---|
| County | Stratum | Facilities | Minimum | Median | Maximum | Total |
| Homa Bay | Public | 5 | 28 | 29 | 33 | 149 |
| | FBO | 3 | 38 | 39 | 42 | 119 |
| | Private | 3 | 31 | 33 | 34 | 98 |
| | Franchise | 4 | 21 | 25 | 25 | 95 |
| Kiambu | Public | 4 | 29 | 29 | 30 | 117 |
| | FBO | 3 | 10 | 39 | 40 | 84 |
| | Private | 4 | 0 | 33 | 52 | 101 |
| | Franchise | 4 | 10 | 25 | 25 | 83 |
| Total | Public | 25 | 10 | 28 | 22 | 655 |
| | FBO | 17 | 6 | 30 | 42 | 481 |
| | Private | 24 | 0 | 23 | 52 | 502 |
| | Franchise | 30 | 0 | 20 | 28 | 535 |

All facilities were required to provide FP for inclusion in the study; however, there were significant differences ($F = 4.11$, $p < 0.01$) in the number of FP methods available, and the number of long acting and permanent methods (LAPM) available ($F = 7.57$, $p < 0.001$), across facility types. A facility was defined as offering a method if the respondent to the facility stated that the method was offered at that facility. A second question asked if that method was available on the day of the survey. Methods may not be available either due to stock-out or due to lack of trained personnel to provide the method. Public facilities offered and had available the highest number of methods, followed closely by franchised private facilities. While public facilities nominally offered the highest number of LAPM, private franchise facilities had the highest number of LAPM available at the time of reporting (**Figure 1**). There was also considerable variation among facility sale of medicines and acceptance of insurance. Public facilities were the least likely to sell medicines, while faith based facilities were the most likely.

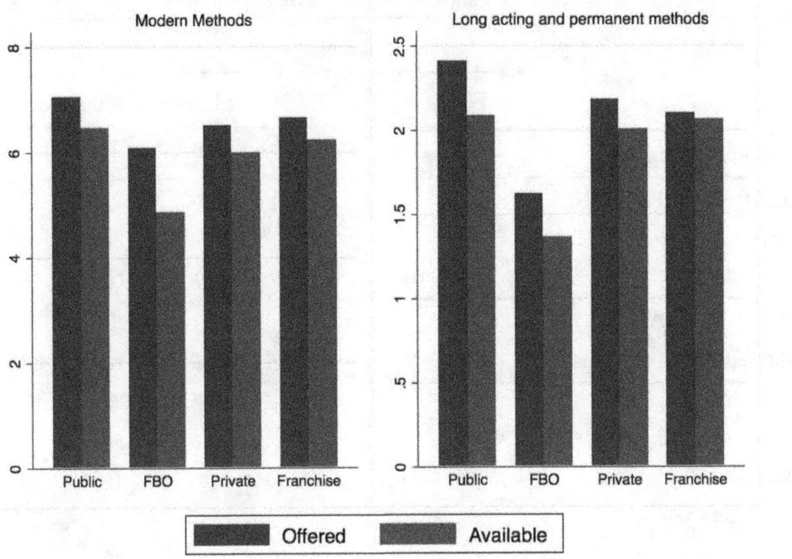


**FIGURE 1.** (Color available online) Mean number of FP methods offered and available by facility type.

There were 919 FP clients and 1,254 child health clients. **Table 2** illustrates the characteristics of study participants by reason for visit (including stratum and county). The relationship between reason for visit and marital status ($\chi_3{}^2 = 10.97$, $p = 0.012$), and education ($\chi_2 = 7.53$, $p = 0.023$) were both significantly different. Since no quota for the number of FP clients per facility or stratum was included, comparing the proportion of FP and child health clients in each stratum indicates if the facility type is more likely to see clients for a particular reason. The row percentages in the last panel of Table 2 were tested to see if they were significantly different from 50%. In private and franchised clinics, there was no significant difference in the proportion of clients interviewed, by reason for visit. Not shown in **Table 2**, the vast majority (88%) of both FP and child health clients had been to the facility they visited before, with no significant differences between groups. Clients were also asked why they chose the health facility, and were able to give multiple answers. Common answers were that the facility was nearby (44.4%), had good quality (40.1%), had the services needed (39.8%), was convenient (24.5%) or that providers were nice/friendly (23.6%).

**TABLE 2.** Client characteristics by reason for visit.

| | Reason for visit | | | | | |
|---|---|---|---|---|---|---|
| | FP ($n$ = 919) | | IMCI ($n$ = 1254) | | Total ($n$ = 2,173) | |
| Client characteristics | $n$ | % | $n$ | % | $n$ | % |
| GENDER OF RESPONDENT | | | | | | |
| Male | 0 | 0.0 | 80 | 6.4 | 80 | 3.7 |
| Female | 919 | 100.0 | 1174 | 93.6 | 2093 | 96.3 |
| MARITAL STATUS* | | | | | | |
| Married/Living together | 758 | 82.7 | 1,075 | 85.9 | 1,833 | 84.6 |
| Never married | 125 | 13.6 | 144 | 11.5 | 269 | 12.4 |
| Divorced/Separated | 30 | 3.3 | 20 | 1.6 | 50 | 2.3 |
| Widowed | 4 | 0.4 | 12 | 1.0 | 16 | 0.7 |
| EDUCATION* | | | | | | |
| No Education | 24 | 2.6 | 15 | 1.2 | 39 | 1.8 |
| Primary School | 351 | 38.2 | 451 | 36.2 | 802 | 37.1 |
| Secondary School and Higher | 542 | 59.1 | 780 | 62.6 | 1,322 | 61.1 |
| COUNTY | | | | | | |
| Nakuru | 214 | 23.3 | 262 | 21 | 476 | 21.9 |
| Mombasa | 93 | 10.1 | 76 | 6 | 169 | 7.8 |
| Machakos | 162 | 17.6 | 223 | 18 | 385 | 17.7 |
| Kakamega | 111 | 12.1 | 186 | 15 | 297 | 13.7 |
| Homa Bay | 183 | 19.9 | 278 | 22 | 461 | 21.2 |
| Kiambu | 156 | 17.0 | 229 | 18 | 385 | 17.7 |
| FACILITY TYPE (ROW PERCENT, *P*-VALUE[a]) | | | | | | |
| Public** | 219 | 33.4 | 436 | 66.6 | 655 | $p < 0.01$ |
| FBO* | 190 | 39.5 | 291 | 60.5 | 481 | $p = 0.04$ |
| Private | 256 | 51.0 | 246 | 49.0 | 502 | $p = 0.84$ |
| Franchise | 254 | 47.5 | 281 | 52.5 | 535 | $p = 0.51$ |
| Total** | | 42.3 | | 57.7 | | $p < 0.01$ |

*[a]Significance testing accounts for survey design.* $^*p < 0.05$, $^{**}p < 0.01$.

**TABLE 3.** Amount paid for services (in Kenyan Shillings), by sector visited or reason for visit.

| Sector | Mean | 25th percentile | 50th percentile | 75th percentile |
|---|---|---|---|---|
| Public | 22.7 | 0 | 0 | 0 |
| FBO | 279.3 | 100 | 150 | 350 |
| Private | 304.8 | 100 | 150 | 350 |
| Franchise | 312.4 | 100 | 150 | 400 |
| FP | 151.5 | 0 | 100 | 150 |
| IMCI | 263.7 | 0 | 100 | 350 |

**TABLE 4.** Distribution of respondents by national and urban wealth quintile ($n = 2157$)[a].

| Quintile | % in national quintile | % in urban quintile |
|---|---|---|
| 1 - Poorest | 5.7 | 19.52 |
| 2 | 6.49 | 15.11 |
| 3 | 11.31 | 19.1 |
| 4 | 27.07 | 22.86 |
| 5 - Wealthiest | 49.42 | 23.41 |
| Total | 100 | 100 |

*[a]16 respondents did not have complete data to calculate their wealth quintile.*

Clients were asked how much they paid for services, and if they had health insurance. Nearly 30% of clients had health insurance, but only 4.7% of them used the insurance for the visit. Client payment was assessed for differences between facility type, and difference between reason for visit. There was a significant difference in mean amount paid between the public sector and the other three sectors ($t \geq 4.73$, $p < 0.001$ for each), but no significant difference between clients of FBO, private, and franchised facilities (**Table 3**). The finding is the same when comparing mean cost of FP or child health services alone, by sector; however, those seeking care for childhood illnesses spent significantly more than those seeking FP, overall (KSH 263.7 vs. 151.5; $F = 15.24$, $p < 0.001$).

**Table 4** outlines the overall wealth distribution of study respondents in comparison to national and urban benchmarks. Although clients are

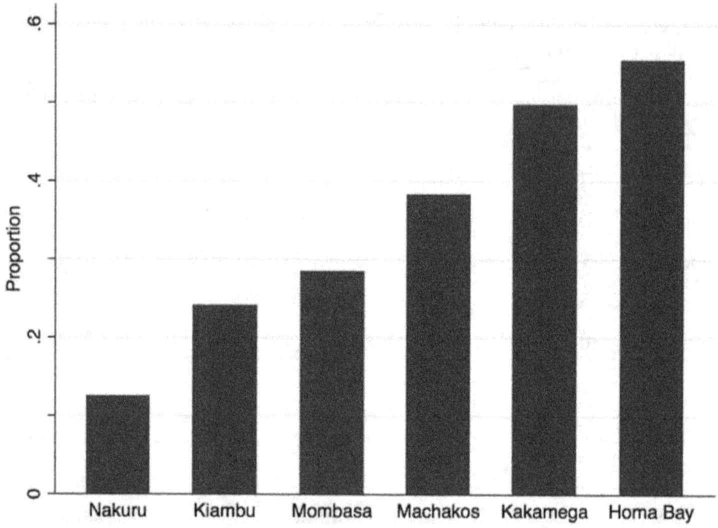


**FIGURE 2.** Proportion of clients in lowest two urban quintiles, by county.

distributed evenly across urban wealth quintiles — used as a default benchmark as the facilities surveyed were urban or per-urban — there are marked regional differences in wealth. Approximately 12% of clients across all 4 sectors in Nakuru are in the poorest 2 urban quintiles vs. 50% of clients in Kakamega and 55% of clients in Homa Bay (**Figure 2**).

## Client Wealth Distribution by Facility Type

**Table 5** shows the distribution of clients by national wealth quintile and facility type. The wealth distribution of clients is significantly different across all four sectors ($F = 4.13$, $p < 0.001$). In pairwise comparisons, wealth distribution between public and private ($F = 11.82$, $p < 0.001$) and public and franchise ($F = 8.89$, $p < 0.001$) sectors are significantly different, using a design-based chi squared test, adjusted for multiple comparisons.

There is a significant difference in the proportion of clients in the bottom two quintiles of the national distribution (those who are in the poorest 40% of the Kenyan population) across all sectors ($\chi_3^2 = 108$, $p < 0.001$). There are also significant pairwise differences between the public and

**TABLE 5.** Proportion of clients in each national wealth quintile, by sector.

| | Type of facility | | | | |
|---|---|---|---|---|---|
| National quintile | Public (%) | FBO (%) | Private for-profit (%) | Franchise (%) | Total (%) |
| 1 (poorest) | 10.92 | 5.70 | 1.20 | 3.55 | 5.70 |
| 2 | 11.54 | 6.54 | 2.41 | 4.11 | 6.49 |
| 3 | 16.46 | 10.34 | 8.43 | 8.60 | 11.31 |
| 4 | 30.92 | 27.64 | 26.71 | 22.24 | 27.07 |
| 5 (wealthiest) | 30.15 | 49.79 | 51.24 | 61.50 | 49.42 |
| Total | 100.00 | 100.00 | 100.00 | 100.00 | 100.00 |

**TABLE 6.** Proportion of clients in each urban wealth quintile, by sector.

| | Type of facility | | | | |
|---|---|---|---|---|---|
| Urban quintile | Public (%) | FBO (%) | Private for-profit (%) | Franchise (%) | Total (%) |
| 1 | 32.77 | 18.78 | 9.64 | 13.27 | 19.52 |
| 2 | 20.46 | 14.77 | 13.05 | 10.84 | 15.11 |
| 3 | 18.77 | 19.20 | 19.28 | 19.25 | 19.10 |
| 4 | 17.38 | 25.11 | 26.10 | 24.49 | 22.86 |
| 5 | 10.62 | 22.15 | 31.93 | 32.15 | 23.41 |
| Total | 100.00 | 100.00 | 100.00 | 100.00 | 100.00 |

private sectors ($t = 3.88$, $p < 0.001$) and between the public and franchise sectors ($t = 2.83$, $p < 0.01$), accounting for survey design and multiple comparisons. The franchise sector serves more of the poorest than the private for-profit sector, but less than the FBO sector, although differences are not statistically significant.

As all facilities surveyed are in urban or peri-urban settings, a more appropriate benchmark may be that shown in **Table 6**, comparing clients only to urban Kenyan households by facility type. There is a significant difference in the urban wealth distribution of clients across all sectors ($F = 4.56$, $p < 0.001$), and between public and private ($F = 11.9$, $p < 0.001$) and public and franchised ($F = 11.79$, $p < 0.001$) facilities, using a design based chi squared test adjusted for multiple comparisons. The difference between public and faith-based facilities is marginally significant ($p = 0.057$), and no longer so when adjusted. When comparing the proportion of clients in the poorest 40% of the urban wealth distribution, the public sector serves significantly more of the poorest than the private ($t = 4.25$, $p < 0.001$) and franchised ($t = 4.08$, $p < 0.001$) sectors, adjusted for multiple comparisons. There is no significant difference between the proportion of poorest urban residents served between the faith based, franchised and private sectors.

## Additional Clients by Facility Type

Among 916 women who came for FP, 10.3% had never used a modern method before, and overall, 15.6% of women were additional users of FP (**Table 7**). There was no significant difference by facility type.

Among child health clients, approximately 25% had never needed a health service before for that issue, with an additional 2.7% of children having been taken to an unqualified provider or no provider for a previous episode of the illness. There were no significant differences in the proportion of additional users across the four facility types (**Table 8**).

**TABLE 7.** Proportion of additional users of FP, by sector.

| Additional FP user | Type of facility | | | | |
|---|---|---|---|---|---|
| | Public (%) | FBO (%) | Private for-profit (%) | Franchise (%) | Total (%) |
| No | 84.47 | 86.32 | 82.61 | 84.65 | 84.39 |
| Yes | 15.53 | 13.68 | 17.39 | 15.35 | 15.61 |
| Total | 100.00 | 100.00 | 100.00 | 100.00 | 100.00 |

**TABLE 8.** Proportion of additional child health clients, by sector.

| Additional child health client | Type of facility | | | | |
|---|---|---|---|---|---|
| | Public (%) | FBO (%) | Private for-profit (%) | Franchise (%) | Total (%) |
| No | 76.28 | 67.96 | 73.06 | 73.38 | 73.08 |
| Yes | 23.72 | 32.04 | 26.94 | 26.62 | 26.92 |
| Total | 100.00 | 100.00 | 100.00 | 100.00 | 100.00 |

## DISCUSSION

This study seeks to understand differences in the patient composition between health service facilities in the public, private, franchised, and faith-based sectors, in urban and peri- urban Kenya, and implicitly to understand if the poor are seeking FP and child health care, and if so from where.

When compared to the national wealth distribution, respondents are predominantly found in the 4th and 5th wealth quintiles overall (**Table 4**); however, the fairly equitable distribution across urban quintiles supports the hypothesis that clients in the facilities, all urban and peri-urban, themselves also came from urban areas, and that the facility-based sample was not, in aggregate, overly skewed toward either the wealthy or poor.

Public sector facilities were found to serve a higher proportion of poor clients than other types of facilities. These findings may be explained in part by the lower price paid for services in the public sector, where over 75% of clients did not pay anything out of pocket. All three non-public facility types served a cross- section of the urban population, but with a leaning toward wealthier patients. The difference in the proportion of poor clients served by the franchise and for-profit private sectors was not meaningful, and both sectors served fewer poor clients than the faith-based sector, although differences were not statistically significant. Assessment of statistical significance in this study is highly influenced by the clustering of clients within facilities and the larger standard errors which result from this design.

No facility type stands out as expanding access to health services more than another, as measured by the two assessments of additional users (for FP and child health services). Understanding the value of a health facility (or facility type) in expanding access may be more meaningful in rural areas, where facilities are further away from each other. In urban areas, such as those where this study took place, all facility types contribute to expanding access.

It is worthwhile reflecting on the unequal distribution of urban poor health care seekers across the six study sites (**Figure 2**). The overall distribution of wealth in our study is very similar to the distribution of wealth among urban dwellers of Kenya, yet the poor are not evenly distributed across urban areas. Additionally, some of the urban areas selected for the study may not be representative of all urban areas within that region. For example, author's analysis of the wealth of care-seekers in Nakuru to those of all urban dwellers in the Rift Valley region show distributions which are starkly different (calculated from 2014 KDHS (10)). There are inconsistencies across regions which cannot be fully explained by the argument that care-seekers overall are wealthier than the population from which they are drawn. A more nuanced explanation for the variations we see may be due to barriers in some regions which inhibit the poor from accessing the formal health system. In Nakuru, Machakos, Kakamega, and Homa Bay, care seekers are generally wealthier than the rest of the urban population and the poorest two quintiles are under-represented among care-seekers. In Mombasa, however, care seekers' wealth mirrors the overall urban population, while in Kiambu, care-seekers are poorer than the general urban population. Possible explanations for these two exceptions might be the limited facility-types surveyed (see following paragraph) and more even socio-economic distribution in Mombasa compared to other regions in Kenya; and that in Kiambu, a relatively poor county neighboring Nairobi, the wealthier members of the community seek care in the nearby city, leaving a poorer cross-section of the county to seek care locally.

This study has three principle limitations. First, it captured facilities in only two of four strata in Mombasa, because permission to conduct research in the public sector was not given, and eligible FBO facilities were not found. In order to achieve the full sample, the sample was reallocated, and proportionality of the sample across regions was somewhat compromised. Second, this study is one of the first to use the EquityTool — a validated, shorter version of the DHS wealth index that compares those sampled to the national and urban wealth distributions. The shorter index was chosen due to the benefits conferred when interviewing outside of the household, including a shorter questionnaire and easier questions, but there is some known mis-categorization between adjacent quintiles (13). When interpreting data, it is advisable to look at the overall wealth distribution, rather than focusing on one quintile alone. Third, by design, the inferences drawn from these findings are limited to those who do in fact seek formal health services. The study does not capture those seeking care at drug shops or pharmacies, and the sampling methodology, reliant upon the Kenya MFL and local providers, meant facilities run by unqualified providers, or unregistered facilities were unlikely to be sampled. Nevertheless, this study is representative of services available to nearly 70% of all urban dwellers in Kenya (calculated from 2009 Census of Kenya) (15).

Taken together, the findings suggest that private providers remain important within the larger health system, more so for FP than childhood illness management. In particular, there are a number of findings with implications for social franchises: they do better at reaching the poor than earlier studies have indicated; however, no better than non-franchised private providers, and somewhat worse than FBO and public facilities. Franchises do a good job of making FP accessible, outperformed in this only by the public sector, which provides access but sees proportionally fewer FP clients. While this study indicates that franchises see clients of similar wealth levels as other private providers, recent research in Kenya has shown that franchise providers see a larger number of FP and child health clients (16). Franchises may thus be able to achieve greater impact through volume of poor seen, rather than proportion of poor within any one clinic.

The results indicate that franchised providers in Kenya have had some successes in leveraging private markets to expand the reach and adoption of FP. The target niche, and related social value, of franchised facilities is evident but not strong: franchised facilities serve more, and more additional, FP users than FBO or public sector providers, but numbers are still low in each facility and the poor are not well-targeted. Greater use of demand side financing initiatives could increase access for the relatively poor.

This is the next challenge for social franchises: how to distinguish their role in the health sector either by reaching more poor (through direct or indirect subsidies, greater outreach, or other methods), or by emphasizing quality and access to a degree that franchised providers increase volumes relative to other sources of care, playing a more important role in overall market expansion than they do currently. This study suggests that both options are open to franchise programs, and that a strategy to distinguish franchises from other provider types would be helpful in explaining the value added to the health system by this delivery model. Ultimately, how franchise programs respond to these findings will be determined by the priority they put upon serving the poor or increasing service adopters.

Perhaps surprising are the findings that faith based facilities are not significantly more pro-poor than for-profit private sector facilities (both franchised and independent). These facilities are organized, most often under the Christian Health Association of Kenya, which provides them with access to technical and human resources, and a national level advocacy body. They have a mission to assure equity in access to health care, yet faith based facilities do collect out-of-pocket payments similar to the other two facility types (17). While service cost may play a role in determining health seeking choices among the poor — especially those who would pay nothing for services at public facilities — there were no significant differences in the mean amount paid by clients of non-public facilities (**Table 3**) — and costs were not reported as important by clients. In fact, women seeking FP services were less likely to visit public sector facilities, despite the lower cost of services and more expansive offering of contraceptive methods. Motivations for selecting providers was not the focus of this study, however; some information can be cautiously inferred. For women seeking FP services, reasons for preferring private and FBO facilities may include real or perceived differences in quality, lower waiting times, or improved provider-client interactions, as established by research in Kenya and elsewhere (18,19). For FP and child health clients alike, access also remains important. The median travel time for careseekers was 20min, with those in the poorest two quintiles traveling longer. While the majority of clients interviewed walked to the facility, suitable formal sector care may not be located near the poorest.

Access to and use of health services is a complicated construct, and it is difficult, if not impossible, to assess all aspects of this construct concurrently. Access for all is an underlying factor in attaining the Sustainable Development Goal of Good Health and Well-Being (Goal 3), especially in achieving universal access to sexual and reproductive health services, and an end to preventable child deaths (20). This study provides additional context for how geographically proximate facilities in urban and periurban Kenya are serving clients of different wealth profiles. While the public sector is charged with ensuring access throughout the country, private and faith based facilities are often located where a perceived market exists. This study captures use by those who do visit formal facilities, and indicates that the market is segmented. Such a study has not previously been conducted in Kenya, and is of interest for specific health system actors, as well as for those charged with the universal healthcare mandate. Furthermore, this study contributes to the literature one of the first comparisons of client wealth across facility type, including franchises.

## AUTHOR CONTRIBUTIONS

NC contributed to the protocol, conducted data collection and analysis, and wrote the manuscript. DM, JW, and CO reviewed the protocol, contributed to analysis, and reviewed the manuscript.

## FUNDING

Data collection in Kenya was undertaken using M4M internal resources. Study design and manuscript preparation was made possible by the generous support of the American people through the United States Agency for International Development, under the terms of USAID Cooperative Agreement No. AID-OAA-A-14-00037 (SIFPO2) to Population Services International. The content and opinions expressed within do not necessarily reflect the views of USAID or the United States Government.

## ACKNOWLEDGMENTS

Authors are grateful to Population Services Kenya, Marie Stopes Kenya, the Christian Health Association of Kenya and the Ministry of Health for facilitating access to study facilities, as well as to the time taken by providers and clients for participating in our study. Authors thank Ms. Karla Feeser for her assistance with this manuscript.

### Conflict of Interest Statement

Two co-authors of this study (JW and CO) are employees of Population Services Kenya, the same organization which manages the Tunza social franchise.

The remaining authors declare that the research was conducted in the absence of any commercial or financial relationships that could be construed as a potential conflict of interest.

## REFERENCES

1. Aday LA, Andersen R. A framework for the study of access to medical care. *Health Serv Res*. 1974.
2. Peters DH, Garg A, Bloom G, Walker DG, Brieger WR, Hafizur Rahman M. Poverty and access to health care in developing countries. *Ann N Y Acad Sci*. 2008 Jul 25;1136(1):161–71.
3. Levesque JF, Harris MF, Russell G. Patient-centred access to health care: conceptualising access at the interface of health systems and populations. *Int J Equity Health*. 2013;12(1):18.
4. Gwatkin D. IMCI what can we learn from an innovation that didn't reach the poor? *Bull World Health Organ*. 2006 Oct 1;84(10):768–768.
5. Chakraborty NM, Sprockett A. Use of family planning and child health services in the private sector: an equity analysis of 12 DHS surveys. *Int J Equity Health*. 2018 Dec;17(1):50.
6. Agha S, Do M. The quality of family planning services and client satisfaction in the public and private sectors in Kenya. *Int J Qual Health Care*. 2009 Apr 1; 21(2):87–96.
7. Basu S, Andrews J, Kishore S, Panjabi R, Stuckler D. Comparative performance of private and public healthcare systems in low- and middle-income countries: A systematic review. *PLoS Med*. 2012 Jun 19;9(6): e1001244.
8. Berendes S, Heywood P, Oliver S, Garner P. Quality of private and public ambulatory health care in low and middle income countries: Systematic review of comparative studies. *PLoS Med*. 2011 Apr 12;8(4):e1000433.
9. Wang W, Wang S, Pullum T, Ametepi P, editors. How family planning supply and the service environment affect contraceptive use: Findings from Four East African Countries. Calverton, MD: ICF International; 2012.
10. National Bureau of Statistics-Kenya and ICF International. Demographic and Health Survey, Kenya. Rockville, MD, USA; 2014.
11. Viswanathan R, Seefeld C. *Clinial Social Franchising Compendium: An Annual Survey of Programs: Findings from 2014*. San Francisco, CA: UCSF; 2015. (Social Franchising Compendium).

12. Metrics for Management. Kenya 2017 [Internet]. Available from: http://www.equitytool.org/wp-content/uploads/2017/02/Kenya-DHS-2014-Factsheet-2017-02-08.pdf.
13. Chakraborty NM, Fry K, Behl R, Longfield K. Simplified asset indices to measure wealth and equity in health programs: A reliability and validity analysis using survey data from 16 countries. *Glob Health Sci Pract*. 2016 Mar 21;4(1):141–54.
14. Holm S. A simple sequentially rejective multiple test procedure. *Scand J Stat*. 1979;6(2):66–70.
15. Kenya National Bureau of Statistics. Kenya Population and Housing Census, Vol 1C [Internet]. Nairobi, Kenya; 2010. Available from: http://www.knbs.or.ke/index.php?option=com_phocadownload&view=category&id=109:population-and-housing- census-2009&Itemid=599#.
16. Chakraborty N, SImmons R, Mbondo M. How Franchising Affects Private Practice. Global Symposium for Health Systems Research.
17. Kagawa RC, Anglemyer A, Montagu D. *The Scale of Faith Based Organization Participation in Health Service Delivery in Developing Countries: Systemic Review and Meta-Analysis*. Beck EJ, editor. PLoS ONE. 2012 Nov 12; 7(11):e48457.
18. Agha S, Karim AM, Balal A, Sossler S. *A Quasi-Experimental Study to Assess the Performance of a Reproductive Health Franchise in Nepal*. Washington, D.C; 2004.
19. Keesara SR, Juma PA, Harper CC. Why do women choose private over public facilities for family planning services? A qualitative study of post-partum women in an informal urban settlement in Kenya. *BMC Health Serv Res*. 2015 Dec;15(1):335.
20. United Nations General Assembly. Transforming our world: The 2030 agenda for sustainable development. 2015.

# Chapter 5

# Prohibit, Constrain, Encourage, or Purchase: How Should We Engage with the Private Health-Care Sector?*

**Dominic Montagu and Catherine Goodman**

## Abstract

This chapter, originally published in *The Lancet* and titled "Prohibit, Constrain, Encourage, or Purchase: How Should We Engage with the Private Health-Care Sector?" sets out a framework for understanding how governments and donor agencies can, and should, work with or regulate the private sector. Authors Dominic Montagu and Catherine Goodman set out the context of the private for-profit sector's prominence in healthcare delivery, concerns about its failures to deliver social benefit, and the resulting search for interventions to improve the sector's functioning. From that starting point, the chapter reviews the evidence for the effectiveness and limitations of such private sector interventions in LMICs and sets out a framework for defining the focus of different interventions.

While few robust assessments are available, some conclusions are possible. Prohibiting the private sector is very unlikely to succeed, and regulatory approaches face persistent challenges in many LMICs. Attention is therefore turning to interventions that encourage private providers to

*This chapter was originally published in "Montagu, D. and Goodman, C. The Lancet, Vol. 388, Issue 10044, (2016) 613–621".

improve quality and coverage (while advancing their financial interests), such as social marketing, social franchising, vouchers, and contracting.

Evidence about the effect on clinical quality, coverage, equity, and cost-effectiveness is inadequate for generalizations. While interventions have been effective in many instances, for example, in addressing a number of specific, focused problems related to cost, access, efficiency, and quality on a restricted scale, challenges remain concerning scalability and scope, indicating the limitations of such interventions as a basis for universal health coverage.

## Introduction

A well-functioning health system can be regarded as one that assures quality, delivers services in response not only to health needs but also to private demand, and guarantees provision of care to both rich and poor people. Although in principle a well-functioning health system can encompass both private and public sectors, private providers can function very poorly, with examples of pharmacy monopolies, price-gouging specialists, induced demand for unnecessary diagnostic tests, purveyors of false medicines or fake miracle cures, and large gaps in coverage. (1,2) These systemic failures are driven by poor information, the misuse of market power, a failure to consider or lack of interest in implications for the broader community such as drug resistance, and inequity in the distribution of income and knowledge.

The private sector's prominence in health-care delivery in much of the world, and the common patterns of failure in many areas of private provision, drives many governments, non-governmental organisations (NGOs), private entrepreneurs, and donor agencies to intervene to improve the sector's functioning. The figure summarises the outcomes of these market failures and the four approaches for engaging with private providers to address them: prohibition of private practice; constraint of its operation through regulation; encouragement and subsidy of private sector delivery for specific services; and purchase of services from the private sector. (3) In this paper we discuss the main methods used under each approach. The figure also draws attention to the fact that the design of methods must reflect the heterogeneity of private sector provision in

**Key messages**

- Engagement with private for-profit providers has taken place on four levels: prohibition, regulation, encouragement and subsidy, and purchase of services.
- Despite experience with a rapidly growing number of interventions, robust assessments are few, though some conclusions are possible.
- Banning the private sector where demand for services is high and capacity to regulate imperfect is very unlikely to succeed, and use of statutory regulation to constrain private providers is inadequate, especially in low-income countries.
- Although some evidence shows that targeted supply-side interventions such as social marketing and vouchers can increase coverage of focused services, less evidence is available for accreditation and contracting, which seek to affect broad areas of service availability and quality.
- For all these interventions little is known about their cost-effectiveness and ability to reach poor people.

terms of the type of goods and services that are targeted and the type of private provider.

Procedures from all these approaches are commonly applied to different parts of the private sector simultaneously — for example, forbidding private abortion services, restricting who may own and operate hospitals, subsidising and encouraging provision of antenatal vitamins through social marketing, and purchasing laboratory or dialysis services as part of the national health strategy.

We review experience with interventions concerning private for-profit providers in low-income and middle- income countries (LMICs) and assess what is known about their effectiveness and limitations. This paper is based on findings from a systematic review of private sector interventions (4) and our analysis of published and grey literature experiences with private sector health system policy activities in LMICs around the world, collected through many years of work in Asia and Africa. The core concepts have been developed through policy training courses in Asia, Europe, and North America with representatives from universities and

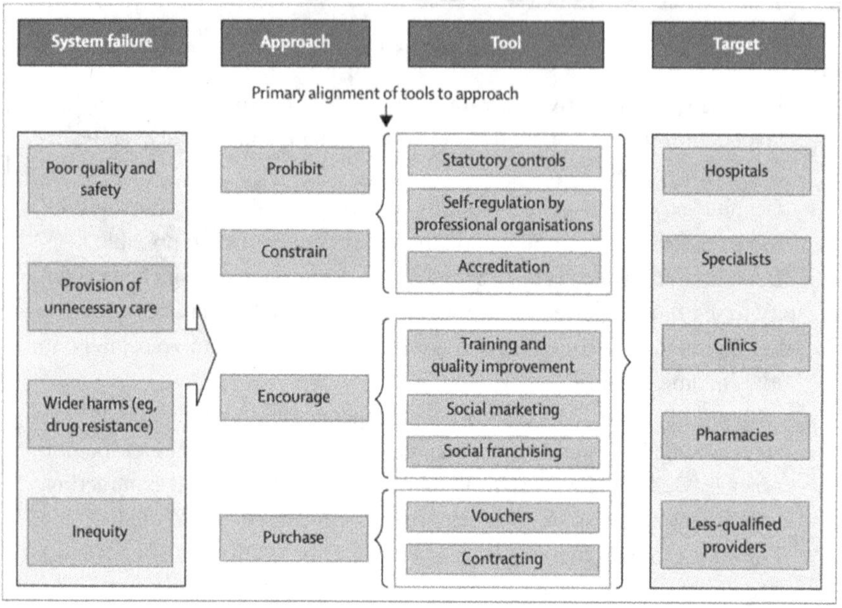


Figure 1. Approaches and devices for private sector engagement

health ministries of many countries. Feedback from these policy makers and analysts has further refined our framework (Figure 1) for understanding the strategies for private sector engagement.

## Approaches

### *Prohibition*

An extreme case of regulation by legal control is a formal ban on some or all forms of private practice. To be effective, any ban requires social support, enforcement capacity, or both. Quite often, neither exists for restricting medical practices in low-income countries, where monitoring challenges mean that prohibitive restrictions are especially difficult to enforce for outpatient services or pharmaceutical sales. By contrast, in many middle-income countries regulatory capacity is sufficient to allow prohibition of some medical practices and an expansion of auditing and enforcement.

Bans on practice by unlicensed providers are often the most visible type of prohibition, but examples of failure are many. In Tanzania, the banning of private providers during the presidency of Julius Nyerere, from independence in 1962 to 1985, forced them to practice undercover and within faith-based organisations but never eliminated private practice. (5) In Cambodia in 2010, the government created a new police force exclusively to impose a ban on private drug sellers. 2 years later no change in practice of these drug sellers was noticed and the force was reputedly allowed to dissolve. Changes in the legal status of abortion services in many countries have forced women to, or away from, informal providers and their unsafe practices, but have had little effect on the overall number of abortions provided. (6). Examples of successful bans are rare in LMICs; they are documented mainly in strongly controlled socialist economies and reversed rapidly as those economies have opened. (7,8)

## Constraint

Although complete prohibition of private health-care providers is rare, some attempt to constrain the activities of private providers is ubiquitous, most commonly through regulation. The term regulation is universally agreed to include statutory rules laid down by government or government-appointed agencies, and also generally considered to include self-regulation implemented by professional bodies. Many commentators emphasise the importance of thinking of regulation more broadly to encompass community accountability, subsidies, contracting arrangements, provider payment systems, and quality improvement or assurance activities. (9–11) Assurance activities in particular are a key part of the hierarchy of so-called responsive regulation, which advocates that regulation should begin with persuasion, dialogue, and voluntary activities, only gradually escalating to mandatory or statutory processes and penalties where required. (12) Although we recognise the importance of this wide range of measures for quality of care, our focus under "Constraint" is more tightly on statutory and self-regulatory constraints, with other strategies to improve private provider performance covered under "Encourage and subsidise" and "Purchase".

Statutory constraints in health care mainly encompass controls on the quality of facilities, human resources, medicines, and equipment, through licensing of pharmacies, clinics, and hospitals and registration of health workers and products. (5,10,13) Other less common constraints aim to counter monopoly power of providers by regulating price, or controlling mergers or collusion. For example, Niger has regulations for wholesale and retail mark-ups for medicines, (14) and in India the government sets ceiling prices for essential drugs. (15) In a few cases regulation is used to address geographical equity: for instance, in Tanzania, legislation restricts registration of new pharmacies in areas where it is deemed there are an adequate number. (5)

Implementation and enforcement of statutory regulations are weak in many African and Asian settings, with some notable exceptions, such as South Africa and the Seychelles. (11,16,17) The regulations are often under- developed and outdated, (11,17) with some countries not having updated their regulatory frameworks for over 40 years. (17) Many governments are not even aware of the scale of the private health-service provision taking place. The operation of unregistered hospitals and clinics is very common; (11) in two Indian states they outnumbered those with formal licences (16) and in Africa only six of 45 countries were reported to have a comprehensive registry of private facilities, with most lists "woefully incomplete and often inaccurate". (17) In some settings, a high volume of medicines is sold by completely unauthorised outlets, such as the market stalls and itinerant vendors in Niger. (15)

There is ample evidence of endemic regulatory infringement by pharmacies and drug stores that are permitted to sell medicines in many low-income and middle-income countries — eg, dispensing prescription- only medicines without a prescription, stocking unauthorised medicines, dispensing insufficient dosages. For example, in Tamil Nadu, India, 61% of prescription- only medicines were dispensed without a prescription, (18) with the range of such medicines often including antibiotics, steroids, narcotic analgesics, psychotropics, antihypertensives, sedatives, tranquillisers, anti-tuber- culosis agents, and abortifacients. A further concern is the quality of medicines, with frequent documentation of both substandard products because of poor manufacture or storage, and deliberately falsified (so-called fake) medicines. (19) Regulation of high-volume, low-cost, pharmaceutical commodities is difficult, and the incentives of pharmacies and retailers make it more so. (7,20) In Colombia, Guatemala, and Mexico, enforcement of prescription laws during the mid-2000s and late-2000s, at the same time as the expansion of pharmaceutical chains, drove a widespread reduction in over-the-counter sales of antibiotics and other prescription-only medicines. (21) This reduction probably reflected both increased regulatory investment and the desire of chains to reduce competition from low-cost, low-quality competitors. (22)

Illegal practices are in some cases a response to demand, with providers who refuse to acquiesce to client requests quickly losing custom to those who will. Inspections are often rare, with some facilities not inspected for over a decade, (16,17) and revocation of hospital licences almost unheard of in many settings. (16,23) One reason could be inadequate capacity of inspection and judiciary agencies, which often do not have the resources for inspections and face severe shortages of staff, (16) who in some case are not even regularly paid. (17) This situation is complicated by overlapping mandates for regulation, which generally encompass national and local public bodies, and require coordination with police and judicial offices to enforce penalties. (16,17) Poor implementation can also indicate lack of incentives for front-line inspectors and their imperfect access to information, and capture of regulatory staff who come to identify with specific interest groups or providers and who could even own infringing retailers or facilities. (11,13,20) For example, in India the conditions for registration of facilities were substantially weakened as a result of challenge by doctors' groups. (16)

Regulators in some settings accept that enforcing standards could increase the cost of provision beyond what can be afforded by poor communities. (24,25) For example, the employment of a pharmacist or even a lower level pharmacy cadre would not be viable for a business in rural Kenya. One possible consequence is a gap between the *de jure* regulation in the country's laws and the de-facto level of regulation that inspectors aim to enforce. (20) The resulting divergence between regulations and common practice provides extensive opportunities for corruption, for example in the form of routine bribe payments to avoid inspection visits or adverse reports. (25)

Little assessment has been done of the introduction or improvement of regulations, with the exception of a few randomised controlled trials in pharmacies. (8,26,27) This gap partly reflects the challenges of conducting controlled assessments of legal changes. However, the use of other approaches such as case studies and qualitative methods for rigorous investigation of regulatory implementation is also rare, (16,25,28) and no evidence about the cost-effectiveness of regulatory strategies exists.

Despite widespread evidence of poor implementation of statutory constraints, in most settings regulation seems to have had some effect on the ordering of private sector provision, and in preventing degeneration into a completely ungoverned free market. For example, in many (though not all) settings most providers will have some form of health qualification, and the sale of medicines is often constrained to specific types of outlets. (29) However, in view of the widespread failures of implementation of statutory regulation, in recent years increasing emphasis has been placed on the benefits of consumer-based regulation, and compulsory and voluntary self-regulation schemes.

Consumer-based regulation can allow consumers to sue providers for adverse experiences and outcomes. In India, a Consumer Protection Act was passed in 1986, to be enforced through dedicated consumer courts. (30) Most studies report high awareness of the legislation by providers, and many complaints have been lodged by consumers. (31) However, the process can be lengthy and costly for consumers, (32) one argument being that outcomes are weighted in favour of defendants, with doctors sometimes receiving the benefit of the doubt. (16)

Self-regulation by professional organisations is common, but also problematic in LMICs. (16) The delegation of regulatory responsibilities to professional groups is based on the rationale that these groups are well placed to assess performance, and that government costs can be reduced and enforcement improved. However, the organisations are often poorly resourced, and not well placed to control providers.10 They also tend to place more emphasis on providing leadership and protection to the medical community, with minimum disciplining of members. (16)

Accreditation, which is the most widespread form of voluntary self-regulation among hospitals, is well established throughout Europe and North America, where it provides a process for combined external and peer assessment of facility standards and quality processes. (33) Accreditation standards are commonly set as targets among many hospitals, and revised regularly to account for widely shared improvements in quality norms. The use of peer assessors from other institutions also facilitates sharing of lessons between facilities.

Accreditation is increasingly common in middle- income countries, where it is often a condition for reimbursement under national health insurance (eg, Thailand, Kenya, Malaysia, Philippines). (34) This conditionality of insurance payments is effective at modifying provider practices in a positive way and, as a result, programmes have often been started after the introduction or expansion of national or social health insurance. (35) The evidence on the effect of accreditation is mixed; some studies find positive effects on clinical quality and patient outcomes whereas others find no effect. (36) However, accreditation works well only if most hospitals in a country take part, and that happens only when participation is linked to reimbursements. Therefore, accreditation in low-income countries is a challenging, and perhaps impossible, proposition. (37) Additionally, accreditation is expensive, and this cost must be borne by participating hospitals, and ultimately their clients. For facilities at the high end of the market, accreditation with global agencies is a good investment. For facilities serving local populations in LMICs or contracted by the public sector, the cost of accreditation can be hard to pass on to patients or purchasers.

Other approaches to providing public information about provider quality include scorecards, surgical outcome comparisons, and know-your-rights campaigns, which are common in countries in the Organisation for Economic Co-operation and Development. These approaches are only now being tested in small ways in LMICs, as in India where the White Ribbon Alliance has piloted a phone-based system for new mothers to assess their delivery providers. (38)

## Encouragement and subsidise

Many governments and NGOs provide positive incentives to encourage the private sector to increase access to key health-care interventions or to improve quality. This support is most commonly done by offering training to private providers, social marketing of commodities, recruiting private providers into a social franchise network, providing targeted tax incentives to encourage investments or reduce end-user prices, or offering subsidies to potential clients. The number of these initiatives has increased substantially over the past two decades, often supported by donor funding.

These strategies aim to reduce reliance on the consumer's imperfect quality assessment and increase the control of quality through supply-side incentives and requirements. The services concerned can include those with benefits for the wider community such as the treatment of infectious diseases, but many do not, justified rather by the need to address inequities in provision. Such expansion in provision can also reduce monopoly power, thus putting downward pressure on prices.

To encourage the use of standard treatment guidelines, the inclusion of private providers in free or subsidised publicly funded training programmes has become increasingly common. (11,39)

This arrangement is premised on the assumption that the main reasons for inadequate care relate to the inadequate knowledge of private providers, which can be addressed through short, focused training sessions. Examples are 2–3 days of training for shopkeepers on appropriate provision of antimalarial medicines in Kenya, (40) short trainings on appropriate management of tuberculosis by private practitioners in India, (41) or 35 days on dispensing and treatment practices for staff in drug shops in Tanzania. (42) Training has often been combined with other strategies, such as community information, prepackaging of medicines, strengthened supervision, or feedback and negotiation sessions (eg, the INFECTOM approach). (20,42–45)

However, extensive evidence of a sizeable know–do gap among private providers remains. For example, whereas only 20% of pharmacists in Vietnam said they would sell antibiotics for a child with a viral upper respiratory tract infection, 83% did so when they were assessed by mystery shoppers. (46) This gap has led many people to question the use of training in isolation, and advocate interventions that draw on techniques and forms of business organisation common in the commercial sector.

Commodity social marketing applies commercial marketing techniques to create demand for products that have high public health value. The promoted commodities are distributed, usually at a subsidised price, through for-profit retail outlets such as pharmacies, shops, drug sellers, and even bars. Social marketing is the most common large-scale private sector intervention model in LMICs, with well over 100 programmes in recent years in more than 70 countries. Family planning commodities were the most frequently socially marketed products throughout the 1970s, 1980s, and 1990s, and vitamins, nutritional supplements, antimalarial drugs, and insecticide-treated mosquito nets have also become common in the past 20 years. For example, social marketing of condoms began as part of family planning efforts, and was substantially expanded in response to the HIV/AIDS pandemic. More recently, artemisinin-based combination therapies have been promoted for the treatment of malaria in the private sector through the Affordable Medicines Facility — malaria (AMFm) which subsidized these medicines at a supranational level. (46)

Many examples of social marketing programmes operate at large and often national scales, and evidence shows that they can increase use of targeted products, including condoms, oral contraceptives, insecticide-treated mosquito nets, oral rehydration therapy, and antimalarial drugs. (32,46–48) In some situations, social marketing is expected to shape the market by establishing new products, changing consumer habits, and stimulating private sector supply, potentially making an unsubsidised market more feasible in future.

By contrast, some have concerns that promotion of own-branded products by a social marketing agency might crowd-out purely private sector alternatives, possibly making the market less viable should the social marketing agency withdraw. (49) In the market for insecticide-treated mosquito nets in Tanzania, this concern led to a switch from a traditional social marketing model to a manufacturers' model, in which the social marketing agency promoted a set of approved products from local manufacturers, but in most programmes the promotion of own-brands has persisted. Other debates have continued about the relative cost-effectiveness and equity effect of social marketing in comparison with alternative commodity delivery strategies such as free public provision and community health worker services. (32,50)

Social marketing focuses on public health commodities that can generally be delivered to end-users with little or no accompanying service by a health-care professional. (51) By contrast, social franchising has been used for enhancing delivery of more complex services, provided principally in clinics or small hospitals. Social franchises "attempt to use franchising methods to achieve social rather than financial goals", (52) by linking pre-existing private health practitioners in a network to provide socially beneficial services under a common brand. (53) Franchises can be stand-alone, in which the franchisee exclusively provides franchised products and services, or fractional, in which the franchisee provides a package of services under both the franchise and unfranchised product lines. (54) Although the franchisor is often an NGO, there are a growing number of government and for-profit social franchises. (55) Franchisees can pay a fee to the franchisor, but aspects of the franchise package such as training and marketing are often funded solely (ie, subsidised) by the franchisor.

Social franchises have been documented in more than 20 countries and their numbers have increased rapidly, doubling every 4 years since 1994, with over 90 tracked by Social Franchising for Health (SF4health) (55,56). The range of services provided through franchised clinics has also increased, with over half of existing programmes supporting multiple services, most commonly including family planning, reproductive health, safe deliveries, and diagnosis and treatment of HIV/AIDS, tuberculosis, malaria, pneumonia, and paediatric diarrhoea. An estimated 15 000–20 000 individual clinics in Asia, Africa, and Latin America now operate as part of social franchise networks. (53)

A key goal of these networks is to provide improved quality of care. Improvements in user satisfaction and perceptions of quality have been documented in most, though not all, franchises studied, but the effect on objectively measured clinical quality of service delivery has been hardly ever demonstrated. (56,57) Social franchising has been shown to increase client volume at franchised clinics, and occasionally has increased overall use at the community level. (56) Key concerns raised about social franchising models include the difficulty of controlling clinical quality, especially for more complex services, and the equity impact, with most evidence showing that franchised clinics tend to serve clients with high socioeconomic status relative to clients of non-franchised clinics or the general population. (56)

## Purchase

The purchasing of some private goods and services is common throughout all public health systems and in most instances is not controversial.

Few would suggest that government health services manufacture their own beds, bricks, or water filters, or their own antibiotics, sterile gloves, or mosquito nets. More complex purchasing commitments, often described with the umbrella term contracting, can be more controversial. Nevertheless, contracting for narrowly defined service components is commonplace. Examples include contracts for dialysis centres in South Africa and the Philippines, and laboratory or pharmaceutical distribution services in Tanzania, Zambia, and Mali. Contracts have also contained a range of financing, construction, and operations models for expansion of hospital infrastructure (and sometimes the provision of clinical services) in Brazil, Mexico, Lesotho, Thailand, and many other countries. (58–60) No systematic evidence from LMICs exists for the quality of contracted private relative to public facilities, (61,62) whereas the evidence from wealthy countries is insufficient and contradictory. (63,64)

Contracting arrangements are sometimes fiscally pragmatic, leveraging private funds for initial infrastructure investments to expand capacity faster than government funds alone allow. In other instances, contracting arrangements are a recognition that private expertise can fill a specialised need better than government can (eg, dialysis or pharmaceutical logistics management), or allow more rapid expansion of service provision. For example, many countries contract NGOs for the provision of family planning and reproductive health services to augment what government clinics alone can provide. Such contracts can be especially favoured where there is an attempt to avoid controversy or serve stigmatised patients, such as sex workers or drug users who might have reasons to be cautious in government facilities.

Contracting for all primary-care provision in a defined geographical area has also been implemented, most commonly in fragile and post-conflict states. Such contracts have been studied extensively in Cambodia, Rwanda, and Afghanistan. (65–69) Although these contract bids were open to for-profit providers, in the end all large-scale contracts of this sort were delivered through non-profit providers. The system of contracting out can, but not always, deliver both effective services and cost-effectiveness, and it has nearly always been used as a temporary solution to assuring public service provision. (70) As soon as stability is assured, governments have shown a strong preference for resumption of traditional primary care that is owned and operated by government. The experience of Cambodia illustrates this system well, where contracting was introduced at the instigation of the Asian Development Bank, and showed many successes, but was rapidly dismantled once the bank requirements were completed and government capacity had grown. (71)

In addition to directly contracting private services, governments can also indirectly purchase services by providing vouchers to users, which can also facilitate targeting subsidies at a particular group such as poor people. In a typical voucher programme, donor or government funds are given to a targeted population for specific goods or services in the form of a paper or electronic voucher that can be used at previously approved public or private providers, who are subsequently reimbursed. A variant of this approach is to base eligibility of users on possession of identification indicating their poverty status, such as the use of the Below Poverty Line card in India. (72) In some cases voucher payment initiatives have been added to established clinic social franchises. Vouchers have been used for family planning services, vaccinations, treatment of sexually transmitted infections, deliveries, antenatal care, and vitamins, and to increase uptake of insecticide-treated mosquito nets. An advantage is that the funds can be targeted to low-income or high-risk individuals in specific geographical areas. One suggestion is that quality of care will also be increased as providers strive to be included in the voucher programme, and in some programmes to compete for the custom of voucher recipients.

Since 1995, the number of voucher programmes has increased rapidly, building on the well-documented experience of the Instituto Centroamericano de la Salud in Nicaragua where targeted payments for treatment of sexually transmitted infections have been in place for 15 years. (73–76) Another well-documented example is the provision of vouchers to women attending public sector antenatal clinics in Tanzania to cover part of the cost of the purchase of insecticide-treated mosquito nets from private retailers. (77–81) Since 2008, 19 voucher programmes are reported in LMICs. (82)

Available evidence shows that vouchers have been associated with increased use of targeted health services. (83–85) Evidence that they can be associated with improvements in quality of care and effective targeting to specific populations is modest, and the effect on population-level health outcomes is inconclusive. (83–85) No clear evidence is available for the cost-effectiveness of vouchers as a method of subsidising health services. Concerns include the potential for fraud around voucher reimbursement, and the costs of identifying accurately both recipients and providers of suitable quality. (82,86,87)

## Discussion and Conclusions

In many LMICs such as China, Cambodia, Paraguay, Senegal, Nigeria, and Ghana, health expenditure is increasing at more than 10% a year. (88) Although the situation in each country is different, they share a challenge common to almost all developing countries — namely, the best way to interact with private providers to create a well functioning health system.

To address this problem, policy makers can draw on several decades of experience with private sector intervention. Unfortunately, much of this experience remains imperfectly documented, with a notable scarcity of robust assessments, which to some extent indicates neglect of this area of research; it also points to the inherent challenges of studying interventions that often require research methods less well accepted than the randomised trials that are the gold standard for much health research.

However, some conclusions are possible from the experience so far. First, we know that some approaches will not work, at least in isolation. Clearly, prohibiting the operation of the private sector, where demand for services is high and capacity to regulate imperfect, is doomed to failure. Furthermore, the ability to constrain private providers through statutory control is inadequate, especially in low-income countries. Self-regulation cannot be relied on to fill the gap because in most settings professional organizations function more like trade unions than effective regulators. We also know that even after training there is often a substantial gap between knowledge and practice. (39,89) That is not to say that regulation and training have no value; training could be an important first step when provider knowledge is highly imperfect, and in many settings regulation prevents a complete free-for-all of so-called quack practitioners and peddlers of fake drugs. Strong regulatory capacity should be the medium-term and long-term priority for low-income countries. In the near term, however, attention is increasingly turning to interventions that encourage private providers to improve the quality and coverage of their care, while advancing their own financial interests.

These approaches include social marketing, social franchising, accreditation, vouchers, and contracting. Evidence shows that social marketing and vouchers can increase coverage of targeted services and commodities, though there are clear limits to the types of interventions that social marketing can deliver, since it is unsuitable for even mildly complex services. By contrast, robust evidence on the effect of social franchising, accreditation, and contracts is less available; despite some positive outcomes, we do not have strong evidence that they can improve technical quality of care and coverage at the community level. For all these interventions, the evidence of their ability to reach poorer groups is weak, (90) and little is known about their cost-effectiveness.

With all interventions in the "Encourage and subsidise" category, key challenges are likely to be the expansion of them in both scale and scope. For example, the intensive nature of support and monitoring of facilities required for social franchising is likely to make rapid geographical scale-up very difficult. Vouchers might work well for a targeted set of services, but would be hard to use for provision of health services more generally. Sustainability is also a concern, since strategies such as social marketing, social franchising, and vouchers require substantial continued subsidy, and are almost entirely funded by extranational donors and implemented through NGOs. Donor preferences for these methods stem from their focused nature, the effectiveness of targeting to prioritised health services or particular populations, and the efficiency gains resulting from funding work outside large, often inefficient, and reputedly ineffective or corrupt, national bureaucracies.

These concerns point to the limitations of the "Encourage and subsidise" methods as a basis for large-scale public–private engagement, and the provision of universal health coverage. Rather they can be thought to function more as band-aids or at best bandages – potentially effective at addressing a focused problem on a restricted scale, but in no way a solution to the systemic, broad-based challenges of the whole health system. Broader-based solutions potentially exist in the form of a combination of accreditation, contracting, and regulation. Though unlikely to be implementable in low-income settings, they are becoming increasingly feasible as incomes and capacity rise in middle-income countries, and collective financing and purchasing can be used to effectively steer private sector development.

The private sector is increasingly hard to ignore, and the costs of ignoring it could be very high in public health terms. A range of devices exists for engagement, and experience with them has rapidly developed in recent years. The choice of appropriate approach will vary substantially, dependent on the health system failures being addressed, the nature of the health-care product or service, the type of provider, and the level of development of the country both in terms of income levels and health system organisation.

## Contributors

Both authors contributed equally to the conception, development, and writing of this article.

## Declaration of interests

Both authors have previously been contracted by Population Services International, an NGO focused on supporting social benefit through private provision of goods and services in developing countries. DM has given talks to, and received honoraria from, other NGOs engaged in private health-care provision.

## References

1. Marriott A. *Blind Optimism: Challenging the Myths about Private Health Care in Poor Countries*. Oxford: Oxfam; 2009. (Oxfam Briefing paper).
2. World Bank. World Bank responds to new Oxfam Health Report. [Internet]. Washington, D.C; 2009 [cited 2016 Apr 18]. Available from: http://go.worldbank.org/FJVS7II3A0.
3. Montagu D, Harding A, Preker A. Harding-Montagu Preker Framework.
4. Montagu D, Goodman C, Berman P, Penn A, Visconti A. Recent trends in working with the private sector to improve basic healthcare: a review of evidence and interventions. *Health Policy Plan*. 2016 Oct 1;31(8):1117–32.

5. Kumaranayake L. How do countries regulate the health sector? Evidence from Tanzania and Zimbabwe. *Health Policy Plan.* 2000 Dec 1;15(4):357–67.
6. Singh S, Wulf D, Hussain R, Bankole A, Sedgh G. *Abortion Worldwide: A Decade of Uneven Progress.* Guttmacher Institute.
7. Chuc N, Tomson G. "Doi moi" and private pharmacies: A case study on dispensing and financial issues in Hanoi, Vietnam. *Eur J Clin Pharmacol.* 1999 Jun;55(4):325–32.
8. Stenson B, Tomson G, Syhakhang L. Pharmaceutical regulation in context: the case of Lao People's Democratic Republic. *Health Policy Plan.* 1997;12(4):329–40.
9. Barnett C, Hort K. Approaches to regulating the quality of hospital services in low- and middle-income countries with mixed health systems: A review of their effectiveness, context of operation and feasibility. Melbourne: Nossal Institute for Global Health, University of Melbourne; 2013.
10. Ensor T, Weinzierl S. Regulating health care in low- and middle-income countries: Broadening the policy response in resource constrained environments. *Soc Sci Med.* 2007;65(2):355–66.
11. Morgan R, Ensor T. The regulation of private hospitals in Asia: Regulation of private hospitals in Asia. *Int J Health Plann Manage.* 2016 Jan;31(1):49–64.
12. Healy J, Braithwaite J. Designing safer health care through responsive regulation. *Med Joural Aust.* 2006;184(Supplement 10):56–9.
13. Bloom G, Henson S, Peters DH. Innovation in regulation of rapidly changing health markets. *Glob Health.* 2014;10(53).
14. AMFm Independent Evaluation Team. Independent evaluation of phase 1 of the Affordable Medicines Facility-malaria (AMFm), multi-country independent evaluation report. Final report. Calverton, Maryland, and London: ICF International and London School of Hygiene & Tropical Medicine; 2012.
15. National Pharmaceutical Pricing Authority. Price Notifications [Internet]. [cited 2015 May 30]. Available from: 2014/08/26/20:47:16. http://www.nppaindia.nic.in/ceiling/.
16. Sheikh K, Saligram PS, Hort K. What explains regulatory failure? Analysing the architecture of health care regulation in two Indian states. *Health Policy Plan.* 2015 Feb;30(1):39–55.
17. Spreng C. Healthy partnerships: how government can engage the private sector to improve health in Africa. Washington, D.C: The World Bank; 2011.
18. Basak S, Sathyanarayana D. Evaluating medicines dispensing patterns at private community pharmacies in Tamil Nadu. *Sothern Med Rev.* 3:27–31.

19. Buckley G, Gostin L. Countering the Problem of Falsified and Substandard Drugs [Internet]. Washington, D.C: Institute of Medicine; 2013. 376 p. Available from: https://doi.org/10.17226/18272.
20. Mills A, Goodman C, Greer G, Unwin A, Brieger W, Meek S. Medicine Sellers and Malaria Treatment in Sub-Saharan Africa: What Do They Do and How Can Their Practice Be Improved? *Am J Trop Med Hyg*. 2007 Dec 1;77(6_Suppl):203–18.
21. Santa-Ana-Tellez Y, Mantel-Teeuwisse AK, Dreser A, Leufkens HGM, Wirtz VJ. Impact of Over-the-Counter Restrictions on Antibiotic Consumption in Brazil and Mexico. Fredricks DN, editor. *PLoS ONE*. 2013 Oct 16;8(10):e75550.
22. Lowe RF, Montagu D. Legislation, regulation, and consolidation in the retail pharmacy sector in low-income countries. *South Med Rev*. 2009;2(2):35–44.
23. Teerawattananon Y, Tangcharoensathien V, Tantivess S, Mills A. Health sector regulation in Thailand: recent progress and the future agenda. *Health Policy*. 63(3):323–38.
24. Attanayake N, Siyambalagoda L. An inquiry into the regulation of pharmaceutical and medical practice in Sri Lanka. London: LSHTM; 2003. (Health Economics and Financing Programme).
25. Wafulaa F, Molyneux C, Mackintosh M, Goodman C. Protecting the public or setting the bar too high? Understanding the causes and consequences of regulatory actions of front-line regulators and specialized drug shop operators in Kenya. *Soc Sci Med*. 2013 Nov;97(SI):220–7.
26. Chalker J, Ratanawijitrasin S, Chuc NTK, Petzold M, Tomson G. Effectiveness of a multi-component intervention on dispensing practices at private pharmacies in Vietnam and Thailand: a randomized controlled trial. *Soc Sci Med*. 2005;60(1):131–41.
27. Chuc NTK, Larsson M, Do NT, Diwan V, Tomson G, Falkenberg T. Improving private pharmacy practice: a multi-intervention experiment in Hanoi, Vietnam. *J Clin Epidemiol*. 55(11):1148–55.
28. Sax S, Marx M. Local perceptions on factors influencing the introduction of international healthcare accreditation in Pakistan. *Health Policy Plan*. 2014 Dec;29(8):1021–30.
29. Goodman C, Kachur SP, Abdulla S, Bloland P, Mills A. Drug shop regulation and malaria treatment in Tanzania why do shops break the rules, and does it matter? *Health Policy Plan*. 2007 Jul 20;22(6):393–403.
30. Bhat R. Regulation of the Private Health Sector in India. *Int J Health Plann Manage*. 1996;11:253–74.

31. Singh G, Gambhir RS, Singh S, Talwar PS, Munjal V. Knowledge and awareness of the Consumer Protection Act among dental professionals in India: a systematic review. *Indian J Dent*. 2014;5(3):146–51.
32. Peters DH, Muraleedharan VR. Regulating India's health services: to what end? What future? *Soc Sci Med*. 2008;66(10):2133–44.
33. Hinchcliff R, Greenfield D, Moldovan M, Westbrook JI, Pawsey M, Mumford V, *et al*. Narrative synthesis of health service accreditation literature. *BMJ Qual Saf*. 2012;21(12):979–91.
34. Shaw CD, Braithwaite J, Moldovan M, Nicklin W, Grgic I, Fortune T, *et al*. Profiling health-care accreditation organizations: an international survey. *Int J Qual Health Care*. 2013 Jul 1;25(3):222–31.
35. Montagu D. Accreditation and other external quality assessment systems for healthcare. DFID Health Systems Resource Centre; 2003.
36. Alkhenizan A, Shaw C. Impact of Accreditation on the Quality of Healthcare Services: a Systematic Review of the Literature. *Ann Saudi Med*. 2011; 31(4):407–16.
37. Bukonda N, Tavrow P, Abdallah H, Hoffner K, Tembo J. Implementing a national hospital accreditation program: the Zambian experience. *Int J Qual Health Care*. 2002 Dec 1;14(90001):7–16.
38. Merck for Mothers. Program Report [Internet]. Merck for Mothers; 2014 [cited 2015 May 30]. Available from: http://www.merckformothers.com/docs/MFM_ProgramReport.pdf.
39. Shah NM, Brieger WR, Peters DH. Can interventions improve health services from informal private providers in low and middle-income countries? A comprehensive review of the literature. *Health POLICY Plan*. 2011 Jul;26(4):275–87.
40. Marsh VM, Mutemi WM, Willetts A, Bayah K, Were S, Ross A, *et al*. Improving malaria home treatment by training drug retailers in rural Kenya. *Trop Med Int Health*. 2004 Apr;9(4):451–60.
41. Bharaswadkar S, Kanchar A, Thakur N, Shah S, Patnaik B, Click ES, *et al*. Tuberculosis Management Practices of Private Practitioners in Pune Municipal Corporation, India. Dowdy DW, editor. *PLoS ONE*. 2014 Jun 4;9(6):e97993.
42. Rutta E, Kibassa B, McKinnon B, Liana J, Mbwasi R, Mlaki W, *et al*. Increasing Access to Subsidized Artemisinin-based Combination Therapy through Accredited Drug Dispensing Outlets in Tanzania. *Health Res Policy Syst*. 2011 Dec;9(1):22.
43. Chakraborty S, D'Souza S, Northrup R. Improving private practitioner care of sick children: testing new approaches in rural Bihar. *Health POLICY Plan*. 2000 Dec;15(4):400–7.

44. Greer G, Akinpelumi A, Madueke L, Plowman B, Fapohunda B, Youssef T, *et al.* Improving management of childhood malaria in Nigeria and Uganda by improving practices of patent medicine vendors. Washington, D.C: BASICS II for the United States Agency for International Development; 2004. Report No.: 264.
45. Chuc NTK, Larsson M, Falkenberg T, Do NT, Binh NT, Tomson G. Management of Childhood Acute Respiratory Infections at Private Pharmacies in Vietnam. *Ann Pharmacother.* 2001;35(10):1283–8.
46. Tougher S, Ye Y, Amuasi JH, Kourgueni IA, Thomson R, Goodman C, *et al.* Effect of the Affordable Medicines Facility – malaria (AMFm) on the availability, price, and market share of quality-assured artemisinin-based combination therapies in seven countries: a before-and-after analysis of outlet survey data. *The Lancet.* 2012 Dec;380(9857):1916–26.
47. Effectiveness, efficiency and equity of social marketing. Review of DFID Approach to Social Marketing. London: DFID; 2003.
48. Sun X, Guo Y, Wang S, Sun J. Social Marketing Improved the Consumption of Iron-fortified Soy Sauce among Women in China. *J Nutr Educ Behav.* 39(6):302–10.
49. Hanson K. Ends versus means: The role of markets in expanding access to contraceptives. *Health Policy Plan.* 2001 May 1;16(2):125–36.
50. De Allegri M, Marschall P, Flessa S, Tiendrebeogo J, Kouyate B, Jahn A, *et al.* Comparative cost analysis of insecticide-treated net delivery strategies: sales supported by social marketing and free distribution through antenatal care. *Health Policy Plan.* 2010 Jan 1;25(1):28–38.
51. Conteh L, Hanson K. Methods for studying private sector supply of public health products in developing countries: a conceptual framework and review. *Soc Sci Med.* 57(7):1147–61.
52. Montagu D. Franchising of health services in low-income countries. *Health Policy Plan.* 2002 Jun 1;17(2):121–30.
53. Schlein K, Montagu D. Clinical Social Franchising Compendium [Internet]. San Francisco, CA: Global Health Group, Global Health Sciences, University of California San Francisco; 2012. Available from: http://www.sf4health.org/sites/sf4health.org/files/reports/Social-Franchising-Compendium-2012.pdf.
54. Bishai DM, Shah NM, Walker DG, Brieger WR, Peters DH. Social Franchising to Improve Quality and Access in Private Health Care in Developing Countries.
55. Viswanathan R, Seefeld C. Clinial Social Franchising Compendium: An Annual Survey of PRograms: findings from 2014. San Francisco, CA: UCSF; 2015. (Social Franchising Compendium).

56. Beyeler N, York De La Cruz A, Montagu D. The Impact of Clinical Social Franchising on Health Services in Low- and Middle-Income Countries: A Systematic Review. Bullen C, editor. PLoS ONE. 2013 Apr 23;8(4): e60669.
57. Nijmeijer KJ, Fabbricotti IN, Huijsman R. Is franchising in health care valuable? A systematic review. *Health Policy Plan.* 2014 Mar 1;29(2):164–76.
58. Coelho C, O'Farrell C. Breaking new ground: Lesotho Hospital Public-Private Partnership – a model for integrated health services delivery. Washington, D.C: World Bank; 2009.
59. Llumpo A, Montagu D, Brashers E, Foong S, Abuzaineh N, Feachem R. Lessons from Latin America: the early landscape of healthcare public-private partnerships. San Francisco, CA: The Global Health Group, Global Health Sciences, University of California San Francisco; 2015. (Healthcare public-private partnership series). Report No.: 2.
60. Montagu D, Harding A. A zebra or a painted horse? Are hospital PPPs infrastructure partnerships with stripes or a separate species? *World Hosp Health Serv Off J Int Hosp Fed.* 2012;48(2):15–9.
61. Berendes S, Heywood P, Oliver S, Garner P. Quality of Private and Public Ambulatory Health Care in Low and Middle Income Countries: Systematic Review of Comparative Studies. *PLOS Med.* 2011 Apr;8(4).
62. Montagu D, Anglemyer A, Tiwari M. Private Versus Public Strategies for Health Service Provision for Improving Health Outcomes in Resource-limited Settings. London: EPPI-Centre.
63. Eggleston K, Shen YC, Lau J, Schmid CH, Chan J. Hospital ownership and quality of care: what explains the different results in the literature? *Health Econ.* 2008 Dec;17(12):1345–62.
64. Sloan F, Picone GA, Taylor DH, Chou SY. Hospital ownership and cost and quality of care: is there a dime's worth of difference. *J Health Econ.* 2001;20(1):1–21.
65. Liu X, Hotchkiss DR, Bose S. The impact of contracting-out on health system performance: a conceptual framework. *Health Policy.* 82(2):200–11.
66. Liu X, Hotchkiss DR, Bose S. The effectiveness of contracting-out primary health care services in developing countries: a review of the evidence. *Health Policy Plan.* 2007 Nov 13;23(1):1–13.
67. Loevinsohn B, Harding A. Buying results? Contracting for health service delivery in developing countries. *The Lancet.* 2005;366(9486):676–81.
68. Mills A, Broomberg J. Experiences of contracting health services: an overview of the literature. Geneva: World Health Organization; (Macro Economics, Health and Development). Report No.: 33.

69. Palmer N. The use of private-sector contracts for primary health care: theory, evidence and lessons for low-income and middle-income countries. *Bull World Health Organ*. 2000.
70. Mcpake B, Hongoro C. Contracting out of clinical services in Zimbabwe. *Soc Sci Med*. 1995 Jul;41(1):13–24.
71. Jacobs B, Thome JM, Overtoom R, Sam SO, Indermuhle L, Price N. From public to private and back again: sustaining a high service-delivery level during transition of management authority: a Cambodia case study. *Health Policy Plan*. 2010 May 1;25(3):197–208.
72. Bhat R, Mavalankar DV, Singh PV, Singh N. Maternal Healthcare Financing: Gujarat's Chiranjeevi Scheme and Its Beneficiaries. *J Health Popul Nutr*. 2009 Sep 15;27(2):249–58.
73. Borghi J, Gorter A, Sandiford P, Segura Z. The cost-effectiveness of a competitive voucher scheme to reduce sexually transmitted infections in high-risk groups in Nicaragua. *Health Policy Plan*. 2005 Jul 1;20(4):222–31.
74. Meuwissen LE, Gorter AC, Kester ADM, Knottnerus JA. Does a competitive voucher program for adolescents improve the quality of reproductive health care? A simulated patient study in Nicaragua. BMC PUBLIC Health. 2006 Aug 7;6.
75. Meuwissen LE, Gorter AC, Knottnerus AJA. Impact of accessible sexual and reproductive health care on poor and underserved adolescents in Managua, Nicaragua: a quasi-experimental intervention study. *J Adolesc Health*. 2006 Jan;38(1):56.e1-56.e9.
76. Meuwissen LE, Gorter AC, Knottnerus JA. Perceived quality of reproductive care for girls in a competitive voucher programme. A quasi-experimental intervention study, Managua, Nicaragua. *Int J Qual Health Care*. 2006 Feb 1;18(1):35–42.
77. Hanson K, Marchant T, Nathan R, Mponda H, Jones C, Bruce J, *et al.* Household ownership and use of insecticide treated nets among target groups after implementation of a national voucher programme in the United Republic of Tanzania: plausibility study using three annual cross sectional household surveys. *BMJ*. 2009 Jul 2;339(jul02 1):b2434–b2434.
78. Khatib RA, Killeen GF, Abdulla SM, Kahigwa E, McElroy PD, Gerrets RP, *et al.* Markets, voucher subsidies and free nets combine to achieve high bed net coverage in rural Tanzania. *Malar J*. 2008 Dec;7(1):98.
79. Marchant T, Schellenberg D, Nathan R, Armstrong-Schellenberg J, Mponda H, Jones C, *et al.* Assessment of a national voucher scheme to deliver insecticide-treated mosquito nets to pregnant women. *Can Med Assoc J*. 2010 Feb 9;182(2):152–6.

80. Mulligan JA, Yukich J, Hanson K. Costs and effects of the Tanzanian national voucher scheme for insecticide-treated nets. *Malar J.* 2008 Dec;7(1):32.
81. Killeen GF, Smith TA, Ferguson HM, Mshinda H, Abdulla S, Lengeler C, *et al.* Preventing Childhood Malaria in Africa by Protecting Adults from Mosquitoes with Insecticide-Treated Nets. Dushoff J, editor. *PLoS Med.* 2007 Jul 3;4(7):e229.
82. Gopalan SS, Mutasa R, Friedman J, Das A. Health sector demand-side financial incentives in low- and middle-income countries: A systematic review on demand- and supply-side effects. *Soc Sci Med.* 2014 Jan;100:72–83.
83. Bellows NM, Bellows BW, Warren C. Systematic Review: The use of vouchers for reproductive health services in developing countries: systematic review: Vouchers for reproductive health services review. *Trop Med Int Health.* 2011 Jan;16(1):84–96.
84. Ensor T. Consumer-led demand side financing in health and education and its relevance for low and middle income countries. *Int J Health Plann Manage.* 2004;19(3):267–85.
85. Meyer C, Bellows N, Campbell M, Potts M. The impact of vouchers on the use and quality of health goods and services in developing countries: a systematic review. London: EPPI-Centre.
86. Bellows BW, Conlon CM, Higgs ES, Townsend JW, Nahed MG, Cavanaugh K, *et al.* A Taxonomy and Results from a Comprehensive Review of 28 Maternal Health Voucher Programmes. *J Health Popul Nutr.* 2013 Dec;31 (4, 2):106–28.
87. Murray SF, Hunter BM, Bisht R, Ensor T, Bick D. Effects of demand-side financing on utilisation, experiences and outcomes of maternity care in low- and middle-income countries: a systematic review. *BMC Pregnancy Childbirth.* 2014 Dec;14(1):30.
88. WHO. Global health expenditure database. Table of key indicators for all the member States [Internet]. Available from: http://apps.who.int/nha/database/Key_Indicators/Index/en.
89. Das J, Holla A, Das V, Mohanan M, Tabak D, Chan B. In Urban And Rural India, A Standardized Patient Study Showed Low Levels Of Provider Training And Huge Quality Gaps. *Health Aff* (Millwood). 2012 Dec;31(12):2774–84.
90. Patouillard E, Goodman CA, Hanson KG, Mills AJ. Can working with the private for-profit sector improve utilization of quality health services by the poor? A systematic review of the literature. *Int J Equity Health.* 2007 Nov 7;6:17.

# Chapter 6

# Recent Trends in Working with the Private Sector to Improve Basic Healthcare – A Review of Evidence and Interventions*

**Dominic Montagu, Catherine Goodman, Peter Berman, Amy Penn, and Adam Visconti**

## Abstract

Building on the framework from Chapter 5, Montagu and Goodman, along with Peter Berman, Amy Penn, and Adam Visconti, use this chapter, "Recent Trends in Working with the Private Sector to Improve Basic Healthcare," to look at the evidence and practice that exists for a set of key private-sector engagement interventions.

A number of interventions in LMICs have, for many years, applied different models of subsidy, support, and engagement to address social and efficiency failures in private healthcare markets. This chapter reports on a review of these models and the evidence in supporting them to better understand what interventions are currently common, and to what extent practice is based on evidence. Using the typology from Chapter 5, we examined five models of intervention with private

---

*This chapter was originally published in "Montagu, D. et al. Health Policy and Planning, Vol. 31, Issue 8, (2016) 1117–1132".

markets for care: commodity social marketing, social franchising, contracting, accreditation, and vouchers.

To bring together the evidence for this evaluation, we conducted a systematic review of both published and gray literature, identifying programs large enough to be cited in publications and studies of the listed intervention types. A total of 343 studies were included in the review, including both published and gray literature. We identified 380 programs, the earliest having begun operation in 1955. Commodity social marketing programs were the most common intervention type, with 110 documented programs operating for condoms alone at the highest period. Existing evidence shows that these models can improve access, utilization, and, possibly, quality; however, for all program types, the overall evidence base remains weak, with practice in private sector engagement consistently moving in advance of evidence. Future research should address key questions concerning the impact of interventions on the market as a whole, the distribution of benefits by socioeconomic status, the potential for scale-up and sustainability, cost-effectiveness compared to relevant alternatives, and the risk of unintended consequences. Alongside better data, a stronger conceptual basis linking program design and outcomes to context is needed.

## Introduction

The private sector provides more than 50% of all healthcare in Sub-Saharan Africa and more than 80% of all healthcare in Asia outside of China[1, 2]. The importance of the private sector is increasingly appreciated by health ministries in LMICs as well as by donors, global health initiatives, and researchers[1, 3, 4], however this attention has not led to greater emphasis on evidence-based translation to policies or interventions. The limited number of programs developed to improve the functioning, integration, or oversight of the private sector are too often put forward as exemplars to be studied, applauded, or replicated without a clear contextual basis, or sound analysis of inputs, outputs, outcomes, and potential for replication.

This paper will address this gap by reviewing recent approaches to working with the private sector in LMICs. "Private" refers to all providers, formal or informal, not employed by government, including those who may be government employee but operate privately after-hours. Although many programs involve faith-based or non-governmental organizations (FBOs and NGOs) as coordinators or intermediaries to for-profit providers, the majority of private providers in LMICs operate as independent, for-profit providers, and this is the focus of this paper (Kagawa *et al.* 2012). The programs identified have varied goals: improving the quality, affordability or coverage of services provided by private providers; using private providers as a means to increase the availability of goods and services critical to public health goals; or using private providers as a more efficient alternative to public provision. All seek to address areas where the prevailing markets for health services fail to meet some widely accepted social priorities.

In global health many commonly practiced interventions have little evidence of effectiveness while other interventions, with a strong evidence base, are not widely adopted. Through this summary we seek to assess the scale of practical experience with private sector engagement interventions in LMICs, and the evidence base for impact behind each intervention type. Understanding the balance between experience and evidence is important for informing both practitioners and policy makers as they contemplate expansion, replication, or modification of existing intervention models.

## Failures in Markets

Government engagement with private providers should be based on careful and explicit analysis of problems in health system performance, and plausible assessment of how working with the private sector will remedy those problems and improve outcomes.[5-7]

In this review we look at healthcare markets from a perspective of social benefit. A healthcare market that functions well, from this perspective, will assure quality or services, deliver services in response to health needs as well as private demand, and ensure that poorer groups are well served. The issues to be addressed therefore include not only the standard "market failures" that prevent the achievement of efficiency from a social perspective, but also those related to inequity in distribution of income and knowledge.

Most common examples of market failures in the health economics literature are problems of under or over consumption related to positive externalities (because consumers do not take into account the benefits of their consumption for others), imperfect information that can allow poor quality providers to flourish or lead to insufficient demand for needed services, and principle-agent incentive problems.

Lack of provision of care to the poor, or use of care by the poor, might be the result of either a market that functions well in economic terms, but poorly in social terms, or a market that fails in both economic and social terms.

These problems may justify government involvement to address inefficiency, inequity, or other socially desirable objectives not adequately addressed by the market, even if the market does not fail.

Few private health providers operate in a completely free market, as there is generally government regulation over health worker qualifications, premises, pharmaceutical products, and sometimes prices[8]. However, such regulation is often limited in scope, poorly implemented, and may work more in the interests of providers than consumers[9–11]. So we remain with markets with an inadequate supply of goods and services important for public health, particularly for the poor; variable and poor quality; high prices; and low responsiveness to outbreaks and ongoing preventative care needs.

One response to these problems has been to call for public provision of health services[12]. However, there is ample evidence that government delivery is not always ideal. Lower income countries are full of examples of government failure to assure supply due to staff absenteeism or commodity stock-outs; inefficient delivery leading to high costs; frequent instances of pilferage and corruption; and free government services going unused due to their perceived poor quality (which may or may not be correct)[13, 14]. The prevalence of government failures, and the preponderance of existing private provision in many countries, together underscore the potential value of alternatives to public care provision. As a result, in recent decades attention has turned to innovative strategies that can enhance the operation of the private sector and address the market and equity failures described above.

## Engaging with Private Providers

International and local organizations committed to providing health services to the poor have been using private sector methods and leveraging existing private sector providers in developing countries for nearly 50 years. However, the number of programs has expanded greatly in recent decades. The instruments used nearly always work through intermediary actors, often NGOs, who are critical for organizing the often-heterogeneous private sector, and providing a necessary channel for facilitated interaction.

The typology of these programs has been documented often[3, 4] and includes:

- Social franchising, where a network of private providers is contracted to provide services under a common brand.
- Commodity social marketing, where commercial marketing techniques are used to create demand for products.
- Accreditation/Certification, a form of external quality review of hospitals, clinics, laboratories, and other facility types.
- Vouchers, given to a specific population for a specific service, to be redeemed at specified providers.
- Contracting, in which the government contracts NGO or commercial providers to deliver services to a certain population.

Such strategies often also include elements of provider training, and subsidies of some aspects of the program.

These strategies generally aim to address the market failures that lead to poor quality of health services by reducing reliance on the consumer's imperfect individual quality assessment and increasing the control of quality through supply side incentives and requirements. The services involved may include those with positive externalities such as the treatment of infectious diseases, but many do not, justified rather by the need to address inequities in provision by expanding the supply of affordable high quality care to poorer groups. Such expansion in provision may also reduce monopoly power, thus putting downward pressure on prices. Contracting primarily addresses government failures, replacing government provision with competitively allocated contracts that are expected to improve quality and lower costs.

In this paper we review the current status of implementation of these interventions, assess the evidence of impact, and highlight key unanswered questions.

## Methods

We conducted a systematic review of the literature to identify evaluations of programs that met definitions for social franchising, commodity social marketing, contracting, accreditation and vouchers (Montagu 2002, Evans 2008, Loevinsohn 2005, Montagu 2003, Sandiford 2002, respectively)[15-19]. We restricted our study to programs operating in LMICs as defined by the World Bank in 2014[20], and to interventions that directly address health-care supply of either commodities or services. The term social marketing can also be used to refer to information, education, and communication (IEC) campaigns conducted through commercial media outlets in order to promote behavior change by a population, without any direct engagement or support to the provision of commodities; such programs were excluded. No limitation on publication date was set.

Searches were conducted using the keywords private, non-state, private sector, independent, non-governmental, NGO, franchising, social franchising, social marketing, voucher, demand-side financing, output based aid, performance-based payment, and combinations of these terms. Our literature review was conducted both in peer-reviewed and grey literature outlets. Formal literature published until April 2014 was identified through keyword searches in English in PubMed, Web of Science, and Google Scholar using Bookends reference software (*Bookends Reference Management Software. Version 11.0.4. Sonny Software. Chevy Chase, MD*) and EndNote citation management (*Endnote. Version 14. Thomson Reuters*). Additional references were found through comprehensive follow-up of citations within previous systematic reviews on interventions or disease specific private sector activities. Grey literature searches were conducted using google.com and through targeted searches of websites belonging to key donor agencies, research institutions, private sector-focused consultancies, NGOs, and academic organizations including: ps4h.org, worldbank.org, usaid.gov, psi.org, psp-one.org, hs2020.org, rhvouchers.org, and dfid.gov.uk.

Studies were required to meet one of the five design criteria developed following procedures documented by Peters *et al.*[21]. Based upon guidelines on study quality and strength of evidence[22-24] we organized studies into a hierarchy of study designs indicating the strength of evidence, following these same criteria:

1. *Reviews*: Systematic reviews, reviews that report their search methodologies, or summary reviews, collected summaries of programs or program results. Of particular note are systematic reviews conducted following guidelines of Cochrane, Campbell, or other internationally recognized formal procedures.
2. *Randomized controlled trials (RCTs)*: Studies which randomly assign intervention and comparison to differing groups, measuring outcomes of interest before and after intervention.
3. *Non-randomized controlled interventions*: Non-random studies with both a before and after measurement that compares results between intervention and comparison groups.
4. *Pre-Post studies*: Studies conducted without a control group, comparing a targeted population before and after introduction of an intervention.
5. *Cross-sectional or descriptive studies*: Studies that describe the effects of an intervention or the operation of a specific intervention at one point in time without a comparison group.

Programs were tallied for years where a citation existed noting their operation. If an included study or review recorded duration of operation for a program, the program was assumed to have operated continuously for the noted duration, or if no duration was mentioned, from the reported initiation time until the date of citation publication.

## Findings

We identified 270 studies in the published literature, and 135 studies in the grey literature that met our search criteria. Of these 80 studies identified were excluded because they focused exclusively on behavior change social marketing. All interventions identified have been the subject of prior systematic or summary reviews (Table 1). The published and grey literature studies are listed in Table 2.

Of the 80 reviews found, 43 were based primarily upon systematic reviews of published literature. Only three, Koehlmoos *et al.* (2009) on social franchising, Lagarde and Palmer (2009) and Witter *et al.* (2012) both on contracting, were registered with a systematic review group.

Table 1. Studies reviewed by intervention type and study design

| | Review | RCT Studies | Controlled Studies | Uncontrolled Studies | Cross-sectional, Descriptive, Case Studies | Total |
|---|---|---|---|---|---|---|
| Social Franchising | 17* | 1 | 8* | 10 | 25* | 61* |
| Commodity Social Marketing | 10* | 5 | 16* | 33 | 20* | 84* |
| Contracting | 26* | 1 | 21 | 16 | 29* | 93* |
| Accreditation | 10* | 1 | 8* | 2 | 32 | 53* |
| Vouchers | 17* | 0 | 22* | 31 | 44* | 114* |
| Total | 80* | 8 | 75* | 92 | 150* | 405* |

*Categories including overlapping articles for other interventions.

*Note*: Harvey and DKT International, 1991-2014 was excluded from Reviews because we chose to only include peer-reviewed literature in the Commodity Social Marketing official count. We did use this information for the program counts in Figure 1. There were 24 of these articles total.

No published studies on vouchers met the highest level of rigor, being based on RCTs. Five social marketing studies and one social franchising study were RCTs. In addition, one study on contracting and another on accreditation have been conducted as RCTs but the results have not been published in peer-reviewed journals.

Non-randomized controlled studies were more common; we identified 75 in all. Uncontrolled pre-post studies were the most frequently identified published studies, numbering 92 in all. A total of 150 cross-sectional, case study, and descriptive studies were found, although this total only includes published studies for commodity social marketing, as the number of grey literature descriptive studies of this type of program numbers in the thousands

The systematic search strategy provided an unbiased basis for identifying programs in each intervention area. While this undoubtedly does not reflect the true number of active programs in LMICs, and in particular undercounts more recent programs due to publication lags, it provides a standardized relative measure of program numbers. The numbers of programs identified within our literature search are graphed in Figure 1; the number of publications in each field is in Figure 2. The earliest contracting

Table 2. Findings from published literature and grey literature (grey literature in italics)

| Private sector strategy | Randomized control trials | Non-randomized control interventions | Uncontrolled (before – after interventions) | Cross-sectional studies or descriptive studies | Reviews | Total |
|---|---|---|---|---|---|---|
| Social Franchising | Aung *et al.*, 2014 | *Khurram Azmat *et al.*, 2013 | Huntington *et al.*, 2012 | *Azmat *et al.*, 2013 | Nijmeijer *et al.*, 2014 | |
| | | Montagu *et al.*, 2013 | Agha *et al.*, 2007b | Bishai *et al.*, 2013 | Schlein *et al.*, 2013 | |
| | | Shah *et al.*, 2011 | Lonnroth *et al.*, 2007 | Azmat *et al.*, 2012 | Beyeler *et al.*, 2013 | |
| | | Ngo *et al.*, 2010 | Hennick and Clements, 2005 | Berk and Adhvaryu, 2012 | Blumenthal *et al.*, 2013 | |
| | | Qureshi, 2010 | | O'Connell *et al.*, 2011 | Sundari Ravindran and Fonn. 2011 | |
| | | *Kozhimannil *et al.*, 2009 | *Frost, 2007* | *Ravindran, 2010 | Koehlmoos, 2009 | |
| | | Bishai *et al.*, 2008 | *Agha, 2006* | Ngo *et al.*, 2009 | *Patouillard *et al.*, 2007 | |
| | | Agha *et al.*, 2007a | *Abt Associates, 2005* | Montagu and Decker, 2007 | Prata *et al.*, 2005 | |
| | | | *Population Services International, 2004* | Stephenson *et al.*, 2004 | Montagu, 2002 | |
| | | | *Agha and Balal, 2002* | Fielder and Wight, 2003 | | |
| | | | *McBride and Ahmed, 2001* | Arango, 1989 | *Viswanathan et al., 2014* | |
| | | | | | *Viswanathan et al., 2013* | |
| | | | | *Population Services International, 2012* | *Schlein K et al., 2012* | |

(*Continued*)

Table 2. (*Continued*)

| Private sector strategy | Randomized control trials | Non-randomized control interventions | Uncontrolled (before – after interventions) | Cross-sectional studies or descriptive studies | Reviews | Total |
|---|---|---|---|---|---|---|
| | | | | *Population Services International, 2011* | *Schlein K et al., 2011* | |
| | | | | *Saeed and Khan. 2010* | **Madhavan and Bishai, 2010* | |
| | | | | *Wexler, 2008* | *Montagu et al., 2010* | |
| | | | | *Tsui et al., 2006* | *Montagu et al., 2009* | |
| | | | | *Crapper, 2005* | **WHO, 2007* | |
| | | | | *Agha et al., 2004* | | |
| | | | | *Plautz et al., 2004* | | |
| | | | | *Sustainable Healthcare Enterprise Foundation, 2004* | | |
| | | | | *Jones and Moore, 2003* | | |
| | | | | *LaVake, 2003* | | |
| | | | | *Ruster, 2003* | | |
| | | | | *Smith, 2002* | | |
| | | | | *Agha et al., 1997* | | |
| | 1 | 8 | 10 | 25 | 17 | 61 |

| Private sector strategy | Randomized control trials | Non-randomized control interventions | Uncontrolled (before – after interventions) | Cross-sectional studies or descriptive studies | Reviews | Total |
|---|---|---|---|---|---|---|
| Commodity Social Marketing | De Allegri *et al.*, 2010 | Dongre *et al.*, 2008 | Kassegne *et al.*, 2011 | Paravani and Orgocka, 2013 | Chapman *et al.*, 2012 | |
| | Garrett *et al.*, 2008 | Agha *et al.*, 2007c | Agha and Meekers, 2010 | Prata *et al.*, 2013 | Hutchinson *et al.*, 2009 | |
| | Muller *et al.*, 2008 | Grabowsky *et al.*, 2007 | Brent, 2009 | Beksinska *et al.*, 2012 | Evans *et al.*, 2008 | |
| | Sun *et al.*, 2007 | Terris-Prestholt *et al.*, 2006 | Wang *et al.*, 2009 | O'Connell *et al.*, 2011 | *Patouillard *et al.*, 2007 | |
| | Rowland *et al.*, 2002 | *Kikumbih *et al.*, 2005 | Shavion and Westley, 2008 | *Ravindran, 2010 | Bertrand *et al.*, 2006 | |
| | | Mathanga *et al.*, 2005 | Fegan *et al.*, 2007 | Freeman *et al.*, 2009 | Stead *et al.*, 2006 | |
| | | Rowland *et al.*, 2004 | Noor *et al.*, 2007 | Banerjee *et al.*, 2007 | Peters *et al.*, 2004 | |
| | | Jacobs *et al.*, 2003 | Maxwell *et al.*, 2006 | Mathanga *et al.*, 2006 | Chapman and Astatke, 2003 | |
| | | Agha, 2002 | Berger *et al.*, 2005 | Purdy, 2006 | Stallworthy and Meekers, 2000 | |
| | | Marchant *et al.*, 2002 | Crape *et al.*, 2005 | Agha and Kusanthan, 2003 | Boone *et al.*, 1985 | |
| | | Agha *et al.*, 2001 | Eloundou-Enyegu *et al.*, 2005 | Howard *et al.*, 2003 | ** | |
| | | *Schellenberg *et al.*, 2001 | Kanal *et al.*, 2005 | Holtz *et al.*, 2002 | | |
| | | Meekers, 2000 | Paulino *et al.*, 2005 | Dunston *et al.*, 2001 | | |
| | | *Schellenberg *et al.*, 1999 | Stevens *et al.*, 2005 | Makutsa *et al.*, 2001 | | |

*(Continued)*

Table 2. (*Continued*)

| Private sector strategy | Randomized control trials | Non-randomized control interventions | Uncontrolled (before – after interventions) | Cross-sectional studies or descriptive studies | Reviews | Total |
|---|---|---|---|---|---|---|
| | | Snow *et al*., 1999 | Agha and Meekers, 2004 | Mong *et al*., 2001 | | |
| | | Vernon *et al*., 1988 | Nathan *et al*., 2004 | Shrestha *et al*., 1990 | | |
| | | | Warnick *et al*., 2004 | Bailey *et al*., 1989 | | |
| | | | Hanson *et al*., 2003 | Fox, 1988 | | |
| | | | Quick, 2003 | Davies *et al*., 1987 | | |
| | | | Brieger *et al*., 2002 | Piet and Hendrata, 1974 | | |
| | | | Zagre *et al*., 2002 | | | |
| | | | Abdulla *et al*., 2001 | | | |
| | | | Meekers, 2001 | | | |
| | | | Valente and Saba, 2001 | | | |
| | | | Crabbe *et al*., 1998 | | | |
| | | | Kipp *et al*., 1998 | | | |
| | | | Janowitz *et al*., 1992 | | | |
| | | | Kenya *et al*., 1990 | | | |
| | | | Ladipo *et al*., 1990 | | | |
| | | | Suyono, 1989 | | | |
| | | | Schellstede and Ciszewski, 1984 | | | |
| | | | Davies and Louis, 1977 | | | |
| | | | Black and Harvey, 1976 | | | |
| | 5 | 16 | 33 | 20 | 10 | 84 |

| Private sector strategy | Randomized control trials | Non-randomized control interventions | Uncontrolled (before – after interventions) | Cross-sectional studies or descriptive studies | Reviews | Total |
|---|---|---|---|---|---|---|
| Contracting | *Bloom et al., 2006* | Bowser *et al.*, 2013 | Heard *et al.*, 2013 | Chirwa *et al.*, 2013 | Witter *et al.*, 2012 | |
| | | Ssengooba *et al.*, 2012 | Arur *et al.*, 2010 | Randive *et al.*, 2013 | Elridge and Palmer, 2009 | |
| | | Cockcroft *et al.*, 2011 | Jacobs *et al.*, 2010 | Zaidi *et al.*, 2013 | Lagarde and Palmer, 2009 | |
| | | Huntington *et al.*, 2010 | Loevinsohn and Harding, 2005 | Heard *et al.*, 2011 | Liu *et al.*, 2008 | |
| | | La Forgia and Harding, 2009 | Mercer *et al.*, 2004 | *Ravindran, 2010 | Palmer *et al.*, 2008 | |
| | | Loevinsohn *et al.*, 2009 | Soeters and Griffiths, 2003 | Nigenda *et al.*, 2009 | Liu *et al.*, 2007 | |
| | | Mills *et al.*, 2004 | Chakraborty *et al.*, 2000 | Ameli and Newbrander, 2008 | *Patouillard *et al.*, 2007 | |
| | | Schwartz and Bhushan, 2004 | Marek *et al.*, 1999 | Macq *et al.*, 2008 | Perrot, 2006 | |
| | | Khan and Ahmed, 2003 | Fiedler, 1996 | Roberts *et al.*, 2008 | Siddiqi *et al.*, 2006 | |
| | | Murthy *et al.*, 2001 | | Palmer and Mills, 2005 | Loevinsohn and Harding, 2005 | |
| | | Mills *et al.*, 1997 | *Chowdhury, 2002* | Jack, 2003 | Palmer, 2000 | |
| | | McPake and Hongoro, 1995 | *Eichler et al., 2002* | Palmer and Mills, 2003 | Mills A, 1998 | |
| | | | *Lavandez et al., 2001* | Abramson, 2001 | McPake and Banda, 1994 | |
| | | *Cercone et al., 2005* | *Barnett and Putney, 2000* | | | |
| | | *Pelletier et al., 2005* | *Connor, 2000* | *SHOPS Project, 2012* | **Gorter et al., 2013* | |
| | | *Broomberg and Mills, 2004* | *Cotlear, 2000* | *Morgan, 2010* | *Khalil, 2013* | |
| | | *La Forgia et al., 2004* | *Nieves et al., 2000* | *Johannes et al., 2008* | **Madhavan and Bishai, 2010* | |

(*Continued*)

Table 2. (*Continued*)

| Private sector strategy | Randomized control trials | Non-randomized control interventions | Uncontrolled (before – after interventions) | Cross-sectional studies or descriptive studies | Reviews | Total |
|---|---|---|---|---|---|---|
| | | *Schwartz and Bhushan, 2004* | | *Bhat et al., 2007* | *WHO, 2006* | |
| | | *Karim et al., 2003* | | *Eichler et al., 2007* | *England, 2004* | |
| | | *Bushan et al., 2002* | | *Ali, 2005* | *Liu et al., 2004* | |
| | | *Mahmud et al., 2002* | | *Danel and La Forgia, 2005* | *Loevinsohn and Harding, 2004* | |
| | | *Keller and Schwartz, 2001* | | *England, 2004* | *Waters et al., 2002* | |
| | | | | *Loevinsohn, 2002* | *Slack and Savedoff, 2001* | |
| | | | | *Barnett et al., 2001* | *Rosen, 2000* | |
| | | | | *Eichler et al., 2001* | *Abramson, 1999* | |
| | | | | *Eichler et al., 2001* | *Bennett et al., 1997* | |
| | | | | *Loevinsohn, 2000* | *England, 1997* | |
| | | | | *Rosen, 2000* | | |
| | | | | *Rosenthal, 2000* | | |
| | | | | *Abramson, 1999* | | |
| | 1 | 21 | 16 | 29 | 26 | 93 |

| Private sector strategy | Randomized control trials | Non-randomized control interventions | Uncontrolled (before – after interventions) | Cross-sectional studies or descriptive studies | Reviews | Total |
|---|---|---|---|---|---|---|
| Accreditation | *Salmon et al., 2003* | Ammar *et al.*, 2013 | Wattanasri *et al.*, 2010 | El-Jardali *et al.*, 2014 | Alkhenizan and Shaw, 2012 | |
| | | Al Tehewy *et al.*, 2009 | Dhatt *et al.*, 2005 | El-Jardali *et al.*, 2013 | Greenfield *et al.*, 2012 | |
| | | *Kozhimannil *et al.*, 2009 | | Sax and Marx, 2013 | Alkhenizan and Shaw, 2011 | |
| | | Quimbo *et al.*, 2008 | | El-Jardali *et al.*, 2012 | Greenfield and Braithwaite, 2008 | |
| | | | | Handoo and Sood, 2012 | *Patouillard *et al.*, 2007 | |
| | | **Bellows et al., 2011* | | Amporfu, 2011 | | |
| | | **Rob et al., 2011* | | Cleveland *et al.*, 2011 | **Madhavan and Bishai, 2010* | |
| | | *Quality Assurance Project, 2005* | | Gershy-Damet *et al.*, 2010 | *Silva, 2007* | |
| | | *Bukonda et al., 2000* | | Opio *et al.*, 2010 | *Mays, 2004* | |
| | | | | Yao *et al.*, 2010 | *Montagu, 2003* | |
| | | | | Ahmad *et al.*, 2009 | *Shaw, 2003* | |
| | | | | Mazziotta, 2009 | | |
| | | | | El-Jardali *et al.*, 2008 | | |
| | | | | Ammar *et al.*, 2007 | | |
| | | | | El-Jardali, 2007 | | |
| | | | | Pongpirul *et al.*, 2006 | | |

*(Continued)*

Table 2. (*Continued*)

| Private sector strategy | Randomized control trials | Non-randomized control interventions | Uncontrolled (before – after interventions) | Cross-sectional studies or descriptive studies | Reviews | Total |
|---|---|---|---|---|---|---|
| | | | | Bukonda *et al.*, 2002 | | |
| | | | | Dhatt and Peters, 2002 | | |
| | | | | Maramba, 2002 | | |
| | | | | Timan *et al.*, 2002 | | |
| | | | | Nandraj *et al.*, 2001 | | |
| | | | | Huang *et al.*, 2000 | | |
| | | | | Whittaker *et al.*, 2000 | | |
| | | | | Arce, 1999 | | |
| | | | | *Mabitsela, 2010* | | |
| | | | | *Banking on Health, 2008* | | |
| | | | | *Hong et al., 2006* | | |
| | | | | *Rafeh and Schwark, 2006* | | |
| | | | | *Rooney and Barnes, 2001* | | |
| | | | | *Blake, 1999* | | |
| | | | | *Newbrander et al., 1999* | | |
| | | | | *Gebaly, 1998* | | |
| | 1 | 8 | 2 | 32 | 10 | 53 |

| Private sector strategy | Randomized control trials | Non-randomized control interventions | Uncontrolled (before – after interventions) | Cross-sectional studies or descriptive studies | Reviews | Total |
|---|---|---|---|---|---|---|
| Vouchers | | Obare *et al.*, 2014 | Bellows *et al.*, 2013b | *Azmat *et al.*, 2013 | Gopalan *et al.*, 2014 | |
| | | Van de Poel *et al.*, 2014 | Agha, 2011a | Brody *et al.*, 2013b | Grainger *et al.*, 2014 | |
| | | Alfonso *et al.*, 2013 | Agha, 2011b | Kanya *et al.*, 2013 | Murray *et al.*, 2014 | |
| | | Amendah *et al.*, 2013 | Ir *et al.*, 2010 | Okal *et al.*, 2013 | Bellows *et al.*, 2013a | |
| | | *Khurram Azmat *et al.*, 2013 | Janish *et al.*, 2010 | Abuya *et al.*, 2012 | Brody *et al.*, 2013a | |
| | | Obare *et al.*, 2013a | Macedo de Oliveira *et al.*, 2010 | de Savigny *et al.*, 2012 | Bellows *et al.*, 2011 | |
| | | Nguyen *et al.*, 2012 | Marchant *et al.*, 2010b | Njuki *et al.*, 2012 | Bhatia and Gorter, 2007 | |
| | | Rahman *et al.*, 2012 | Marchant *et al.*, 2010a | Ahmed and Khan, 2011a | *Patouillard *et al.*, 2007 | |
| | | Ahmed and Khan, 2011b | Webster *et al.*, 2010 | Gingrich *et al.*, 2011 | Worrall *et al.*, 2005 | |
| | | Bauhoff *et al.*, 2011 | Bhat *et al.*, 2009 | Minh *et al.*, 2010 | Ensor, 2004 | |
| | | Ekirapa-Kiracho *et al.*, 2011 | Hanson *et al.*, 2009 | Schmidt *et al.*, 2010 | | |
| | | Killeen *et al.*, 2007 | McKay *et al.*, 2006 | Baume *et al.*, 2009 | **Gorter et al., 2013* | |
| | | Meuwissen *et al.*, 2006c | Meuwissen *et al.*, 2006a | Hanson *et al.*, 2008 | *Meyer et al., 2011* | |
| | | Meuwissen *et al.*, 2006d | Meuwissen *et al.*, 2006b | Khatib *et al.*, 2008 | *Gupta et al., 2010* | |
| | | *Kikumbih *et al.*, 2005 | Grabowsky *et al.*, 2005 | Mulligan *et al.*, 2008 | **Madhavan and Bishai, 2010* | |
| | | Erulkar *et al.*, 2004 | Nathan *et al.*, 2004 | Kweku *et al.*, 2007 | *Arur et al., 2009* | |
| | | Marchant *et al.*, 2002 | Sandiford *et al.*, 2002 | Gorter *et al.*, 2006 | **WHO, 2007* | |
| | | *Schellenberg *et al.*, 2001 | Robey, 1987 | Meuwissen *et al.*, 2006e | *Gorter, 2003* | |

(*Continued*)

Table 2. (*Continued*)

| Private sector strategy | Randomized control trials | Non-randomized control interventions | Uncontrolled (before – after interventions) | Cross-sectional studies or descriptive studies | Reviews | Total |
|---|---|---|---|---|---|---|
| | | *Schellenberg *et al.*, 1999 | Chow, 1970 | Tami *et al.*, 2006 | | |
| | | | Cernada and Chow, 1969 | Borghi *et al.*, 2005 | | |
| | | **Bellows et al., 2011* | | Howe *et al.*, 2005 | | |
| | | **Rob et al., 2011* | *Bajracharya et al., 2013* | Mushi *et al.*, 2003 | | |
| | | *Hatt et al., 2010* | *Crape et al., 2011* | | | |
| | | | *Bellows and Hamilton, 2010* | *Armstrong, 2012* | | |
| | | | *Bellows et al., 2010* | *Bellows, 2012* | | |
| | | | *Gorter et al., 2009* | *GROPBA, 2012* | | |
| | | | *Rahman et al., 2009* | *Corby, 2011* | | |
| | | | *Bellows et al., 2008* | *Donaldson and Thiede, 2011* | | |
| | | | *Bellows, 2007* | *Boler and Harris, 2010* | | |
| | | | *Ngu, 2007* | *Kilonzo et al., 2010* | | |
| | | | *Bhat et al., 2006* | *Truzyan et al., 2010* | | |
| | | | *Leisher and Nachuk, 2006* | *Aneesa et al., 2009* | | |
| | | | | *Bashir et al., 2009* | | |
| | | | | *Kundu et al., 2009* | | |

| Private sector strategy | Randomized control trials | Non-randomized control interventions | Uncontrolled (before – after interventions) | Cross-sectional studies or descriptive studies | Reviews | Total |
|---|---|---|---|---|---|---|
| | | | | *Bellows, 2008* | | |
| | | | | *Donaldson et al., 2008* | | |
| | | | | *Koehlmoos et al., 2008* | | |
| | | | | *NCAPD, 2008* | | |
| | | | | *Salvetto and Alvarado, 2008* | | |
| | | | | *Bhat et al., 2007* | | |
| | | | | *Krishna, 2007* | | |
| | | | | *Lowe and Bellows, 2007* | | |
| | | | | *Islam, 2006* | | |
| | | | | *Tan et al., 2005* | | |
| | | | | *Gorter et al., 1999* | | |
| | 0 | 22 | 31 | 44 | 17 | 114 |

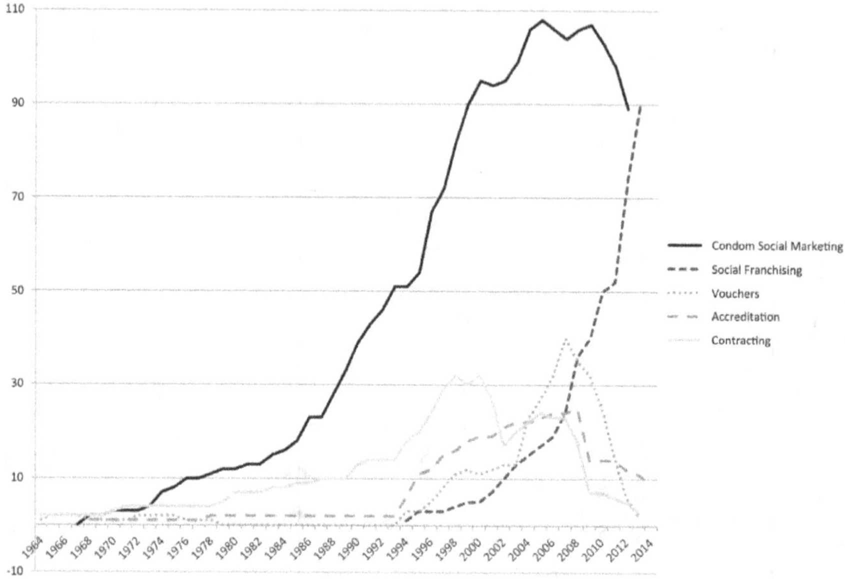


Figure 1. Programs in existence, by year (measured as referenced as existing at that time in published or grey literature).

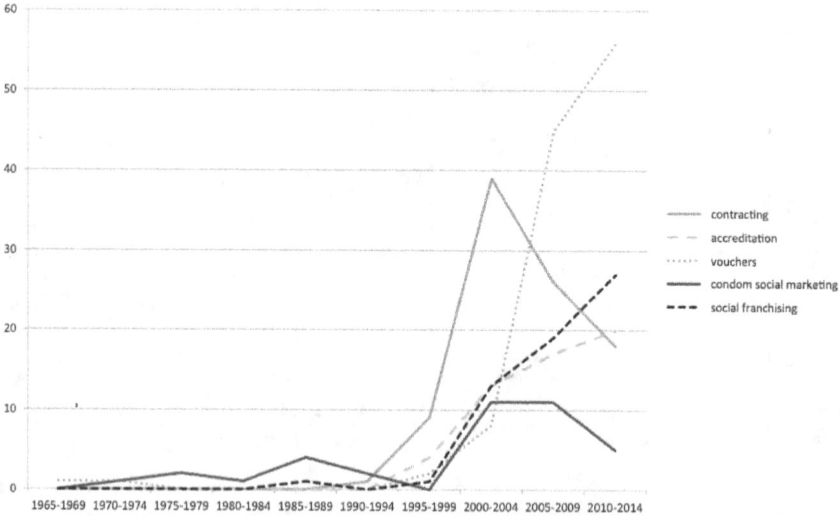


Figure 2. Published and grey literature papers by topic area and year.

programs documented dated from 1955 in Zimbabwe[25] and 1960 in Uruguay[26]. The earliest voucher programs identified date to 1964 and 1965 in Taiwan and South Korea respectively[27–29]; only two more were documented between 1979 and 1995. Social marketing programs were first documented in 1968 in both India and Uruguay; accreditation programs in the Philippines in 1968 (Philippine Society of Pathologists)[30]; and social franchising programs in Nepal in 1994 and India and Pakistan in1995[31].

Below we introduce each intervention in turn, describing the extent of implementation experience or practice, and the evidence on effectiveness, organizing the evidence using the hierarchy of study designs described above.

## Social Franchising

A social franchise encompasses a network of pre-existing private health practitioners linked through contracts to provide socially beneficial services under a common brand. Most often operated by NGOs, social franchises "attempt to use franchising methods to achieve social rather than financial goals."[17] A central goal of franchising private providers is that it allows rapid scaling up of service delivery points, and builds upon preexisting infrastructure[31].

### *Practice*

Social franchises have been documented in over 40 countries[32]. The number of social franchises is increasing rapidly, nearly doubling every four years since 1994. The range of services provided through franchised clinics has also increased, with over half of currently active social franchise programs supporting multiple services, most commonly including family planning, reproductive health, safe deliveries, and diagnosis and treatment of HIV/AIDS, TB, malaria, pneumonia, and pediatric diarrhea. Over 95,000 providers currently operate in Asia, Africa, and Latin America as part of social franchise networks[31].

### *Evidence*

A 2009 systematic review on social franchising found no studies meeting Cochrane inclusion criteria[33]. Non-randomized controlled studies from

Vietnam, Pakistan and the Philippines demonstrated increases in franchised clinic use overall, and in use of targeted family planning and reproductive health services[34]. In Myanmar, Lonnroth *et al.* showed franchised delivery of TB care led to an overall increase in TB diagnosis and treatment after adjusting for non-franchised provision[35]. In the Philippines, Kozhimannil *et al.* found franchised midwife services associated with a statistically significant increase in prenatal care, but not with giving birth in an institution. Franchising was furthermore found to be less effective at reaching the poor and rural populations than the national health insurance program[36]. In Pakistan, Bishai reports that franchised facilities provided higher quality services than other private facilities surveyed, served a higher proportion of poor clients than government facilities, and served clients more efficiently than government facilities[37]. In Nepal, Agha noted a significant increase in client satisfaction in franchised clinics compared to non-franchised clinics[38].

## Commodity Social Marketing

Commodity social marketing (CSM) applies commercial marketing promotion strategies to create demand for products such as contraceptives, mosquito nets, malaria medicines, and vitamins that have high public-health value. At the same time, the promoted commodities are distributed through for-profit channels: pharmacies, shops, drug-sellers, bars, etc., usually at a subsidized price, making them more affordable to the end user.

### *Practice*

Social marketing programs are the one of the most common large-scale private sector intervention model in LMICs, although social franchising programs have nearly surpassed it (Figure 1). In 2005 and 2009, 110 CSM programs were active, and declined to 94 by 2013, making the number of social marketing programs nearly equivalent to social franchising programs. Throughout the past fifty years we have identified 156 different social marketing programs operating in 83 countries (Figure 1). While family planning commodities were the most commonly socially marketed products throughout the 70s, 80s, and 90s, vitamins, nutritional supplements, anti-malarials, and mosquito nets have also become common in the past twenty years.

## *Evidence*

While the evidence for the effectiveness of large-scale behavior change campaigns is strong[15, 39, 40], the evidence base for CSM is more mixed. Supporting CSM a 2003 review by Chapman and Astatke concluded that "the effectiveness of social marketing for increasing the use of products and services is well established in the areas of HIV/AIDS, maternal and child health and family planning and reproductive health."[41] The review summarized data from 16 studies, and found evidence to suggest that social marketing programs can increase the use of a variety of health commodities, including condoms, oral contraceptives, insecticide treated nets (ITNs) and oral rehydration therapy. A review from 2000 by Stallworthy and Meekers reviewed subsidy cost per unit for 23 condom social marketing programs. They found that market size and program maturity were the most important determinants of lower subsidy per unit needed.[42] However, more recently, Peters *et al.* found insufficient evidence to conclude that social marketing was or was not more effective at delivering products or services than other health interventions.[21] A 2009 review of the impact of rural contraceptive social marketing programs also found insufficient evidence to confirm impact.[43] A 2012 review, however, found that commodity social marketing improved availability of condoms in the private sector and use of condoms in high-risk sex.[44]

An RCT comparison of socially marketed vs. free ITNs in Burkina Faso found no difference in cost-effectiveness of the two delivery methods.[45] In an RCT in China, Sun *et al.* found a 30% increase in purchase of iron-fortified soy sauce in social marketing locations compared to control areas. Three other RCTs focused primarily on the behavior change aspects of commodity-linked social marketing programs and did not provide guidance specific to effective commodity social marketing.[46–48]

Of the 16 non-randomized controlled studies, eight compared populations offered socially marketed products to control populations who received no intervention. Five studies reported on bednet programs, three on contraceptive programs, one on water purification, and one on both contraceptives and HIV/AIDS behavior change. The programs took place in Botswana, Cameroon, Columbia, Ghana, Guinea, India, Kenya, Malawi, Mozambique, South Africa, Tanzania, and Uganda. Nine of the studies showed positive results (eg: greater uptake of family planning commodities, higher rates of appropriate treatment for pediatric diarrhea) in the socially marketed sites compared to areas not receiving social marketing. Two studies reported negative effects on product usage in social marketing programs compared to alternative delivery methods used elsewhere (free provision through clinics or community based distribution).

Thirty-three pre-post analyses of social marketing programs were found. Of these 13 reviewed programs focused on family planning, seven of them condoms specifically. A further seven studied supplement programs, six ITNs, two malaria treatment, and one each for social marketing programs targeting water purification, STI treatment, oral rehydration, and treatment of intestinal worms. Twenty-four of the studies reported positive results (eg: increased rates of appropriate treatment) resulting from the social marketing interventions. A further seven studies indicated positive outcomes, but were unclear as to the attributable impact of social marketing in achieving the outcomes. Two studies did not report positive outcomes from social marketing.

Analysis of CSM in Tanzania found it to be socially beneficial, with a benefit-cost ratio of between 1.31 and 1.72[49]. A study in Malawi found social marketing of ITNs to be effective at reaching vulnerable populations and noted that subsidy costs per net decreased rapidly as volume increased.[50]

Two well designed studies of subsidized malaria treatment programs in Tanzania and Kenya have demonstrated the potential success of market based subsidized supply at increasing access and lowering costs of treatment, particularly among low income populations[51–53]. However, these programs had limited branding and marketing components, and did not self-identify as social marketing programs and so are not included in this overall review. Their success nevertheless adds support to the evidence based for commodity social marketing given the close similarities of the intervention models.

## Contracting

Contracting is defined as the provision of healthcare services by private providers on behalf of the government. Contracting with the private sector is implemented in two ways: through contracting out, in which private organizations are engaged to take on government financed services outside of the government health system; or contracting in, in which private organizations are engaged to manage or directly delivery services provided within existing government facilities.

### *Practice*

Contracting out of some aspects of health delivery are understood to be common in many LMICs. For example, hospital and clinic support services such as cleaning and security are routinely contracted to private suppliers, and contracting of ambulance transportation and emergency response is not unusual[54, 55]. However, large scale contracting in, or out, appears to remain relatively rare. We have identified 49 contracting experiments operating since 1955 in 30 countries. The number of concurrent programs peaked in 1998 and 2000 with 32 contracting initiatives functioning, and has since declined to 18 in 2008 (Figure 1). Twenty-four of the identified studies were from Latin America, more than twice as many as from any other region of the world (Figure 1). Lack of governmental capacity may, as Lagarde and Palmer conclude, make contracting a particularly attractive alternative in some settings. However, the reputation of contracting as a delivery option most suited for fragile or post-conflict settings[56, 57] appears to be contradicted by the existing evidence of widespread contracting application in non-conflict settings.

### *Evidence*

The evidence for contracting for health services has been better assessed than for other private sector interventions. A Cochrane Collaboration systematic review of contracting for health services in LMICs was published in 2009. Based on findings from the three studies meeting its inclusion criteria the review found that contracting was effective at increasing access and use of services, and that "contracting out may be an appropriate response to scale up service delivery in particular settings, such as post-conflict or fragile states." The review did not find evidence on the relative effectiveness of contracting compared to government provision or other delivery methods.[56] A second Cochrane review in 2012 focused on paying for performance, in the context of contracted delivery. The review found that the evidence base was weak to draw definitive conclusions on paying for performance in LMICs.[58] Earlier reviews with less restrictive inclusion criteria have been generally more positive in their findings. Liu *et al.* (2008) include 16 studies of 13 programs in their review of contracting out.[59] Their findings confirmed those of Loevinsohn and Harding (2005) that contracted out services consistently provided better access than government provided services.[16] Liu *et al.* found that contracting had the potential to increase equity of care, but that insufficient evidence existed to confirm that it was more effective at this than other methods of financing or delivery services. The authors found insufficient evidence to indicate whether contracting out led to differences in quality of care or efficiency of provision when compared to alternatives. Prior literature reviews by Mills (1998), England (2004), and Patouillard (2007) found insufficient evidence to assess contracting effectiveness at improving outcomes, access, utilization or cost.[4, 55, 60]

Comparisons between the effectiveness of different methods of contracting have shown no difference or limited difference in outcomes.[61, 62] A recent study from Cambodia has both shown positive productivity results from contracting of care, and also documented the process of transitioning from a post-conflict contracting effort to a more traditional system of direct government service provision.[63]

## Accreditation

Accreditation is a form of external quality review, based upon published standards, administered by an independent body, and focused on benchmarking and process improvements. In general, accreditation is only applied to hospitals and, rarely, to blood banks or laboratories. In most instances accreditation programs are participatory: representatives from the accredited institutions are involved in the accreditation of other institutions. Accreditation of hospitals expanded in the 1980s, and is common in most OECD countries[18, 64, 65] While quality certification programs exist in most countries, these differ in important ways from accreditation initiatives, being externally driven, often department-focused rather than comprehensive reviews of institutional practices, having less emphasis on benchmarking and continuous improvement, and often being more expensive.[66] Certification programs do not fit an agreed upon typology and so are excluded from this review.

### *Practice*

Accreditation programs in LMICs have been documented in hospitals or clinics in Argentina, Brazil, Colombia, Egypt, Ghana, Indonesia, Kyrgyzstan, Lebanon, Liberia, Malaysia, Philippines, South Africa, Tanzania, Thailand, and Zambia. Laboratory accreditation programs have been documented in Argentina, Pakistan, Philippines, South Africa, Thailand, and Uganda. At least one accreditation program is reported to have closed down in the last 10 years, however program websites and the International Accreditation Programme of the International Society for Quality in Health Care indicate that the number has been stable since 2005.

### *Evidence*

There have been reviews of accreditation programs in LMICs summarizing their operations or their potential for impact[18, 65], and we found three reviews of research on accreditation from LMIC. We found eight controlled studies of healthcare accreditation in LMICs in our review. Two pre-post studies without controls were identified[67-69], both for laboratory services, however none contain sufficient data to demonstrate attributable impacts of accreditation, ruling out external factors. Three papers from the grey literature report quality improvements in hospitals as a result of accreditation in Zambia.[70, 71] A number of cross-sectional and qualitative studies have reviewed the experience of individual accreditation programs, nearly all donor-supported. These have found positive results.[70, 72, 73] A second focus for qualitative studies has been on laboratory accreditation, often evaluated as part of a promotion campaign by the World Health Organization or other international agencies.[69, 74-76]. These experiences are also reported to have led to quality improvements.

## Vouchers

Vouchers are one form of consumer-led, or demand-side financing. In a typical voucher program, donor or government funds are given to a targeted population for a targeted service or set of services in the form of a credit. This credit, in the form of a paper or electronic voucher, is distributed to the target population and can be reimbursed at a limited number of previously approved providers. Vouchers have been used for family planning services, vaccinations, treatment of STIs, deliveries, ante-natal care and vitamins, and to increase uptake of ITNs.

### *Practice*

The first documented voucher programs for healthcare delivery in LMICs that we identified were initiated in 1964 and 1965 in Taiwan and South Korea respectively.[77] Only two new voucher programs are reported in the literature for the following 30 years, one in Costa Rica and one in Iran. Since 1995, however, voucher programs have grown rapidly in number (Figure 1), building upon the well documented experience of ICAS in Nicaragua[78-82] and the interest and availability of financial support from the World Bank-housed Global Program for Output Based Aid (GPOBA) and the German Development Bank (KfW). Seven voucher programs started since 2005 are voucher payment initiatives added on to already-established clinic social franchises. As of 2008, 40 voucher programs are reported in LMICs at its peak (Figure 1).

### *Evidence*

We found 17 reviews of voucher programs in both published and grey literature. Only the Bellows *et al.* and Brody *et al.* studies were systematic reviews. Bellows *et al.* studied the evidence of vouchers used for reproductive health services, examining the impact on cost, quality, service utilization, and health impact. They identified 15 quantitative studies of 13 voucher programs, and concluded that there was positive, but limited, evidence of increase in use of reproductive health services in areas served by voucher programs. Similarly positive but inconclusive evidence was found for population-level health outcomes and changes in quality resulting from voucher programs. The review was hampered by the dearth of long-established voucher programs for reproductive health. Brody *et al.* examined if voucher programs in developing countries effectively target specific populations, increase use of services or goods, have cost-efficiency, and improve quality and health outcomes. They identified 24 studies of 16 voucher programs, but only found moderate to robust evidence that vouchers target specific populations, increase use of services and health care goods, and improve quality of care.

A 2004 non-systematic review by Ensor included a broader range of consumer-led demand side financing programs, focusing on all health services, and finding a similar positive but weak indication for increases in use as a result of voucher programs, no evidence for differences in quality, and positive but potentially confounded evidence for improvement in health outcomes following initiation of a voucher scheme in Mexico.[83]

An ongoing challenge with the evaluation of voucher programs is the difficulty of adjusting for confounding factors in what is inevitably a distal relationship between payments, provision and use of services, and the effect of those services at a population level.

As a payment-focused intervention, vouchers are often considered explicitly in terms of their potential for delivering efficient subsidy to targeted sub-populations. Three studies examined relative cost-effectiveness of vouchers as a method of subsidizing health services or of financing public health improvements.[78, 84, 85] Borghi *et al.* (2005) conducted a cost-effective analysis of a competitive voucher scheme in Nicaragua compared to the absence of vouchers. They found that the voucher scheme was both effective, because it treated 92% of common STIs compared to 15% in the absence of vouchers, and cost-effective: the cost to cure STI was cheaper with a voucher.[78] Hatt *et al.* (2010) found that in Bangladesh, maternal health demand-side financing programs supported by vouchers were significantly associated with rates of deliveries with qualified providers twice that found in control sites.[84] Alfonso *et al.* (2013) analyzed the cost-effectiveness of a voucher scheme with health system strengthening versus the standard of care in rural Uganda. The voucher scheme had a cost-effectiveness ratio of US$302 per DALY averted, and cost per death averted of $20,756.[85]

## Discussion

We have set out to measure interventions in private healthcare markets in two complementary ways. First, by culling published and grey literature for references, systematically searching the internet, donor and program websites, and conducting key informant interviews, we have assessed the scale of implementation of the major forms of direct private-sector engagement in LMICs in the past 50 years. Second, by building on a number of systematic reviews and individual studies we have consolidated the evidence on their impact.

Strategies for working with private providers are not limited to those we have investigated. Other approaches include provider training, liaising with professional associations and strengthening regulation.[86, 87] However, we chose to focus on these five areas as they involve direct engagement with private providers and have received growing attention in recent decades.[88]

It is immediately obvious that practice remains far in advance of research. The academic basis for supporting franchised delivery of public health services remains weak[33], but policy makers, program implementers, and a host of private, bilateral, and national funders are investing in it for a growing range of services in a growing number of countries[31]. The same dichotomy exists for social marketing, contracting, voucher-based funding initiatives, and accreditation programs.

Why this should be the case is not clear, but we posit a few possible explanations. First, the evaluation methods used for clinical health are not well adapted to public health policies and as result often bypassed by policy makers and program managers alike[89]. Second, there is a strong bias among donor agencies and development specialists towards 'success stories' and so positive experiences, even if not rigorously assessed, lead rapidly to replication and expansion. Third, the interventions here all have in common their reliance on extra-governmental actors as the principal agents for implementation. For many donors and technical support agencies the benefits of avoiding what are often perceived as excessively bureaucratic and corrupt government agencies may outweigh doubts about proven effectiveness. Fourth, the free-market preferences of some funding agencies may provide a pre-existing bias to support private-sector activities regardless of evidence. Finally, there may simply be a frustration with the counterfactual: government supported financing or delivery of care that also is nearly always pursued without evaluations of the kinds we have examined in this study.

In the introduction we noted that key goals of these interventions were to address the failure of markets to delivery social benefits in the private health care sector, particularly related to poor quality and inequality in utilization of basic services. There is evidence that CSM, contracting and vouchers can improve access and utilization, and some indication that franchising can improve quality, but the evidence remains limited. In 2004 Peters *et al.* wrote that "little is known about how to use tools that affect consumer behavior or restructure health markets" and lamented that the Cochrane Group on Effective Practice and Organization of Care (EPOC) only studied developed country examples.[21] The EPOC group now has a focus area on LMIC reviews. Other changes have been slower. Controlled studies of private sector interventions remain rare, and comparisons with other intervention types are nearly non-existent. Healthcare provision is highly dependent on context, and yet the study of given mechanisms in different contexts, such that context could be controlled for and better understood, is nearly unknown.

The available data leave a number of key questions unanswered – questions that are often the subject of heated debates in the policy arena. These include the following:

**Adding or shifting demand:** The evidence shows that the strategies tend to increase use of the providers involved, but is this an overall increase in coverage or does it reflect "crowding out" of public sector provision or the existing unsubsidised private sector?

**Unintended Consequences:** Are there risks that working with private providers may actually damage rather than improve quality? For example, does giving additional training or certification to private providers with relatively low health qualifications encourage them to overreach themselves and begin to act like fully trained doctors? Does encouraging less qualified private providers to provide medicines under CSM risk poor drug use practices such as under- or over-treatment due to the dominance of profit motives?

**Excluding the poorest:** Does working with the private sector mean that interventions are less likely to reach the poor? Most programs aim to increase access for vulnerable groups but there is concern that the poorest will be unable to afford private providers and that the benefits of such initiatives will therefore be disproportionately reaped by better off groups. Patouillard *et al* reviewed the evidence on this issue, finding little evidence on the socio-economic distribution of benefits from these interventions, but considerable evidence that such interventions had worked successfully in generally poor communities.[4]

**Is large scale impact possible:** Are these programs capable of operating at scale? While CSM has often been implemented on a national scale, other programs tend to start small, and there are concerns that their positive effects may not be sustained following expansion, if it is not possible to retain the same level of oversight.

**Sustainability:** Are the effects sustainable in the long term? For example, will the quality standards required for franchising and accreditation be maintained, even if this means expelling some providers from the scheme for non-compliance? Will vouchers become subject to fraud and mis-use?

**Cost Effectiveness:** Are these programs good value for money? Very little information is available on the cost-effectiveness of these approaches, despite the scale of resources invested in them.

**Counterfactual:** Finally would public and donor resources be better targeted at strengthening the public sector, than in trying to develop and improve the private sector? Oxfam have argued that publicly financed and delivered services dominate in countries with higher performing, more equitable health systems.[12]

While our review found no evidence to indicate that any of these negative effects were occurring as a result of private sector initiatives, we also found little or no evidence that they are being examined.

To improve the comparability of programs in the context of low levels of evidence we propose a set of metrics that donors and host governments should insist on when supporting private sector interventions.

**Scale and duration**: the number of patients served, providers engaged, and diseased diagnosed and treated for each year in operation.

**Effectiveness** of the program, measured in health outcomes at the community level as well as in terms of goods or services provided, and, critically, measured in comparison to what occurred before the program was introduced.

**Costs** and **cost-effectiveness** in comparison to other ways of delivering the same goods or services, whether through alternative private sector initiatives or through strengthening of government services.

**Distribution of costs and benefits** of interventions, reflecting the socio-economic status of beneficiaries and the economic burden on patients.

## Conclusion

The core principle of what makes an effective public health intervention is that it identifies a known source of social or economic market failure and seeks to address it, and that public health goals and provider goals are aligned. It remains unclear whether the current strategies for working with private sector providers can and do achieve these aims. The field of private healthcare engagement in LMICs is moving more quickly than research. As we try to understand what interventions have been conducted with private providers around the world it is evident that many pilots have been developed on the basis of intuition than rigorous evidence.

As engagement with the private sector in LMICs continues to grow in importance, more research must be directed at large-scale programs, drawing on study designs at the upper end of the "hierarchy" of evidence i.e. controlled before and after designs, using randomization where feasible and appropriate. Although more operational research, and 'learning by doing' is still needed, a parallel body of studies should be designed to assess not only immediate outputs but also the broader range of unanswered questions outlined above.

Working with private providers has the potential to address important public health goals. Existing limited evidence shows that the strategies examined in this review can improve access and utilization, and possibly quality. Given the wide interest in these approaches, there is a need to both generate more and more rigorous evidence about their impact, and the need to encourage standardization of metrics across programs to assure better decision making among implementers and policy makers while academic evidence catches up to practice.

## Bibliography

1. Marek T, O'Farrell C, Yamamoto C, Zable I. Trends and Opportunities in Public-Private Partnerships to Improve Health Service Delivery in Africa: Human Development Sector, Africa Region, The World Bank; 2005.
2. UCSF Global Health Group. The Private Sector in Health: iHEA 8th World Congress Pre-Congress Symposium: Conference Report. Toronto, Canada; 2011.
3. Bennett S, McPake B, Mills A. Private health providers in developing countries: serving the public interest? London, U.K.: Zed Books; 1997.
4. Patouillard E, Goodman CA, Hanson KG, Mills AJ. Can working with the private for-profit sector improve utilization of quality health services by the poor? A systematic review of the literature. *Int J Equity Health*. 2007; **6**: 17.
5. Preker AS, Harding A. Private Participation in Health Services: The World Bank; 2003.
6. Roberts M, Hsiao W, Berman P, Reich M. Getting health reform right: a guide to improving performance and equity: Oxford University Press; 2004.
7. World Health Organization. The world health report 2000 - Health systems: improving performance. Geneva, Switzerland: The World Health Organization, 2000.

8. Kumaranayake L, Mujinja P, Hongoro C, Mpembeni R. How do countries regulate the health sector? Evidence from Tanzania and Zimbabwe. *Health Policy Plan.* 2000; **15**(4): 357–67.
9. World Bank. Healthy Partnerships: How Governments Can Engage the Private Sector to Improve Health in Africa Washington D.C.: World Bank; 2011.
10. Ensor T, Weinzierl S. Regulating health care in low- and middle-income countries: Broadening the policy response in resource constrained environments. *Soc Sci Med.* 2007; **65**(2): 355–66.
11. Ensor T, Witter S. Health economics in low income countries: adapting to the reality of the unofficial economy. *Health Policy.* 2001; **57**(1): 1–13.
12. Marriott A. Blind Optimism: Challenging the Myths about Private Health Care in Poor Countries. London: Oxfam International; 2009.
13. Banerjee AV, Glennerster R, Duflo E. Putting a Band-aid on a Corpse: Incentives for Nurses in the Indian Public Health Care System. *J Eur Econ Assoc.* 2008; **6**(2-3): 487–500.
14. Nylander PP, Adekunle AO. Antenatal care in developing countries. *Baillieres Clin Obstet Gynaecol.* 1990; **4**(1): 169–86.
15. Evans WD, Blitstein J, Hersey JC, Renaud J, Yaroch AL. Systematic review of public health branding. *J Health Commun.* 2008; **13**(8): 721–41.
16. Loevinsohn B, Harding A. Buying results? Contracting for health service delivery in developing countries. *Lancet.* 2005; **366**(9486): 676–81.
17. Montagu D. Franchising of health services in low-income countries. *Health Policy Plan.* 2002; **17**(2): 121–30.
18. Montagu D. Accreditation and Other External Quality Assessment Systems for Healthcare.: Department for International Development Health Resource Centre 2003.
19. Sandiford P, Gorter A, Salvetto M. Vouchers for health: using voucher schemes for output-based aid. Public Policy for the Private Sector, an online journal of the World Bank. 2002.
20. World Bank. Country and Lending Groups. 2014 [cited August 26, 2014]; Available from: http://data.worldbank.org/about/country-and-lending-groups.
21. Peters DH, Mirchandani GG, Hansen PM. Strategies for engaging the private sector in sexual and reproductive health: how effective are they? *Health Policy Plan.* 2004; **19 Suppl 1**: i5–i21.
22. (AHRQ) AfHRaQ. Systems to Rate the Strength of Scientific Evidence: Summary: Agency for Healthcare Research and Quality; 2002.
23. Oxford Centre for Evidence-Based Medicine. Levels of Evidence. 2009 [cited 2014 Sept 7]; Available from: http://www.cebm.net/oxford-centre-evidence-based-medicine-levels-evidence-march-2009/.

24. Guyatt GH, Sackett DL, Sinclair JC, Hayward R, Cook DJ, Cook RJ. Users' guides to the medical literature. IX. A method for grading health care recommendations. Evidence-Based Medicine Working Group. *JAMA*. 1995; **274**(22): 1800–4.
25. McPake B, Hongoro C. Contracting out of clinical services in Zimbabwe. *Soc Sci Med*. 1995; **41**(1): 13–24.
26. Slack K, Savedoff W. Public Purchaser-Private Provider Contracting for Health Services: Examples from Latin America and the Caribbean. Sustainable Development Department, Technical Papers Series. Washington, DC: Inter-American Development Back; 2001.
27. Robey B. Community-based contraceptive distribution: a Korean success story. *Asia Pac Pop Policy*. 1987; (4): 1–4.
28. Cernada G, Chow LP. The coupon system in an ongoing family planning program. *Am J Public Health Nations Health*. 1969; **59**(12): 2199–208.
29. Chow LP. Family planning in Taiwan, Republic of China: Progress and prospects. *Popul Stud (Camb)*. 1970; **24**(3): 339–52.
30. Maramba TP. Accreditation of clinical laboratories in the Philippines. *Southeast Asian J Trop Med Public Health*. 2002; **33 Suppl 2**: 79–82.
31. Viswanathan R, Schatzkin E, Sprockett A. Clinical Social Franchising Compendium: An Annual Survey of Programs: Findings from 2013. San Francisco, CA: The Global Health Group; 2014.
32. Viswanathan R, Schatzkin E. Clinical Social Franchising Compendium: An Annual Survey of Programs: findings from 2012. San Francisco, CA: The Global Health Group; 2013.
33. Koehlmoos TP, Gazi R, Hossain SS, Zaman K. The effect of social franchising on access to and quality of health services in low- and middle-income countries. *Cochrane Database Syst Rev*. 2009; (1): CD007136.
34. Ngo AD, Alden DL, Pham V, Phan H. The impact of social franchising on the use of reproductive health and family planning services at public commune health stations in Vietnam. *BMC Health Serv Res*. 2010; **10**: 54.
35. Lonnroth K, Aung T, Maung W, Kluge H, Uplekar M. Social franchising of TB care through private GPs in Myanmar: an assessment of treatment results, access, equity and financial protection. *Health Policy Plan*. 2007; **22**(3): 156–66.
36. Kozhimannil KB, Valera MR, Adams AS, Ross-Degnan D. The population-level impacts of a national health insurance program and franchise midwife clinics on achievement of prenatal and delivery care standards in the Philippines. *Health Policy*. 2009; **92**(1): 55–64.

37. Bishai D, Shah N, Walker D, Brieger W, Peters D. Social franchising to improve quality and access in private health care in developing countries. *Harvard Health Policy Review*. 2008; **9**(1): 184–97.
38. Agha S, Karim AM, Balal A, Sosler S. The impact of a reproductive health franchise on client satisfaction in rural Nepal. *Health Policy Plan*. 2007; **22**(5): 320–8.
39. Evans W, Haiderm M. Public Health Brands in the Developing World. Public Health Branding: Applying Marketing for Social Change. Oxford, U.K.: Oxford University Press; 2008. p. 215–32.
40. Stead M, Gordon R, Angus K, McDermott L. A systematic review of social marketing effectiveness. *Health Education*. 2007; **107**(2): 126–91.
41. Chapman S, Astatke H. Annex 5: Effectiveness, Efficiency, and Equity of Social Marketing. London: DFID Health Systems Resource Centre; 2003 September 2003.
42. Stallworthy G, Meekers D. An analysis of unit costs in selected condom social marketing programs, 1990-1996. *Social Marketing Quarterly*. 2000; **6**(4).
43. Hutchinson P, Do M, Bunde E, Peacock E, Clodfelter C. An Assessment of Rural Contraceptive Social Marketing Programs PSP-one; 2009.
44. Chapman S, Jafa K, Longfield K, Vielot N, Buszin J, Ngamkitpaiboon L, *et al*. Condom social marketing in sub-Saharan Africa and the Total Market Approach. *Sex Health*. 2012; **9**(1): 44–50.
45. De Allegri M, Marschall P, Flessa S, Tiendrebeogo J, Kouyate B, Jahn A, *et al*. Comparative cost analysis of insecticide-treated net delivery strategies: sales supported by social marketing and free distribution through antenatal care. *Health Policy Plan*. 2010; **25**(1): 28–38.
46. Garrett V, Ogutu P, Mabonga P, Ombeki S, Mwaki A, Aluoch G, *et al*. Diarrhoea prevention in a high-risk rural Kenyan population through point-of-use chlorination, safe water storage, sanitation, and rainwater harvesting. *Epidemiol Infect*. 2008; **136**(11): 1463–71.
47. Muller O, De Allegri M, Becher H, Tiendrebogo J, Beiersmann C, Ye M, *et al*. Distribution systems of insecticide-treated bed nets for malaria control in rural Burkina Faso: cluster-randomized controlled trial. *PLoS One*. 2008; **3**(9): e3182.
48. Rowland M, Webster J, Saleh P, Chandramohan D, Freeman T, Pearcy B, *et al*. Prevention of malaria in Afghanistan through social marketing of insecticide-treated nets: evaluation of coverage and effectiveness by cross-sectional surveys and passive surveillance. *Trop Med Int Health*. 2002; **7**(10): 813–22.

49. Brent R. A cost-benefit analysis of a condom social marketing programme in Tanzania. *Applied Economics*. 2009; **41**(4): 497–509.
50. Stevens W, Wiseman V, Ortiz J, Chavasse D. The costs and effects of a nationwide insecticide-treated net programme: the case of Malawi. *Malar J*. 2005; **4**(1): 22.
51. Sabot OJ, Mwita A, Cohen JM, Ipuge Y, Gordon M, Bishop D, *et al*. Piloting the global subsidy: the impact of subsidized artemisinin-based combination therapies distributed through private drug shops in rural Tanzania. *PLoS One*. 2009; **4**(9): e6857.
52. Cohen JM, Sabot O, Sabot K, Gordon M, Gross I, Bishop D, *et al*. A pharmacy too far? Equity and spatial distribution of outcomes in the delivery of subsidized artemisinin-based combination therapies through private drug shops. *BMC Health Serv Res*. 2010; **10 Suppl 1**: S6.
53. Kangwana BP, Kedenge SV, Noor AM, Alegana VA, Nyandigisi AJ, Pandit J, *et al*. The impact of retail-sector delivery of artemether-lumefantrine on malaria treatment of children under five in Kenya: a cluster randomized controlled trial. *PLoS Med*. 2011; **8**(5): e1000437.
54. Figueras J, Robinson R, Jakubowski E. Purchasing to improve health systems performance: European Observatory on Health Systems and Policies; 2005.
55. Mills A, Broomberg J. Experiences of Contracting Health Services: an Overview of the Literature. London: Health Economics and Financing Programme, London School of Hygiene and Tropical Medicine; 1998.
56. Lagarde M, Palmer N. The impact of contracting out on health outcomes and use of health services in low and middle-income countries. *Cochrane Database Syst Rev*. 2009; (4): CD008133.
57. La Forgia G, Mintz P, Cerezo C. Contracting for basic health services: A case study of the Guatemalan experience. Washington DC: World Bank. 2004.
58. Witter S, Fretheim A, Kessy FL, Lindahl AK. Paying for performance to improve the delivery of health interventions in low- and middle-income countries. *Cochrane Database Syst Rev*. 2012; **2**: CD007899.
59. Liu X, Hotchkiss D, Bose S. The effectiveness of contracting-out primary health care services in developing countries: a review of the evidence. *Health Policy Plan*. 2008; **23**(1): 1–13.
60. England R. Experiences of Contracting with the Private Sector: a selective review. London: DFID HSRC. 2004.
61. Soeters R, Griffiths F. Improving government health services through contract management: a case from Cambodia. *Health Policy Plan*. 2003; **18**(1): 74–83.

62. Arur A, Peters D, Hansen P, Mashkoor M, Steinhardt L, Burnham G. Contracting for health and curative care use in Afghanistan between 2004 and 2005. *Health Policy Plan.* 2010; **25**(2): 135–44.
63. Jacobs B, Thome J, Overtoom R, Sam S, Indermuhle L, Price N. From public to private and back again: sustaining a high service-delivery level during transition of management authority: A Cambodia case study. *Health Policy Plan.* 2010; **25**(3): 197–208.
64. Shaw CD. Accreditation in European health care. *Jt Comm J Qual Patient Saf.* 2006; **32**(5): 266–75.
65. International Society for Quality in Health Care (ISQua), World Health Organization. Quality and Accreditation in Health Care Services: A Global Review. Geneva: World Health Organization; 2003.
66. Shaw C. Quality and accreditation in health care services-A global review. Ed ISQua-WHO, Geneva. 2003.
67. Alba S, Hetzel MW, Goodman C, Dillip A, Liana J, Mshinda H, *et al.* Improvements in access to malaria treatment in Tanzania after switch to artemisinin combination therapy and the introduction of accredited drug dispensing outlets - a provider perspective. *Malar J.* 2010; **9**: 164.
68. Dhatt G, Burnett D, Peters S, Van Rijswijk A. A survey of non-conformances raised during accreditation inspections of medical laboratories in South Africa. *Accreditation and Quality Assurance.* 2005; **10**(6): 295–9.
69. Wattanasri N, Manoroma W, Viriyayudhagorn S. Laboratory accreditation in Thailand: a systemic approach. *Am J Clin Pathol.* 2010; **134**(4): 534–40.
70. Quality Assurance Project. The Zambia Accreditation Program Evaluation. Operations Research Results.: USAID; 2005.
71. Bukonda N, Abdallah H, Tembo J, Jay K. Setting up a national hospital accreditation program: the Zambian experience: Quality Assurance Project; 2000.
72. Hong R, Mishra V, Fronczak N. Evaluating a national family planning quality improvement program in Egypt. APHA 134th Meeting; 2006.
73. Newbrander W. Accreditation of Providers for the National Health Insurance Fund of Tanzania. Management Sciences for Health; 1999.
74. Rooney A, Barnes K. Assessing the Cost Effectiveness of Hospital Accreditation in Two Developing Countries. . Joint Commission Resources (JCR) and The Joint Commission, Council for Health Services Accreditation of South Africa, KwaZulu Natal Province, and Zambian Central Board of

Health, University Research Col, LLC/Center for Human Services for the Quality Assurance Project, WHO, USAID; 2001.

75. Gershy-Damet GM, Rotz P, Cross D, Belabbes el H, Cham F, Ndihokubwayo JB, *et al*. The World Health Organization African region laboratory accreditation process: improving the quality of laboratory systems in the African region. *Am J Clin Pathol*. 2010; **134**(3): 393–400.
76. Yao K, McKinney B, Murphy A, Rotz P, Wafula W, Sendagire H, *et al*. Improving quality management systems of laboratories in developing countries: an innovative training approach to accelerate laboratory accreditation. *Am J Clin Pathol*. 2010; **134**(3): 401–9.
77. Ross JA, Han DW, Keeny SM, Cernada GP, Hsu TC, Sun TH. Korea/Taiwan 1969: report on the national family planning programs. *Stud Fam Plann*. 1970; (54): 1–16.
78. Borghi J, Gorter A, Sandiford P, Segura Z. The cost-effectiveness of a competitive voucher scheme to reduce sexually transmitted infections in high-risk groups in Nicaragua. *Health Policy Plan*. 2005; **20**(4): 222–31.
79. Gorter A. Targeting voucher to underserved populations in Nicaragua. 36th Annual Global Health Conference; 2009 May, 2009.
80. Meuwissen L, Gorter A, Kester A, Knottnerus J. Does a competitive voucher program for adolescents improve the quality of reproductive health care? A simulated patient study in Nicaragua. *BMC Public Health*. 2006; **6**: 204.
81. Meuwissen L, Gorter A, Knottnerus A. Impact of accessible sexual and reproductive health care on poor and underserved adolescents in Managua, Nicaragua: a quasi-experimental intervention study. *J Adolesc Health*. 2006; **38**(1): 56.
82. Meuwissen L, Gorter A, Knottnerus J. Perceived quality of reproductive care for girls in a competitive voucher programme. A quasi-experimental intervention study, Managua, Nicaragua. *Int J Qual Health Care*. 2006; **18**(1): 35–42.
83. Ensor T. Consumer-led demand side financing in health and education and its relevance for low and middle income countries. *Int J Health Plann Manage*. 2004; **19**(3): 267–85.
84. Hatt L, Nguyen H, Sloan N, Miner S, Magvanjav O, Sharma A, *et al*. Economic Evaluation of Demand-Side Financing (DSF) for Maternal Health in Bangladesh. Review, Analysis and Assessment of Issues Related to Health Care Financing and Health Economics in Bangladesh, project. Bethesda, MD: Abt Associates Inc.; 2010.

85. Alfonso YN, Bishai D, Bua J, Mutebi A, Mayora C, Ekirapa-Kiracho E. Cost-effectiveness analysis of a voucher scheme combined with obstetrical quality improvements: quasi experimental results from Uganda. Health Policy Plan. 2013.
86. Smith F. Private local pharmacies in low- and middle-income countries: a review of interventions to enhance their role in public health. *Trop Med Int Health*. 2009; **14**(3): 362–72.
87. Bennett S, Hanson K, Kadama P, Montagu D. Working with the Non-State Sector to Achieve Public Health Goals. Geneva: World Health Organization; 2005.
88. Janovksy K, Peters D. Improving health services and strengthening health systems: Adopting and implementing innovative strategies: An exploratory review in twelve countries. Geneva: World Health Organization; 2006.
89. Yamey G, Feachem R. Evidence-based policymaking in global health – the payoffs and pitfalls. *Evid Based Med*. 2011; **16**(4): 97–9.

# Part 3

# Lessons from the Field

# Chapter 7

# Private Patients Prelude: The Poor Health of Health Programs

April L. Harding

## Abstract

This chapter shifts from the larger "systems" perspective to a focus on healthcare delivery, the programs which focus on specific services, and the beneficiaries of those programs. Data, however well collated, cleverly analyzed, and thoughtfully interpreted, can only provide a skeleton on which to hang our understanding of private healthcare delivery in low- and middle-income countries: how the private sector is viewed by clients; what it means for providers, both those working full time in the private sector and those employed both in the public and private sectors; and how governments and international development agencies think about and react to the private sector.

This chapter provides an introduction to the views and priorities of patients in selecting care for themselves or their loved ones, what factors matter, and when and how real people deal with difficult choices.

In 2002–2003, I was working with a team analyzing health service delivery in Bangladesh. Our analysis was generating some conflicts. While Bangladesh's health authorities run a traditional "national health service," some researchers were arguing that private services had grown to play an important role. Government officials and officials from some aid agencies were adamant that the private sector was not significant – just a few private clinics and hospitals, catering mostly to the well-off. As such, policy efforts and the team's analysis should rightly focus on the public network. At last, we obtained data from a survey which had asked people throughout the entire country where they went for healthcare, and their answers surprised even the researchers: 9 out of 10 encounters were private. The health system Bangladeshis encountered in their day-to-day lives, the real health system, bore little resemblance to the comprehensive public service model that figured so prominently in officials' minds. Besides private for-profit and NGO clinics and hospitals, people were going to licensed practitioners, unlicensed practitioners, pharmacies, drug sellers, and traditional healers. When we examined poor people's responses, we learned they too were seeking care from private sources, as were people living in rural areas. Private providers and retailers clearly played a huge role – ensuring access to services; though, we found very little information about the quality of services. It suggested quality was unreliable. The team sifted through this information, trying to make sense of it, in hopes of identifying some policies and actions health officials could take that reflected this reality.

At the same time, another team was launching a local program under a global initiative to improve child health: the Integrated Management of Childhood Illnesses (IMCI). The initiative aimed to target countries with poor child health and to help them take action to improve child health in their country. Child mortality rates were high in Bangladesh; 73 of every 1,000 children born died before they turned five. The strategy involved targeting the illnesses generating the most child mortality. In Bangladesh, that was diarrhea, pneumonia, and fever. The child health program team explained that their program would train all health workers in public clinics to properly deal with these "big killers," and they would help clinics ensure drugs were in stock and strengthen staff supervision. The key, they said, was to focus efforts on the priority illnesses and to get their quality-improving intervention rolled out to all public clinics. Officials anticipated that by improving care for these key childhood illnesses, they would achieve large reductions in child illness and death. And it would… if that better care reached all sick children. The recent data showed that, in Bangladesh, it would not be so simple.

Our team pointed out that few sick children were taken to public clinics and urged officials to rethink the strategy, to consider ways to engage private practitioners, pharmacies, and drug sellers to do better on pneumonia, diarrhea, and malaria, and to take some steps to reflect the newly recognized reality of Bangladesh's service delivery network – without success. When pressed, the IMCI team members admitted that many sick children were taken to private providers rather than the public network for care. They pointed out that there was virtually no reliable information about the private sector, which meant any effort to involve them in the child health initiative would delay implementation. They'd have to go out themselves and collect information on private service providers; their strategy would have to be adjusted. NB: the IMCI "tools" were not adapted or appropriate for working with private practitioners. These efforts would involve unacceptable delays in starting the program. And, in any event, they were confident that caregivers would quickly switch once IMCI improved public services. So, they implemented the global IMCI "solution" to excess child mortality as designed, despite how ill-suited it was to the local realities. I was surprised and disappointed. How, I wondered, could program managers pursue such an ill-fitting strategy? As part of an evaluation study, the IMCI solution/strategy were fully implemented in some facilities in the Matlab district. After six years of implementation and six years of improving public services, the researchers confirmed the strategy generated measurable improvements in service quality. Better-quality care did not, however, reduce child illness and death. And how could they? At the end of the program, as at the start of the program, caregivers still took less than 1 of every 5 sick children to these improved public clinics. All other children continued to be seen in private clinics without the benefit of IMCI improvements. This would not be the last time I would see a program pursue a "packaged" global strategy, seemingly blind to the private activities that make up a large part of people's daily reality in developing countries, and which would achieve little for that reason.

## 1. The Health Sector in Developing Countries: The Individual Perspective

When a Nigerian or Indian person gets sick, just like an American or German person, they consider their options. They try to determine the most promising treatment options. Maybe they live near a good public hospital in a big city, and they go there. Or maybe, they live out in the country but are lucky enough to live near a public clinic in which they have confidence. When you ask them, you will learn that, very often, they go elsewhere.[1] Where do they go? They go to a range of private practitioners and medicine retailers: the good, the bad, and the in-between. They may be able to afford good-quality private care or benefit from the charitable activities of mission hospitals or socially oriented businesses, such as Narayana Hrudayalaya Hospital or LifeCare in India. Like you or me, their ailment may be something simple, and a trip to the pharmacy and some over-the-counter medicine will do the trick. Quite likely, they will turn to an informal pharmacy or "drug seller" for medicine. They may get the right drugs for their illness, or not. They may get good drugs, or they may get counterfeit or poor-quality drugs. Many will get poor-quality medicines and care, which doesn't help them. It may even endanger their lives. They may pay a little or a lot. If they are sick for a long time, the cost may throw them and their family into poverty. This is the reality people face every day in developing countries when dealing with their health problems.

Private practitioners and retailers play a significant role in the lives of people in developing countries. Without them, far fewer people would have access to healthcare and medicine. They often provide poor care and medicines though and undoubtedly contribute to poor outcomes. In addition, paying for these services sometimes makes poor people even poorer.

Given this reality, which strategies can health programs support to improve access to needed services? Which can address the most serious quality problems? Most importantly, what can they do to improve healthcare? Which strategies will be most successful in reaching the poor, who bear so much of the burden of ill health in developing countries?

These are important questions for a country's policymakers. They are equally important questions for international donors because donors are big players in the health policies and health systems of these countries. Rich countries and philanthropists channel US$12.5 billion per year to health programs, a substantial portion of all aid worldwide. In some countries, donors provide over half of public spending on health. Done well, the programs help people obtain more, and better, healthcare. They help people take more effective steps to protect their and their families' health. Done poorly, they accomplish much less.

---

[1] Households in developing countries are surveyed every four or so years about when and where they seek care when ill in the Demographic and Health Surveys (https://dhsprogram.com/).

## 2. How Did We Make Things Better for Ourselves?

But how can policy practitioners deal with this complex picture? We are not asking this question for the first time. This current developing-country reality looks a lot like the developed-country past. Back then, their newspapers carried stories of sick people dying for lack of money (see Box 1) and stories of egregious medical errors and fake medicines. How did we get out of it? How did our societies curb the worst practitioners and facilities? How did we ensure people with little money could access healthcare?

**Box 1. Their present ... and our past**

In Canada, the 1946 Toronto *Globe and Mail* reported a woman in labor who was refused help by three successive physicians, apparently because of her inability to pay. In Australia, a 1954 letter published in the Sydney *Morning Herald* sought help for a young woman who had lung disease. She couldn't afford to refill her oxygen tank and had been forced to ration her intake "to a point where she is on the borderline of death."

*Source*: *The New Yorker*, Atul Gawande.

Policymakers responded to the challenges by building, incrementally, on the existing service system, taking steps to construct service provision and drug distribution networks that served all people. They built financing mechanisms that reduced payments as a barrier and ensured people would not be wiped out from healthcare costs. Public agencies in most countries ended up taking on certain responsibilities (disease surveillance, etc.), where private initiative was infeasible or had little to offer. Hospitals, too, ended up under the ownership or strong influence of government in many countries. Hospitals need significant capital, and services are hard to buy. For many activities, financing and regulation were expanded over the years to achieve social goals, though private entities continued to perform the activities. The provision of primary care services in most countries is a messy mix of public and private. Other aspects of care, such as pharmacies and dentists, are predominantly private in nearly all countries in the world.

Health systems can work with more, or less, "private-ness." They can roll out health programs working with their existing systems, building on the governance platforms that exist and the service systems, public and private, that people encounter in their daily lives. Indeed, that is likely the only way to do so (Levy, 2014).

## 3. Are Poor Countries Different?

But what makes sense when resources are very scarce, as they are in many developing countries? What about when you have only a fraction as much as rich countries to spend on healthcare? And public sector capacity is weak? In such challenging environments, does a more-public model have an advantage? Perhaps such a model might allow a government to focus on delivering basic services until they have the capacity to manage such tasks as contracting and regulation – tasks that seem intuitively more complex to manage than direct care provision.

While it is plausible that "more public provision" would work better than "more private provision" in developing countries, evidence doesn't support the intuition. Boone and Zhan asked this question in a 2006 study (Boone and Zhan, 2006). Comparing 45 developing countries side-by-side, both groups do equally well, or, in many cases, unwell, in meeting health needs. The oft-noted bias to serve elites and urban dwellers in public systems keeps the more-public systems from doing better at reaching the poor. A more recent analysis of European health systems found no difference in health system quality based on how public or private delivery of care was (Montagu, 2021).[2]

So, where does this leave us? More importantly, where does it leave developing countries? It leaves them with the systems that they have and what the small changes that can be made to make things better. And perhaps this is a good starting point because, in reality, policy changes and health reforms will work, or not, depending on how well they fit the current reality of the existing system. A clear understanding of the starting point is critical to choosing a good way to move forward, whatever the goals.

[2]The results do not confirm causation (e.g. that more utilization of private services causes better access and equity), but they do undermine the presumption that a more-public strategy will work better to improve health and reach the poor.

## 4. (Private) Beauty is in the Eye of the Beholder

We can't really link a large private health sector with health outcomes, equity, or any of the other things we care about. We see it in well-performing developed countries; we see it in better and worse performing developing countries. But many developing countries continue to be unable to ensure access to health services, and patients continue to be impoverished by healthcare costs.

Some important actors in global health see efforts to engage the private sector as misguided. Oxfam argues that "to achieve universal and equitable access to decent health care … the public sector must be made to work as the main provider. There is no shortcut and no other way." And they suggest, "aid is wasted on private healthcare" (Marriott, 2009).

Others, like the IFC, argue that the private sector can play a critical role in "meeting the need for more and higher-quality healthcare" in developing countries (*Business of Healthcare in Africa, 2008*). A recent analysis of sources of care across Western Europe shows that ownership has very little correlation to quality of care, health outcomes, or citizens' satisfaction with their healthcare services (Montagu, 2021).

Discussions about this topic generate strong emotion and lots of rhetoric about the wisdom, or even morality, of engaging private providers and retailers in health programs.

Despite the shouting among global experts and advocacy organizations in global meetings, on the ground there is very little engagement, interaction, or even communication between the private part of countries' health systems and the public, much to the detriment of the people who need help when they are sick. In fact, program managers and donors often appear unaware that the private sector exists, or that it might contribute to solving some of the problems they are trying to solve.

At the global level, there is much talk of engaging the private sector, but often the "private sector" donors and global health agencies end up engaging with is comprised solely of international NGOs and global corporations. The local private health sector – the pharmacies, labs, and private practices where so many people are receiving whatever healthcare they get – is simply not on their radar screen. And certainly, representatives from these private sector actors are rarely present in global discussion forums or in country-level discussions regarding health challenges and strategies.

## 5. Recurring Themes

Part 3 of this book examines global health programs and how planners and public officials involved in these programs relate to the private health sector. Looking across the programs, a pattern emerges of systematic errors they make with respect to the private health sector. These errors undermine programs' success, especially in the many countries where the private sector plays a large role in health service and product delivery. The errors reflect outmoded mental models and myths about developing countries' health systems.

### 5.1 *The myth of what is going on with a country's health system*

Program managers and agency officials widely believe that programs can reach most people, and certainly the poor, through public services. Bangladesh's experience with the global child health initiative is not unique. It is but one manifestation of a common way of thinking among health policy practitioners in the developing world. The mental model of the health system which exists and within which programs and projects are developed and implemented bears little resemblance to the complicated reality described above. The premise underlying these programs is one of a comprehensive, and reasonably functioning, public delivery system. At the top, there is a health ministry, which is responsible for identifying priorities, allocating resources, recruiting and managing staff, managing procurement and distribution of supplies, supervising operations, and taking steps to address problems as they emerge. They administer referral hospitals linked to mid-level clinics, which in turn are linked to and support basic health facilities spread throughout the countryside. When people are sick, as the thinking goes, they turn to their nearby clinic for care. If need be, they are referred to a higher-level facility. Their medical problems are identified and dealt with at one of these facilities. When people need condoms, oral rehydration salts, or mosquito nets to protect their health, the staff of these facilities will give them, explain why and how to use them, and the people will do so.

Health programs, such as those targeting child health, TB, and malaria, are designed to be implemented through this mythical system.

For years, programs have continued, not noticing their omissions and not adding strategies to reach people beyond the public system.

## 5.2 *The myth of what ought to be done to achieve health objectives*

Many program managers and agency officials believe the only proper way to deliver health services is via a publicly run service network. They mistake the need for dominant public funding for the need for public ownership and operation. Many wealthy countries achieved their health goals by building pluralistic, mixed delivery systems, as noted above. Further, "more public" systems in general perform no better, nor worse, than "more private," either in wealthy or developing nations. Yet, the idea that the only way to achieve health goals is through a comprehensive public provider network drives policymakers to dismiss exploring ways to work with the private providers that are serving the very people programs are striving to reach.

Health services, both public and private, in developing countries, especially the poorest countries, suffer serious quality problems. However, the private sector in a specific country appears to be no worse, and possibly better, than the public sector often is.

## 5.3 *The myth that pressing health problems justify ignoring local systems*

Information about the private domain of the health system is rarely available in developing countries. Private providers are poorly covered in authorities' information systems. In contrast with developed countries, professional associations and industry groups infrequently participate in policy or public health forums. Policymakers seeking to engage them face a considerable burden to pull together even a modicum of the information needed to do so productively. Generally, this time-consuming upfront work is deemed too burdensome, and this is especially the case for initiatives with short time horizons.

Donor-supported health initiatives often have short time horizons. This makes it difficult to pursue any strategies that require upfront work to analyze and understand the local health services context, and this especially inhibits effective work with the private health sector, given the lack of information and poor data about private provision in most LMIC settings.

## 5.4 *The myth that capital investment is the key to harnessing private contributions to healthcare*

The four health program experiences in this book confirm improvements in healthcare and product provision can be achieved by engaging with the small businesses and NGOs that provide these services to so many people. Small businesses and NGOs provide extensive health services in almost all well-functioning health systems. While growing corporate activity in health service provision may sometimes contribute to health goals, there is little evidence of this thus far in developing countries.

## 5.5 *The myth that more of the same will achieve better results*

Family planning programs were the first major global health programs – with most starting in the early 1960s and 1970s. Like their successors, they were aiming to reach as many people as they could with their products and services, which in this case would enable people who wished to delay childbearing to do so. In the early years, many programs focused almost exclusively on a public distribution model, believing that public and mostly free distribution would enable them to reach most couples. The first phase of Pakistan's FP program did just this, and distribution numbers were very high. The program was proclaimed a success. It was used as a model for other programs. In the late 1960s, a population survey determined that there had been no change in contraception use during the time of the project. Despite these findings, in the 1970s, the same single strategy was again tried, but with more intensity, in the "ill-fated inundation" scheme. Millions of condoms and pill cycles were imported and distributed, while contraceptive use continued to be virtually unchanged (Robinson and Ross).

Often, as with Pakistan's FP program, the response to other health program shortcomings has been couched in terms of additional resources needed, presuming that additional resources will predictably expand reach and impact. That is, while the program proposals discuss expanding coverage of, say, treatment for pneumonia, the underlying strategy is more training, more drugs, and other supplies to generate the increases.[3] There is rarely consideration of the need or potential impact of alternative strategies or deploying resources in different ways, which might, in the circumstances, more effectively achieve the desired increases in coverage. Certainly, consideration of reaching people using private providers by working with their providers happens infrequently.

## 6. Learning from the Innovators

Some programs managed to kick these unhealthy habits. This book reviews four major global health programs in malaria, TB, child health, and family planning and presents some insights on these issues.

### 6.1 *Chapter 9: Examining the experience with malaria programs*

Malaria programs devote considerable effort and resources to getting people sleeping under insecticide-treated mosquito nets (ITNs). Historically, most programs sought to distribute nets through public supply chains and clinics. Supply chain and clinic inventory management problems were widespread and often intractable. Recently, donor-supported programs started distributing nets through temporary nation-wide "campaigns." These campaigns succeeded in distributing nets widely and increased their use in a number of countries. These achievements are commendable. However, they have rarely contributed to building countries' own systems for ensuring wide use of mosquito nets. Nets last about three years; hence, sustained coverage depends heavily on continued, or expanded, donor support.

[3]For example, a 2010 WHO Malaria Report acknowledges that even in countries where large numbers of ITNs have been distributed, rates of net use are still often quite low. The strategy suggested to deal with this is to hand out even more nets. This overlooks considerable evidence that many households have nets they are not using (see the references in Chapter 9 on malaria).

Tanzania took another route; they managed to increase net use and build a more resilient system for ensuring access to nets by collaborating with the private sector. Starting in 2000, Tanzanian authorities established a national collaboration with private net producers, distributors, and retailers to build their distribution capacity. They deployed considerable efforts to increase Tanzanians' understanding of treated nets and to increase their demand. The program used vouchers to target subsidies and to make sure that high-risk people (children and pregnant women) would be able to purchase nets. They took steps to improve the business environment for net manufacturers and distributors. Declining production costs and intensified competition brought prices down, from US$6–10 (1999) to US$3–4 (2007). Nets became widely available throughout the country, sold by a network of 200 wholesalers and 6,400 retailers (Koenker *et al.*, 2013). Tanzanians steadily increased their use of treated mosquito nets, and this helped bring down malaria-related illness and deaths. Not only had they increased coverage and use, Tanzania had established a sound country-wide distribution and retail system and a mechanism that allowed them to subsidize nets, while tapping households' own contributions to the cost. As a result, Tanzania's net platform is more resilient to the ups and downs of donor funds. Chapter 9 examines malaria programs like Tanzania's for further insight into the opportunities and challenges involved with engaging the private sector to increase the use of mosquito nets as well as access to effective treatment.

## 6.2 *Chapter 10: Examining the experience with TB programs*

Properly diagnosing and treating all patients suspected of TB is essential to TB control. The disease is concentrated in a few countries where health services are dominated by private provision. Bringing TB under control in these countries demands that programs find ways to ensure TB sufferers who seek private care are properly treated. Most programs have made limited efforts to engage private practitioners, pointing to their unreliable quality as an insuperable barrier. Some programs have, nevertheless, reached out to engage private practitioners, including Bangladesh's. Bangladeshis, especially poor Bangladeshis, suffer from one of the highest burdens of TB in the world. Program managers made considerable efforts, starting in 1993, to reach all TB sufferers with the highly effective directly observed treatment, short-course (DOTS) regime. However, because most TB patients were still seeking care from private practitioners outside the program, detection and cure rates remained disappointingly low. The Damien Foundation, an implementing partner in the program, recognized that they would need to mobilize private "village doctors" to expand the reach of the program. Village doctors are neither qualified, nor registered. Their training is minimal. Nevertheless, they are the largest group of providers and are especially important in rural areas. In 1998, the foundation launched a collaboration which involved training, access to TB drugs, and supervision. Within five years, 20–45% of patients in the partnership areas were being treated by village doctors (Salim, 2006) – a significant expansion in the program's reach. Surprisingly, patients treated by these village doctors experienced a slightly higher cure rate even than those treated in the traditional public program (Salim, 2006). Chapter 4 examines TB programs like Bangladesh's for further insight about the opportunities and challenges involved with engaging the private sector for TB treatment and control.

## 6.3 *Chapter 11: Examining the experience with family planning programs*

Increasing access to contraceptive products and services is essential to the success of family planning programs. In the 1980s, the Indonesian family planning program was faced with disappointing results despite considerable investment in delivering contraceptive products and services via public channels. When Haryano Suyono was named head of the Indonesian National Family Planning program, he added alternative channels for access to family planning services and products, including private sector channels, under the Blue Circle program. The Blue Circle initiative trained private doctors and midwives, so they could provide good-quality family planning services to people. The program also involved considerable efforts to increase people's understanding of and, thereby, demand for and willingness to pay for contraception. As a result, substantial progress was made in family planning coverage and contraceptive prevalence. The strength of the private supply system, people's increased willingness to self-pay, and the familiarity of the population with private sources for family planning services and products made the program resilient. When public funding plummeted following the Asian financial crisis, contraceptive prevalence remained stable, as formerly public clients simply switched to private sources (Schoemaker, 2005). When hit with drops in funding, other programs have not proven so resilient, as we shall see. Chapter 5 examines family planning programs like Indonesia's for further insight about the opportunities and challenges involved with engaging the private sector to increase and sustain access to family planning services and products.

## 6.4 *Chapter 12: Examining the experience with child health programs*

Sometimes, programs pursue child health improvements using specified interventions, as in Bangladesh's IMCI initiative. Often, though, they pursue child health improvements as part of a broader effort to improve population health by strengthening frontline primary care services. As in Bangladesh, such initiatives tend to limit their efforts and attention to the public network, forgetting to check what is really going on in terms of service provision and utilization. In selecting a strategy and designing their program, officials rarely take a clear-eyed look at the starting point; they rarely examine what capacity exists and where people are seeking care. There are exceptions, however.

Coming out of more than 20 years of civil conflict, in 2002, the Afghan population's health was very poor, and the health system was in shambles. Health officials and donor agencies considered trying to expand services by building up the public network. However, a quick scan of the situation made it clear that the network was highly deteriorated; few people received services from public clinics. Officials not only needed to expand service provision, they urgently needed to increase the proportion of female health workers, and they needed to get health workers to locate in isolated places. Officials recognized that public sector workforce management processes would hamper these efforts. Their scan also revealed that local and international NGOs were providing services throughout the country, but there was no coordination. In some regions, there were many service providers; in others, there were none; each provided different services. Officials determined that these providers constituted a platform they could build on. So, they established a system to contract NGOs to provide services in identified areas, to recruit staff, and to provide a specified service package. They identified important performance indicators and tied a portion of reimbursement to meeting them. The NGOs, assured of steady income, and with clearly defined responsibilities, succeeded in rapidly expanding services in a coordinated fashion. They deployed a range of creative employment strategies to recruit and deploy large numbers of female health workers and to motivate staff to locate in isolated areas. These efforts rapidly improved service availability (measured as the ratio of facilities to population, which increased by about 30%, and the share of facilities providing antenatal care, which rose by 45–75%), and institutional delivery rates (which roughly doubled). They also contributed to a remarkable reduction in child mortality (from 257 deaths per 1,000 live births in 2000 to 161 in 2007) (Arur *et al.*, 2010).

In the chapters that follow, we look at experiences within each program of such innovations. We examine how innovators have fared with breaking the mold, and what insights can be gleaned about the strategies they deployed. We also examine programs that have not sought to engage the private sector, even where evidence suggests it is necessary, to shed light on the factors sustaining the pursuit of such unpromising strategies.

## 7. Learning Lessons

Part 3 of this book provides a window into private sector engagement strategies and experiences *across programs* and, hence, makes it possible for practitioners to learn from *other* programs.

Even aid professionals with no interest in health policy or health development assistance will benefit from reading the studies that follow, as they provide insights into some of the most common problems with implementing development assistance in general, especially with regard to strengthening service provision.

A clear pattern emerges when donors use aid to help a country achieve health goals – an intense focus on the public sector through all phases of designing and implementing health programs. This bias leads to predictable problems in the way the programs work. The fact that donors work with and through government makes sense; indeed, they must do so, as government agencies *must* be the stewards of the health system to guide it toward meeting the populations' health needs and toward achieving priority health goals. In many countries, however, the private sector plays a substantial role in the health system. In many places, the private sector provides most care and medicines. Overlooking this reality and failing to find ways to engage the private sector clearly limits the success of policies and programs.

The studies that follow review how four global health programs work in the context of developing-country health systems; they examine how and when they engage or, more often, overlook the private health sector. They examine how this happens and how these strategies contribute to or undermine program impact.

Before diving into the programs in the following chapter, we explore in more detail the private health sector's role in developing countries and the issues that arise from it.

## References

A. Arur, D. Peters, P. Hansen, M. A. Mashkoor, L. C. Steinhardt and G. Burnham. (March 1, 2010). Contracting for health and curative care use in Afghanistan between 2004 and 2005. *Health Policy and Planning* **25**(2): 135–144.

P. Boone and Z. Zhan. (2006). *Lowering Child Mortality in Poor Countries: The Power of Knowledgeable Parents.* London. Discussion Paper No. 751. Centre for Economic Performance. ISBN: 978-0-7530-2057-9

*Business of Healthcare in Africa.pdf* [Internet]. Washington, DC: International Finance Corporation, World Bank Group; 2008. Report No.: 44143. http://documents.worldbank.org/curated/en/878891468002994639/The-business-of-health-in-Africa-partnering-with-the-private-sector-to-improve-peoples-lives.

H. M. Koenker, J. O. Yukich, A. Mkindi, R. Mandike, N. Brown, A. Kilian, *et al.* (December 2013) Analysing and recommending options for maintaining universal coverage with long-lasting insecticidal nets: The case of Tanzania in 2011. *Malaria Journal* **12**(1): 150.

B. Levy. (2014). *Working with the Grain* [Internet]. New York: Oxford University Press. p. 266. https://doi.org/10.1080/00220388.2015.1058563.

A. Marriott. (2009). *Blind Optimism: Challenging the Myths About Private Health Care in Poor Countries.* Oxford: Oxfam. (Oxfam Briefing paper).

D. Montagu. (March 15, 2021). The provision of private healthcare services in European Countries: Recent data and lessons for Universal Health Coverage in other settings. *Frontiers in Public Health* **9**: 636750.

W. Robinson and J. Ross. (eds.). *The Global Family Planning Revolution: Three Decades of Population Policies and Programs*. (2007) Washington, DC: The World Bank.

M. H. Salim. (June 1, 2006). Turning liabilities into resources: Informal village doctors and tuberculosis control in Bangladesh. *Bulletin of the World Health Organization* **84**(6): 479–484.

J. Schoemaker. (September 2005). Contraceptive use among the poor in Indonesia. *IFPP* **31**(3): 106–114.

# Chapter 8

# Private Sector: Here, and Here to Stay

**Dominic Montagu**

## Abstract

In this chapter, Dominic Montagu provides the opposite context: exploring what is known about the providers who deliver services in LMICs. As the chapter title states, "Private Sector: Here, and Here to Stay." Private sector healthcare providers, in all but the most dysfunctional failed states, function within a health system that is measured, regulated, and policed. This chapter sets out, in brief, the ways in which governments think about the private sector, categorize the different parts of it, and regulate it (well or badly). This is, in turn, influenced by clear trends in market functioning, which drive how different components of the private sector function.

There are a few rules of thumb which hold true in nearly all countries. Products – medicines, self-administered test kits, and beauty products – are all more likely to be sold by private providers than public providers. These might be shops, drug vendors, patent-medicine sellers, chemists, or pharmacies, depending on the product and the country, but the source will almost invariably be private.

Ambulatory care is more likely to be private than public. That's particularly the case with dentists and non-clinical specialists (psychiatrists, optometrists, etc.), but it is also true for primary care doctors. In most LMICs, most primary care doctors work in solo practices, and while they might have a "day job" in a government facility, most of their time is spent in their private clinics, and most of their income comes from that after-hours private practice.

Hospitals, by contrast, are likely to be public in most countries – subsidized by governments, absorbing a large portion of the national health budget, and being a visible indicator of public healthcare assurance. Uncertain regulations and duplicative or complex subsidies (i.e. hospitals sometimes pay for infrastructure from on budget, salaries from a second budget, and consumables from yet a third source) make public services likely to be continued even when questions about their comparative advantages over the private sector exist.

In financing and in oversight, government attitudes toward the private sector influence what services are delivered where, to whom, and by whom. The framing of this chapter sets the scene for the following case studies.

## 1. What is the Private Health Sector? What is It Doing? How is Its Role Changing?

The private health sector is many things: for-profit, non-profit, secular, religious, self-employed, corporate, or formal/ informal. The sector – everything that isn't government – includes the good, the bad, and the ugly.

The phrase "private health sector" refers to a wide variety of private actors. Within the for-profit sector, this includes both small businesses and corporate entities. It includes non-profit, religious, secular, international, and community-based organizations. It includes the self-employed midwife, or the traditional birth attendant operating in the community, as well as traditional healers and other informal providers.

Though sometimes less at the forefront of thinking by policymakers and international donors, private wholesalers, distributors, and retailers almost always play a significant role in developing countries' health systems. The availability of privately distributed products is more widespread than privately provided healthcare because even people who seek care in public clinics may obtain their medicine from a private pharmacy or drug dispenser.

The heterogeneity of private provision exists around the world, not only in LMICs. The wealthy countries of the world all have complex mixtures of public and private provision, always including private pharmacies, almost always private dentists, and a varying mix of public and private hospitals. As data on the private sector, and analysis of the data which may always have existed unexamined, become more widely shared and discussed in journals and policy fora, it is increasingly evident that lumping all components of the private sector together is a barrier to good measurement, good policy-making, and good governance.

There are a few rules of thumb which stand in nearly all settings. Products – medicines, self-administered test kits, beauty products – are all more likely to be sold by private providers than public providers. These might be shops, drug vendors, patent-medicine sellers, chemists, or pharmacies, depending on the product and the country, but the source will almost invariably be private. Ambulatory care is more likely to be private than public. That's particularly the case with dentists and non-clinical specialists (psychiatrists, optometrists, etc.), but it is also true for primary care doctors. In most LMICs, most primary care doctors work in solo practices, and while they might have a "day job" in a government facility, most of their time is in their private clinics, and most of their income comes from that after-hours work. Hospitals, by contrast, are likely to be public in most countries.

Across all levels of care, curative services are more likely to be private, and preventative services (family planning, vaccines, etc.) are more likely to be public. While prevention is the centerpiece of public health, there are few policies and fewer subsidies to include private practitioners in ensuring access to them in most countries. Behavior economics 101 makes it obvious why, absent strong regulation and well-designed subsidies, a profit-motivated provider would focus on treatment, rather than prevention: people will pay to get better or to fix an injury. They will be ambivalent about paying to avoid an unlikely, hypothetical future illness or issue.

Because of profit motivation and population densities, private services are more likely to be urban than rural, again reflecting the effects of market forces and the lack of countervailing policy or subsidy efforts in nearly all settings.

A number of analyses have been conducted on the size and trends of private sector health providers in LMICs in the past 10 years. A study by Karen Grepin in 1994 confirmed the importance of the private sector as a source of primary care, and found that between 1990 and 2013 (across 224 surveys in 77 countries), half the population turned to the private sector when seeking care for sick children and between 1998 and 2013, even among the poorest 40% of the population in each country, two out of

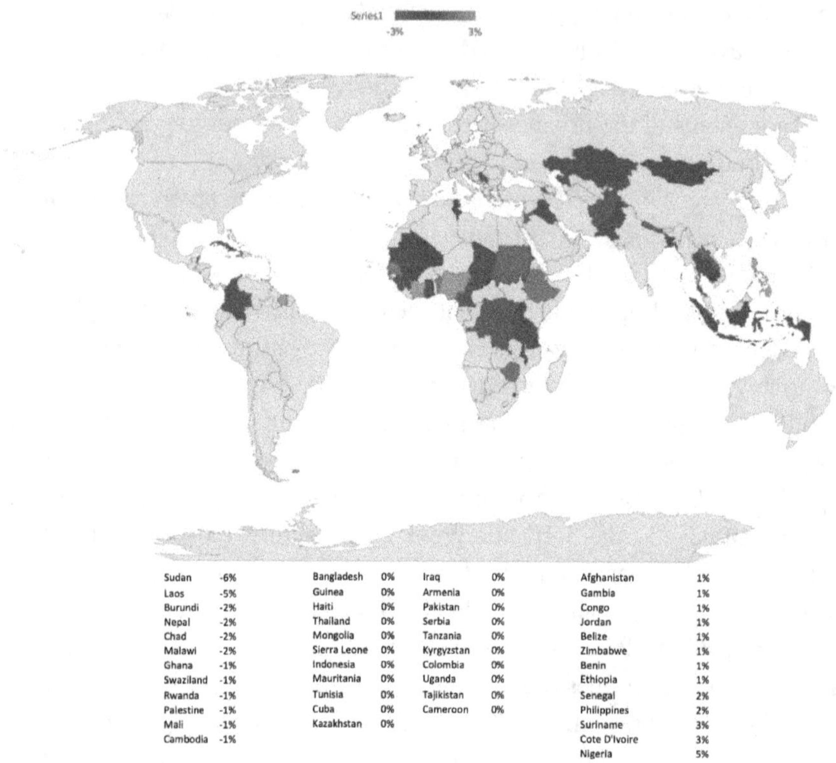


Figure 1. (Color available online) Change in percent of inpatient healthcare delivered by the private sector.

*Source*: From Montagu and Chakraborty's report to WHO, 2020.

every five households sought private care (Grépin, 2016). More recently, a study by Montagu and Chakraborty (2021) using data from 2010 to 2019 found "[no] regional or global trends towards or away from private care in LMICs," as illustrated in Figure 1.

Though some think the private sector is important only for better-off people, in fact the poor often use the private sector as much or more than the wealthy, driven by opening hours, which matter when one can't take time off from work to visit a clinic; by privacy concerns; by shorter wait times; and often by perceptions of more polite and responsive care. This is not true in all countries or all settings, but the private sector is important enough for all income groups that, nearly everywhere, health programs implemented exclusively through public sector channels will miss many of the poor. This is particularly true for health programs which demand ongoing engagement between patients and treatment centers: programs such as family planning, diabetes and hypertension management, or treatment for malaria and tuberculosis.

While the rich and the poor both use private providers for care, the poor often use different providers than the wealthy. While well-off households visit doctors and hospitals, poor households, in low-income countries in particular, are likely to initially seek care at traditional healers, informal providers, drug sellers, and pharmacies, and only after those sources of care prove insufficient will patients move on to doctors, clinics, and hospitals. Because of these varied patterns of use, donors, programs, and governments opting to work with or target a group of providers implicitly determine which users they will reach. For example, in designing a large-scale intervention in Cambodia, improving the quality of private hospitals would improve the healthcare of better-off people; working with drug shops or CHWs could greatly influence the health of poor people. Providers that are informal – unlicensed, unregistered, and of uncertain levels of training – along with a large number of small providers, poor documentation about service delivery points, and limited capacity for management and accounting all contribute to the result that health programs infrequently engage the private providers most heavily used by the poor. It is understandable, and it leaves the poor unsupported as they seek care.

## 2. What Accounts for Private Sector Existence?

Path dependency is an enormously important determinant in the development of systems for governance, property ownership, financing, and health systems, among many other aspects of national governance organizations. The history of health systems in OECD countries is better documented than that of LMICs' healthcare systems. This history makes it clear that, in most cases, today's healthcare financing and delivery systems are the inheritors of systems that began a hundred or more years ago. Where care was private and government intervention was small, as in the US, that private-sector bias continues to this day. Where government intervention to support workplace healthcare guilds began early, as in Prussia and then Germany in the mid-1800s, employment-based financing for care, directed through strong government regulation and oversight, remains the core of care systems to this day.

Major changes in healthcare systems seem to happen infrequently and mostly when major social upheavals are occurring. The UK National Health Services grew out of the government takeover of all hospitals as part of the home-front mobilization during World War II. Canada's social healthcare system came about after a two-year doctor's strike in one small midwestern province.

Barring major shocks, systems evolve slowly. Markets respond to demand for care. Where markets exist, people have choices, and some will choose private providers for reasons of cost, efficiency, perceived or demonstrated quality, hours of operation, or anonymity. Government hospitals and clinics in many LMICs are notorious for stock-outs of critical medicines, long wait times, overworked and underpaid staff and providers with all that that implies, and restrictive hours of access. They are also usually free and have a predictable level of quality, which is frequently better than alternative private facilities that serve lower-income populations.

The result is that people seeking care make the same trade-offs all around the world. As I sit here in California, if I sprain my ankle, I could go to a hospital, public or private, emergency room to have it X-rayed. That would take many hours of waiting and cost me the deductible fee from my insurance. Or, I could go to the pharmacy, buy a bandage, and hope it gets better by itself. That will cost a small amount of money and fifteen minutes. We all make healthcare choices all the time.

Often, of course, markets and regulations develop together and become increasingly complex as they do so. Private drug sellers in Nigeria, called "patent and proprietary medicine vendors" (PPMVs), are licensed by local governments, overseen by national pharmacy boards, and regulated for quality compliance with standards by the national ministry of health. Pharmacists dislike them because they compete to sell many of the same drugs despite not being legally permitted to do so. But pharmacies are also allowed to sell drugs in bulk to PPMVs, and this makes a huge profit for many pharmacists, putting regulation and oversight into a zone of conflict of both professional and financial interests. Adding to this, the ministry of health, state licensing officials, and pharmacist councils are all in conflict – because the relevant regulations overlap and are broadly written and, as a result, frequently contradictory – about who has final oversight authority over PPMVs. And no one agency cares enough to bring the fight to the Nigerian Supreme Court: oversight over PPMVs is a curse, not a prize, so no agency will battle to own it.

Similar intersecting interests, business relationships, and established norms exist in all countries. The result of this kind of complexity is that the growth and slow evolution of current market norms are almost always more common than a dramatic change.

The result is that, all around the world, the private sector persists, growing at times in some countries while shrinking at times in others. Governmental policies to adjust financing for healthcare, such as the current global push for universal health coverage, can slowly tilt systems toward improvements in equity, access, and quality. But the key word will always be "slowly," and as the Netherlands, Belgium, Germany, Japan, and many other countries have shown us, universal health coverage can be delivered through private providers and private hospitals as effectively as through government providers and facilities if financing and a strong enough governance and regulatory system exists.

## 3. Key Issues

The private health sector induces strong emotions because of its role in enhancing or decreasing overall quality, inequity, cost, and impoverishment. Quality is often poor: many of the people selling pharmaceuticals are untrained, and many of the "village doctors" around the world have never gone to medical school. But quality is often also very good: the best hospitals in most countries – from Mexico to India, from Kenya to Vietnam – are usually private. And where quality is poor, it is often poor in both public and private settings. A recent study from India looked at *the same* providers seeing clients in the public health clinics and after hours in their private health clinics, and it concluded that while the quality was poor in both settings, it was significantly better in the private setting, largely because the doctors asked on average one additional question and spent a tiny number of additional minutes with each patient (Das *et al.*,

2012). Healthcare quality is an issue in LMICs but is an issue everywhere, not just among private providers.

The financial barriers to healthcare access and threats to impoverishment resulting from care are problematic anywhere that payment is required for healthcare services: inherent issues deriving from both the *need* for care during times of illness and the information differential between patients and providers. Most wealthy countries address this problem by separating the issues of ownership of care and payment for care. Private providers treat patients and are then paid by national health insurance, thereby eliminating the power differential and the information differential. It isn't a perfect solution, and it requires strong data systems and governance systems, both of which are weak in less wealthy countries. So, well-managed private care serving the public good as a component of an organized effort to ensure universal health coverage … is rare.

## 4. Underlying Issues: Ignorance and Bias

Because of the slow evolution of health system structures noted above, the challenges that are inevitably present with private commodity and care provision are challenges that governments – regardless of ideology – must learn to manage. Happily, the past century of experience from OECD countries shows that good management of the private sector is possible and that, with good governance, the private sector can contribute greatly to the satisfaction, health, and well-being of all parts of a nation's population.

Unhappily, the most common response to the reality of large private sector participation in healthcare markets in LMICs is to give in to anti-private biases – to ignore it and talk loudly about growing and strengthening public services. That trick, as they say, never works. Just as private sector growth within a structured system is rare or slow, so too is public-sector growth. National health delivery systems involve thousands or millions of people and established institutions, depending on the country, each with a vested interest in the continuation of the existing system. That means private hospitals, pharmacists, drug manufacturers or importers, public regulators and medical schools, public and private blood banks, laboratories, and ambulance services, along with the many, many people who staff and supply each. From the most powerful hospital group to the least powerful corner-store drug vendor, there is a common thread of having built relationships, incomes, regulations, and careers upon the *status quo*. That does not change – in any direction – easily. This makes wishfully ignore the reality of large-scale private provision, where it exits, ineffective.

With large-scale systemic change unlikely, recognizing, understanding, and overcoming fears and both pro (free market, competition, and innovation) and con (profiteering, self-interested, and low-quality) biases toward private care provision are a key first step to collecting and acknowledging data on private care and building a role within the larger health system for private hospitals, doctors, nurses, blood banks, pharmacies, and the rest.

## 5. Engagement, Thoughtful Engagement, is Necessary

The slow-moving nature of health systems in the absence of wars or other cataclysmic social changes leads to the conclusion that planned, well-staffed, well-organized, and sustained engagement between the public and private sectors is necessary to assure governments accomplish their mandate for overall system governance and that the private sector works in coordination with the public to advance the overall public good.

Private sector expansion or strengthening through greater subsidies, lowered barriers to entry or growth, or the waiver of regulatory oversights can incentivize a larger private sector for health but not a better functioning one. Healthcare goods and services, because of the high information differential between providers (pharmacies, doctors, clinics, and hospitals) and clients (patients, consumers of care, and preventative care seekers), require governmental interventions to be safe and effective. Well thought out government intervention is needed to ensure that education standards, reporting accuracy, effective referrals, allocative efficiency, quality assurance, and transparent pricing all work well both on their own and in coordination across the overall system.

Strategies for improving both health and healthcare must be based on understanding the local context, building upon effective public provision where this exists, and upon effective private provision where that exists. But this kind of analysis of context is rarely done.

## 6. Engagement Takes a Special Effort

The reasons for this are complex, and both widespread biases and large gaps in information are common drivers for gaps in analysis. In many LMICs, the governance systems created at the end of the colonial period were not developed to separate core functions of government, such as service provision and financing. The result in many countries is a governmental health sector with strong incentives to continue assuring maximum funding to its own internal delivery systems and which – even were there the will – is likely grossly underfunded and underprepared to effectively regulate care provision at any level outside of the command-and-control models possible internal to government care. The basic scaffolding upon which core policy apparatus can build regulatory and financing systems has, in many countries, been anemic for many years.

This poses a challenge for governments and for development assistance. Outputs such as attended deliveries or bed nets delivered to protect against malaria are used as proxies for health outcomes. But doing this can often leave the underlying problems with system communication and coordination invisible. Directly funded outputs can be easier to drive than indirectly improved systems of communication and coordination, which will, in the long run, be needed to sustain and effectively govern the mixed health system.

## 7. Analytical Approach and Structure of the Book

The following chapters set out to explore these issues, their effects, and possible solutions in depth through a number of programmatic examples across key healthcare issues facing developing countries. We look at programs where attention, experience, and significant global funding combine to provide well-documented cases of successes and challenges.

We strongly believe that there are common lessons to be learned across programs, from family planning to HIV/AIDS to TB, and so on. The chapters of this book return again and again to the application of effective institutional analysis as a foundation needed to develop and apply good policies and effective regulations, financing plans, and service delivery programs. These regulations, policies, and programs must be system-wide: applied to both public and private delivery channels with equivalence and equity. Through the cases set out in this book, we look to explore and elucidate how to accomplish this. We have made every effort to aggregate lessons and bring a summary of evidence forward in ways that highlight the commonalities.

Inevitably, the application of lessons from this book will imply adaptation, often significant adaptation, to other settings, other health areas, and other regulatory needs. As the information about private sector importance in developing countries grows and the transparency of OECD experiences funding and regulating private provision in effective coordination with publicly provided care becomes more widespread, we believe the result will be more attention to the needs of thoughtful and wholistic public–private coordination and more understanding of the examples in this book and beyond, which can serve a wide range of policymakers, students, researchers, program directors, development partners, and care providers as they work to assure private care advances global health, as it both can and should.

## References

J. Das, A. Holla, V. Das, M. Mohanan, D. Tabak and B. Chan. (December 2012). In urban and rural India, a standardized patient study showed low levels of provider training and huge quality gaps. *Health Affairs* **31**(12): 2774–2784. https://doi.org/10.1377/hlthaff.2011.1356.

K. A. Grépin. (July 2016). Private sector an important but not dominant provider of key health services in low- and middle-income countries. *Health Affairs* **35**(7): 1214–1221. https://doi.org/10.1377/hlthaff.2015.0862.

D. Montagu and N. Chakraborty. (April 12, 2021). Standard survey data: Insights into private sector utilization. *Frontiers in Medicine* **8**: 624285. https://doi.org/10.3389/fmed.2021.624285.

# Chapter 9

# The Private Sector and Malaria

**Albert Kilian**

## Abstract

Albert Kilian describes the complexities of diagnosis, treatment, and prevention in this chapter. Malaria is a major killer in the developing world. In 2012, approximately 207 million episodes of clinical malaria occurred, leading to the deaths of an estimated 627,000 people – mostly African, mostly children, and mostly poor. Programs to reduce malaria mortality focus on prevention, often mosquito abatement or the use of nets to prevent mosquito bites at night, or treatment, increasingly with effective combinations of effective medicines.

This chapter examines the experience with malaria programs and private sector engagement to shed light on when and how the private sector can contribute to delivering malaria interventions. We examine how the habits and operating norms of the agencies and people involved in the global malaria effort have influenced the consideration and deployment of such strategies.

Through a series of case studies, we argue that while malaria programs have achieved remarkable increases in net ownership and use deployment, they have faced rather more difficulty increasing treatment coverage. This is at least, in part, because national malaria programs' focus on speed, product procurement, and distribution has discouraged the development of strategies to mobilize private drug sellers, net producers, distributors, and retailers. Program managers and donors, in many countries, need to shift to diversifying their strategies, adding private sector channels, so that programs can achieve broader goals.

## 1. Introduction: Malaria and the Role of the Private Sector

Malaria is a major killer in the developing world. In 2012, approximately 207 million episodes of clinical malaria occurred, leading to the deaths of an estimated 627,000 people – mostly African, mostly children, and mostly poor (WHO, 2013). Programs to reduce malaria mortality focus on prevention, often mosquito abatement or the use of nets to prevent mosquito bites at night, or treatment, increasingly with effective combinations of effective medicines.

This chapter examines the experience with malaria programs and private sector engagement to shed light on when and how the private sector can contribute to delivering malaria interventions. This chapter examines how the habits and operating norms of the agencies and people involved in the global malaria effort have influenced the consideration and deployment of such strategies.

## 2. The Challenge of Malaria Control

Malaria is a complex disease caused by a group of parasites, among which *Plasmodium falciparim* is the most deadly and most common in Sub-Saharan Africa. Malaria is transmitted among people when they are bitten by infected night-flying mosquitoes.[1] Typical symptoms include fever, headache, vomiting, and other flu-like symptoms. Absent effective treatment, the infection can lead to death when the parasite invades and damages red blood cells or blocks the capillaries that carry blood to the brain or other organs. Because of the role mosquitoes play, malaria control can be pursued by targeting infections in people or by targeting mosquitoes to reduce their biting and infecting of people, also known as *vector control*.[2,3]

[1] Mosquitoes are referred to as the *vector* for malaria transmission.

[2] Vector control refers to activities to control a disease by combating the means of transmission from person to person.

[3] In contrast to the standardized strategies for treatment, efforts to reduce transmission by mosquitoes must reflect local patterns of mosquito behavior and breeding, as well as the environment and weather.

Unlike many diseases, where a small proportion of the population is affected, in malaria-endemic areas, most people are infected. But by the age of five, infected people develop stronger immune systems and suffer less from the disease. This is why children, with their weaker immune systems, suffer so much from malaria. Pregnant women and their unborn children are also harmed by malaria;[4] it contributes to the death of newborn children in this way. With many types of malaria, the symptoms escalate slowly, giving people or their caregivers time to find treatment. However, this is not always the case: some forms of malaria generate rapid deterioration and death, making quick access to treatment critical.

## 2.1 *Malaria programs: The activities and how they are supposed to work*

While the disease and its transmission are complex, the essential components of donor-supported[5] malaria control programs are fairly straightforward, focusing on preventing infection and ensuring malaria sufferers are treated promptly and appropriately.

More recently, donor-supported programs have focused on more vertical strategies, such as indoor residual spraying (IRS). This involves once- or twice-yearly spraying of the inner walls of homes with insecticide. Insecticide residue kills mosquitoes which land on the walls. Recent prevention activities have also sought to increase the use of mosquito nets, especially insecticide-treated nets (ITNs), which are significantly more effective than untreated nets in preventing bites. All these strategies work by reducing the number of people bitten and infected. By reducing infection in individuals, they also reduce transmission since fewer mosquitoes bite fewer infected people. Treatment activities aim to increase access to and appropriateness of treatment for people sick with malaria, reducing the number of ill and deceased patients as well as reducing transmission. Treatment initiatives can be further distinguished

---

[4]Pregnancy generates anemia in women, which, combined with malaria-generated anemia, undermines the development of the fetus.

[5]Note that locally led malaria control programs (e.g. China and Italy) deployed more integrated approaches to malaria control, involving changes in housing and agriculture practices as well as management of wetlands and waterways (see Jobin, 2014; Webb, 2014).

between those that aim to improve the treatment of active cases of malaria and those that aim to increase prophylactic treatment, such as intermittent presumptive treatment in pregnant women (IPTp) and intermittent presumptive treatment in infants (IPTi) and children (IPTc). Malaria programs strive to increase coverage of all these interventions; however, the role of the private sector is most important with respect to two control strategies: curative treatment and mosquito nets. This chapter focuses on these topics.

Children and pregnant women suffer the most severe harm from malaria, so program activities are often targeted at them, as well as targeting the poor, whose poverty undermines their access to products and services. Individual targeting, however, is not central to reducing malaria transmission, as this is done by reducing mosquitoes' opportunities to bite infected people. Irrespective of which individuals are covered, population coverage rates of at least 50%, and ideally 80%, generate a "mass effect," rendering protection to all people whether or not they are using a net (Killeen *et al.*, 2007). In contrast to many health program targets, net coverage targets derive from epidemiological factors (see Box 1). Prevention and treatment interventions are complementary, and successful programs include high treatment and prevention coverage. The central challenge of all malaria control programs is to expand and sustain coverage of these proven interventions. The critical distinction between products or clinical interventions that work and delivery strategies that work to get the

### Box 1. Some targets are aspirational, others epidemiological

Some health program targets relate to coverage levels which generate disproportionate reductions in disease (e.g. immunization and "herd immunity," TB prevalence, and the "mass effect" of net coverage in malaria vector control) (Snow *et al.*, 1997; Marsh and Snow, 1999; Howard *et al.*, 2000). Other targets, such as most of the Millennium Development Goals, are aspirational. They are set to focus donors' and local policymakers' attention on a health problem. Malaria program prevention coverage targets are epidemiological; significantly higher health gains can be achieved at high coverage rates.

interventions to the people who need them is often overlooked (see Box 2). People think that because we have nets and drugs which work, controlling malaria is straightforward, but as discussed in the following, this is patently not the case. In the following section, I examine the range of delivery strategies that programs use to increase access to treatment and then the use of mosquito nets.

**Box 2. Programs may not work, even when the products do**

Mosquito nets reduce malaria when used; but mosquito net programs may or may not be effective in getting nets available and used. Effective drugs will cure malaria, but medicines procured or shipped may or may not reach most people with malaria. While we know which products and clinical interventions can control malaria, it is much more complicated to choose delivery strategies which will work in real-world conditions to achieve high and sustainable levels of coverage and use. It is these much more complicated decisions about delivery strategies that must be improved if programs are to work. Program effectiveness is largely determined by these choices. The weak link in malaria programs is the patchy effectiveness of the most commonly used delivery strategies on the ground.

## 3. The Role of the Private Sector in Malaria Treatment

### 3.1 *Malaria treatment: The issues*

Timely treatment with effective medicine is central to malaria control, and programs make considerable efforts to increase access. However, often the use of the most effective medicines remains low, which constitutes one of the biggest problems hampering malaria control.

All control programs include activities to enhance access to effective treatment. Improving treatment creates three kinds of benefits: it reduces harm to people suffering from malaria; it reduces the likelihood that others get malaria; and it makes drugs last longer by slowing the development of resistance.[6] Program activities typically aim to increase the use of

[6]Ineffective or incomplete treatment hastens resistance by exposing the parasite to the treatment – but not enough to clear the infected person's system of the parasite.

effective drugs in public clinics.[7] Since public clinics suffer frequent drug stockouts, malaria programs often include efforts to improve government malaria medicine procurement and supply chain management. Programs typically include efforts to improve the quality of treatment, often through case management training, that is, through training frontline providers to properly identify malaria and give the right drugs and dosage. Like many efforts to improve service delivery in frontline public clinics, these efforts have often had disappointing results (Juma and Zurovac, 2011). While some programs succeed in improving case management, the problems of supply chain management (procurement, leakage, and pilfering) have proven intractable in a number of countries (Mikkelsen-Lopez *et al.*, 2014). Improvements in access to medicines in public clinics have been rare and often short-lived (Rao *et al.*, 2013). Even when drugs are available, people typically don't go there for treatment when they are sick with malaria, saying public clinics are too far away, often not open, have long waits, and that staff treat them unkindly (Rutebemberwa *et al.*, 2009).

As a result, despite substantial increases in efforts and resources, the use of artemisinin-based combination therapies (ACTs), the most effective treatment for malaria, remains low. Many people who seek care receive inappropriate treatment. Although this is slowly improving, in 2012, in 12 of 16 endemic African countries, less than 60% of antimalarial drugs used by children with fever were ACTs (Tougher *et al.*, 2012). Access to effective treatment is a critical bottleneck in many countries striving to improve malaria control.

Efforts often have limited impact even when they succeed in increasing medicine availability in public clinics, as so many people seek treatment elsewhere. Many, often most, people who are sick with malaria turn to pharmacists, private practitioners, and medicine sellers[8] (Goodman *et al.*, 2007a). Overall, the WHO estimates that 63% of people with

---

[7]The appropriate drug to treat malaria in a country or region varies depending on how much resistance has built up to the least expensive drugs. In the majority of countries, malaria parasites have developed resistance to cheaper drugs and the need to resort to the much more expensive artemisinin-based medicines.

[8]Following Goodman *et al.* (2007), we define "medicine sellers" to include all commercial retailers supplying fever/malaria drugs, except formal pharmacies that are required to be staffed by a qualified pharmacist.

malaria seek treatment in the private sector (WHO, 2008). Moreover, these care-seeking patterns are persistent (Grépin, 2016).

Private outlets and practitioners are providing treatment, of a sort, to many people who are sick with malaria. People almost invariably pay for these medicines out of pocket, as few low-income countries subsidize essential medicines distributed through private retail outlets and supply chains. Also, as both regulation and professional self-regulation are weak, private clinics' case management and dispensing practices are frequently poor. Many people use informal medicine-selling outlets, and their practices are even worse. These sellers are prone to responding to the specific request of the patient (e.g. "give me the pink pills"). These self-paying customers are quite cost-conscious and sometimes short on cash. So, these medicine sellers often dispense cheaper, less effective malaria medicines (e.g. chloroquine) or provide smaller dosages or shorter treatments. They rarely give instructions on how to use the medicines. Since poor people and rural inhabitants rely the most on these providers, they bear most of the harm from the poor-quality treatment provided by informal medicine sellers. Fake drugs with too little, or none, of the active ingredient, are also a growing problem in many countries, especially in Asia (Bate and Hess, 2010).

A regulatory crackdown to stop informal providers dispensing malaria medicine might seem tempting. This strategy can diminish poor dispensing. However, it may also diminish access to malaria medicines for these outlets' customers unless accompanied by actions which increase their access through some other channel. In Tanzania, this regulatory strategy was tried. It compelled private medicine sellers to stop stocking the most effective medicines, thereby *reducing access* to effective medicine overall since people continued to get their medicine from private outlets (Hetzel *et al.*, 2006).

Despite these problems, malaria programs rarely make efforts to work with private distributors and retailers to address these problems. This is unfortunate because to improve treatment for the majority of people with malaria (who consistently seek treatment in the private sector), making sure they get drugs that work and improving dispensing practices is critical. The failure to engage with private providers and to recognize the importance of this platform for reaching people who are sick with malaria has contributed to the declining malaria treatment rates. To be effective in most countries, any strategy to expand access to high-quality malaria treatment will need to work both in the public sector and through the network of private distributors and retailers (Arrow *et al.*, 2005; Fraser and Druce, 2006). What we need to know then is, how? How can malaria programs work with private providers, pharmacists, and medicine sellers to expand access to effective treatment? This is discussed in the following.

### 3.2 *Harnessing the private sector in malaria treatment*

Many people who are sick with malaria obtain medicines from private drug shops, ranging from pharmacies to informal, and often unregulated, medicine sellers (Wafula and Goodman, 2010).[9] Efforts to improve the supplies and dispensing practices of these providers are challenging. These outlets are small, dispersed, fragmented, and hard for programs to reach. Public officials have attempted regulatory actions to close down informal drug shops (Cambodia) or to stop their dispensing of malaria medicines (Goodman *et al.* 2007b) with little success. In some cases, as noted above, it can reduce access to the best medicines. Beyond this, health programs have made limited efforts to work with these providers. Wafula and Goodman conducted a systematic review of such initiatives in 2010, finding 10 studies which met their inclusion criteria. They found that all the engagement strategies focused on educating these providers, often complemented by efforts to influence treatment seekers. Most were implemented on a small scale, and the time elapsed until endline data collection was fairly brief. The evidence must be interpreted in that light.

While there are relatively few studies, the findings are encouraging. Only three initiatives targeted dispensing and advice related to malaria (Oshiname and Brieger, 1992; Greer *et al.*, 2004; Nsimba, 2007); however, the other initiatives sought to change dispensing behavior in ways similar to those needed to improve malaria treatment and outcomes. Their findings are relevant for judging the potential of strategies to engage these types of providers with regard to malaria. The review found that the education initiatives consistently improved knowledge.

[9] In this section, we discuss outlets dispensing medicines (what Wafula and Goodman refer to as "specialized drug shops"), not general shops that sell medicines.

However, results were mixed on communication with clients and referrals. Surprisingly, drug vendors exhibited desired changes in dispensing, even when this reduced their income. Nevertheless, educational interventions which took into account the income effects of targeted practice changes achieved greater success. Taken together, the evidence suggests that "knowledge and practices of pharmacies and drug shops can be improved across a range of diseases," including malaria (Wafula and Goodman, 2010, p. 316).

Control programs have used other strategies to improve provider dispensing behavior, including malaria treatment, accreditation, and social franchising. Tanzania's establishment of an accredited network of drug shops is particularly promising. Valimba *et al.* (2014) found that training interventions with these shops improved knowledge, communication, and patient medicine use significantly.

The notable successes of TB programs, described in Chapter 10, in engaging private providers to implement appropriate diagnostics and DOTs for TB patients further confirm the feasibility of working with private providers to improve treatment. Since the DOTs protocol is much more complex to administer and achieve adherence, success with engaging private providers to implement DOTs confirms the feasibility of engaging private providers to improve the much simpler malaria treatment (refer to the discussion on TB in Chapter 10). Likewise, the small scale but promising experience with franchising in reproductive health services indicates there are yet more instruments that can work to influence even small, unorganized providers to improve the quality of care (Bishai *et al.*, 2008). While the fragmentation and heterogeneity of the broader range (including much less skill and education) of malaria treatment providers make them challenging to work with, there is some evidence that *less* trained providers may be easier to influence through the use of protocols than are more trained. In Bangladesh, for example, low-skilled village health workers complied more frequently with the recommended TB treatment protocol than other more highly trained providers (Hamid *et al.*, 2006). The success of both malaria and other interventions indicates that this susceptibility to influence could well be a potential advantage; that is, it may be quite feasible to improve the treatment of even low-skilled, informal private providers.

In recent years, another serious problem has emerged, further threatening access to effective malaria medicine. The effectiveness of the two main inexpensive malaria drugs – chloroquine and sulfadoxine-pyrimethamine – has diminished, leaving artemisinin-based drugs as the sole remaining effective treatment in many places. The cost of these drugs is up to 15 times that of chloroquine. The high cost of artemisinin-based drugs has meant that, as the effectiveness of the cheaper drugs has waned, access to effective medicines has further declined because people cannot afford the drug which works best.

The problem facing the global malaria community and country control programs now is even more complex. Not only must the practices and products of private medicine sellers be improved, but people who rely on commercial distribution systems must somehow receive a much more expensive drug, whose local market prices they can ill-afford. Absent action, the use of effective medicine will remain low. In addition, people seeking treatment in local markets at an affordable price often buy artemisinin drugs as monotherapy. Pills with only artemisinin as an active ingredient accelerate the development of the parasite's resistance.[10] Resistance to artemisinin is a grave danger, as no new malaria medicines are anticipated in the near future.

This looming tragedy mobilized the global community to develop an innovative market-shaping strategy, whereby subsidized product distribution would be extended to include commercial distribution systems.[11] The aim is to shift the balance of malaria medicines flowing through the markets in commercial distribution systems toward artemisinin-based combination therapy (ACT) drugs, or to crowd out the use of other medicines. The Affordable Medicines Facility for Malaria (AMFm), launched in 2010, deploys three tools to achieve this shift. First, the facility involves a factory-gate subsidy to reduce the retail price of the drugs, and it uses the

---

[10]Pills which combine a second active ingredient more often succeed in killing the parasite rather than allowing it to recover and multiply in a form more likely to be resistant to subsequent treatment.

[11]Market-shaping strategy is a set of policy actions to alter health market(s) functioning as a means of achieving health goals.

leverage of the subsidy and expanded sales to reduce the price for private importers.[12] It also includes communication activities to promote proper use and influence retail pricing. The factory-gate subsidy subsidizes ACTs at the point they leave the factory; the drugs then flow through public and private supply chains, gaining the usual price markups, to be dispensed in private clinics, pharmacies, and medicine shops.

The strategy was implemented in eight pilot countries. An independent review of the results found that it achieved substantial reductions in quality-assured ACT prices and in absolute markups in six of the eight countries (Tougher *et al.*, 2014). Studies of the Tanzania results using household surveys found that the strategy led to high availability even in very rural, remote areas (Yadav *et al.*, 2012) and confirmed that the subsidies are reaching all socioeconomic quintiles, even the poor (Cohen *et al.*, 2013).

Despite this well-documented success, AMFm ended after its start-up period when the primary funder, the global funds to fight AIDS, Tuberculosis and Malaria, decided not to continue funding it. No replication, continuation, or duplication of other medicines has ever been attempted. The reasons for AMFm's demise are not public but appear to have been strongly influenced by participating governments' preferences for malaria control funds to go directly to government-delivered programs and not to private subsidies. The politics of malaria control and development health subsidies remain central to private sector engagement or exclusion from national strategies and donor funding.

## 4. The Role of the Private Sector in Preventing Malaria with Mosquito Nets

### 4.1 *Preventing malaria with mosquito nets*

People have long used mosquito nets to prevent insect bites. With the innovation of treating mosquito nets with insecticides (ITNs) and then mixing the insecticide with the net fibers (long-lasting insecticide treated nets, or LLINs), the nets achieved high and sustained rates of protection.

[12]Public sector purchasers had already achieved substantial price reductions.

These nets protect people sleeping under them twice as well as untreated nets and protect others in the community by killing mosquitoes which touch the nets. In ideal conditions, treated net use can halve malaria episodes and reduce child deaths by 20%. They have become a staple of malaria control in developing countries.

To understand the challenges associated with mosquito net programs, we need to dig deeper into what success looks like; we need to understand which ingredients add up to a successful malaria program.

## 4.2 *Net program mechanics*

Before we discuss the effectiveness of different strategies used to get people sleeping under mosquito nets, we must clarify what programs need to accomplish. Clearly, they must get the majority of people sleeping under ITNs. For all the reasons discussed above, programs must include activities to increase current use or help "catch up" to the targets of high population use. It is also important, though, that people are able to obtain nets on an ongoing or continuous basis. Malaria can't be prevented by having people sleep under a mosquito net for one night, one week, or even one year. Coverage rates achieved have to be sustained indefinitely. And, stability of coverage requires that people have continuous access to nets nearby in their community. So, net programs must also be judged for how they contribute to "keep up" net use, that is, the degree to which they enhance *continuous access* to mosquito nets.[13] Access, even net ownership, does not protect people from mosquito bites though; for that, they must use the nets consistently and properly. We know that many people don't sleep under nets, even when they have them. There are many documented instances of distributed nets going unused or being used for other purposes, so activities which increase demand for and propensity to use nets are a critical factor in a successful net program (Fegan *et al.*, 2007; Grabowsky *et al.*, 2007; Hassan *et al.*, 2008).

To paraphrase Hippocrates, malaria is long, aid is short.[14] Eradication is feasible in very few places; control is the goal, and malaria is going to

[13]The important concepts of "catch up" and "keep up" were introduced in the Roll Back Malaria 2005 report.

[14]The original quote is *Ars longa, vita brevis*, or Art is long, life is short.

be around for the foreseeable future in most countries. Moreover, public and donor expenditures on malaria, as with all health initiatives, rise and fall. Even though global funding for malaria is at a record high, available funds still fall well short of what's needed to adequately cover countries with populations at risk.[15] Net programs therefore must promote higher levels of supply and use, even when aid and donor-supported malaria efforts diminish. In addition, they must be judged for how much of individuals' willingness to contribute to their own protection they tap. That is, programs must be judged for their sustainability and for the changes achieved in local capacity and behaviors which will contribute to net use next year and the following year, beyond the contributions and activities of donors. Next, we review the evidence for strategies used in net programs, assessing how well each strategy does with respect to these four goals. The characteristics are synthesized in Table 1.

Table 1. Key performance indicators for net programs.

| Performance Indicator | Explanation |
|---|---|
| Current access | How are net prices associated with the strategy? How broad is the reach of strategy? How rapidly does the strategy typically increase access? How much does the strategy typically reduce financial barriers and reach the poor? |
| Ongoing access | How much does the strategy contribute to continuity of access? How close is supply to people on an ongoing basis? How does the strategy affect the density and reliability of net supplies in communities? |
| Demand | How effective is the strategy at reaching communities with effective demand and behavior change messages? How much does the strategy contribute to the choice of nets? |
| Sustainability | How sustainable are the achievements of the strategy (beyond program funding and/or donor support)? What proportion of supply improvements will continue without or with lower levels of external support? What portion of any price reductions achieved would continue in the absence of program support? What portion of net use is independent of donor efforts? |

[15] Snow *et al.* (2010) found that resources available were sufficient to cover approximately 40% of needed interventions.

## 4.3 *Delivery strategies*

The range of strategies for promoting net coverage is broad, encompassing approaches which rely fully on the public sector and others which engage private actors (e.g. importers, distributors, and retailers, as well as social marketing organizations) relatively more.

### 4.3.1 *Public clinic distribution*

Many early net initiatives distributed nets via frontline public clinics (both general primary care and antenatal care clinics), with net prices either partly or fully subsidized (Tables 2 and 3). Clinic staff was intended to give the nets to people coming to the clinic and explain why and how to use the nets. These initiatives relied on centrally administered public supply systems to procure and distribute nets to clinics. Many initiatives experience serious problems with supply chains. Evaluations in Kenya and Eritrea found that logistical and oversight problems emerged,

Table 2. Free net distribution via clinics.[a]

| Performance Indicator | Score | Comment |
|---|---|---|
| Current access | Medium | Abolished financial barriers; lack of co-payment reduces the motivation of clinic staff to distribute and reduces clinic resources for restocking; coverage increases range from low to moderate |
| Ongoing access | Medium | Access is enhanced for people living near public clinics; stockouts are common |
| Demand | Low | Behavioral change communication is typically provided only when people come to a public clinic; not broadly effective in changing net-related behavior; typically no choice of nets |
| Sustainability | Low | Availability relies on the effectiveness of centrally administered public supply systems, which are typically weak; no funds are available in clinics for restocking; often, low sustainability occurs in the absence of program support |

*Note*: [a]See Annex for tables of net program evaluations (for all the net strategy tables).

Table 3. Subsidized net distribution via clinics.

| Performance Indicator | Score | Comment |
|---|---|---|
| Current access | Medium | Reduce financial barriers; clinic staff is often more motivated to distribute nets due to co-payment; facilities are better able to restock because of the availability of co-payment funds |
| Ongoing access | Medium | Access is enhanced for people living near public clinics; supply problems are common |
| Demand | Low | Behavioral change communication is typically provided only when people come to a public clinic; not broadly effective in changing net-related behavior; typically no choice of nets |
| Sustainability | Medium | Availability relies on the effectiveness of the centrally administered public supply system; net co-payments generate some funds in clinics for restocking |

however, and programs struggled to make nets consistently available at clinics (Grabowsky *et al.*, 2007; Guyatt and Ochola, 2003; Guyatt *et al.*, 2004; Nyarango *et al.*, 2006; Goldberg *et al.*, 2008). In addition, even for the nets that did reach households, many went unused. Behavioral change communication efforts were insufficient and often ineffective. Recipients often didn't appreciate the benefits of the nets enough to use them for malaria prevention (see Box 3).[16] A wide variety of uses and misuses of mosquito nets were documented, from fishing nets to wedding veils, to fencing for small livestock.

### 4.3.2 *Traditional social marketing*

Programs recognized they needed better approaches to delivery and more sophisticated education and demand promotion efforts. A number of

[16]Propensity to use nets varies greatly across, and even within, countries. Gambian citizens, for example, have long used nets fairly extensively, while in Nigeria, net use has been low and very hard to increase.

**Box 3. Why is it so hard to get people sleeping under nets?**

- In some settings, people think malaria isn't a serious illness; everyone gets it, and most cases go away on their own.
- People attribute some deaths (e.g. from cerebral malaria) to other causes and don't think nets will prevent those deaths (Maslove *et al.*, 2009).
- It is uncomfortable sleeping under nets, especially in hot weather.
- People don't think mosquitoes transmit malaria (Maslove *et al.*, 2009).
- People don't like the nets that are available or given to them.
- Available nets may have negative local connotations (e.g. white nets resembling burial shrouds).
- Available nets may not suit sleeping spaces (e.g. they are hard to hang and then store during the day).
- Nets may have higher value in other uses (fishing and drying fish, as wedding veils, or for privacy).
- Nets may not repel or kill non-malarial mosquitoes – so people think they don't work.

countries started to adapt traditional social marketing strategies (widely deployed in family planning programs since the early 1960s – see Chapter 5). Traditional social marketing differed from previous public distribution efforts in three ways (Table 4). First, distribution activities were "outsourced" to existing private distributors and retailers. Rather than paying for these services, programs set prices for the products; in this way, wholesalers', distributors', and retailers' margins motivated them to stock and sell the products (Harvey, 1999) just as they did for their commercial activities. In addition, they complemented the alternative distribution strategy with an innovative communication approach. TSM used sophisticated marketing strategies borrowed from the advertising industry to "sell" insecticide-treated mosquito nets and, indirectly, to educate about the considerable benefits of using nets to protect oneself from mosquitoes and malaria. These tools were more strategic than earlier communication efforts. They involved analyzing people's attitudes and behaviors, identifying groups ("market segments") which were least using mosquito nets,

Table 4. Traditional social marketing (and distribution of subsidized nets by participating retailers).

| Performance Indicator | Score | Comment |
|---|---|---|
| Current access | Low | Subsidy reduces net prices; increases access in limited number of locations; doesn't affect access at non-participating retailers; positive price restricts use by low-income people |
| On-going access | Medium | Outlets have high-quality nets in stock on an ongoing basis but doesn't affect access at non-accredited retailers |
| Demand | High | Highly effective demand promotion |
| Sustainability | Medium | Can "crowd out" local, spontaneous supply sources; requires continued support to maintain supply increase; increased demand may continue; positive prices motivate continued stocking by distributors and retailers |

and identifying the beliefs or misunderstandings that were keeping them from doing so. Traditional social marketing communication deployed messages tailored to target groups and local beliefs.

The campaigns typically involved marketing a specific brand of net ("Use Serena Mosquito Nets!"). Evaluations from Malawi, Kenya, and Afghanistan found that the strategy was effective at increasing demand for and use of nets (Holtz *et al.*, 2002; Noor *et al.*, 2006). But some people still didn't buy nets, saying they couldn't afford it, and there were still relatively few places to buy nets (Agha *et al.*, 2007; Schellenberg *et al.*, 2001; Holts *et al.*, 2002; Noor *et al.*, 2006). Moreover, participating distributors' and retailers' supplies depended on continued shipments from donor-supported suppliers.

These social marketing campaigns increased the use of branded nets supplied by their program, but the impact on *total* net use was unclear. Some people using the branded nets appeared to have shifted from other nets to the program-supplied nets (Muller *et al.*, 2008; Agha *et al.*, 2007). Reflecting this, some programs shifted to strategies to promote net use in general rather than of a specific brand, and they shifted to monitoring the total market for nets – encompassing information on all sources of nets (including the commercial sector unaffiliated with the program), not just those supplied by control programs. These social marketing-style demand promotion activities were clearly effective in increasing people's understanding and use of nets; the challenge which remained was finding strategies to establish broad and sustainable supply systems for nets.

### 4.3.3 *Growing commercial delivery*

The experience with traditional social marketing showed that when people's demand for nets increased, private distributors and suppliers could play a role in meeting that demand. Studies of the total market for nets revealed that many, often most, nets people were using came from private suppliers (Webster *et al.*, 2007); that is, program-provided nets were only covering a portion of the people sleeping under nets. Commercial retailers sell mainly untreated nets, which are only half as effective as treated nets. Nevertheless, these sales didn't rely on program support, and in the face of unreliable program funding, this was appealing. Health ministries, always facing constrained funding, saw some benefit in capturing people's willingness to pay for nets (all or partly). These privately sold nets, paid for by individuals, contributed to putting net coverage on a more sustainable financial footing. Some programs, especially in Tanzania (see Box 3), started experimenting with strategies to grow commercial delivery of mosquito nets (Magesa *et al.*, 2005). They encouraged the proliferation of private net producers, importers, distributors, and retailers, including in rural areas. They did this through reducing barriers to entry and production (e.g. reducing taxes and tariffs) (Khatib *et al.*, 2008) and by targeting subsidized nets to diminish "crowding out" private supplies. They also undertook generic marketing efforts to promote demand for all nets (rather than promoting the use of specific brands of nets) (Abdulla *et al.*, 2001), as well as working with private producers to upgrade production technology so that local manufacturers could produce treated nets (Magesa *et al.*, 2005). This strategy was successful in increasing ongoing access, especially broad geographical access, and competition, which led to lower market prices (Khatib *et al.*, 2008). An important advantage of this strategy was that it let private organizations do the hard work of distribution and retail, including tracking where stocks are running low and managing shipments to replenish local

Table 5. Growing commercial delivery.

| Performance Indicator | Score | Comment |
|---|---|---|
| Current access | Low | Moderate rates of increase in net coverage; positive price restricts use by low-income people |
| On-going access | High | Increased number and widely distributed outlets have nets in stock on an ongoing basis |
| Demand | Medium | Reasonably effective demand promotion; promotes demand of all nets, not just branded ones; range of net choices increases use |
| Sustainability | High | Promote local/spontaneous supply; requires small amount of outside support to maintain supply increase; increased demand may continue |

inventories. This combination of activities generated increased use, on-going access, and sustainability (Table 5).

### 4.3.4 *Vouchers*

While growing commercial delivery efforts could achieve broader ongoing access and sustainability, current use was still too low to meet targets or achieve a "mass effect" protection of non-users. The strategy still left some people unable to afford a net. For this reason, Tanzania (Magesa *et al.*, 2005; Khatib *et al.*, 2008) and Ghana (Grabowsky *et al.*, 2005a) added vouchers to reduce the price for targeted individuals. Voucher programs provide target users (often pregnant women and children) with a voucher to cover part or all of the price of a treated mosquito net purchased from one of the participating private distributors and retailers (Table 6). This reduces financial barriers, increases use among target groups, and also supports the market development of distributors and suppliers:

Tanzania – success; Ghana – failure in implementation.

### 4.3.5 *New technology, new money, new delivery strategies: LLINs, campaigns, and free nets*

Programs applied the strategies described above when relatively little funding was available; the activities were thus smaller in scale. Even

Table 6. Vouchers as a complement to a growing commercial delivery strategy.

| Performance Indicator | Score | Comment |
|---|---|---|
| Current access | High | Reduces financial barriers to net use; increases access broadly by incentivizing stocking and sales |
| On-going access | High | Outlets have nets in stock on an ongoing basis |
| Demand | High | Effective demand promotion; can target financial support to target populations |
| Sustainability | Medium | Promotes local/spontaneous supply; ability to target limited funding (and tap others ability and willingness to pay) may contribute to sustainability |

successful programs achieved slow increases in coverage. In the early 2000s, things changed. LLINs became more widely available. Moreover, donor funding started to grow rapidly (PMI, DfID, Global Fund, and World Bank Booster Program; see Figure 1). The leading agencies decided that rapid increases in net coverage were a priority objective. Yet, many malarial countries had weak health systems, which constrained their ability to absorb the large sums available. Officials deployed a new strategy to rapidly increase current access, or "catch up": free distribution of nets via mass campaigns (Table 7). A group of international non-governmental organizations started working together to rapidly increase net use by adding net giveaways to existing donor-supported immunization campaigns. They did this through international procurement, shipping the nets to the aid-receiving country. They also set up temporary supply chains or linked up with the supply arrangements deployed for mass immunization campaigns, mobilizing immunization campaign workers to hand out nets to families coming for vaccination. In some countries, mass campaigns for nets alone were implemented. The supply strategy, while temporary, had the virtue of not relying on the public, centrally administered supply chains, whose weakness undermined success in earlier programs.

In countries where earlier demand promotion activities were sufficiently effective, campaigns achieved sizable increases in use (Noor *et al.*, 2007; Fegan *et al.*, 2007; Grabowsky *et al.*, 2005a; CDC, 2005; Grabowsky *et al.*, 2005b). But in other countries, demand for and value of nets were weak; campaign distribution initiatives lacked the time to analyze and address attitudes and behaviors regarding net use. In these cases, only a

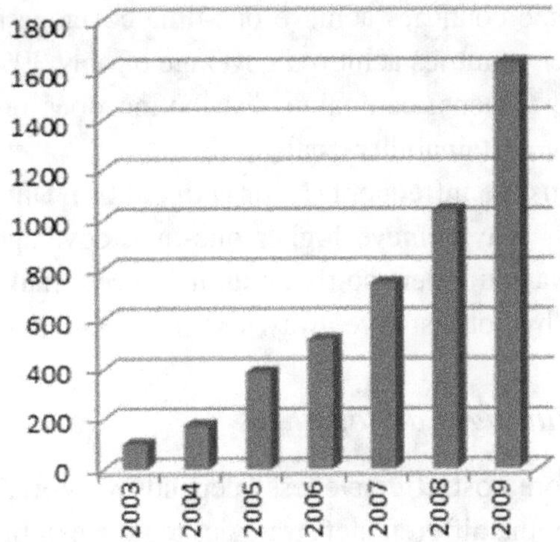


Figure 1. Malaria funding commitments 2003–2009 (in US$ millions).

*Source*: Malaria Funding and Resource Utilization: The First Decade of Roll Back Malaria (Roll Back Malaria Partnership 2010).

Table 7. Free net campaign distribution.

| Performance Indicator | Score | Comment |
|---|---|---|
| Current access | High | Gets nets to large number of people quickly (though limited by campaign coverage limits, e.g. 50% of children on average) |
| On-going access | Low | Does not promote broad distribution and stocking; may "crowd out" private net distributors and retailers |
| Demand | Low | Usually does not include demand promotion due to short duration |
| Sustainability | Low | Does not promote and may crowd out local/spontaneous supply; requires continued outside support to maintain operation of campaigns and to cover full cost of nets |

limited portion of the nets distributed have ended up being used (Grabowsky *et al.*, 2007; Khatib *et al.*, 2008; Goldberg *et al.*, 2008). Also, in these situations, some nets ended up being used for other purposes (Grabowsky *et al.*, 2005a; Afolabi *et al.*, 2009).[17] The result of these differences is that cam-

[17] Since campaigns are utilized most often after a number of other strategies have been implemented, high use rates following campaigns are sometimes mistakenly attributed solely to the campaign rather than to the multiple strategies that have been applied.

paigns helped some countries achieve one-time coverage rates as high as 80%, though other countries achieved coverage of only 30%.

For all these reasons, campaign distribution does not contribute to ongoing access or sustainability goals.

Net campaigns are infrequent (Noor *et al.*, 2007). Untargeted (or universal) giveaways may achieve higher one-time coverage but may also "crowd out" private suppliers so that ongoing access may even be weakened (see Box Why not just give away nets?).

## 4.4 *Insights: Putting it all together*

Cost (and therefore cost effectiveness) depends very much on the local context. However, the different net strategies tend to exhibit similar ranges of cost effectiveness (Yukich *et al.*, 2008; Kilian *et al.*, 2010).

Each strategy has its own strengths and weaknesses. Compared to public distribution, traditional social marketing approaches are good at tapping private distributors and retailers to do the hard work associated with net distribution, and they are good at stimulating demand and getting people to use the nets they have. Growing commercial delivery may reduce net prices in a sustainable way and increase the locations and reliability of net sources. Voucher mechanisms can reduce financial barriers to use and provide a platform for targeting the scarce financial resources of those who will especially benefit from nets (children and pregnant women) or people for whom financial barriers are the biggest constraint — the poor. "Catch up" mass campaign distribution can rapidly increase net ownership at a point in time, which, when complemented by the demand promotion typically associated with the other strategies, increases use as well. To achieve high and ongoing use and sustainability, net programs have to apply multiple strategies, including social marketing, growing commercial delivery, and, if possible, vouchers (Lengeler and de Savigny, 2007). Expert reviews facilitated by RBM and the WHO have, unsurprisingly, come to the same conclusion (see RBM and WHO Guidelines), as has a recent meta-analysis of net program impact evidence (Kilian *et al.*, 2010).

### 4.4.1 *Results and issues with net initiatives*

Some programs have achieved notable coverage increases. Four countries have achieved ownership rates in excess of 80%; another six have

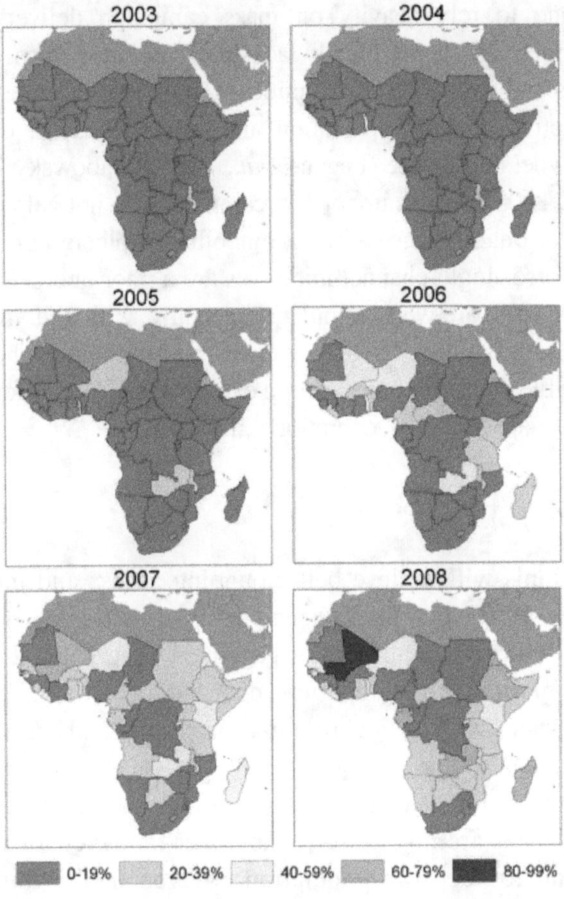


Figure 2. (Color available online) Annual maps of household net ownership 2003–2008.
*Source*: Flaxman *et al*. (2010).

coverage between 60% and 80% (see Figure 2). Yet, use is still much lower than the ownership of nets. As a result, ownership coverage figures overstate the protection people are getting from malaria by using mosquito nets. The majority of people at risk for malaria are still not protected by nets (Flaxman *et al*., 2010). Equally importantly, coverage levels achieved are fragile, as the continuity of access and sustainability of many delivery arrangements are low.

*Program activities are narrow and "catch-up" focused.* While the evidence and guidelines confirm the need for multi-channel antimalaria programs, many continue to rely heavily on mass campaign delivery strategies. Campaign implementation typically lacks the time or platform to do a situation analysis and so link to communities. Campaigns are rarely accompanied by effective demand promotion and, by themselves, do poorly at converting ownership to use (Fegan *et al.*, 2007; Grabowsky *et al.*, 2007; Hassan *et al.*, 2008). Just as important, campaigns do not help establish the foundations for ongoing access or sustainability (Golberg *et al.*, 2008). By themselves, these single-channel initiatives are a poor public health investment, though they are very popular, especially with the implementing INGOs. This gap between "better practice" and the approaches programs deploy is notable. The following section explores this gap, followed by possible links with aid agencies' operational imperatives.

### 4.4.2 *Conclusion*

Control programs will achieve better ongoing access and more sustainability if they pursue multiple channels for net coverage. Often, these programs will involve significant engagement of private actors – local mosquito net producers and importers, distributors, and retailers. In many settings, they can play a critical role in a successful and sustainable mosquito net program.

Since the donor and government funds available in malaria-endemic countries are not sufficient to cover the levels of nets needed now, let alone to keep the population covered in the future, private demand and, importantly, supply are much needed in the short and medium terms. Failure to take this need into account and inadvertently "crowding out" private distribution and private sale and payment can reduce the overall use of nets, now and in the future. Many early family planning programs similarly failed to consider the implications of programs' product distribution strategies on local supply and demand (see Chapter 6).[18] These programs generated serious dependency

[18]This approach in family planning programs led to serious drops in access and use of contraceptives when program funding declined in (the late 1990s); see Chapter 11, Family Planning, for further discussion.

problems, manifested in large drops in supplies and use when donors diminished or withdrew their support.

We next discuss malaria development assistance efforts in the past 20 years. We examine its features and changes which influence malaria programs. We focus our attention on how donors' operations and approaches interacted with the consideration and implementation of strategies to mobilize the private sector.

**Box 4. Multiple strategies can lead to sustainable success: Tanzania's net initiative**

Tanzania's malaria burden in the late 1990s was very high; as many as 100,000 people died every year, 80% of whom were under five. With less than $1 million per year available for malaria control, yet a strong commitment to combating the disease, TZ officials decided to explore a strategy which could harness private producers, distributors, and retailers to contribute to their aims of increasing access to and use of mosquito nets. They studied these markets, including people's attitudes toward and understanding of malaria and nets. They tested out different mechanisms for demand creation. In 2000, they established a national collaboration with private stakeholders focused on "growing the market," that is, expanding private businesses' contribution to ITN production, distribution, and retail. They slowly built a nation-wide voucher program that allowed them to target their limited subsidies on high-risk people. The vouchers allowed people to obtain subsidized nets from private retailers. By improving the enabling environment, several businesses were persuaded to start up ITN production. The government reduced tariffs on inputs (e.g. yarns) for ITN production as well as on ITNs themselves. Market competition and lower costs combined to reduce costs and prices substantially (from $6–10 in 1999 to $3–4 in 2007). By 2008, the four top firms, employing 3,000 workers, were producing more than 10 million nets annually, which were sold by a network of 200 wholesalers and 6,400 retailers. Distribution capabilities grew considerably stronger. ITN sales grew steadily throughout 2001–2008 from 1 to 3 million, as shown in Figure 3 (left), with approximately 50% of these nets provided by the commercial retail market.

(*Continued*)

*(Continued)*

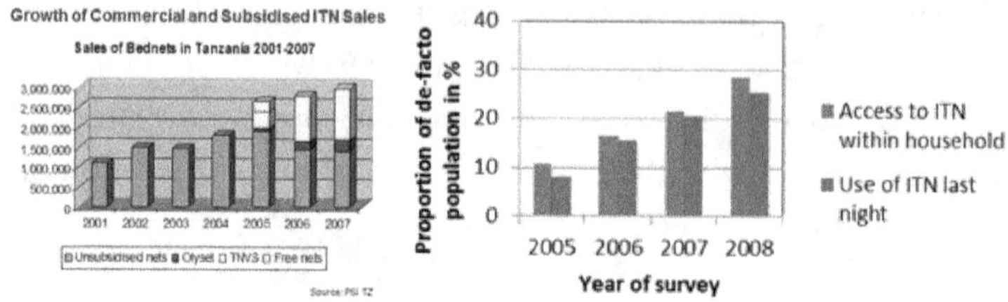


Figure 3. (Color available online) Trends in growth, access, and use of ITNS

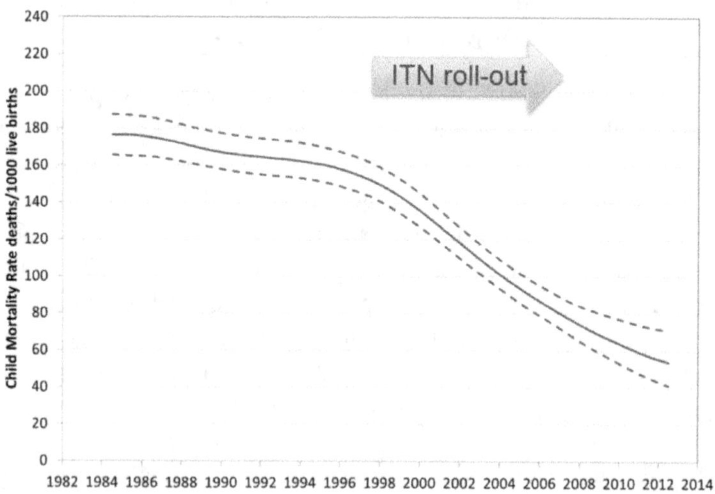


Figure 4. Reductions in malaria related illness and death contribute to declines (starting in 2000) in child mortality

*See*: Kilian "Markets for Health" Case, 2014.

Access to ITNs within Tanzanian households likewise grew steadily from 11% in 2005 to 29% in 2008 (see Figure 3, right). More importantly, between 77% and 94% of those who could use an ITN also did so, demonstrating Tanzanians had acquired a solid culture of net use.

These efforts helped reduce malaria-related illness and death (see Figure 4). Tanzania had achieved increases in coverage and use and established a sound country-wide distribution and retail system. At the same time, the voucher mechanism enabled them to strategically target available funds on high-risk people while tapping households' own contributions to the cost of nets.

## 5. Sources of and Constraints to Progress

### 5.1 *Aid influences program design*

As noted in Chapter 2, the mechanics of providing development assistance directly influence the design and implementation approaches of donor-supported programs (Gibson *et al.*, 2005; Ostrom *et al.*, 2002; Ramalingam, 2013). This influence is stronger when aid funding constitutes a large portion of total spending on an initiative.

We have long known that malaria control programs need to engage the private sector. The 2005 RBM evaluation concluded that control programs would not achieve their goals without deploying strategies to work with the private sector on access to drugs and mosquito nets. Yet, programs infrequently do so, and in the case of net efforts, strategies have shifted in the opposite direction. If malaria programs are to do better, we must understand what lies beneath this tendency. This section of the chapter delves into the global architecture and implementation arrangements for malaria programs, seeking to understand how they may have contributed to these missed opportunities and to identify actions or changes which could reduce the divergence and enhance the programs' effectiveness and sustainability.

### 5.2 *Malaria actors and funding mechanisms*

To understand why malaria control programs are designed and implemented the way they are, we examine key agencies' organizational imperatives and operating processes. The Global Fund, the US President's Malaria Initiative, DfID, and the World Bank are the largest funders for malaria programs.[19] The WHO and RBM are the leading

[19]GF has funded, through Round 7, $5.5 billion for malaria control (World Bank, 2009). The US President's Malaria Initiative was launched in 2005. They have allocated $1.2 billion between 2005 and 2010 for malaria in 15 countries (World Bank, 2009). The World Bank has allocated $470 million for malaria in Africa between 2005 and 2008 (World Bank, 2009).

technical agencies.[20] We have already confirmed their guidelines recommend programs include strategies to work with the private sector to improve access to treatment and mosquito nets. The guidelines are not to blame. However, these agencies also influence program design through the processes they use for preparing projects and grants and by allocating technical staff to contribute to project and grant proposal preparation, as well as helping select program monitoring metrics. We examine these influences also.

As discussed above, control programs frequently leave out private sector engagement strategies. The patterns' breadth and persistence suggest many or all the key agencies are contributing to the problem. RBM's evaluation found that they overlook the "important role of the local private sector in product and service delivery at the country level". The Global Fund evaluation found that the local private commercial sector has not by and large been included in Global Fund–supported program implementation (GF evaluation). A USAID review had similar findings for PMI. Under their Malaria Booster Program, the World Bank too has shifted in this direction, especially if you examine the volumes of funding (the majority of funds go to drugs distributed via public clinics and mosquito nets distributed via INGO-managed mass campaigns). The pattern holds regardless of the country context with respect to people's habits to seek care from private sources and without regard for private product distribution and retail systems.

The question, of course, is why. Several factors appear to be at work, among them: time pressures; a "production mentality," which conflates products purchased with health impact; and, relatedly, program monitoring indicators that obscure private sector operation. In addition, donor-supported projects rarely give weight to sustainability and ongoing access, the very performance features to which private sector engagement can contribute.

[20]RBM is a multilateral partnership organization whose founding partners include WHO, UNDP, UNICEF, and the World Bank. The goal of the initiative is to mobilize more attention toward malaria, resources for malaria programs, and progress toward malaria control. RBM's main tools are global advocacy activities and country-level support for designing, implementing, and monitoring malaria programs.

### 5.2.1 *Metrics*

All three major malaria funders, as well as the technical agencies, monitor these production indicators and often conflate them with the broader set of program achievements required for sustained malaria control. The Global Fund, PMI, and World Bank malaria programs all focus primarily on product delivery and little on capacity building and sustainability (Roberts, 2007; Natsios, 2010). For Global Fund and PMI, at least part of this production focus comes from the need to show results to supervisory bodies to ensure continued funding is forthcoming (Natsios, 2010).

Virtually all donors use indicators to monitor programs which track program activity but are not indicative of reaching people or any aspect of program sustainability. Rather, they monitor nets procured and distributed, drugs procured and distributed, and diagnostic kits procured and distributed (see Table 8). The term "distributed" typically refers to the product entering the campaign or public sector supply chain. That is, these funders are monitoring how much is being done, not how much is being achieved. Nets distributed overstates nets used by 2.5 times (Flaxman *et al.*, 2010). ACTs may be procured and distributed through public clinics, but this does not tell us what proportion of people with malaria are receiving the medicine.

The Global Fund evaluation team underscored the danger of mistaking products procurement for impact on the ground:

> "The findings related to ACTs are the most perplexing and worrisome of the four primary malaria interventions because they show the least improvement." While there are data showing that most countries have purchased large amounts of ACT, *there is little or no evidence of a corresponding increase in the use of ACT for treatment of children [p ES-38]* (Study Area 3).

Programs monitored using these metrics look more successful than they are. Tracking such figures makes it easy to conclude that a single channel for net or medicine supplies is sufficient. Program documents may refer to additional indicators, net ownership, and usage data from household surveys, for example. However, reporting on program performance metrics is frequently limited to activity indicators. Program

Table 8. What is and what should be monitored in malaria programs.

| What is monitored? | What is recommended by Roll Back Malaria's Monitoring and Evaluation Reference Group to be monitored? | What needs to be monitored? |
|---|---|---|
| Nets, ACTs, diagnostic kits procured (from program data)<br>Nets, ACTs, diagnostic kits distributed (from program data) | Coverage of nets, treatment from representative household surveys | Coverage from household surveys<br>Supply sources (nets and ACTs) public and private<br>Quality of treatment public sector<br>Quality of dispensing private sector<br>Quality of drugs available (public and private)<br>Bio-markers of disease from HHS |
| *Source*: PMI annual reports; Flaxman *et al.* | *MERG Guidance Note*: Assessing the Impact of Malaria Control Activities on Mortality among African Children Under 5 Years of Age | *Sources*: Strengthening Monitoring and Evaluation of Malaria Control Programmes: Report of an Inter-country Consultation (SEARO, 2004); MERG ppt |

performance is not linked to metrics measuring their influence on ongoing or continuous access (e.g. how far must people go to buy a net?), nor do they use data on overall population access to ACTs (e.g. how far must people go to get the recommended malaria medicine? how much do they cost? and how often does the nearby outlet have the medicine available). They rarely collect or use information on non-program nets. That is, nets purchased privately rarely show up in program monitoring data, even though historically this has been an important source of coverage (Webster). Hence, any "crowding out" of private purchase and sale is not captured.

Why did the programs use such problematic metrics? Research is rarely done examining linkages between aid agencies' operating context and the structural parameters of their assistance; and, indeed, none has examined this aspect of malaria assistance. Nevertheless, several factors stand out as likely culprits. First, in the mid-2000s, a strong sense of urgency about combating malaria emerged (see Sachs, 2008). Many articles refer to extremely short time horizons for malaria efforts. The possibility of achieving rapid increases in coverage of "proven" technologies seemed to make even elimination possible, a vision which naturally diminished attention to sustainability.[21] This urgency likely discouraged efforts to build diverse, multi-channel programs which could contribute not just to rapid scale-up but also to ongoing access to nets and ACTs (WB Incentivizing report; Roberts, 2007, Jobin, 2010, 2012). Strategies to collaborate with private net producers, wholesalers, and retailers inevitably require upfront analysis of the local context, including, especially, private actors' capabilities, constraints, and potential for contributing to program goals. It also requires an analysis of people's care-seeking patterns and demands. Programs have to establish and sustain communication channels with private actors as well as broader approaches to monitoring which capture private activity. Donors and implementers strongly focused on speed face considerable difficulty pursuing such strategies.

The massive and rapid increase in funding flows created pressure to move the money and diminished attention to program effectiveness. Existing capacity and absorption constraints at the country level encouraged the use of project-related supply systems, such as campaigns' temporary distribution arrangements.

Monitoring a full set of indicators is critical. The context and epidemiology of malaria vary across countries and over time in response to environmental changes as well as program control activities. Well-designed strategies may or may not be working to increase coverage of priority interventions; some populations may be getting reached, others not. Coverage, once high, may be deteriorating more rapidly than anticipated. Adapting programs based on a clear understanding of strategy implementation and community-level impact is critical to success. The MERG has developed a set of program monitoring indicators which includes indicators of program activities (or inputs and outputs) as well as

[21] Some activists and funders pushed to make malaria elimination the goal, even while malaria experts quietly pointed out that the goal ran counter to the long experience with malaria control in Africa (Webb, 2014, p. 146) and could potentially distort program strategies away from features important for sustainability.

impact and outcomes. However, by and large, program monitoring looks at program inputs and outputs and focuses on current or one-time access without regard to other important aspects of program performance. For example, programs do not monitor the density and breadth of net supply sources, which are important for ongoing access to nets. Nor typically do they collect information on private practitioners' case management. Many do not monitor the availability of ACTs at private pharmacies and dispensers, even though most people seek help there.

The indicators currently used to monitor malaria programs make a program which procures and distributes a lot of items look successful without reference to the proportion of people reached by the program or the impact on the overall access and use of nets or drugs a program may have. That is, they leave out performance indicators, which would reveal important elements of program effectiveness. A mechanism for meaningful monitoring, learning, and adapting program strategies is weak or missing in many programs. This broken feedback loop doubtless contributes to continuing, unchanged, and flawed programs; we simply don't know what's going on for important elements.

We've seen that monitoring practices make it easy to misperceive the reach and success of malaria programs under implementation. This makes it easy to think it is not worthwhile to go to all the trouble of working with private providers and suppliers to achieve sustained malaria control.

### 5.2.2 *Time pressures*

Compared to the components monitored in most programs, devising and implementing strategies to work with the local private sector takes a very long time. Growing commercial delivery strategies, which work through altering market operations, take even longer to unfold. However, the recent surge of attention and support for malaria control has been framed with a great sense of urgency. This urgency translates into very short time horizons for country programs and aid projects to deliver results. Traditionally, development assistance initiatives have had 5–10-year time frames to achieve their results; recent malaria programs have been pushed to show results in 1–2 years. Andrew Natsios, who led USAID during the establishment of the US' flagship malaria initiative, the "President's

Malaria Initiative" (PMI), wrote that PEPFAR and PMI were approached as humanitarian or crisis responses, and the programs were designed accordingly (Natsios, 2010). At the country level, the GF has to make decisions about funding continuation in the second year of grant funding, and a country's progress toward "results" is clearly important for that decision. Such time horizons and pressures often discourage or preclude any analysis of local private sector capacity or the establishment of context-appropriate engagement strategies to harness private sector capacity. In fact, the time pressures make it hard to do anything other than procure and distribute products. And that is precisely what the programs focus on. Natsios describes how widespread this "production" mentality has become in aid projects, and malaria programs are a perfect example.

### 5.2.3 *Public agencies' role*

Several other factors predispose malaria programs to exclude private sector engagement. Typically, with other categories of external support, health ministries prefer to have resources flow to and through their system (Hozumi *et al.*, 2009). So, allocating drugs via private pharmacies and drug dispensers is opposed.

### 5.2.4 *Policy economy*

In the case of the large informal sector (drug dispensers), formal, trained providers often oppose strategies to engage them, suggesting they may elevate their status, drawing more people to seek medicine from these sources.

### 5.2.5 *Narrow range of consultation in strategy development*

Observers of Globa l Fund Country Coordinating Mechanisms (CCMs)[22] note that their operation often predisposes to the exclusion of private producers, distributors, pharmacies, and practitioners. CCMs exhibit a consistent tendency toward program activities implemented by governments

[22]The body responsible for the content and oversight of implementation of GF financed activities in a country.

and NGOs/CSOs, which are overseen by a small group of INGOs which participate in CCMs (OIG Global Fund, 2009).

### 5.2.6 *Skill shortages*

Several analysts point out that mobilizing the capacity of private actors requires program management capabilities (e.g. to do private sector analysis, develop collaboration strategies, and manage monitoring, which includes private activity), which are usually weak (DfID NAO Malaria review). They suggest the relatively low amount of donor support for local technical capacity for control program management (partly as a result of the shift to budget support via sector-wide approach blended funding mechanisms) may have contributed to the decline in efforts to mobilize private sector contributions.

## 5.3 *Lessons*

Malaria programs have achieved remarkable increases in net ownership and use deployment, especially mass campaign efforts with their effective, but temporary, supply chains. Programs have faced rather more difficulty increasing treatment coverage with narrow, mainly public sector distribution platforms. However, programs' focus on speed and product procurement and distribution has discouraged the development of strategies to mobilize private drug sellers, net producers, distributors, and retailers. Program managers and donors need to shift to diversify their strategies, adding, in many countries, private sector channels, so that programs can achieve broader goals (including ongoing access and sustainability).[23]

This shift, though, won't occur until program funders and managers start to monitor performance indicators which more accurately capture what programs need to achieve (e.g. use statistics and access point data), sustained decreases in prices (e.g. lower market prices), and choice of nets. Keeping an "eye on the ball" of meaningful performance indicators

---

[23] Sustainability here encompasses both the local capacity to undertake the tasks associated with delivering products and services and the adequacy of locally available resources to sustain the desired level of activity.

will serve to correct programs that aren't working, including those that aren't working due to the omission of private sector engagement when it is necessary.

In reviewing programs' progress and the effectiveness of their assistance, donors should be cognizant of a broader set of performance objectives, beyond activity and current "coverage." Donors should examine their metrics to ensure they are capturing factors such as ongoing access and financial as well as implementation sustainability.

## References


S. Abdulla, J. A. Schellenberg, R. Nathan, O. Mukasa, T. Marchant, T. Smith, M. Tanner and C. Lengeler. (2001). Impact on malaria morbidity of a programme supplying insecticide treated nets in children aged under 2 years in Tanzania: Community cross sectional study. *BMJ* **322**(7281): 270–273.

B. M. Afolabi, O. T. Sofola, B. S. Fatunmbi, W. Komakech, F. Okoh, O. Saliu, P. Otsemobor, O. B. Oresanya, C. N. Amajoh, D. Fasiku and I. Jalingo. (2009). Household possession, use and non-use of treated or untreated mosquito nets in two ecologically diverse regions of Nigeria – Niger Delta and Sahel Savannah. *Malaria Journal* **8**(1): 30.

S. Agha, R. Van Rossem, G. Stallworthy and T. Kusanthan. (2007). The impact of a hybrid social marketing intervention on inequities in access, ownership and use of insecticide-treated nets. *Malaria Journal* **6**(1): 13.

K. Arrow, C. Panosian and H. Gelband (Eds.). (2004). *Saving Lives, Buying Time: Economics of Malaria Drugs in an Age of Resistance*. Institute of Medicine, National Academies of Sciences, United States.

S. Basu. (2006). Implementation Completion Report on a Credit in the Amount of SDR SDR 119.2 Million to India for a Malaria Control Project.

R. Bate and K. Hess. (2010). Anti-malarial drug quality in Lagos and Accra – a comparison of various quality assessments. *Malaria Journal* **9**: 157.

D. Bishai, N. Shah, D. Walker, W. Brieger and D. Peters. (2008). Social franchising to improve quality and access in private health care in developing countries. *Harvard Health Policy Review* **9**: 184–197.

W. Brieger, A. Unwin, G. Greer and S. Meek. (2004). *Interventions to Improve the Role of Medicine Sellers in Malaria Case Management for Children in Africa*. Consultative Meeting on Interventions to Improve the Role of Medicine Sellers in Case Management of Malaria (Fever) in Children Under 5.

Centers for Disease Control and Prevention (CDC). (2005). Distribution of insecticide-treated bednets during an integrated nationwide immunization campaign – Togo, West Africa, December 2004. *MMWR Weekly* **54**(39): 994–996.

J. L. Cohen, P. Yadav, C. Moucheraud, S. Alphs, P. S. Larson, J. Arkedis, J. Massaga and O. Sabot. (2013). Do price subsidies on artemisinin combination therapy for malaria increase household use? Evidence from a repeated cross-sectional study in remote regions of Tanzania. *PloS One* **8**(7): e70713.

G. W. Fegan, A. M. Noor, W. S. Akhwale, S. Cousens and R. W. Snow. (2007). Effect of expanded insecticide-treated bednet coverage on child survival in rural Kenya: A longitudinal study. *The Lancet* **370**(9592): 1035–1039.

A. D. Flaxman, N. Fullman, M. W. Otten, Jr., M. Menon, R. E. Cibulskis, M. Ng, C. J. Murray and S. S. Lim. (2010). Rapid scaling up of insecticide-treated bed net coverage in Africa and its relationship with development assistance for health: a systematic synthesis of supply, distribution, and household survey data. *PLoS Medicine* **7**(8): e1000328.

N. Fraser and N. Druce. (2006). Partnerships for malaria control: Engaging the formal and informal private sectors, HLSP Institute for UNICEF/UNDP/World Bank/WHO Special Programme for Research and Training in Tropical Diseases (TDR), in Collaboration with the Working Group on Financing and Resources of the Roll Back Malaria Partnership, Chaired by The World Bank.

C. C. Gibson, K. Andersson, E. Ostrom and S. Shivakumar. (2005). *The Samaritan's Dilemma: The Political Economy of Development Aid*. Oxford University Press, Oxford, UK.

S. Githinji, S. Herbst, T. Kistemann and A. M. Noor. (2010). Mosquito nets in a rural area of Western Kenya: Ownership, use and quality. *Malaria Journal* **9**: 250.

C. Goodman, W. Brieger, A. Unwin, A. Mills, S. Meek and G. Greer. (2007a). Medicine sellers and malaria treatment in sub-Saharan Africa: What do they do and how can their practice be improved? *American Journal of Tropical Medicine and Hygiene* **77**(6 Suppl): 203–218.

C. Goodman, S. P. Kachur, S. Abdulla, P. Bloland and A. Mills. (2007b). Drug shop regulation and malaria treatment in Tanzania–why do shops break the rules, and does it matter? *Health Policy and Planning* **22**(6): 393–403.

M. Grabowsky, N. Farrell, W. Hawley, J. Chimumbwa, S. Hoyer, A. Wolkon and J. Selanikio. (2005a). Integrating insecticide-treated bednets into a measles vaccination campaign achieves high, rapid and equitable coverage with direct and voucher-based methods. *Tropical Medicine & International Health* **10**(11): 1151–1160.

M. Grabowsky, T. Nobiya, M. Ahun, R. Donna, M. Lengor, D. Zimmerman, H. Ladd, E. Hoekstra, A. Bello and A. Baffoe-Wilmot. (2005b). Distributing insecticide-treated bednets during measles vaccination: A low-cost means of achieving high and equitable coverage. *Bulletin of the World Health Organization* **83**: 195–201.

M. Grabowsky, T. Nobiya and J. Selanikio. (2007). Sustained high coverage of insecticide-treated bednets through combined catch-up and keep-up strategies. *Tropical Medicine & International Health* **12**(7): 815–822.

G. Greer, A. Akinpelumi, L. Madueke, B. Plowman, B. Fapohunda, Y. Tawfik, R. Holmes, J. Owor, U. Gilpin, C. Clarence and B. Lennox. (2004). Improving Management of Childhood Malaria in Nigeria and Uganda by Improving Practices of Patent Medicine Vendors. Arlington, VA, BASICS II for the US Agency for International Development.

K. A. Grépin. (2014). The role of the private sector in delivering maternal and child health services in low-income and middle-income countries: An observational, longitudinal analysis. *The Lancet* **384**: S7.

H. L. Guyatt, A. M. Noor, S. A. Ochola and R. W. Snow. (2004). Use of intermittent presumptive treatment and insecticide treated bed nets by pregnant women in four Kenyan districts. *Tropical Medicine & International Health* **9**(2): 255–261.

M. A. Hamid Salim, M. Uplekar, P. Daru, M. Aung, E. Declercq and K. Lonnroth. (2006). Turning liabilities into resources: Informal village doctors and tuberculosis control in Bangladesh. *Bulletin of the World Health Organization* **84**(6): 479–484.

P. D. Harvey. (1999). Let every child be wanted: How social marketing is revolutionizing contraceptive use around the world. Westport, Conn., Auburn House.

S. E.-D. H. Hassan, E. M. Malik, S. I. Okoued and E. M. Eltayeb. (2008). Retention and efficacy of long-lasting insecticide-treated nets distributed in eastern Sudan: A two-step community-based study. *Malaria Journal* **7**(1): 85.

M. W. Hetzel, J. J. Msechu, C. Goodman, C. Lengeler, B. Obrist, S. P. Kachur, A. Makemba, R. Nathan, A. Schulze and H. Mshinda. (2006). Decreased availability of antimalarials in the private sector following the policy change from chloroquine to sulphadoxine-pyrimethamine in the Kilombero Valley, Tanzania. *Malaria Journal* **5**: 109.

T. H. Holtz, L. H. Marum, C. Mkandala, N. Chizani, J. M. Roberts, A. Macheso, M. E. Parise and S. P. Kachur. (2002). Insecticide-treated bednet use, anaemia, and malaria parasitaemia in Blantyre District, Malawi. *Tropical Medicine & International Health* **7**(3): 220–230.

S. C. Howard, J. Omumbo, C. Nevill, E. S. Some, C. A. Donnelly and R. W. Snow. (2000). Evidence for a mass community effect of insecticide-treated bednets on the incidence of malaria on the Kenyan coast. *Transactions of the Royal Society of Tropical Medicine and Hygiene* **94**(4): 357–360.

D. Hozumi, L. Frost, C. Suraratdecha, B. Pratt, Y. Sezgin, L. Reichenbach and M. Reich. (2009). The role of the private sector in health: A landscape analysis of global players' attitudes toward the private sector in health systems and policy levers that influence these attitudes. Technical Partner Papers, Results for Development.

W. Jobin. (2010). *A Realistic Strategy for Fighting Malaria*. Boston Harbor Publishers, Boston, MA.

W. R. Jobin. (2012). *Improving the US Presidential Malaria Initiative*. Boston Harbor Publishers, Boston, MA.

W. Jobin. (2014). Increased economic productivity after suppressing malaria transmission in 14 African countries. *Africa Policy Journal*.

E. Juma and D. Zurovac. (2011). Changes in health workers' malaria diagnosis and treatment practices in Kenya. *Malaria Journal* **10**(1): 10.1186.

R. A. Khatib, G. F. Killeen, S. M. Abdulla, E. Kahigwa, P. D. McElroy, R. P. Gerrets, H. Mshinda, A. Mwita and S. P. Kachur. (2008). Markets, voucher subsidies and free nets combine to achieve high bed net coverage in rural Tanzania. *Malaria Journal* **7**: 98.

A. Kilian, N. Wijayanandana and J. Ssekitoleeko. (2010). Review of delivery strategies for insecticide treated mosquito nets: Are we ready for the next phase of malaria control efforts? *TropIKA.net* **1**(1).

G. F. Killeen, A. Tami, J. Kihonda, F. O. Okumu, M. E. Kotas, H. Grundmann, N. Kasigudi, H. Ngonyani, V. Mayagaya, R. Nathan, S. Abdulla, J. D. Charlwood, T. A. Smith and C. Lengeler. (2007). Cost-sharing strategies combining targeted public subsidies with private-sector delivery achieve high bednet coverage and reduced malaria transmission in Kilombero Valley, southern Tanzania. *BMC Infectious Diseases* **7**: 121.

C. Lengeler and D. deSavigny. (2007). Programme diversity is key to the success of insecticide-treated bednets. *The Lancet* **370**(9592): 1009–1010.

C. Lengeler, M. Grabowsky, D. McGuire and D. deSavigny. (2007). Quick wins versus sustainability: Options for the upscaling of insecticide-treated nets.

*American Journal of Tropical Medicine and Hygiene* **77**(6 Suppl): 222–226.

S. M. Magesa, C. Lengeler, D. deSavigny, J. E. Miller, R. J. Njau, K. Kramer, A. Kitua and A. Mwita. (2005). Creating an "enabling environment" for taking insecticide treated nets to national scale: The Tanzanian experience. *Malaria Journal* **4**: 34.

Malaria Consortium. (2002). Final Report of the External Evaluation of Roll Back Malaria. Liverpool, United Kingdom.

K. Marsh and R. W. Snow. (1999). Malaria transmission and morbidity. *Parassitologia* **41**(1–3): 241–246.

I. Mikkelsen-Lopez, W. Shango, J. Barrington, R. Ziegler, T. Smith and D. deSavigny. (2014). The challenge to avoid anti-malarial medicine stock-outs in an era of funding partners: The case of Tanzania. *Malaria Journal* **13**: 181.

S. Mookherji, L. Ryan, J. Ricca, M. Bize and T. Dye. (2008). Evaluation of the Global Fund Partner Environment, at Global and Country Levels, in Relation to Grant Performance and Health Systems Effects, Including 16 Country Studies, Macro International.

O. Müller, M. De Allegri, H. Becher, J. Tiendrebogo, C. Beiersmann, M. Ye, B. Kouyate, A. Sie and A. Jahn. (2008). Distribution systems of insecticide-treated bed nets for malaria control in rural Burkina Faso: Cluster-randomized controlled trial. *PLOS One* **3**(9): e3182.

National Audit Office. (2013). Report – Value for Money: Malaria, Department of Health and Social Care, United Kingdom.

A. Natsios. (2010). The Clash of the Counterbureaucracy and Development. Washington DC, Center for Global Development.

A. M. Noor, A. A. Amin, W. S. Akhwale and R. W. Snow. (2007). Increasing coverage and decreasing inequity in insecticide-treated bed net use among rural Kenyan children. *PLoS Medicine* **4**(8): e255.

S. E. D. Nsimba. (2007). Assessing the impact of educational intervention for improving management of malaria and other childhood illnesses in Kibaha District-Tanzania.

Office of the Inspector General (Global Fund). (2009). Report on the Review of Local Fund Agent Tendering Process.

F. O. Oshiname and W. R. Brieger. (1992). Primary care training for patent medicine vendors in rural Nigeria. *Social Science & Medicine* **35**(12): 1477–1484.

E. Ostrom, C. Gibson, S. Shivakumar and K. Andersson. (2002). Aid, Incentives, and Sustainability: An Institutional Analysis of Development

Cooperation — Summary Report. SIDA Studies in Evaluation, Swedish International Development Agency.

A. M. Pierre-Louis. (2008). Intensifying the Fight against Malaria: The World Bank's Booster Program for Malaria Control in Africa, World Bank.

B. Ramalingam. (2013). *Aid on the Edge of Chaos: Rethinking International Cooperation in a Complex World*. Oxford University Press, Oxford, UK.

V. B. Rao, D. Schellenberg and A. C. Ghani. (2013). Overcoming health systems barriers to successful malaria treatment. *Trends in Parasitology* **29**(4): 164–180.

L. Roberts. (2007). Combating malaria. Battling over bed nets. *Science* **318**(5850): 556–559.

M. Rowland, J. Webster, P. Saleh, D. Chandramohan, T. Freeman, B. Pearcy, N. Durrani, A. Rab and N. Mohammed. (2002). Prevention of malaria in Afghanistan through social marketing of insecticide-treated nets: Evaluation of coverage and effectiveness by cross-sectional surveys and passive surveillance. *Tropical Medicine & International Health* **7**(10): 813–822.

E. Rutebemberwa, A. A. Kinengyere, F. Ssengooba, G. W. Pariyo and S. N. Kiwanuka. (2014). Financial interventions and movement restrictions for managing the movement of health workers between public and private organizations in low- and middle-income countries. *Cochrane Database of Systematic Reviews* **2**: CD009845.

J. D. Sachs. (2008). A deadline on malaria. *Scientific American* **299**(1): 36.

J. R. Schellenberg, S. Abdulla, R. Nathan, O. Mukasa, T. J. Marchant, N. Kikumbih, A. K. Mushi, H. Mponda, H. Minja, H. Mshinda, M. Tanner and C. Lengeler. (2001). Effect of large-scale social marketing of insecticide-treated nets on child survival in rural Tanzania. *The Lancet* **357**(9264): 1241–1247.

J. Sherry, S. Mookherji and L. Ryan. (2009). Five-Year Evaluation of the Global Fund – Synthesis Report.

J. Simon, K. Yeboah-Antwi, A. Schapira, M. Kabir Cham, R. Barber-Madden and M. I. Brooks. (2011). External Evaluation of the President's Malaria Initiative: Final Report, USAID.

R. W. Snow, J. A. Omumbo, B. Lowe, C. S. Molyneux, J. O. Obiero, A. Palmer, M. W. Weber, M. Pinder, B. Nahlen, C. Obonyo, C. Newbold, S. Gupta and K. Marsh. (1997). Relation between severe malaria morbidity in children and level of Plasmodium falciparum transmission in Africa. *The Lancet* **349**(9066): 1650–1654.

D. Socheat, L. Chanthap and V. V. R. Seshu Babu. (2005). Piloting of a Strategy for Collection of Malaria Information from the Private Sector, Cambodia,

National Centre for Parasitology Entomology and Malaria Control, GTZ BACKUP Initiative.

J. Stevenson. (2001). Mapping local rehabilitation and intermediate care services. A Whole Systems Approach to Understanding Service Capacity and Planning Change, Kings Fund.

T. A. Taylor and P. Yadav. (2011). Subsidizing the distribution channel: Donor funding to improve the availability of products with positive externalities. Citeseer.

The Lancet. (2000). Donor responsibilities in rolling back malaria. *Elsevier*. **356**: 521.

S. Tougher, Y. Ye, J. H. Amuasi, I. A. Kourgueni, R. Thomson, C. Goodman, A. G. Mann, R. Ren, B. A. Willey and C. A. Adegoke. (2012). Effect of the affordable medicines facility—malaria (AMFm) on the availability, price, and market share of quality-assured artemisinin-based combination therapies in seven countries: A before-and-after analysis of outlet survey data. *The Lancet* **380**(9857): 1916–1926.

S. Tougher, A. G. Mann, Y. Ye, I. A. Kourgueni, R. Thomson, J. H. Amuasi, R. Ren, B. A. Willey, D. Ansong, K. Bruxvoort, G. Diap, C. Festo, B. Johanes, A. Kalolella, O. Mallam, B. Mberu, S. Ndiaye, S. B. Nguah, M. Seydou, M. Taylor, M. Wamukoya, F. Arnold, K. Hanson and C. Goodman. (2014). Improving access to malaria medicine through private-sector subsidies in seven African countries. *Health Affairs* (Millwood) **33**(9): 1576–1585.

R. Valimba, J. Liana, M. P. Joshi, E. Rutta, M. Embrey, M. Bundala and B. Kibassa. (2014). Engaging the private sector to improve antimicrobial use in the community: Experience from accredited drug dispensing outlets in Tanzania. *Journal of Pharmaceutical Policy and Practice* **7**(1): 1–7.

F. N. Wafula and C. A. Goodman. (2010). Are interventions for improving the quality of services provided by specialized drug shops effective in sub-Saharan Africa? A systematic review of the literature. *International Journal for Quality in Health Care* **22**(4): 316–323.

J. L. A. Webb. (2014). *The Long Struggle against Malaria in Tropical Africa.* Cambridge University Press, New York, NY, USA.

J. Webster, J. Lines, J. Bruce, J. R. Armstrong Schellenberg and K. Hanson. (2005). Which delivery systems reach the poor? A review of equity of coverage of ever-treated nets, never-treated nets, and immunisation to reduce child mortality in Africa. *The Lancet Infectious Diseases* **5**(11): 709–717.

J. Webster, J. Hill, J. Lines and K. Hanson. (2007). Delivery systems for insecticide treated and untreated mosquito nets in Africa: Categorization and outcomes achieved. *Health Policy and Planning* **22**(5): 277–293.

World Health Organization (WHO). (2008). World Malaria Report. World Health Organization. Geneva, World Health Organization.

World Health Organization (WHO). (2013). World Malaria Report. Geneva, World Health Organization.

P. Yadav, J. L. Cohen, S. Alphs, J. Arkedis, P. S. Larson, J. Massaga and O. Sabot. (2012). Trends in availability and prices of subsidized ACT over the first year of the AMFm: Evidence from remote regions of Tanzania. *Malaria Journal* **11**: 299.

J. Yukich, F. Tediosi and C. Lengeler. (2007). Operations, costs and cost-effectiveness of five insecticide-treated net programs (Eritrea, Malawi, Tanzania, Togo, Senegal) and two indoor residual spraying programs (Kwa-Zulu-Natal, Mozambique). USAID Report.

J. O. Yukich, C. Lengeler, F. Tediosi, N. Brown, J. A. Mulligan, D. Chavasse, W. Stevens, J. Justino, L. Conteh, R. Maharaj, M. Erskine, D. H. Mueller, V. Wiseman, T. Ghebremeskel, M. Zerom, C. Goodman, D. McGuire, J. M. Urrutia, F. Sakho, K. Hanson and B. Sharp. (2008). Costs and consequences of large-scale vector control for malaria. *Malaria Journal* **7**: 258.

# Chapter 10

# The Private Sector in TB Programs

**Mukund Uplekar**

## Abstract

This chapter by Mukund Uplekar describes drawing on his many years leading the World Health Organization's work to guide private sector engagement with national TB programs around the world. Developing country governments and global agencies have responded to TB's resurgence as a serious health threat with stepped-up resources and attention to control programs. Initially, donor-supported TB programs sought to reach patients primarily through public facilities. Where most TB sufferers were seeking private care, the results were disappointing.

Based on considerable evidence that private engagement can accelerate TB control, global health organizations now advocate engaging private practitioners, and some countries have taken important steps in this direction. Programs which pursue engagement frequently succeed, for example, in improving private providers' practices. Still, the magnitude of the effort falls short of the private sector's potential contribution to TB control. A number of countries with a high TB burden are unlikely to achieve the desired reductions in TB cases without expanding the engagement of private providers. Donors and technical agencies may accelerate progress by refining this dimension of TB program strategy in countries where private providers play a large role in the healthcare provision system.

Developing country governments and global agencies have responded to TB's resurgence as a serious health threat with stepped-up resources and attention to control programs. Initially, donor-supported TB programs sought to reach patients primarily through public facilities. Where most TB sufferers were seeking private care, the results were disappointing. Based on considerable evidence that private engagement can accelerate TB control, global health organizations now advocate engaging private practitioners, and some countries have taken important steps in this direction. Programs which pursue engagement frequently succeed, for example, in improving private providers' practices. Still, the magnitude of the effort falls short of the private sector's potential contribution to TB control. A number of countries with a high TB burden are unlikely to achieve the desired reductions in TB cases without expanding the engagement of private providers. Donors and technical agencies may accelerate progress by refining this dimension of TB program strategy in countries where private providers play a large role in the healthcare provision system.

## 1. Introduction: TB and the Role of the Private Sector

Tuberculosis (TB) is the world's second-most deadly infectious disease, after HIV/AIDS, killing more than 1.3 million people in 2012 (World Health Organization (WHO), 2013). Once a scourge covering much of the world, most now-wealthy nations managed to wipe out the disease through improved living conditions and treatment. As a result, TB control attracted little attention and few resources for many years, even as the disease resurged in poorer countries. A landmark 1993 World Bank review of health interventions' cost-effectiveness identified TB control as highly effective. At the same time, strains resistant to standard first-line treatment, or multi-drug-resistant TB (MDR-TB), started to appear. With increased travel, wealthy countries recognized that TB poses a threat even to their own citizens. In 1994, the WHO declared TB a global emergency, and the disease became a focus of global health and development assistance. New funding and attention reenergized countries' national control programs. These efforts have likely contributed to saving 22 million lives since 1993. Nevertheless, prevalence and incidence are declining painfully slowly, no more than 2% per year. Moreover, given that the population is growing at about 2% per year, the number of new cases continues to rise (Dye and Williams, 2010). Drug-resistant strains are emerging ever more frequently. These worrying figures suggest we examine the barriers to better TB control, which we turn to in the following.

The burden and misery of TB falls most heavily on poor people and poor countries (Gandy and Zumla, 2002). TB is concentrated in 22 countries – often referred to as the *high-burden countries*.[1] Together, these countries account for more than 80% of TB cases worldwide. Private providers provide substantial care in most of them. In 10 of them, sick people turn more often to private than public sources for care.[2] This is confirmed by the large amounts of TB drugs which flow through private channels, likewise confirming the magnitude of private TB treatment (Wells *et al.*, 2011). Nevertheless, for many years, programs have done little to engage the private sector, focusing efforts on reaching and curing people through public facilities. Unsurprisingly, in many countries, programs struggle to reach many people sick with TB in a timely way, perpetuating long delays in diagnosis.

TB experts have recognized the importance of mobilizing private practitioners to properly diagnose and treat TB patients since the late 1990s. Global guidelines encouraged private sector engagement starting in 2002 (Uplekar, 2003; WHO, 2007). The 2006 *Stop TB Strategy* underscored the importance of engaging the private sector, making it

---

[1]India, China, Indonesia, South Africa, Pakistan, Afghanistan, Bangladesh, Brazil, Cambodia, the Democratic Republic of the Congo (DRC), Ethiopia, Indonesia, Kenya, Mozambique, Myanmar, Nigeria, the Philippines, the Russian Federation, Thailand, Uganda, the United Republic of Tanzania, Vietnam, and Zimbabwe. Together, they account for more than 80% of cases and 83% of deaths. Global support for TB control targets these high-burden countries (HBCs).

[2]Pakistan (86% private utilization), Bangladesh (86%), Cambodia (77%), India (77%), Nigeria (69%), Indonesia (71%), Uganda (65%), the DRC (56%), Kenya (56%), and the Philippines (52%). Figures are from the most recent demographic and health household surveys for the respective country.

one of six principle components of TB control. The 2006 *International Standards of TB Care* likewise endorse working with private practitioners so that their patients receive care of adequate quality. Moreover, national control programs have initiated some efforts to reach patients via private practitioners. Still, the scale of these efforts is small relative to the number of patients cared for privately (Lal *et al.*, 2011). Rampant mismanagement of patients by private practitioners persists and contributes to the emergence of drug-resistant strains (see Box 1). Privately run lab networks have emerged with the capacity to test for drug-resistant TB, a key bottleneck in efforts to reduce the transmission of resistant strains. To date, few programs have tapped into these services. There is both a challenge and an opportunity with respect to the private sector's role in TB control.

**Box 1. Mumbai's private practitioners are still mismanaging TB**

A recent study found that when 106 private practitioners in a Mumbai slum were asked to write a prescription for a patient with TB, they prescribed 63 different drug regimens, only six of which were appropriate. The study replicated a 1991 study in the same place (the Uplekar study). Little has changed in two decades. The control program ignores private practitioners, and practitioners mismanage patients.

*Source*: Udwadia *et al.* (2010).

This chapter examines TB programs' experiences with private sector engagement to shed light on how such initiatives can contribute to TB control. We examine the most common program strategies and the mechanics of their implementation at the country level. We also examine the evidence on private sector engagement strategies' effectiveness when applied to the key services and goals of TB control programs. We examine the way programs are designed and implemented, the role of funding and technical agencies, and how they help or hinder private sector engagement.

## 2. The Challenge of TB Control and the Role of the Private Sector

TB is caused by the *mycobacterium tuberculosis* bacteria, which spreads from person to person through airborne droplets. Although TB can infect other organs in the body, including the bones, lymph nodes, and central nervous system, most frequently it infects the lungs. This form of the disease, called pulmonary TB, causes the persistent cough so widely associated with the disease. Pulmonary TB is the infectious form, as it is the cough that allows the bacteria to become airborne. Someone with this form of TB will on average infect one person per month. TB control programs focus on detecting and treating people suffering from pulmonary TB to reduce the spread of the disease.

People with active TB[3] usually suffer debilitating symptoms. Eventually, most seek treatment. Their symptoms are initially not easily distinguishable from other illnesses; frequently, the first provider they see fails to make a correct diagnosis. Getting the majority of patients with a long-lasting cough tested, and tested promptly, is critical to controlling TB. Faster, more accurate diagnostic tests exist but are relatively costly. In resource-constrained settings, diagnosis is commonly done by sputum microscopy.[4]

Since bacilli don't always appear in sputum, patients must give multiple samples at different times.[5] Typically, patients must travel to a diagnostic center and return to receive their results. Both patients and practitioners find this process burdensome, and many practitioners don't trust microscopy's accuracy. Private practitioners frequently use chest X-rays, which many can perform themselves; however, by itself, the test is not specific (e.g. shadows can be caused by other things in addition to TB). Blood tests are used in a number of countries; they are quicker but

[3]Many people have the bacteria present in their bodies but are neither sick nor spread the disease; this state is referred to as latent TB.

[4]Chest X-rays can provide additional useful information to support the diagnosis.

[5]Patients infected with extra-pulmonary TB, in particular, typically have low levels of bacteria in the lungs and are therefore hard to diagnose with sputum microscopy.

not accurate in high-prevalence settings (Grenier *et al.*, 2012). As a result, many people with active TB are not diagnosed and remain untreated, and many who don't have TB are incorrectly diagnosed and treated.

Once diagnosed, most TB infections respond to a standardized six-month regimen comprising a combination of four so-called first-line drugs. Treatment is costly, posing a considerable barrier to access. Treatment costs, combined with the costs of transport and lost wages, can easily impoverish a TB patient and their family in many countries. The drugs have unpleasant side effects and are expensive. Patients must take them for a minimum of six months; yet, they often feel better after a few weeks of treatment and are tempted to stop taking the medication or to take them less regularly. Private providers often prescribe ineffective drug combinations and make little effort to follow up on patients' adherence to treatment. As a result, patients don't get better; even more worryingly, the still-present bacteria may rebound as a drug-resistant strain, which they spread to others.

TB control efforts must reach most people with active TB and get them diagnosed *promptly* and *accurately* and treated *fully*. Patients seeking care must be referred for timely diagnosis, and patients must be able to access the proper drugs without undue difficulty. Commonly, treatment involves some form of supervision, whereby a provider or family member observes the patient taking their medication. As drug-resistant strains emerge, control is becoming more challenging. Providers must quickly identify patients who aren't responding to first-line treatment and test for drug resistance. Diagnostic tests for resistant strains are expensive, often complex to do, and time-consuming. When resistant strains are identified, patients must switch to a much more complex and costly regime of second-line medications. Even countries with relatively strong primary care systems[6] struggle with these tasks.

[6]Primary care refers to first-contact services (diagnosis and treatment of acute and chronic illnesses, health promotion, disease prevention, health maintenance, counseling, and patient education) for people provided in a variety of healthcare settings and accessed through self-referral. These services can be provided by primary care physicians and nurses or other types of professionals.

## 2.1 *TB programs: The activities and how they are supposed to work*

Unfortunately, most TB sufferers live in countries with weak primary care systems. Primary care is provided by public facilities of varying degrees of functionality along with a wide range of private providers. In public facilities, drug stock-outs are common. Many health workers use poor diagnostic practices (Pai and Das, 2013), clinics lack systems for patient monitoring and reporting, and staff have weak links with community workers who could help monitor patients' drug-taking near where they live. Though clinics receive public funding, patients often pay formal and informal fees and face other barriers to getting services. People often complain of poor treatment and attitudes, long waits, and a lack of privacy, an important concern for people suffering from a stigmatized disease such as TB (Zafar Ullah, 2012). Accessing public services often involves significant travel time, a barrier exacerbated by clinics' limited and uncertain opening hours. Public systems often have insufficient diagnostic capacity, especially newer diagnostic technologies; if a patient is suspected of suffering from TB, they must travel multiple times to a center with the needed lab services. Public lab systems often have very limited capacity to test for drug-resistant TB; therefore, for patients who aren't responding to treatment, testing them for drug resistance is often very difficult.[7]

On the other hand, private providers are heterogeneous, ranging from highly skilled doctors, specialists, quality-assured labs, and non-profit hospitals to informal practitioners with little training, including pharmacies and drug sellers. Private providers tend to be highly accessible; they are located more widely and have longer, more convenient opening hours (Das *et al.*, 2012; Kim, 2006; Hamid Salim *et al.*, 2006; Sinanovic, 2006). Waits are short. Often, patients trust private providers more because they know them (e.g. their family doctor) and, in part, because they are paying them, which may give them a feeling of leverage or empowerment in their interaction. But practitioners' fees are often higher than those in the public sector; drug prices are frequently multiples of those paid by public organizations (Wells

[7]For example, India's TB control program must scale up drug susceptibility testing (given the growth of drug resistance). Yet, scale-up remains slow.

*et al.*, 2011). Social insurance coverage is limited in most high-burden countries, and private patients are rarely able to access either subsidized drugs or drugs obtained at discounted priced.[8] Instead, most private patients pay the full cost out-of-pocket. In addition to the considerable expenses involved, the "full-on" market incentives associated with TB care are particularly problematic with regard to care quality. Providers receive more income from X-rays and blood-based tests than from the recommended sputum microscopy. Few private practices are configured to monitor patients, say, by employing a part-time community nurse, and patients are rarely inclined to pay for such services, even if offered. Unsurprisingly, diagnostic practices are often poor, as are arrangements for monitoring and following up with patients (Uplekar and Shepard, 1991, Uplekar, 1998; Nshuti *et al.*, 2001; Chengsorn *et al.*, 2009; Udwadia, 2010).

Poor people tend to use the poorest-quality private providers (e.g. drug sellers, untrained practitioners) because they are closer, cheaper, and sometimes will allow them to pay over time. Patients who are pressed for cash may forgo the clinical consultation altogether and buy antibiotics directly from pharmacies and other drug sellers.

These characteristics make TB control particularly challenging. They are exacerbated in countries with weak primary care systems involving out-of-pocket payments and unreliable primary care provision.[9]

Control programs strive to overcome these problems by selectively strengthening primary care in the areas most critical for TB control. Typically, they include activities to:

- train practitioners to improve diagnosis and treatment;[10]
- tap external procurement and logistics support for TB drugs to ensure steady and widespread availability of drugs;

[8] Many TB programs obtain drugs at relatively low prices via the Stop TB Global Drug Facility.

[9] The weakness of health services provision is commonly referenced as a major constraint to accelerating progress on TB control. See, for example, the *Report on the Meeting of the Second Ad Hoc Committee on the Tuberculosis Epidemic*. 2004. Geneva: World Health Organization. p. 22.

[10] Including following the International Standards for TB Care.

- access donor and public funding for drugs to provide drugs at a low price or for free;
- build diagnostic capacity with widespread access (e.g. microscopy diagnostic services for regular TB, diagnostic services to identify drug-resistant TB);
- develop arrangements to monitor patients' treatment within the community.

To check their performance, programs collect figures on the number of active TB patients providers have diagnosed ("cases detected") as well as the number of patients who have completed treatment.[11] These activities could, in principle, control TB even in weak health systems. However, they are extremely challenging to implement and rarely implemented across the whole primary care system in developing countries, as we discuss in the following.

Most TB control activities are designed to be implemented through public facilities. While such an approach can be effective in settings where most people use public services, it doesn't work well when the public system reaches only a part of the population. In these settings, such strategies miss many patients. Officials are well aware of the problems with private TB care. The logic underlying their response is, in essence, substitution: private providers should refer their patients for public treatment. Many programs' fundamental engagement with the private sector consists of regulatory directives requiring private providers to report suspected cases and refer them for treatment in the public sector. The regulations' content ignores practitioners' practice settings and incentives. Rates of referral are, unsurprisingly, limited.

Beyond such regulations, private practitioners are largely left out of program efforts. With such limited interaction, it is impossible to properly plan TB control activities, let alone find collaborative arrangements to

[11] *Cases detected* are defined as the number of active TB cases which have been properly diagnosed and reported to the program; *cases successfully treated* are defined as the number of reported cases which have completed proper treatment, tested negative, and reported to the control program.

**Box 2. Complementing private provision with public health nurses**

Private practitioners provide most primary care in Japan, South Korea, and Taiwan. Private practices are poorly configured to undertake patient supervision and follow-up. All three countries deploy public health nurses to perform these activities, while the patients remain in their physician's care (Seita, 2004; Kim *et al.*, 2009; Lo *et al.*, 2011). Universal insurance coverage removes service payments as a barrier to treatment. However, Japan brought their TB epidemic under control in 1945–1960, when they were much poorer, and most people paid for care out-of-pocket. This suggests that a strategy of strategically providing support to complement private primary care is relevant for developing countries (Seita, 2004).

improve patient management by private practitioners. Program efforts to expand public diagnostic services, especially drug-susceptibility testing, face great difficulties,[12] yet very few consider tapping into private lab services.

A few countries have built sound TB control programs by complementing private primary care's characteristic weaknesses (e.g. patient supervision, tracking, reporting) (see Box 2), while some countries have established mechanisms to allow privately treated patients access to discounted drug supplies (e.g. Bangladesh, see Gospodarevskaya *et al.*, 2014). This suggests that alternative paths are possible.

Since 2002, the global health agencies leading on TB (e.g. WHO, Stop TB) have actively encouraged the integration of private practitioners into control programs via the "public–private mix" strategy.[13] A number

[12]In 2010, 8 of the 22 HBCs did not meet the benchmark of 1 microscopy center per 100,000 population. And, among the 36 countries in the combined list of 22 HBCs and 27 high MDR-TB burden countries, 20 had less than the benchmark of 1 laboratory capable of performing culture and drug susceptibility testing per 5 million population (Global Tuberculosis Control Report, WHO, 2011).

[13]Part of the Integrated Standards of TB Care and Control Guidelines.

of programs pursued such approaches with considerable success. Only a few have been scaled-up, however, and private diagnostic services are rarely tapped. We discuss these experiences and the insights which can be gleaned from them in the following.

## 3. How Can the Private Sector Contribute to TB Control?

### 3.1 *Harnessing the private sector in TB treatment*

In this section, we discuss how the private sector can be engaged for TB control. We examine the mechanics of strategies to influence private actors, and we review evidence on how they work in practice. Then, we discuss the implications.

### 3.2 *What private sector engagement needs to do to contribute to TB control?*

A range of strategies have been developed to engage the private sector. Engagement strategies have naturally sought to reach the many TB sufferers who go to private practitioners to improve their diagnosis and treatment.

Most initiatives aim to engage private practitioners to get them to more often do proper diagnosis, treatment, and reporting to countries' control programs.[14] Since programs' traditional educational activities focus on public services, many private practitioners are not even aware of recommended TB protocols (Shinde *et al.*, 2012). Others know about them but don't trust them. Hence, efforts to improve private practitioners' diagnostic, treatment, and referral practices often involve educational activities adapted for private practitioners. This can be very challenging as

---

[14]Control programs monitor their own performance by tracking the number of TB cases that are identified and properly treated/cured. So, when they work with private practitioners, they try to establish reporting relations so the cases they detect and treat can be included.

Table 1. Attitude and incentive barriers in private TB treatment.

| Practitioner increases… | Practitioner incentive issues | Patient incentive issues |
|---|---|---|
| Diagnosis via sputum microscopy | (–) Low trust of microscopy; (–) patient loss due to diagnostic referral; (–) loss of lab kick-back payments from private labs for non-recommended tests | (–) Inconvenience of travel to microscopy center multiple times, (–) waiting for test results. |
| Recommendation of correct (DOTS) therapy | (–) Low trust of program therapy guidelines; (–) aversion to displeasing patient (could lose patient/income); inconvenience of intermittent, DOT regimens; loss of gifts/incentives from chemists and pharmaceutical companies for writing antibiotic prescriptions | (–) Frequent travel to supervision site; (–) having someone watch them take medicine |
| Proper monitoring of own-administered therapy | (–) Patient supervision time-consuming; hard to follow up on defaulters (lose value of their time; and may not have support staff to follow up on defaults) | (–) Frequent travel to supervision site; (–) having someone watch them take medicine |
| Proper monitoring of therapy via referral to program provider | (–) Low trust of program services; (+) increase patient loyalty by getting them access to valued treatment; (–) lose patient/income | (+) Access to free or discounted treatment; (–) frequent travel to supervision site; (–) having someone watch them take medicine; (–) patients may be treated poorly at program centers |
| Application of proper therapy by helping patient access free/subsidized drugs from practitioner | (+) Enhanced patient loyalty by getting them access to valued drugs; (+) income from treatment (accompanying free or discounted drugs) | (+) Discounted/free drugs |
| Reporting or notification of TB cases to the national control program (active TB diagnosis patients; fully treated/cured via DOTS) | (–) Inconvenience and lost time filling out and sending forms; possible concerns about stigma and confidentiality if NTP attempts to contact private clients | N/A |

private providers are often highly fragmented and the numbers are very large.

Getting private practitioners to change their behavior and implement recommended diagnostics and treatment faces a number of challenges, relating to their incentives and attitudes as well as those of their patients. For example, many private practitioners do not trust sputum microscopy. Some prefer costly and inaccurate blood-based tests. Many practitioners do not trust control program protocols (Fochsen, 2007). Private practitioner engagement strategies must address these incentive and attitude issues to succeed. They must also address patient incentives. Most patients are significantly and negatively impacted by the frequent travel required for 2–6 months of supervised administration of medicine and also dislike being watched as they take their medicine (Pinto and Udwadia, 2010). Often, shorter travel distances can make private providers more attractive to patients, but the pay-for-service relationship can also make ensuring completion more challenging. The most common incentive and attitude barriers, both for practitioners and patients, are outlined in Table 1.

Full treatment of TB is very costly. When compelled to pay out-of-pocket, people often delay seeking care until their illness is advanced or stop partway through the six-month treatment regimen. Few countries with a high TB burden have mechanisms which fund private services. None deploy regulatory policies, such as market authorization or promotion of consolidation, which are designed to reduce drug costs in private outlets. While control programs have brought down their own drug costs through the Global Drug Facility's pooled procurement, very few national programs have used this resource to bring down drug prices for private patients. There are a few notable, mostly small-scale exceptions, where programs have provided TB drugs free-of-charge to providers. Such arrangements are useful where they exist, giving control programs leverage, as practitioners value the ability to supply their patients with drugs free or at a discount but often prefer not to refer their patients to the public sector.

In countries with social insurance, such as Estonia, Latvia, and South Korea, the package of covered services includes TB treatment and drug costs, ensuring patients do not have to pay, regardless of whether they seek care from private or public providers (Koppel *et al.*, 2008; Kim, 2006). Under social insurance, health agencies fund providers under contractual mechanisms, which gives them leverage to influence providers' behavior, including those related to TB control. In these systems, health officials and providers' representative bodies hold regular consultations, during which they can share information and come to a common understanding of challenges faced and options for resolving them. They use these platforms to discuss and coordinate responses to priority issues, such as TB. The consultations appear to be important, contributing to the adaptation of guidelines to fit the local setting, higher degrees of "buy-in" to, and compliance with guidelines and protocols.

Control program staff and other officials frequently lack both motivation and capabilities to engage the private sector. Agencies' operating routines and information systems are ill-suited to coordination, let alone collaboration, with private organizations. Nor do they have forums where issues of common interest (e.g. new diagnostic methods, the evolution of drug resistance) can be discussed among private and public stakeholders. Exacerbated by this lack of interaction, public officials and private practitioners often distrust each other, sometimes extremely. This is especially true in India. Pai and Das note this and urge public officials to move beyond a narrative of "blame," where every new TB crisis is predictably assigned to the actions of the private sector in India (Pai and Das, National Med J of India, 2013). Establishing regular forums for dialogue across the public–private divide is essential to any efforts to engage the private sector for TB control.

The practitioners who need to be engaged in TB control are often extremely heterogeneous, ranging from informal, untrained providers to lung specialists to NGO hospitals. Program strategies to engage private providers must necessarily be adapted to work with these distinct types of providers. Standardized strategy templates, successful in public sector TB control activities, will rarely work. Instead, each country's policymakers will need to develop a strategy which reflects the types of practitioners they need to engage and the context within which they operate.

Reviewing the experience with private sector engagement in TB control in developing countries reveals the constituent mechanisms of the most common strategies are financial incentives, mediating bodies, "soft contracts," and subsidized drugs. Next, we present evidence from countries which have engaged private providers in applying the strategies outlined in the PPM for TB Care and Control guidelines.[15] Then, we briefly discuss other approaches that countries have used to engage the private sector in TB control.

It is challenging to synthesize evaluation findings for complex system interventions, such as private sector engagement in TB control[16] (see Box 3) (Malmborg *et al.*, 2011). The interventions invariably contain distinct features.

A review by Malmborg and colleagues evaluated private sector engagement interventions in TB control (Malmborg *et al.*, 2011). The remainder of this discussion draws on that review.

Almost all the studies they found showed that private practitioners' engagement made a measurable contribution to both reaching more TB sufferers and improving the quality of their care. Only the designs of four studies, all involving for-profit providers, supported attribution of the results to the private sector engagement (e.g. they had control arms), and all found increased case detection.[17] No NGO engagement studies had controls, though they also documented increases in case detection. Examining the mechanisms observed across successful interventions, they found strategies consistently relied on either *paying financial incentives* or having in place *a mediating NGO* to achieve improvements. When these mechanisms were removed, the gains diminished. The four studies which supported attribution found sizable improvements in treat-

[15]WHO and the Stop TB Partnership developed this template.

[16]Simple health service delivery interventions sufficiently resemble the nature and analytics of clinical interventions that medical methodologies are reasonably useful. Complex health system interventions necessitate the use of evaluation methods which are harder to aggregate in a sound manner.

[17]For example, in New Delhi, India, they achieved a near doubling of case detection compared to the control area. In Myanmar, new smear positives rose from 46 to 85 per 100,000 between 2001 and 2004, compared to 23–36 in the same period in the control area.

**Box 3. Better practice for assessing evidence for complex system interventions**

In contrast to clinical interventions, there are no agreed criteria for systematic reviews of complex system interventions (Malmborg *et al.*, 2011). Moreover, inappropriately applying criteria for clinical interventions can generate nonsensical and misleading results. Experts generally agree that such a review should:

- specify and apply inclusion/exclusion criteria reflecting studies' soundness of analytical framework and measurement of intervention and impact variables;
- distinguish studies which have stronger grounds for attributing the impact observed to the intervention (e.g. degree of internal validity);
- establish meaningful groupings of evaluations to illuminate how the interventions' constituent mechanisms lead to the desired outputs and outcomes and identify important context characteristics that appear to interact with the intervention to generate the results (e.g. conditions of external validity).

ment success across very different health system settings (e.g. New Delhi in India, Vietnam, and Nigeria).[18] Where subsidized drugs were provided, patients' costs were markedly reduced. For example, a New Delhi intervention engaging qualified for-profit providers reduced patient costs by two-thirds. Lonnroth *et al.* conducted a similar analysis of intervention mechanisms and found that most successful engagement initiatives

[18]New Delhi, India: The PPM intervention area successful treatment rate (81%) was 69% higher than the treatment rate of private providers in the non-intervention area, and the rates were indistinguishable from those at the Government Chest Clinic. In Vietnam, treatment success increased from 49% to 62%. In Nigeria, engaged NGO providers achieved slightly higher successful treatment rates than the public sector and had fewer patients defaulting.

established relationships with providers, which they characterized as "soft contracts" exchanging drugs for performance (Lonnroth *et al.*, 2006).[19]

It is clear that engaging private providers can increase access to and quality of care. Studies also found private sector engagement can contribute to reaching the poor and reduce financial barriers. However, to do so, the strategies must include a component to reduce costs (e.g. through subsidies and/or reducing market prices). Strategies which target the providers they use also help to reach more poor people. However, few programs have engaged informal practitioners, which are so important for poor people. An initiative in Bangladesh successfully worked with informal practitioners to increase case detection and improve the quality of treatment (Hamid Salim *et al.*, 2006). Much more effort and analysis is needed to document mechanisms that target the poor (Malmborg *et al.*, 2011). Indonesia, Myanmar, and India, have experimented with contracting diagnostic services, though these experiences have yet to be evaluated.

The evidence, taken as a whole, strongly supports these approaches to private sector engagement. Some features of the interventions and the process for preparing and implementing them appear critical. Strategies typically require practitioners to adjust their behavior significantly and to do additional work related to patient follow-up and program reporting. Financial incentives and subsidized drugs are valuable mechanisms to motivate private practitioners to follow clinical, referral, and reporting guidelines. Operationalizing this relationship through "soft contracts" works well across health system settings. Reducing drug costs helps poor patients' access to treatment and complete therapy and reduces the significant financial burden TB places on patients and their families. Control programs also struggled to find mechanisms to manage their interactions with the inevitably large number of private practitioners. Most utilized an intermediary, usually a socially oriented private organization or professional body, to take on critical stewardship activities, such as accreditation,

---

[19]The authors use the phrase "soft contract" to distinguish the agreements between practitioners and program agencies or intermediaries about actors' responsibilities from "hard contracts," which are enforceable agreements under a country's contract law and commercial code.

service verification, reimbursement, and supply coordination (Uplekar review; Malmborg).

How initiatives were implemented is just as important as the strategy or intervention. Successful programs took time and made efforts to identify a "right fit" strategy. They engaged in dialogue with private stakeholders to come to a common understanding of the setting and the problems the initiative aimed to address. They often negotiated to find mutually agreeable options for resolving the problems. Strong mixed health systems' policy apparatus contains platforms for such exchanges. The policy apparatus in high-burden countries rarely do (Zafar Ullah *et al.*, 2012). Each initiative found ways to compensate for these missing platforms. They undertook sufficient public–private dialogue to adapt mutually agreeable strategies that fit the local setting and enabled their collaboration for TB control (Zafar Ullah, 2012). Practitioners' compliance is influenced by even seemingly small adjustments to the intervention, for example, altering training to reduce time away from work or easing the administrative burden associated with reporting or referral (Zafar Ullah, 2012).

Given the significance of the private sector and the evidence that programs can successfully engage it, efforts to do this are relatively limited (Lal *et al.*, 2011). This "engagement gap" is evident when the small numbers of TB cases reported by private practitioners are compared with the large numbers of people turning to them for care.[20] In the early 2010s, a number of country programs reported the proportion of cases the private sector had reported (as a proportion of the total, see Table 2). Nigeria did the best since 39% of cases reported came from the private sector, while approximately 69% of people seek care privately. Pakistan and the Philippines are more typical: Pakistan's private practitioners reported 20% of cases, while seeing approximately 86% of all healthcare patients. In the Philippines, where more than half of sick people go to private providers, only 7% of reported TB cases came from them. In India, private practitioners contribute no more than 3% of cases detected (WHO, 2011).

[20]It is challenging to avoid double counting; for example, people who may be diagnosed in the private sector and then go to the public sector, where they are re-diagnosed in order to get the drugs for free.

Table 2. The "engagement gap": Privately reported cases compared to private sector utilization.

| | Private utilization (most recent household survey) (%) | Proportion of total cases reported by private actors (%) |
|---|---|---|
| India | 80 | 2–3 |
| Nigeria | 69 | 39 |
| Pakistan | 86 | 20 |
| Philippines | 52 | 7 |

*Source*: WHO Global Tuberculosis Control Report, 2011.

Global Fund TB grants likewise reveal relatively few private sector engagement activities, even in places where private practitioners are treating many people with TB (Lal *et al.*, 2011). In the following, we discuss the factors likely constraining engagement, including the role of funding and technical agencies in influencing program design and implementation.

## 4. Sources of and Constraints to Progress

TB experts have recognized the importance of private sector engagement for many years. TB programs have made more progress in implementing private sector engagement activities than programs for child health, AIDS, or malaria. While the scale of these efforts is limited, it is useful to examine the factors which may have led to their emergence. Here, we explore the factors that appear to have encouraged the deployment of engagement strategies. Then, we examine factors that constrain programs from pursuing such strategies more broadly and from scaling up successful initiatives. We explore the functioning of the "feedback loop" that emerges from the reporting and monitoring systems for TB control at national and global levels.[21] We do this to see how the feedback loop encourages adaptation in programs which are off-track,

[21] "Feedback loop" refers to the processes for monitoring program progress against expected benchmarks, the mechanisms for assessing barriers to progress, and the decision-making mechanisms for taking corrective action.

including dealing with performance gaps that are associated with overlooking the private sector.

## 4.1 *Country-level and program factors enabling or constraining engagement*

Common features of developing countries' health systems make private sector engagement challenging. Private primary care providers (e.g. clinics, labs, and professionals) often have few connections to public agencies or policy processes (Spreng, 2011). Government agencies focus most of their attention on the facilities they administer; leaving their broader stewardship responsibilities to the side (Lagomarsino *et al.*, 2009). Private practitioners are disorganized and highly fragmented, especially the primary-care practitioners so critical for TB control. Bodies representing private providers are often weak, as are their formal relations with government agencies. These agencies rarely have accurate information about the private sector, lacking even basic information about their location and capacity (Spreng, 2011; Hozumi *et al.*, 2009). Frequently, even disease surveillance systems omit the private sector (Spreng, 2011). Nor do they have systems for sharing information about drug effectiveness or recommended protocols.

Public officials' attitudes are often a barrier to collaboration. Many are suspicious of the private sector and don't wish to share scarce resources with actors they perceive as not part of their system and not their responsibility (Hozumi, 2009). And consistently, public officials do not have the skills and agencies don't have the capabilities to take on new roles involved with engaging the private sector, including especially managing contracts and reimbursement (Hozumi *et al.*, 2009). Public officials rarely have access to information about engagement strategies, nor do they know how these strategies have been applied or if they have been successful elsewhere (Hozumi *et al.*, 2009). In addition, public officials rarely have anywhere they can turn for training and other capacity development support (England, 2008).

## 4.2 *Global-level factors enabling or constraining engagement*

As with all health programs, the technical and funding agencies supporting TB control influence program design and implementation, including private sector engagement. They are very influential in TB due to their dominance in funding. For example, in Pakistan, in 2011, there was no government funding of the control program, and in Afghanistan, Bangladesh, and Cambodia, domestic funding is 10% or less of total TB program costs. External agencies are dominant funders in all countries. The funding agencies exert influence through the organizational imperatives surrounding their projects and grants, which are their primary means of supporting countries' TB control efforts. Agencies also influence the design and implementation of TB control activities through their staff attitudes, capabilities, and behavior.

WHO and the Stop TB Partnership are the most influential technical entities.[22] They support the development and implementation of TB control in a number of ways. The Stop TB Partnership functions primarily as a platform for collaboration among global- and country-level actors working to combat TB. They disseminate technical material to country officials, often in the form of standardized guidelines. They bring country officials together to update them on practices and enable them to share experiences.

The partnership's working groups constitute an important platform for interacting with country officials. The groups hold global and regional meetings, which enable technical experts and country officials to interact around specific topics and program activities (e.g. laboratory strengthening, expanding coverage of appropriate treatment). National agencies report their anti-TB activities to the WHO. These data feed into working group discussions about performance and how to improve program performance. The working groups greatly influence program strategies (McKinsey and Company, 2008).

The DOTS Expansion[23] Working Group strives to ensure that programs are undertaking activities to reach more TB sufferers and ensure proper diagnosis and treatment. The group's yearly meeting for program managers provides an opportunity to monitor progress, share experiences, and stimulate action to alter approaches where necessary.

---

[22] Stop TB is a multi-lateral partnership organization whose founding partners include WHO, UNDP, UNICEF, and the World Bank.

[23] DOTS refers to directly observed treatment – short- course, the recommended treatment regime for TB.

The group also conducts country visits, during which they undertake technical reviews of program activities. It possesses considerable knowledge on critical operational topics and has actively supported private sector engagement. A well-organized "public–private mix" subgroup supported programs to implement learning pilots. They constructed a strong operational evidence base containing practical information on how to engage the private sector. The group used case detection targets to do "performance benchmarking"; they used such calculations to prod local officials to consider private sector engagement when rates were stagnating through public sector activities alone. WHO and Stop TB also established a mechanism to provide technical support for preparing Global Fund grants (Mookherji *et al.*, 2008). This mechanism allows country officials to tap into global technical expertise, including private sector engagement, during the development of TB grant proposals.

The Global Fund, the US government, and concessional World Bank loans are the largest sources of external funds for TB control and, thereby, the most influential funding agencies. Agencies' funds flow once they receive and approve a proposal for TB control activities for which the funds will be used. The World Bank staff manages project preparation together with government officials, and their loans flow exclusively to governments. The Global Fund allocates grants, and proposal preparation is managed by special-purpose country-level governance bodies (country coordinating mechanisms (CCMs)). Typically, expert consultants are hired, and they may tap input from WHO and Stop TB experts via the mechanism mentioned above. The procedures for preparing and approving these proposals strongly influence the content of each agency's support and, through this, influence program strategy and activity.

The World Bank's health sector strategy and staff attitudes are relatively positive toward private sector engagement (1997, 2007 strategies). However, the World Bank's only counterpart in country support is the government (by statute), and the bank's funds flow only to the government. This has proven a significant constraint on the World Bank's private sector policy support and engagement (Axelsson *et al.*, 2003; Stout and Johnston, 1999). Between 1997 and 2007, for example, only 4% of projects included activities to support policy strengthening with respect to private sector engagement (Ainsworth, 2009). The Global Fund, despite relating to a broader group of country-level stakeholders and being able to allocate funds to private actors, has likewise provided relatively little support for private sector engagement in TB control (Lal *et al.*, 2011). Relevant private sector representatives are frequently excluded from the bodies managing GF grants, which biases programs against activities to engage, for example, private practitioners or laboratories (Mookherji *et al.*, 2008).[24]

As noted above, most country officials lack knowledge and skills related to private sector engagement. A survey of public health practitioners at the global and country levels suggests that global agency staff and, likewise, public health experts involved in project and grant preparation lack this expertise (Hozumi *et al.*, 2009).[25] Even when agencies have such expertise, they struggle to break down internal silos to enable it to be applied across program areas (e.g. reproductive health expertise applied to TB programs; Bowers *et al.*, 2010).[26]

Additional issues emerge in the on-the-ground process of defining activities to be supported by external agencies. The process of preparing proposals is typically highly time- and resource-constrained. Since information about and analysis of the private sector is rarely available, it is difficult to quickly develop sound engagement activities.[27] Unlike clinical guidelines, service provider engagement strategies require substantial adaptation to the local context. While contextualization is critical for strategies to influence public or private service providers, the challenges are often greater for private providers, given their greater heterogeneity and the frequent absence of a body ready to play an intermediary role. And strategies must be adapted to be implementable by national and local health agencies that manage and supervise engagement activities. This need

---

[24]International and Domestic Non-Governmental Organizations (NGOs) are often represented and influence decision-making; but not representatives from the private practitioner and lab sector.

[25]Even developed countries' private sector engagement in health and other social services has involved considerable capacity building for public officials involved in implementation.

[26]As noted in Chapter 11, family planning experts have more knowledge of private sector engagement, but the knowledge rarely flows to other program areas (e.g. malaria, TB).

[27]Personal communication with Preker and Waty.

for extensive adaptation of engagement activities to the local context makes global guidelines for private sector engagement less directly applicable and has discouraged people from exploring them (Portero and Rubio, 2003).

Successful private sector engagement requires "soft" forms of support: on-the-job training of public officials and program staff, and other forms of organizational development activities, such as information and management systems, are critical. Support for the development and operation of public–private dialogue forums is likewise necessary. Yet, technical agencies and funders provide little such support (Mookherji *et al.*, 2008; Bowers *et al.*, 2010; Natsios, 2010). External agencies often find it easier to finance the procurement and distribution of goods and the building or upgrading of facilities.

As is evident from the programs discussed in this book, almost all country-level programs start out with a public-sector-centric design. Moreover, programs face barriers to change, especially those related to private sector engagement. Programs change this approach only in response to considerable pressure. In particular, decision-makers alter programs to include private sector engagement when they face pressure to achieve performance goals and when such change is not extremely difficult. Functioning feedback loops about program performance are central to private sector engagement in health programs. A feedback loop's functionality depends on three linked characteristics related to program management and accountability: the soundness[28] of indicators used to track performance; the soundness of the data collection and reporting process; and the degree to which performance problems generate adaptive pressure. Each program has a characteristic "feedback loop" stemming from how external agencies monitor projects and interact with country officials on performance issues, depending on the nature of the information systems and how local program managers use performance information in program design decisions. We discuss how TB programs perform, on average, on each of these:

---

[28] In this case, indicator soundness encompasses their comprehensiveness (e.g. coverage of private activity).

- Indicator soundness – moderate. Programs commonly use case detection relative to incidence to monitor performance, a relatively sound indicator.[29] Incidence estimates are derived from population surveys. Hence, survey frequency determines the indicator's usefulness as a marker of program effectiveness. Many countries have done surveys too infrequently to render much insight for decisions on program strategy. (McKinsey and Company, 2008). However, survey frequency is increasing (Macro International, 2009). For diagnostic services, programs track the number of microscopy centers and labs with drug susceptibility (WHO, 2011); these figures give little insight on program performance.
- Indicator comprehensiveness – low. Private sector diagnosis and treatment are not tracked to any meaningful degree. Countries are slowly increasing the collection of case detection data in the private sector. Programs do not track data on drug and diagnostic distribution, sales, and pricing in the private sector, despite the valuable insight it provides.[30] Nor do they collect and use such information for diagnostics.
- Soundness of the collection and reporting process – poor. The quality of the reporting process is generally poor. TB program agencies typically collect and report data, and they have latitude over which data to collect and report (e.g. leaving out private activity). This enables them to obscure problems. Program performance information from validated sources is rarely collected or analyzed. This enables control programs to maintain their public-sector focus simply by not collecting and presenting information on what is taking place in the private sector. From a disease control perspective, what is happening with respect to the evolving TB epidemic in the private sector is critically important. This is especially true with respect to tracking

[29]These measures contrast favorably with those used in IMCI (see Chapter 12) and malaria bed-net coverage (see Chapter 9), which monitor production and output data (e.g. clinics where staff have been trained to properly treat sick children and bed nets procured or distributed).

[30]Wells *et al.* (2011) illustrate the valuable insights generated from examining data on drug distribution, sales, and pricing. Pai *et al.* (2009) illustrate the insights generated from examining diagnostic distribution, sales, and pricing data.

**Box 4. Indian public officials don't welcome private reports of drug resistance**

While India's program has not developed surveillance relationships or systems with private providers, some private providers nevertheless take the initiative to report their encounters with drug-resistant strains. Recently, in India, the private Hinduja hospital reported a case of XDR-TB, an event of great public health significance. Public officials, evidently not welcoming public dissemination of news that reflected poorly on their program, have been persecuting the person and institution that made the report.

*Source*: BMJ commentary, January 2012; Akbar, *The Caravan*, 2013.

drug resistance.[31] However, agencies, whose performance is judged by how well they are controlling TB, have little incentive to gather and share this information, as it can reflect poorly on them (see Box 4). If TB surveillance expanded to track private activity, performance in many countries would look considerably worse, a fact that is undoubtedly clear to public officials in India and beyond.

Allowing control programs to collect and report the data used to assess their performance creates a profound conflict of interest that undermines the soundness of TB control program monitoring. Control program organizations have the ability and, often, the incentive to take decisions about reporting which obscure performance problems. These incentives discourage monitoring private sector activity. Private provision (including widespread mismanagement of private diagnosis and treatment) is frequently not monitored, and drug-resistant cases seen by private providers are not tracked.

- Enabling adaptation – poor to moderate. Ideally, identified performance gaps lead to changes in program strategies. In practice, TB programs alter strategies too little in general and especially when it comes to private sector engagement. External agencies help, as the

[31] In some countries, with very large numbers of patients treated in the private sector and with mismanagement rife, drug-resistant TB is emerging at an accelerated rate.

PPM subgroup's informal "performance benchmarking" illustrates, but not enough. (McKinsey and Company, 2008).

### 4.3 *Lessons*

Donors and program managers can learn from the small successes of private sector engagement in TB control, and they can learn from how limited these initiatives have been.

The development of technical guidelines to support engagement, combined with a mechanism to provide technical expertise during Global Fund grant preparation, clearly enabled positive change. And the DOTS Expansion Working Group's subgroup helped nudge program managers and policymakers with their performance benchmarking and regular meetings, which provided practitioners with fora for sharing their experiences and practical skills acquired for engagement strategy implementation.

Nevertheless, the limited engagement in countries with extensive private health services suggests inertia is keeping programs on an unproductive track, and it suggests that there is too little support and limited external or internal pressure for change. While guidance from technical agencies emphasizes engagement when needed, policymakers and program staff have little support for building the capabilities to do so. Funding agencies' operational imperatives and staffing sometimes limit the amount of pressure or even support they provide for such changes.

Program reporting and performance monitoring should encourage, or even require, altering or adding engagement strategies when needed to reach TB sufferers or provide access to critical diagnostic services. However, current monitoring systems can obscure program performance. Even where programs are seen to be performing poorly, program managers' decisions appear to experience only mild pressure to take corrective action.

## 5. Conclusions and Insights for Funders

Though well-documented strategies for engaging the private sector in TB control exist, programs deploy them to a very limited degree. Absent changes in program design and management, private sector activity will continue unchanged. Widespread mismanagement of TB patients will persist, risking turning the TB epidemic into an MDR-TB epidemic. People, especially the poor, will continue to delay and discontinue treatment; many will be impoverished by the costs. Opportunities to accelerate access to timely and reliable diagnosis and treatment will be missed. Nowhere is the potential of engagement, nor the risks of inaction, greater than in the high-burden countries with substantial private care-seeking.

In a time of falling international funding flows for health, global agencies should take action to enable programs to adapt toward more effective strategies, including engaging the private sector.

A few key points are as follows:

- External agencies can and should do more to support the actions outlined above through their many interactions with public officials and program managers.
- They should support the expansion of data collection to include the private sector and encourage the expansion of the program dashboards to include metrics which capture the private sector.
- External agencies should the support piloting and evaluation of innovative private sector engagement mechanisms, such as contracting and outsourcing, to harness private lab capacity.
- These agencies can help accelerate these developments by supporting capacity building for the range of capabilities agencies and officials need to undertake the range of challenging tasks involved with private sector engagement.

These agencies themselves are struggling to build their own capabilities to provide such support. They will likely have to address these internal constraints to be able to contribute productively to the agenda outlined here.[32]

TB programs show great potential to improve effectiveness by shifting program design and implementation toward more engagement of the private sector. Donors and technical agencies can contribute

[32]According to the DfiD Malaria Review, they are taking action to fill these gaps (DfID Comptroller and Auditor General, 2013).

through proactive support for private sector engagement. Agencies will need to make some changes to their own operations to provide such support.

## References

H. Axelsson, F. Bustreo and A. Harding. (2003). *Private Sector Participation in Child Health: A Review of World Bank Projects 1993–2002*. Health, Nutrition and Population Discussion Paper Series. Washington DC: World Bank.

G. Bowers, F. Feeley and B. Ravenholt. (2010). *A Review of USAID's Experience with the Private Sector in Health: 1968–2009*. Arlington, VA, USA. QED Group.

C. Dye and B. G. Williams. (2010). The population dynamics and control of tuberculosis. *Science* **328**(5980): 856–861.

R. England. (2008). *Informal Opinion Survey*. Washington DC, USA. Center for Global Development.

G. Fochsen, (2007) Encounters with Power: Health Care Seeking and Medical Encounters in Tuberculosis Care: Experiences from Ujjain District, India. Karolinska University Press. Sweden. ISBN 978-91-7357-447-1. Dissertation.

M. Gandy and A Zumla. (2002). The resurgence of disease: Social and historical perspectives on the 'new' tuberculosis. *Social Science and Medicine:* **55**(3): 385–396.

E. Gospodarevskaya, O. Tulloch, C. Bunga,S. Ferdous, A. Jonas, S. Islam, M. Rahman, M. A. Hussain, M. N. Haque, S. Egwaga, E. Gardiner, G. PrayGod, M. A. Islam, G. H. Mann, W. A. Wells, S. B. Squire. (214) *The International Journal of Tuberculosis and Lung Disease*, **18**(7): 810–817.

J. Grenier, L. Pinto, D. Nair, K. Steingart, D. Dowdy, A. Ramsay and M. Pai. (2012). Widespread use of serological tests for tuberculosis: Data from 22 high-burden countries. *European Respiratory Journal* **39**(2): 502–505.

M. A. Hamid Salim, M. Uplekar, P. Daru, M. Aung, E. Declercq and K. Lonnroth. (2006). Turning liabilities into resources: Informal village doctors and tuberculosis control in Bangladesh. *Bulletin of the World Health Organization* **84**(6): 479–484.

D. Hozumi, L. Frost, C. Suraratdecha, B. Pratt, Y. Sezgin, L. Reichenbach and M. Reich. (2009). The role of the private sector in health: A landscape analysis of global players' attitudes toward the private sector in health systems and policy levers that influence these attitudes. Washington DC: *Results for Development Institute*. ISBN 978-0-9788790-8-2.

H. J. Kim. (2006) Current Situation of Tuberculosis and its Control in Korea. *Journal of the Korean Medical Association.* **49**(9): 762-772.

H. J. Kim, G-H. Bai, M. K. Kang, S. J. Kim, J. K. Lee, S-I. Cho, W. J. Lew. (2009) A Public-Private Collaboration Model for Treatment Intervention to Improve Outcomes in Patients with Tuberculosis in the Private Sector. *Tuberculosis and Respiratory Diseases* **66**(5): 349–357.

A. Koppel, K. Kahur, T. Habicht, P. Saar, J. Habicht, E. Ginneken. (2008). Estonia: Health system review. World Health Organization. Regional Office for Europe. World Health Organization. Regional Office for Europe, European Observatory on Health Systems and Policies. https://iris.who.int/handle/10665/107891.

G. Lagomarsino, D. de Ferranti, A. Pablos-Mendez, S. Nachuk, S. Nishtar and S. Wibulpolprasert. (2009). Public stewardship of mixed health systems. *Lancet* **374**(9701): 1577–1578.

S. S. Lal, M. Uplekar, I. Katz, K. Lonnroth, R. Komatsu, H. M. Yesudian Dias and R. Atun. (2011). Global Fund financing of public-private mix approaches for delivery of tuberculosis care. *Tropical Medicine & International Health*, **16**(6): 685–692.

H-Y. Lo, S-L. Yang, P. Chou, J.-H. Chuang, C-Y. Chiang. Completeness and timeliness of tuberculosis notification in Taiwan. *BMC Public Health* **11**: 915.

K. Lonnroth, M. Uplekar and L. Blanc. (2006). Hard gains through soft contracts: Productive engagement of private providers in tuberculosis control. *Bulletin of the World Health Organization* **84**(11): 876–883.

Macro International. (2009). *Final Report: Global Fund Five-Year Evaluation: Study Area 3. The Impact of Collective Efforts on the Reduction of Burden of Disease of AIDS, TB and Malaria*. The Global Fund. Calverton, MD, USA.

R. Malmborg, G. Mann and S. B. Squire. (2011). A systematic assessment of the concept and practice of public-private mix for tuberculosis care and control. *International Journal for Equity in Health* **10**(1): 49.

McKinsey and Company. (2008). Independent External Evaluation of the Stop TB Partnership. Accessed on Jan 28, 2024 at: https://www.stoptb.org/sites/default/files/stop_tb_evaluation_final_report_exhibits_annexes.pdf.

S. Mookherji, L. Ryan, J. Ricca, M. Bize and T. Dye. (2008). Evaluation of the Global Fund Partner Environment, at Global and Country Levels, in Relation to Grant Performance and Health Systems Effects, Including 16 Country Studies, Macro International. Accessed on Jan 28, 2024 at: https://archive.theglobalfund.org/media/2983/archive_terg-sa2macro_report_en.pdf.

A. Natsios. (2010). *The Clash of the Counterbureaucracy and Development.* Washington DC: Center for Global Development.

M. Pai and J. Das. (2013) Management of tuberculosis in India: time for a deeper dive into quality. *The National Medical Journal of India.* **26**(2): 65–68.

M. Pai, J. Minion. H. Sohn, A. Zwerling, M. Perkins. Novel and Improved Technologies for Tuberculosis Diagnosis: Progress and Challenges. *Clinics in Chest Medicine* **30**(4): 701–716.

L. M. Pinto. and Z. F. Udwadia. (2010). Private patient perceptions about a public programme; what do private Indian tuberculosis patients really feel about directly observed treatment? *BMC Public Health* **10**: 357.

J. L. Portero and M. Rubio. (2003). Private practitioners and tuberculosis control in the Philippines: Strangers when they meet? *Tropical Medicine & International Health* **8**(4): 329–335.

A. Seita. (2004). "Think PHC, Do TB": Integration-based scale up of tuberculosis control in Japan. Harvard University. https://www.hsph.harvard.edu/wp-content/uploads/sites/114/2012/10/rp217.pdf.

C. Spreng. (2011). *Healthy Partnerships: How Governments Can Engage the Private Sector to Improve Health in Africa.* Washington DC: World Bank — International Finance Corporation.

S. Stout and T. Johnston. (1999). *Development Effectiveness in Health, Nutrition, and Population: Lessons from World Bank Experience.* Washington DC: World Bank.

Z. F. Udwadia. (2010). Tuberculosis management by private practitioners in Mumbai, India: Has anything changed in two decades? *PLoS One* **5**(8): e12023.

A. N. Z. Ullah, R. Huque, A. Husain, S. Akter, A. Islan, and J. N. Newell. (2012). Effectiveness of involving the private medical sector in the National TB Control Programme in Bangladesh: evidence from mixed methods. *BMJ Open.* **2**(6):e001534.

M. Uplekar. (2003). Involving private health care providers in delivery of TB care: Global strategy. *Tuberculosis (Edinb)* **83**(1–3): 156–164.

M. Uplekar and D. S. Shepard. (1991) Treatment of tuberculosis by private general practitioners in India. *Tuberculosis.* **72**(4): 284–290.

M. Uplekar, S. Juvekar. S. Morankar. S. Rangan. P. Nunn. (1998). *International Journal of Tuberculosis and Lung Disease.* **2**(4): 324–329.

W. A. Wells, C. F. Ge, N. Patel, T. Oh, E. Gardiner and M. E. Kimerling. (2011). Size and usage patterns of private TB drug markets in the high burden countries. *PLoS One* **6**(5): e18964.

World Health Organization (WHO). (2007). *PPM for TB Care and Control: A Tool for National Situation Assessment.* Geneva: WHO. WHO/HTM/TB/2007.391.

World Health Organization (WHO). (2011). *Global Tuberculosis Control Report.* Geneva. WHO. WHO/HTM/TB/2011.16. ISBN 978-92-4-156438-0.

# Chapter 11

# Family Planning and the Role of the Private Sector

**Ruth Berg and April L. Harding**


## Abstract

Ruth Berg and April L. Harding draw on years of experience with program design and management in this chapter on "Family Planning and the Role of the Private Sector." Like many health innovations, access to and use of contraceptives in the developing world initially lagged far behind that in wealthier countries. In the 1960s, several aid agencies and philanthropies mobilized to address this gap via support for developing countries' family planning (FP) programs. From the mid-1960s to the mid-1990s, average fertility in the developing world fell from six to three children per woman. Some estimates attribute 43% of the decline in world fertility during this period to FP programs.

Today, the local private sector contributes considerably to FP efforts in many developing countries. In addition to large numbers of unaffiliated providers and retailers, private non-profit organizations contribute to FP through a range of strategies, including social marketing, social franchising, and vouchers, as well as through more systemic mechanisms, such as insurance coverage and contracting. Private distributors, pharmacies, and retail outlets make it easy for people to pick up condoms, pills, spermicides, and other products. Many social insurance organizations cover FP services provided by public and private providers. In some countries, health agencies contract with private providers for a service package which includes FP. Private organizations perform critical stewardship activities too. Under social marketing, they often manage health communication activities and coordinate private distributors' and retailers' efforts. Under social franchising, they accredit and monitor providers. Under social insurance and voucher schemes, they verify whether services have been provided and manage reimbursements.

Whether they live in rich or poor countries, people value the ability to limit their number of children. For poor couples in developing countries, having the family size they desire can be the difference between minimal economic security and unremitting poverty. High frequency and poor spacing of births undermine the health of children and women, the more so in countries with weak health services. When couples' fail to avoid unwanted pregnancies, women may seek unsafe abortions; as a result, many die (Grimes *et al.*, 2006). At the society level, high fertility can constrain economic growth and social development (Levine, 2004; Das Gupta *et al.*, 2011). At a personal level, women's ability to manage their fertility can improve their lives by allowing them to obtain more education and better jobs.

The development of modern contraceptive products, such as condoms and pills, and services, such as IUD insertion, implants, and sterilization, made it relatively easy, in principle, for people to have the number of children they desire. The availability of contraception and new attitudes about family size combined with economic growth and education to bring about the "demographic transition" in which fertility and family size declined rapidly in high- and middle-income countries around the world between 1920 and 1980 (Das Gupta *et al.*, 2011). Like many health innovations, access to and use of contraceptives in the developing world initially lagged far behind that in wealthier countries. In the 1960s, several aid agencies and philanthropies mobilized to address this gap via support for developing countries' family planning (FP) programs. From the mid-1960s to the mid-1990s, average fertility in the developing world fell from six to three children per woman. Some estimates attribute 43% of the decline in world fertility during this period to FP programs (Bongaarts, 1995; Robinson and Ross, 2007; Das Gupta *et al.*, 2011).

Today, the local private sector contributes considerably to FP efforts in many developing countries. In addition to large numbers of unaffiliated providers and retailers, private non-profit organizations contribute to FP under a range of strategies, including social marketing, social franchising, and vouchers, as well as more systemic mechanisms such as insurance coverage and contracting. Private distributors, pharmacies, and retail outlets make it easy for people to pick up condoms, pills, spermicides, and other products. Many social insurance organizations cover FP services provided by public and private providers. In some countries, health agencies contract with private providers for a service package which includes FP. Private organizations perform critical stewardship activities too. Under social marketing, they often manage health communication activities and coordinate private distributors' and retailers' efforts. Under social franchising, they accredit and monitor providers. Under social insurance and voucher schemes, they verify whether services have been provided and manage reimbursements.

Such pluralism of strategies and implementing organizations was uncommon in early FP programs. Many programs sought to increase contraceptive use mainly through public supply chains and provider networks, even in countries in which public services had limited capability and reached only part of the population. Over time, the limitations of this approach became clear, and programs added strategies to reach underserved people through private outlets and providers. Beyond expanding coverage, the private sector came to be recognized as important for stretching program dollars and eventually for sustaining coverage as demand grew and donor support diminished.

While many programs have been successful, in a number of countries, mostly in Sub-Saharan Africa, large numbers of people don't yet understand contraceptive methods and don't have access to FP products and services. Many women want to limit childbearing and yet are not using contraception. Global efforts such as FP2030 seek to facilitate a coordinated approach to measuring and supporting efforts to address this. The better these efforts reflect lessons from past programs, including those related to engaging the private sector, the more successful they will be. This chapter reviews the private sector engagement experiences aimed at achieving FP goals to gain insight into how and when engagement can contribute to program objectives. Other health programs have only begun experimenting with private sector engagement, and many insights from the long and rich experience within FP programs are useful for them as well.

These experiences make it clear that donor practices matter. Certain features of aid agencies' behavior encouraged integration of private sector capacities; some features made it easy to overlook opportunities to engage the private sector. This chapter examines these linkages and points to those which may be most relevant for donors who wish to support private sector engagement in FP and other health programs where appropriate.

## 1. A Short History of Family Planning Programs

In rich and poor countries, understanding and use of contraceptive products and services lagged behind their development. Conservative social attitudes about women's roles and about sexuality and reproduction slowed uptake. Even where knowledge spread, attitudes changed, and the desire to manage fertility grew, healthcare providers' and public officials' ignorance and conservatism constrained access to contraceptive products and services. Public services and social insurance were slow to add FP coverage.

Organized efforts within wealthy nations to promote FP started in the 1920s and 1930s. Advocates linked contraceptive access to women's ability to control their reproductive lives and to help women avoid abortions. Non-governmental organizations (NGOs), such as the American Birth Control League, the UK's National Birth Control Council, and France's Maternité Heureuse (Happy Motherhood), emerged and worked to educate people about contraception. They educated health professionals, often collaborating with professional associations and education institutions. They worked to remove regulations blocking the advertising, distribution, and retail of contraceptives. Advocacy organizations prodded policymakers to extend public services to include FP. Slowly, public and private providers expanded the provision of FP counseling and services.

In insurance-based systems, legislators bowed to pressure and added FP to service packages provided through public and private providers. Equally importantly, they removed regulations blocking the distribution of contraceptives. Private pharmacies and the commercial distribution systems on which they relied increased their offer of condoms, pills, and spermicides as demand grew.[1]

Despite such changes, people's access to services often grew slowly; practitioners were slow to change and slow to provide FP advice and services. NGOs engaged in advocacy and education often transform into or establish social enterprises[2] to fill gaps in availability left by traditional health services and distribution systems. Relying on a mix of fees, private donations, and public funds, they used cross-subsidy and price discrimination to ensure fees didn't discourage poor people from accessing contraception (Glass, 1966). As FP acceptance grew, some social enterprises established relationships with traditional health services, eventually entering into public and insurance contracts for their services (e.g. Marie Stopes in the UK, Planned Parenthood in the US). These patchwork funding and provision arrangements evolved to provide broad coverage across wealthy nations.

Developing countries initiated their FP programs later, often with considerable external support. The Ford and Rockefeller Foundations started working to foment and support FP programs in developing countries in the 1950s and 1960s (Seltzer, 2002. Large-scale funding from bilateral agencies, especially USAID and SIDA, started shortly after, followed by multilateral agencies such as UNFPA and the World Bank in the late 1960s and early 1970s (Robinson and Ross, 2007). Many of these organizations were motivated by concerns about population growth and also supported FP as a mechanism to promote development (Seltzer, 2002 Robinson and Ross, 2007).

[1]With very few exceptions, in wealthy countries, drugs and other medical consumables are distributed by private companies, and pharmacies are privately operated.

[2]See Glossary: Social enterprise.

In most countries, donors worked with government agencies to develop and implement projects that supported the countries' programs.[3] In several countries, mostly in Latin America, local NGOs played an influential role in program formulation and implementation, and they often channeled considerable donor funds for FP activities.

## 2. Family Planning Programs in Developing Countries

Though FP programs varied across countries, they had common elements: activities to extend contraceptive services and products and communication efforts to generate demand (Tsui, 1996; Seltzer, 2002).[4]

Most program efforts focused on expanding the supply of products and services (Seltzer, 2002). Public sector administration and clinic-based provision of services and products constituted the core of many programs. FP programs implemented activities to make services and supplies available through clinics and the staff who worked there. And programs tried to make condoms, pills, and other products available.

Before programs commenced operation in developing countries, people typically knew little about contraception, especially people from disadvantaged groups, such as the poor, less educated, and rural inhabitants. Cultural attitudes, especially women's low status and influence, discouraged their use of FP services in many countries. Women commonly had unfounded fears about side effects and risks. Programs often implemented communication activities to educate people about contraception and its benefits.[5] In addition to educating the public, programs sought to educate and change the attitudes of health practitioners. Doctors and other health workers often didn't understand and even opposed the use of contraceptive products and services, discouraging women from using them. Some promulgated misinformation about side effects and risks.

Programs recruited and trained staff to provide clinical and counseling services within public clinics. FP programs also worked to get clinic staff

---

[3] See Glossary for distinction between a health program and a health project.

[4] Policy advocacy was another important element.

[5] The public health literature refers to these as *behavior change communication (BCC)*.

to undertake outreach activities (e.g. to go out into communities, educate people about contraception, distribute supplies, and refer them to clinics for services).

Some donor projects provided considerable technical support, including resident advisors, to the government agencies managing these efforts. Moreover, they provided contraceptive products, sometimes most or all of the products distributed by a national program. Early on, a few contraceptive manufacturers were located in developing countries. Projects procured products externally, either globally or sometimes within the aid-giving country.[6] They also organized product shipment to the aid-receiving country, similar to the mechanisms deployed for mosquito nets. Implementing these activities was difficult and slow. Some governments established separate oversight boards; many established separate service networks to accelerate implementation (Seltzer, 2002).

## 3. How Family Planning Programs Came to Engage the Private Sector

### 3.1 *The early days (1960s–early 90s)*

#### 3.1.1 *Strategies for products*

While many programs relied heavily on public-sector platforms to implement FP activities, a few utilized private-sector supply chains from the outset. Colombia's NGO-led FP initiative sought to use the commercial distribution network, which supplied pharmacies throughout the country.[7] They worked to get more affordable products flowing through these channels. Early on, they bulk-purchased condoms and oral contraceptives from international manufacturers and then sold these at concessionary prices to commercial distributors. Commercial distributors and pharmacies did the work of transport, distribution, and

---

[6]For example, "Buy America" regulations required substantial portions of USAID funding be used to purchase supplies and services from US companies.

[7]Sensitivity to social institutions in some regions (e.g. the Catholic Church in Latin America and the Philippines) motivated governments to give NGOs strong roles in FP programs.

retail. They directly distributed low-priced contraceptives in rural and slum areas through their own networks (Seltzer and Gomez, 1998). Most demand promotion consisted of print advertising and interpersonal promotion by community-based workers. Over time, they expanded the range of products they procured and bought more from local manufacturers (Seltzer and Gomez, 1998). Their success in making a wide range of contraceptives (pills, condoms, vaginal methods, and injectables) widely available at moderate prices in pharmacies throughout the country contributed to Colombia's notable increases in contraceptive prevalence and fertility declines in the 1970s and 1980s (Seltzer and Gomez, 1998). Commercial channels evolved under a regulated markup regime to make moderately priced products available in much of Brazil as well (Cromer *et al.*, 2004).[8] While this platform contributed to Brazilians' rapid increase in contraceptive use in the 1970s and 1980s, mechanisms to make contraceptives available to the poor were weak. As a result, access for low-income people increased more slowly, as did their use of contraceptives.

Such approaches were the exception, however. Early on, most programs sought to distribute contraceptive products through public clinics and relied on public systems to distribute the products. Some programs, such as India's and Kenya's, struggled for years to energize sclerotic public supply chains to make products reliably and widely available. At the same time, developing commercial distribution systems made simple consumer products widely available. Indeed, by the mid-1960s, drugstores and other retail outlets were increasingly stocking condoms and other simple contraceptive products in many of these countries. They were concentrated in urban areas, though, and prices were often high, limiting their contribution to contraceptive coverage (Harvey, 1999). "Social marketing," perhaps the best known private-sector engagement strategy, emerged in the mid-1960s to create an additional product delivery channel by tapping into this capacity.

[8]They had several manufacturers of condoms and pills who paid no royalties, hundreds of distributors, and thousands of retail pharmacies selling moderately priced contraceptives through 1992; when price regulations were abolished in 1992, market prices for contraceptives tripled.

**Traditional social marketing** strategies involve activities to distribute and promote the use of simple health products, where: distribution is outsourced to private distributors and retailers who are reimbursed via product fees; health communication based on commercial marketing techniques is deployed; and, typically, management of both sets of activities is professionalized by, for example, outsourcing management or allocating management to an autonomous agency.

### 3.1.2 *A new approach to product distribution*

Traditional social marketing (TSM) differed from previous public distribution efforts in three ways. First, distribution activities were "outsourced" to existing private distributors and retailers. Rather than paying for these services, programs set prices for the products; in this way, wholesalers', distributors', and retailers' margins motivated them to stock and sell the products (Harvey, 1999) just as they did for their commercial activities.[9] The aim was to distribute contraceptives to as many people as possible, including the poor. Hence, programs set prices as low as possible, generating revenue to cover part of the distribution and marketing activities' costs (Armand, 2003).[10]

TSM's second key component was marketing. Programs' early health communication efforts were often simplistic, reflecting little understanding of or distinctions among, potential users' attitudes toward contraception. TSM complemented its alternative distribution strategy with an innovative communication approach. Wealthy countries' public health programs had achieved remarkable improvements in diet, drug use, and smoking behaviors by using sophisticated marketing tools from the advertising industry in what came to be called "social marketing".[11] TSM

[9]Peter King, an MIT professor working in India with the Ford Foundation, is credited with coming up with the concept in 1964 (Harvey, 1999; Robinson and Ross, 2007).

[10]As most TSM initiatives were distributing donated products, covering the products' costs was unnecessary.

[11]Commercial *marketing* techniques were used to change people's behavior for *social* goals — hence *social marketing*.

**Box 1. Bangladesh's successful shift from communication to marketing**

In the early phase (1965–1980) of Bangladesh's FP efforts, the program used traditional communication approaches and strategies which disseminated the generic message "a small family is a happy family." It achieved little. In 1981, the program brought in marketing experts to assess the problem. They studied potential users as consumers, and their research revealed that men's attitudes were the main constraint on contraceptive use. A mass media campaign was implemented, targeted to influence male audiences. Within a year, men's attitudes shifted significantly, and contraceptive use rose. *Source*: Reducing Fertility in Bangladesh. Case 13 in Levine (2004).

borrowed and adapted these tools to "sell" contraceptives and, indirectly, FP. These tools were more strategic than earlier communication efforts. They involved analyzing people's attitudes and behaviors, identifying groups ("market segments") which were least using contraceptives, and identifying the beliefs or misunderstandings that were keeping them from doing so (see Box 1). Social marketing communication deployed messages tailored to target groups and local beliefs. They complemented traditional messages on the desirability of small families and birth spacing with advertising to stimulate demand for products. Most initiatives sought to increase demand for contraception by increasing demand for branded products. That is, they developed brands for the products they distributed and advertised them, focusing on the brand's quality and attractiveness, just as commercial product advertisements do.[12] TSM's final distinguishing feature was the professionalization of management, often accomplished through "outsourcing."[13] Weak management of distribution and health communication activities had contributed to early disappointments. Under TSM, programs typically allocated responsibility for communication activities to the private organizations managing

[12] Strategies promoting branded products also involve repackaging the products.

[13] Commonly, an INGO was funded by a donor to do these tasks.

distribution activities.[14] These independent organizations identified capable private distributors and retailers interested in distributing program products.[15] They consulted potential distributors and retailers to better understand their capabilities and to ascertain the conditions under which they might be willing to distribute program products. They developed mutually agreeable affiliation relationships. They delivered promised products and fulfilled other commitments to affiliated distributors and retailers. They managed marketing activities, adapting them based on insights from sales data. They took steps to adjust their agreements (e.g. markups and reporting) where necessary (Harvey, 1999). Both communication and distribution benefited enormously from more flexible, responsive, and professional management.

*Results and what was learned*: TSM's capacity to achieve widespread national distribution through private distributors and retail shops was evident. In many countries, strong management and effective communication strategies combined with the vitality of private distribution and retail networks accelerated the distribution and use of program condoms. Several reviews confirmed that this approach was more efficient and often cost-effective than public distribution (Meadley *et al.*, 2003; Bishai and Madhavan, 2010).[16] Donors appreciated that TSM's typical organizational setup somewhat insulated their activities from public agencies' frequent operational problems.

Beyond the effectiveness of the TSM "package," the experience revealed that programs could use pricing and markups to tap into the vitality of private distribution and retail networks for distributing priority health products. TSM's successes underscored the importance of adding delivery channels to increase availability and expand access. Communication initiatives managed by private entities performed better than those managed by government agencies. The TSM experience demonstrated how to apply commercial marketing techniques to health behavior changes.

---

[14]This first evolution of social marketing approaches is often referred to as the "distribution model," or, as most social marketing organizations were NGOs, the "NGO model".

[15]Some programs did not outsource distribution and promotion to retailers.

[16]Effectiveness and cost analysis were primarily based on total sales as against total program costs — often expressed as a cost per "couple year of protection." See Meadley *et al.* (pp. 17–19) for an overview of the data limitations and methodological challenges.

It showed also that, for behaviors linked to commodities, product advertising could be effectively used to change health behavior. Other health programs have applied these insights to many other behaviors and products (e.g. oral rehydration solution, breastfeeding, hygiene, and nutrition). Social marketing organizations often performed important stewardship-related activities, including assessing, consulting, and negotiating with private organizations, as well as monitoring their activities. These efforts were essential to the strategies' effectiveness.

### 3.1.3 *Strategies for services*

Contraceptive *services* are also essential elements of FP programs. As with product distribution, a few early programs opted to involve the private sector in public FP activities from the outset. When Taiwan and South Korea launched their programs in the 1950s and 1960s, respectively, most people used private services and paid out-of-pocket. Program managers aspired to rapidly increase coverage of FP services. Consultations with private practitioners' associations helped convince them that private services could be a platform for rapidly expanding coverage. They decided to focus program efforts on communication activities and target subsidies for services for low-income people. They hoped their communication efforts would persuade better-off people to seek services while covering their own costs. To target program funds at low-income people, they gave them vouchers so that they could obtain FP services (e.g. sterilization and IUD insertion) from private providers. Community health workers distributed vouchers to low-income people, who used the vouchers to obtain services without payment from a clinic of their choice. These initiatives rapidly expanded access to and uptake of services and contributed to their rapid increases in contraceptive prevalence (Robey, 1987). By targeting scarce resources, they were able to contain program costs within the parameters of available public funding.

In a number of countries, local NGOs, often affiliates of the International Planned Parenthood Federation, played important roles in administration and service provision; in such programs, private providers were sometimes contracted to fill gaps in service provision. This was demonstrably the case in Colombia, Ecuador, and Chile, where large numbers of private providers were contracted to provide FP services (Seltzer, 2002). In Bangladesh, approximately 20% of FP clients were served by contracted NGOs (Levine, 2004).

Most programs aimed to expand FP services through public service networks. This was not easy. They faced serious problems in supervising and motivating staff to deliver FP services in the context of general service delivery. Management and supervision problems were common. Public sector human resource management arrangements made it difficult to motivate staff to provide FP services; indeed, in some countries, even motivating staff to come to work regularly was difficult. Public workers were often busy with existing duties and not eager to take on additional FP-related tasks, especially those that necessitated going out into communities. The nature of public administration, with its emphasis on accountability for inputs and following rules for the use of funds or hiring staff, made it hard to generate motivation or accountability for expansions in FP coverage.[17] Problems with service access and use persisted through years of program efforts. Programs found it especially challenging to get public health workers to go out into communities, provide information, contraceptive products, and referrals to clinics for services. And these services were critical for program effectiveness. Economic recessions, reduced public expenditures, and distortionary political responses (e.g. informal retrenchment and reduction in non-wage expenditure) throughout the 1980s and early 1990s undermined public services, which made them an even more problematic platform for expanding the coverage of FP services.

The problems related not only to getting public providers to offer services; often people didn't want them even when they were available. Potential users of contraceptives often found public services unresponsive, and this made people use them less (Seltzer, 2002). Women especially chose private clinics over public ones because of the convenient hours of service and perceived quality, including more privacy and respectful treatment (Levine, 2004). Young and unmarried people, who are often not "supposed" to be sexually active, preferred private providers

[17]Targets and bonuses were sometimes used to focus public-sector staff on FP service provision (e.g. the Philippines).

for their privacy and confidentiality. Private services were more responsive to clients and delivered higher consumer quality and client satisfaction compared to public services; as a result, they generated higher uptake and continuation of contraception.

Public agencies generally avoided contracting, and when they did pursue it, they limited it to contracting outreach work, where health workers go out into communities to educate people about contraception, distribute supplies, and make referrals. While contracting for outreach services was successful in some settings, government agencies often struggled with contract management.

### 3.2 *Moving toward sustainability and integration*

Throughout the 1970s and 1980s, programs adapted and deployed strategies to achieve notable increases in use of FP products and services (Robinson and Ross, 2007; Seltzer, 2002). Demand for FP was growing, and programs were not able to meet it. The 1980s brought pressures to broaden programs' objectives, in particular, to reduce dependence on publicly provided contraceptives and also on donor assistance.[18]

Early FP efforts paid little attention to either operational or financial sustainability[19]; donor funding was relatively plentiful and stable. This changed, as assistance for FP stagnated in the late-1970s and subsequently declined.[20] In addition, many aid recipients' economies had grown stronger. Program managers and donors grew more interested in increasing *local contributions to the cost* of contraceptives. Donors desired that governments would adequately fund contraceptive products. However, in many countries, it was clear that increasing private payments would be necessary to sustain, let alone increase, coverage.

---

[18]Programs were also encouraged to broaden their focus from FP to reproductive health.

[19]For example, USAID projects through 1990 devoted little attention to sustainability, with only 3% of project documents explicitly mentioning sustainability. This increased to 15% after 1994 (Esselman, 1994).

[20]More than 2% of development assistance funds flowed toward FP between 1960 and 1976, but the decline was rapid, and by the 1980s, FP funding averaged only 1.3% of development assistance.

As noted, substantial portions of contraceptive supplies in a number of countries were provided by projects. Sharp declines in contraceptive availability due to declines or delays in donor support revealed the risks of such dependence. When Bangladesh's FP assistance declined in the late 1980s, for example, market prices for condoms doubled, while contraceptive use fell by 30% between 1989 and 1990 (Ciszewski and Harvey, 1994). Hence, program managers and donors prioritized increasing *alternative contraceptive supplies*.

Program managers scrutinized their contraceptive coverage strategies, seeking to understand their influence on operational and financial sustainability.[21] TSM initiatives' had resolved management and distribution problems. However, most relied on aid agencies for supplies and operational funding and were managed by donor-funded organizations; their coverage achievements were tenuous. In addition, their pricing, product, promotion, and distribution strategies often constrained the development of alternative supply sources.

*Pricing formulas and product branding*: Most TSM initiatives promoted and distributed highly subsidized and undifferentiated products. The large subsidies ensured the poor could afford the products, but they were heavily utilized by higher-income people too. Unless they could find a way to increase higher-income people's payments for their contraceptives and thereby target program subsidies to lower-income people, programs could achieve little financial sustainability in terms of coverage.

Most TSM initiatives had increased contraceptive demand by skillfully promoting brands. This strategy links people's demands for a specific brand rather than the product. Companies use brand marketing to create loyalty to their products and make it hard for potential competitors to attract their customers. Unfortunately, it has the same effect in health product markets, thereby discouraging the entry and growth of other suppliers. Program managers recognized that alternative promotion and pricing strategies would be necessary to enable and encourage the growth of alternative contraceptive supplies (Bulatao, 2002).

---

[21] Operational sustainability refers to the capacity of local actors to ensure the delivery of products and services; financial sustainability refers to the capacity of locally available resources to sustain the desired level of activity.

### 3.2.1 *Striving to harness markets for product delivery*

In the 1990s, programs explored new approaches to contraceptive coverage, aiming for greater operational and financial sustainability. Similar to Colombia's early efforts, programs experimented with alternative pricing and procurement strategies to make affordable products available; they experimented with approaches to encourage private businesses to expand their import, production, distribution, and retail activities. Programs studied the environment in different markets; they consulted business people to learn which elements of the market environment were most important for investment and other decisions related to increasing commercial activity. Some features of the enabling environment were outside program influence: urbanization, income, and the general business environment (e.g. business registration, access to finance, and labor market constraints). Programs could influence some elements of the enabling environment, such as taxes and tariffs on contraceptive products. Program advocacy led Brazil to abolish taxes on all commercial activities related to condoms in 1997. Mediated by their well-developed commercial distribution and pharmacy network, the decline in condom prices helped increase access to contraceptive products. Others advocated removing restrictions on product advertising, which limited demand promotion efforts. Some worked to stimulate competition to reduce prices. For example, some programs funded product testing and pushed for the removal of regulatory barriers to reduce the cost for businesses to bring new products to market, especially low-cost products. In some instances, programs worked out cooperative agreements with commercial suppliers, paying for advertising to generate enough demand to justify companies' expansion.

The most important factor programs could influence was often the suppressive effect of highly subsidized program-distributed contraceptives as well as their brand-linked contraceptive marketing activities.

**Growing commercial delivery** strategies are market system interventions aimed at expanding private activity in priority health markets. Health communication based on commercial marketing techniques is deployed to increase demand, and, typically, a body constituted of public officials and representatives of relevant private stakeholders monitors market evolution.

Programs made considerable efforts to develop alternative approaches without undermining coverage for low-income people. To get better-off people to pay for contraception, programs tested mechanisms to target subsidies on poorer people through "market segmentation." Poor people were to get free contraceptives from public outlets, while higher-income people would pay a range of prices and buy their contraceptives from both public and private outlets. Getting higher-income people to pay for contraceptives was essential to increasing financial sustainability of contraceptive coverage. Moreover, reducing untargeted subsidies and the uncertainty generated by program-distributed contraceptive supplies would encourage private businesses to expand their production, distribution, and retail activities.[22] Programs also experimented with alternative approaches to demand generation, most notably generic demand generation.[23]

Growing commercial delivery (GCD) strategies are market system interventions which work by generating changes in the operation of markets. To bring about these changes, programs monitor the relevant market, track responses to policy actions to better understand the forces influencing market behavior, and ascertain the need for further actions. Over time, they "enact iterative and 'bespoke' policy and program activities" to shift market operations in the desired direction. Compared to traditional strategies (e.g. public distribution or TSM), market-shifting approaches take longer to unfold, and benefits are generated more indirectly. Donor-supported programs have pursued such strategies relatively rarely.[24]

GCD strategies were deployed in pursuit of distinct objectives from previous efforts, notably operational and financial sustainability. And they were mostly deployed in middle- rather than low-income countries. These strategies work partly or wholly through altering the market environment

---

[22] Such strategies frequently included collaboration with commercial manufacturers and are often referred to as the "manufacturers' model" of contraceptive social marketing (Armand, 2003).

[23] Generic demand creation activities promote the use of a class of products (e.g. condoms) rather than a branded product. Colombia utilized generic demand creation in their FP program.

[24] USAID was the largest donor for most FP programs. They were compelled to provide programs in-kind supplies rather than to fund purchases from local or regional suppliers.

and engendering private organizations' responses. Hence, they are inherently difficult to assess. Nevertheless, compared to direct distribution strategies, evidence suggests some programs were able to increase the sustainability of contraceptive coverage through applying GCD approaches. They did so by increasing local manufacturing, distribution, and retail, as well as by increasing local contributions to contraceptive costs (Seltzer and Gomez, 1998). Furthermore, some programs were able to craft their approach to deploy these strategies without creating barriers for low-income people (Seltzer and Gomez, 1998).

Implementing these strategies required distinct capabilities on the part of program managers. Monitoring systems which capture how the relevant market or markets are evolving are essential. Sustained dialogue with private sector stakeholders is necessary to identify key features of the market environment which limit commercial activity as well as potential areas for collaboration. Some strategies required public and private stakeholders to come to a common understanding about what was happening in the relevant markets, to identify gaps and areas of mutual interest, and to formulate agreements about who would do what to fill those gaps (Cromer *et al.*, 2004).[25] Very often, for GCD associated with FP products, both had to be built from scratch (Cromer *et al.*, 2004). As with other strategies, success with GCD initiatives often involved conscious efforts to fill these "stewardship gaps."

### 3.2.2 *New approaches to services*

Programs' struggles to increase access to FP services, as well as concerns about dependence and sustainability, compelled reconsideration of strategies toward the delivery of FP services and products. Sometimes, the resulting course changes included efforts to engage the private sector (Cromer *et al.*, 2004).

Programs directly applied two engagement strategies to make services available: *vouchers* and *social franchising*. One appealing characteristic

[25] While forums for communication among public and private stakeholders are common in wealthy countries' mixed health systems, they were rare in developing countries (Palmer, 2006).

of vouchers was the potential to provide support to particular users who experienced particular barriers (e.g. the poor and stigmatized groups). Program managers also wished to explore whether targeting mechanisms could contribute to the sustainability of coverage, even where donor funds might be declining. Some countries also sought to increase coverage and sustainability through public contracting and social insurance.

Some programs had involved NGOs in service delivery from the beginning. Like TSM distribution, contracted private providers were often more efficient than the public ones. Donors frequently contracted service provider organizations directly, as they did TSM management organizations. However, donor-funded FP contracting, like all donor-funded services, may collapse when aid funds diminish (Palmer, 2006). In addition, dependence was a serious concern across countries where contracted NGOs provided substantial FP services in the face of declining FP aid.

Programs worked hard to "localize" these NGOs in hopes of sustaining their services. The NGOs pursued domestic funding via contracting by public agencies or social insurers. In a few countries with financing mechanisms supporting service purchasing from independent providers (e.g. Colombia, Bolivia, and the Philippines), NGOs transitioned to a sustainable footing partly by obtaining contracts. NGO providers sought to increase local funding in other ways. They pursued local donations; they charged higher-income patients for services; and they raised income by selling more-demanded products and services, such as condoms, to subsidize others (often, clinical contraceptive services). Some entities succeeded in generating enough revenue from richer patients and more-demanded services to stabilize their delivery of priority FP services under this "social enterprise" business model. Colombia's ProFamilia illustrates such a transition.

*Contracting*: In the 1980s and 1990s, programs shifted service strategies to support broader basic service packages and away from FP alone.[26] In the broader context of primary care service provision, health workers often focus their time and attention on curative services; little time and

[26]This reflects the shift within the FP global community from FP to reproductive health, which, among other things, emphasized the importance of integrated services and also reflects the emphasis on integrated primary care outlined in the 1978 Alma Ata Declaration.

**Contracting** strategies involve activities to expand or sustain access to priority health services through local funding agencies contracting for services.

**Insurance coverage and contracting** strategies involve activities to expand or sustain access to priority health services and products through social insurance coverage of services.

attention is given to preventive services, especially those which require workers to go out into the community.[27] These frontline incentive problems are hard to address within public systems. Contracting mechanisms, in contrast, can be structured to link funding to coverage indicators, including FP coverage. Cambodia, Bangladesh, and Afghanistan contracted NGO providers for primary care service packages and included FP performance indicators; this contributed to achieving higher coverage rates than those achieved via public delivery.

*Insurance coverage and contracts*: Where insurance mechanisms exist, they can be used to expand access to FP services via private providers. However, insurance schemes can poorly cover FP; where donor-funded programs operated, schemes could more easily omit coverage. In a few instances, programs' advocacy efforts persuaded employers and social insurance organizations to expand FP coverage. While the populations covered were often small, the coverage usually continued after donor support ended (Skibiak, 1991).

Beyond the boundaries of FP programs, reforms establishing social insurance create an opportunity to improve access to services, including FP. Estonia was able to do this in the mid-1990s. They used the leverage of their new contracting instruments, combined with people's ability to choose their providers, to expand the use of contraception and reduce abortion. Observers note that education for the newly private doctors

[27]Recall that FP services demand more community outreach and that patients'/users' motivation to seek services is much greater for curative than preventative services.

> **Voucher** strategies encompass mechanisms which allocate subsidies to user-selected providers to expand the provision of priority services or products; typically, a voucher administration organization is involved. Vouchers are often implemented as part of a growing commercial delivery strategy.

emphasized FP, and this played an important role in their expansion of FP services. Similarly, when Colombia established a social insurance system in the mid-1990s, the service packages included FP.[28] Initially, the government struggled to verify whether insurers were providing adequate coverage; as regulatory capacity improved, use of services expanded, even as FP aid sharply declined (Seltzer and Gomez, 1998). Experience with social insurance confirms that contracting and provider choice are mechanisms which can be deployed to expand access to FP. Several factors mediate the effect, including providers' knowledge, monitoring of insurers' performance with respect to coverage, incentives in reimbursement contracts, and co-payments permitted for services.

Throughout the 1990s, private provision was growing — responding to growing demand and, in many countries, deteriorating public spending and services. In the early 2000s, FP programs started experimenting with strategies to harness these providers as a means to expand coverage of FP services. They experimented with vouchers, which South Korea and Taiwan had used in the 1950s and 1960s to rapidly expand FP services via private providers. They also experimented with social franchising and other mechanisms to network private providers to increase the provision of good-quality FP services.

*Vouchers*: Despite Taiwan's and South Korea's successes in the 1950s and 1960s, in the ensuing years, neither FP nor other programs manifested much interest in targeting or vouchers. This changed in the 2000s. Health officials increasingly recognized the extent of private provision, including the widespread use of private providers by poor people with little money to spare. Developed and developing country governments were deploying

[28] Insurance coverage for poor people is publicly funded.

**Box 2. Quality assurance is critical for contraceptive services**

FP products and services vary greatly in terms of their complexity. The complexity influences potential users' ability to assess quality and has important implications for potential harm. Condoms are somewhat easier to judge the quality of (for users); and the risk of harm from a poor-quality condom is a small increase in the likelihood of an unplanned pregnancy or contraction of an STD. Insertion of an intra-uterine contraceptive device and sterilization are both procedures with greater potential harm from poor practices. In the case of condoms, the market, even left to its own devices, may well do much more good than harm by increasing access to and use of contraceptives by people who wish to use them. However, there are much greater dangers from poor-quality assurance with private contraceptive services. This danger makes it critical that effective interventions to ensure the quality of private services are identified and implemented.

choice mechanisms, where public funds were allocated to providers based on users' selections in health and other social services. Moreover, aid was falling, giving targeting mechanisms greater appeal. FP programs' rediscovery of vouchers may have been inevitable.

In many countries, poor women utilize fewer FP and reproductive health services. Even where such services are, in principle, available in public clinics, many are not using them. Bangladesh, China, Kenya, India, Indonesia, Nicaragua, and Uganda deployed vouchers as a means to target subsidies for the poor and other underserved groups. While strategies vary, they all distribute vouchers to cover a portion of service costs for low-income women. And they all empanel providers which meet quality standards. Providers are reimbursed for seeing voucher-bearing patients. Vouchers allow recipients to choose their provider while still accessing financial support. Private services are widespread in these countries, and people often prefer to obtain services from private providers. Hence, the programs included private providers in the accredited supply networks to increase the likelihood that services would be available and that people would seek care.

These initiatives succeeded in expanding access and utilization, especially for poor and marginalized people (Bellows *et al.*, 2011). Some successfully used their leverage to motivate quality improvements among providers (Bellows *et al.*, 2011). By targeting program funding, vouchers can increase equity and coverage sustainability. Vouchers are deployed for the decentralized, choice-based provision of social services throughout the world and, at a sufficiently large scale, can be cost-effective compared to alternative mechanisms. Decentralized, choice-based delivery of health services in national systems is typically done in an integrated fashion (e.g. socially funded service packages) rather than for specific services. Hence, their cost-effectiveness for health service delivery on a national scale is unknown.[29]

While the mechanisms can work, they can be used for a limited range of services and products (e.g. products or services with fixed or predictable costs). In addition, they rely on the availability of a well-run organization to undertake the management of voucher distribution, verification, and reimbursement. As few developing countries have reliable accreditation or licensing systems for healthcare providers, they must find an alternative arrangement to assess provider quality. Furthermore, recent voucher initiatives have been implemented with donor support. They will have to develop links to domestic financing to sustain their benefits.

*Social franchising*: As noted above, many programs struggled to expand services via public-sector channels. For example, only 24% of Pakistan's population had access to FP services in 1995, despite having one of the oldest programs. The program had in place a well-functioning organization, Social Marketing Pakistan, managing the product distribution and promotion components of the program.[30] They decided to build on this foundation, adapting the strategy of affiliating distributors and pharmacies

[29]Vouchers have also been successfully at a national scale for *product* delivery (e.g. to increase access to mosquito nets while building sustainable local distribution systems, see Chapter 9: Malaria).

[30]The organization was well-structured to receive funds, report on activity and results, and manage relations with a large number of private providers.

**Social franchising** strategies strive to expand access to and use of services by affiliating private providers, who are reimbursed via service fees; health communication based on commercial marketing techniques is typically deployed by NGO intermediates.

to create a network of private practitioners to provide FP services. Social Marketing Pakistan developed a social franchise business model to network private providers. Similar to TSM, the strategy established a network of existing providers. The network is created when providers join the franchise, agreeing to comply with the franchisees' quality standards.[31] They received support from the franchisor to improve services, as well as receiving discounted supplies.[32] Similar to distributors and pharmacies participating in a TSM distribution network, they anticipate an increase in customers deriving from the franchisor's advertising, and they keep markups on sales of the lower-priced supplies.[33] These gains motivate providers to do the hard work of achieving and maintaining franchise quality standards.

Program managers recognized that quality assurance is considerably more challenging for services than for selling condoms and other products (see Box 2). Therefore, the relationship between the franchisor and franchised providers is necessarily more intense than that between social marketing organizations and affiliated distributors and pharmacies. Social franchising's critical advantage is that it may make it possible to improve service quality among the fragmented providers who provide so much care, including to poor people (Montagu, 2002).[34] Social Marketing

[31] In the case of social franchising, a franchisor is an intermediary organization used to establish sustained relationships with health service providers. See Glossary.

[32] Programs have utilized primarily fractional franchises, where only the FP portion of services provided by a general service provider is franchised.

[33] Like social marketing supply strategies, social franchising relies on user payments rather than free distribution.

[34] Such structures are critical to quality assurance in well-performing mixed health systems but are usually absent in developing countries.

Pakistan's Greenstar franchise has grown to 8,540 franchisees, providing more than 3.4 million visits in 2012 (Schlein Montagu, 2012). The model has since been adapted and applied in many other countries.[35] Many programs have successfully deployed social franchising approaches to tap into private providers' capacity to increase access to good-quality FP services (Bishai and Madhavan, 2010). However, social franchising requires training, monitoring, and the ability to kick non-performers out (Montagu, 2002; Bishai *et al.*, 2008; Bishai and Madhavan, 2010). Likewise, the NGOs which have managed the development and operation of these networks are an essential ingredient; where social franchising succeeds, there is always a well-functioning, socially oriented NGO acting as franchisor.[36] The precise parameters of the relationship between the franchisor and its provider-members vary, reflecting the distinct country and market contexts. Also, it takes time, negotiation, and adjustment to find a balance between the "value proposition" the franchise offers its members and the burden associated with complying with quality, pricing, and reporting. There is no template.

Social franchises have proven useful for harnessing private providers' capacity and for improving the mix and quality of services for the many people who use these providers. Though they can reduce the prices that customers pay for quality-assured services and products, franchises do rely on patient payment. Hence, some financial barriers to access remain, which may discourage use by the very poor. Initiatives to test social franchising combined with vouchers are ongoing.[37]

## 3.3 *Insights and lessons*

### 3.3.1 *Lessons about strategies*

Some features of FP programs eased collaboration with the private sector: NGOs' involvement in program formulation and the ease with which

[35] See Schlein Montagu (2012).

[36] Typically, the franchisor is a former social marketing organization (as in Pakistan); sometimes it is a service provider organization, such as Marie Stopes, and local affiliates.

[37] See the African Health Markets for Equity initiative.

products might flow through private channels are the most notable. As a result, FP programs provide a wealth of insight about private sector engagement. Compared to public distribution alone, the TSM experience demonstrates that programs can expand access by adding a channel which taps into the existing capacity of private distribution networks. Often, this is more efficient than public distribution. Providers are harder to network, and service quality is more challenging to monitor. Nevertheless, programs' experiences with social franchising suggest that the strategy can expand the provision of prioritized services, while ensuring service quality, and it can work even with the small, unorganized providers which are so heavily used by the poor. Where public or social insurance contracting is infeasible, vouchers can tap into private providers to increase services for specific groups and can enable the targeting of subsidies to increase programs' financial sustainability.

In terms of more systemic approaches, contracting integrated service packages with performance contracting, linking funding to FP service provision, can contribute to coverage. Moreover, where social health insurance mechanisms are present, they can be a sound platform for increasing FP coverage. GCD strategies can nudge market development to increase contraceptive coverage and enhance sustainability, though programs often struggle to implement these approaches.

Insights about strategies deployed in FP to harness the private sector are relevant to other programs. Indeed, variations of TSM strategies have been deployed in numerous other programs. Child health programs, as you will read in Chapter 12, have successfully used TSM strategies to promote and distribute oral rehydration, zinc, products for household water treatment, and soap. Malaria programs, as we saw in Chapter 9, have deployed both TSM as well as GCD strategies to expand access to mosquito nets and malaria medicines. Maternal health programs have successfully used social marketing strategies to distribute iron/folic acid supplements, vitamins, and safe delivery kits.

### 3.3.2 *Broader insights*

*Management and coordination*: Poor performance of public services and supply chains is often linked to health agencies' weak management. Yet, managing engagement with the private sector often relies on sound management and coordination. Many successful engagement initiatives overcame this gap by involving private organizations, often INGOs and NGOs, in the management of these activities. Analyses of implementation underscore the importance of this component.

*Intermediary organizations*: Policy practitioners increasingly recognize private organizations' role in distribution and provision. Many engagement experiences reviewed here reveal that private organizations are also filling "*stewardship*" *gaps*. With remarkable frequency, we see private organizations acting as intermediaries in the operationalization of these strategies. Within social marketing efforts, private organizations coordinated the distribution of supplies and managed relationships with distributors and retailers. In social franchising initiatives, private organizations "networked" fragmented providers to achieve quality improvements and expand FP services and products in a manner congruent with their operation as small businesses. In voucher initiatives, private organizations took on the responsibility of checking to see if services were delivered and reimbursed providers. FP program experience suggests that private nonprofit organizations are contributing a great deal by filling stewardship gaps in addition to providing supplies and services directly. This suggests engagement is more likely to succeed where program managers identify the most critical gaps and consider how and by whom they can be filled.

*Contextualization and adaption*: The content of similarly named engagement strategies varies considerably from place to place. Successful implementation and impact are frequently linked to how well programs altered strategies to "fit" important local features (Cromer *et al.*, 2004; Seltzer, 2002). Given how varied the makeup, capacity, and attitudes of the local private sector are, this is not surprising.

Well-documented experiences frequently characterize the implementation of these strategies as adaptive. That is, the specific policy approach and the parameters of the relationship with the private sector are iteratively identified and implemented based on observations of private providers' and customers' responses to previous actions and market adjustments. Often, the intermediary organization does much of the work of monitoring, iterating, and negotiating to find a stable, productive relationship with the private actors involved. Many commentators draw attention to the importance of this adaptation for success (OED, 1991; Cromer *et al.*, 2004; Seltzer, 2002; Robinson and Ross, 2007). They attribute the need for adaptation to the lack of information about the private sector with which most initiatives start off, as well as would-be private collaborators' considerable independence to determine their responses. In general, any strategy whose effect is mediated through a market requires adaptive implementation; hence, it is unsurprising that observers remark on its importance for many FP initiatives' efforts to engage private actors.[38]

We next discuss FP development assistance efforts since they emerged in the 1950s. We examine its features and changes which influence FP programs. We focus our attention on how donors' operations and approaches interacted with the consideration and implementation of strategies to mobilize the private sector.

## 4. Sources of and Constraints to Engagement

Wealthy Western countries' FP efforts reflected their health system pluralism. Private pharmacies and their suppliers, private clinics and practitioners, as well as non-profit social enterprises, undertook most product retail and distribution and provided many services. Many developing countries' early efforts deployed public sector strategies exclusively. What might explain this? Private distribution systems, retail outlets, and services were undoubtedly weaker than they had been in wealthy countries 20–30 years earlier. However, public systems were likewise weaker.[39] In hindsight, the heavy reliance on the public sector to provide services, especially to distribute products, appears excessive. In this section, we explore which factors may have contributed to programs' early emphasis on public sector delivery. And we examine the factors which appeared to facilitate engagement, which, as noted above, became more common in the 1980s–1990s.

---

[38]With the plausible exception of TSM, the engagement strategies qualify as complex interventions which generate their impact through changes in complex systems, which generally demand adaptive implementation.

[39]This weakness became clear once care-seeking behavior was examined using household surveys.

*Aid influences program design*: As noted in Chapter 2, the mechanics of providing development assistance directly influence the design and implementation approaches of donor-supported. This influence is stronger when aid funding constitutes a large portion of total spending on an initiative. Given the dominant role donors played in many FP programs, it is not surprising that numerous sources mention their influence on program design and implementation (Robinson and Ross, 2007; Seltzer, 2002).

In the following, we examine the operational features of the most influential aid agencies' relationships with country-level actors, including their rules, incentives, and habitual processes.[40] We examine features which influence the design and management of aid projects and, through this, influence the strategies pursued within the FP programs they supported.[41] Agencies' reporting structures likewise influence the strategies they tend to support. We point out where this relationship has been linked to private sector engagement.

## 4.1 *The public sector focus*

*Public agencies' role*: Government agencies and public officials are natural counterparts for development assistance. And they were important counterparts for most early FP projects. In many countries, USAID and other influential donors worked with and through public agencies to formulate projects to support the countries' programs. Even international NGOs and foundations often relied on their relationships with government agencies for implementation (Robinson and Ross, 2007). These agencies and officials are familiar with service and product delivery approaches that are implemented within the public sector; few are familiar with alternatives. Stewardship mechanisms for identifying and implementing private sector engagement strategies are often weak or absent. Often, officials prefer strategies which funnel external resources through public agencies.

---

[40] Gibson *et al.* (2005) lay out a similar framework, emphasizing the interface between SIDA's characteristic operating processes and the features of strategies in the programs they support.

[41] See Glossary for definitions of programs versus projects.

*Narrow participation in program development*: The parameters of FP programs and strategies frequently emerged from discussions between government agencies and external organizations (Robinson and Ross, 2007; Seltzer, 2002). Where broader sets of stakeholders participated in these discussions, programs often pursued more pluralistic strategies. In countries like Colombia, Ecuador, Chile, and Brazil, where health professionals' associations and NGOs were involved in program formulation and management, private actors were invariably involved in implementation (Robinson and Ross, 2007; Seltzer, 2002). South Korea's and Taiwan's inclusion of professional associations in program formulation appears to have contributed to the involvement of private practitioners in service delivery. Limited involvement of domestic stakeholders with awareness or interest in the private sector in the early phase of donor-supported FP programs in many countries likely contributed to overlooking potential opportunities to mobilize private sector actors.

*Aid agencies' preference for expedience*: External agencies generally prefer program strategies which can be quickly implemented and this preference was certainly present for the agencies supporting FP. Identifying strategies to work with private actors is relatively time-consuming, and most private sector engagement strategies take more time to unfold and generate desired gains. USAID's preferences for public sector-focused strategies were often driven by the pressure the agency felt to rapidly prepare and implement assistance activities while the World Bank support also noted that too-short time horizons for projects discouraged the deployment of such strategies.

*Coverage goals*: Most FP projects and programs aimed to increase the coverage and use of contraceptives.[42] Early project documents rarely referred to efficiency or sustainability. When individuals and organizations designing aid projects are not concerned with efficiency or sustainability, opportunities to mobilize the private sector are less often considered. Given their objectives, it was natural, if not inevitable, to select strategies which could be implemented within the public system.

[42] Aided by household survey data, many programs now target the poor, who often have lower coverage than the rest of the population.

*Aid agencies' tools for support*: Considerable health development assistance during this period consisted of funding "lumpy investments" or "bricks and mortar," such as facility upgrading and construction and equipment, a predilection also present in FP support (Robinson and Ross, 2007; OED, 1991). The benefits from these investments rely on public sector staffing and operation; hence, they are invariably linked to public service delivery.

Aid agencies provided considerable support for contraceptive products. Typically, they allocated funds for external procurement and shipment to the country; often, they funded external organizations to distribute products (Bowers *et al.*, 2010).[43] This procurement approach was typically efficient, as the well-managed international large-volume tenders obtained low prices.[44] Donors often funded public agencies and, under TSM, INGOs to manage distribution. Aid focused on distributing shipped products constituted a poor platform for building public agencies' capabilities to understand and exercise stewardship across the broader private sector, and it often discouraged local and regional manufacturers, importers, distributors, and retailers from expanding their delivery of contraceptives.

*Agency culture*: Staff attitudes and the organizational culture of influential technical agencies, such as the UNFPA and WHO, are sometimes tied to preference for public sector-implemented strategies. Some observers noted that their involvement contributed to overlooking opportunities to engage the private sector in FP programs (Robinson and Ross, 2007).

*An era of popularity for government solutions*: The 1950s, 1960s, and early 1970s were a "golden period" of welfare state expansion. Wealthy countries strived to improve their own citizens' access to social services, often by expanding public services. Most aid agencies and technical advisors believed and promoted the idea that state bureaucracies should play the dominant role in development (Stone 65; Siffen 76, quoted in Batley).

[43] In particular, USAID and UNFPA.

[44] Though, recall that USAID assistance typically supported the procurement of US products, due to "Buy America" restrictions.

Developing-country governments manifested a similar orientation. This orientation was reinforced in countries where post-independence governments were struggling to build their legitimacy by, among other things, delivering social services. The prevalence of relatively statist attitudes during this period undoubtedly contributed to FP programs' focus on public-sector strategies.

In these respects, early FP programs are similar to other health programs. And these tendencies manifest across the programs discussed here and elsewhere (La Fond, 1995). FP programs aren't unique in how they started, but rather in what happened later. Despite starting off with a public sector focus, many programs did change course. They added strategies to harness local private sector capacities to address program gaps or weaknesses. Many of these changes involved tapping into private sector capacities, which had initially been overlooked. What may explain this?

## 4.2 *Family planning programs and aid adapts*

*Declining confidence in government solutions*: During the late 1970s and 1980s, prevailing thinking about the role of government shifted toward a more minimalist view. Recessions and fiscal crises in wealthy countries led to efforts to cut back and streamline government activity. Wealthy countries sought alternatives to public bureaucracies to achieve social policy goals. And these attitudinal shifts were likewise reflected in the provision of development assistance. Like other programs, FP programs faced challenges related to the decline of public spending in the 1980s and the resulting deterioration of public services.

*Importance of products*: When a program sought new approaches to increasing contraceptive use, it was relatively straightforward to pursue the private distribution of simple products, such as condoms, spermicides, and resupply of pills. In contrast to clinical services, these products can be safely distributed by unskilled personnel. Arguments that only public workers could be trusted to provide them, commonly deployed to deter collaboration with private practitioners, were less persuasive.

*Early engagement generates "how-to" knowledge base*: A number of programs pursued engagement early on. Taiwan's and South Korea's use of vouchers in the 1950s and 1960s enabled private practitioners to play a major role in extending services. Colombia's product distribution efforts from the early 1970s showed how commercial producers, distributors, and retailers could contribute to contraceptive access. Early experiences with TSM informed the subsequent development of the social franchising strategy. These experiences, complemented by significant investments in operational research, constituted a foundation of knowledge about how to engage the private sector, on which later FP efforts drew. Having this knowledge base made it easier for programs to identify and implement strategies to engage the private sector (Robinson and Ross, 2007).

*Construction and use of holistic information sources*: FP programs and donor projects bore an unusual degree of scrutiny. Oversight agencies and many development experts doubted FP programs could affect such deeply engrained, culturally, and personally driven behaviors as those relating to contraception (Robinson and, 2007). This skepticism generated demands for sound evidence of effectiveness. As a result, aid organizations, in particular, USAID, invested heavily in operational research and devoted considerable resources to developing and implementing repeated surveys to track populations' contraceptive use and fertility (Fabic *et al.*, 2012; Robinson and Ross, 2007).[45] These surveys generated information about people's contraceptive behaviors, which could be tracked over time to gain insight on programs and strategies' effectiveness. These holistic information sources were invaluable for flagging program performance problems. Since they could shed light on populations' contraceptive behaviors, they could be used to analyze the use of private sources.

[45]Implementation of the Demographic and Health Surveys started in 1984; they represent the next evolution of two earlier household survey programs: the World Fertility Surveys and Contraceptive Prevalence Surveys. The World Fertility Surveys took place from 1973 to 1984, and the Contraceptive Prevalence Surveys took place from 1977 to 1985. It was initially funded jointly by the United States Agency for International Development (USAID) and the United Nations Population Fund (UNFPA), with assistance from the governments of the United Kingdom of Great Britain and Northern Ireland, the Netherlands, and Japan.

Observers point out that these data sources played a critical role in making the case for engaging the private sector and enabling implementation (Robinson and Ross, 2007; Tsui, 1996). Others urge further investments in such information sources to expand private engagement and contributions (OED, 1991).

*Objectives shifted*: Private sector engagement strategies received an even bigger boost when donors expanded project objectives to include not just the *use* of contraceptives but also *efficiency* and, eventually, *sustainability*. While early FP programs focused primarily on increasing the use of contraceptives, when FP aid stagnated and eventually declined starting in the 1980s, donors increasingly emphasized sustainability, both operational and financial. Throughout the late 1980s and 1990s, continuing into the 2000s, FP projects struggled to adapt strategies to increase both the financial and organizational sustainability of their projects. Efforts to engage the private sector very often refer to these objectives as the foundation for considering private sector engagement. Relatedly, programs grew increasingly interested in targeting support for particular people — either because of declining aid volumes or concerns with disparities in access. As programs worked to target subsidies for lower-income people, they often sought to nudge better-off people to cover their own costs. Expanding private provision for non-targeted groups was often part of such efforts.

*Aid challenges*: Whatever factors facilitated increased private sector engagement, overall, efforts appear modest. Numerous references to the need to shift support to expand support for private sector engagement confirm that the frequency falls short of agencies' intentions and judgments. Clearly, aid agencies struggled to support private sector engagement. Public officials' lack of interest and other country-level factors were doubtless barriers. However, agencies' operational imperatives sometimes contributed. While GCD strategies can contribute to shifting contraceptive use in a country to a sustainable footing, their impacts are slower to unfold, harder to measure, and less attributable to donors' activities. Compared to funding supplies, demand-stimulation efforts perform badly in the "beauty contest" among strategies to attract donor support and are systematically underutilized. Programs can fairly quickly increase demand for branded, program-provided products. However, demand support strategies (general demand promotion, social insurance, and contracting), which work via a market supply response, take longer and are harder to track and attribute. Donors often prefer to fund products and supply support in general, a bias that discourages support for sustained activities related to adapting policies, as well as platforms for consultation among public and private stakeholders. Support tools tend to require expedient disbursement and implementation; monitoring often prioritized direct attribution for benefits delivered (OED, 1991).

Donors, especially USAID, devoted considerable funding to projects aiming to support GCD strategies. Nevertheless, most reviews remark on the persistent reliance on public, untargeted distribution.

## 5. Conclusions and Insights for Funders

FP programs' experiences provide insight about strategies to engage the private sector, as well as about aid agencies' influence on the consideration and deployment of such strategies.

### 5.1 *More and better private sector engagement can help family planning programs accelerate progress*

Experience within these programs suggests that private sector engagement can contribute to program objectives, including expanding access, efficiency, and sustainability. The experience suggests FP initiatives can improve their effectiveness by more frequently considering and pursuing engagement. Just as important, it gives some insight about better practices for implementing these strategies.

*Engage more*: Traditional social marketing and social franchising strategies can help tap into private capacity; working with private distributors, retailers, and providers can increase the efficiency of program activities. Programs can overcome barriers to coverage expansion by adding private delivery channels. Absent public contracting or insurance mechanisms, vouchers can help expand access and target program subsidies for particular groups.

*Pursue systemic approaches*: More systemic strategies are essential for the sustainability of FP program achievements. Wherever public contracting and/or social insurance platforms are available, programs should endeavor to work through these mechanisms to ensure the delivery of FP services and products. Strategies to increase commercial delivery of products by private manufacturers, distributors, and pharmacies can be critical for programs' operational and financial sustainability. Private sector engagement can be a much-needed tonic for some programs' current dependence-generating approaches.

*Focus on demand, less on supply*: Programs will be more effective and sustainable, and the private sector can contribute more.

*Build holistic monitoring systems*: DHS and other household surveys have been invaluable. The information from the surveys can be used more often to good effect.

*Mind the gap*: Many developing countries' health agencies lack information and technical knowledge to understand the private sector, and they lack mechanisms for information exchange, and mechanisms for communicating with private sector representatives are weak. They lack the fora for sustaining collaborative relationships inherent in all engagement strategies. Many successful instances of engagement within FP programs relied on sustained efforts to fill these stewardship gaps. Programs which devote conscious attention to identifying and filling these "stewardship gaps" are likely to work better.

*Plan for adaptation*: Most of the engagement strategies deployed within FP programs required considerable alteration to suit the local context; this contextualization demands analysis of local markets as well as local stewardship institutions and their shortcomings. Engagement strategies typically required considerable adaptation upon implementation. Programs will achieve more if they recognize the importance of contextualization and adaptation and integrate this recognition into their diagnostics, policy formulation, and implementation. There are, alas, no templates.

## 5.2 *Better aid can help this happen*

*Support holistic project and strategy development*: FP programs with broader participation in analysis and strategy formulation more often identified opportunities to tap into private sector capacities. Virtually all engagement initiatives found a means of gathering information about private sector capacities and perspectives to inform their approach to collaboration.

*Invest in, and use, holistic monitoring systems*: FP donors' considerable investments in the DHS and its predecessors proved invaluable. The surveys made it possible to track populations' contraceptive-, care-, and product-seeking behaviors. These data made it possible to learn about programs' performance beyond tracking activity. In many countries, the data drew attention to the need to engage the private sector and have been used to learn about the effectiveness of different strategies. Similar investments in developing a survey tool to track provider and retailer markets are urgently needed. Absent such investments, it is unlikely that private sector engagement strategies will be well implemented and that they will attract much support.

*Examine supply-push, direct-delivery biases*: Donors supporting FP have worked long and hard to expand private sector engagement. This has given them more time, and greater grounds, for reflecting on their halting progress. A structural bias in aid provision toward supporting supply-expanding strategies and the delivery of products is the factor most often singled out. Agencies which wish to support private sector engagement will benefit from examining their own operating processes and operational imperatives to identify and address such biases.

*Help fill stewardship gaps*: Many developing countries' health agencies lack mechanisms for information exchange and fora for communication and collaboration among public and private stakeholders. FP programs' engagement successes often relied on activities which filled these gaps in creative ways. Support for such activities can be overlooked, especially when donors focus on narrowly defined and directly attributable "results." Hence, donors should take care that they provide support for filling "stewardship gaps."

*Build agency and staff capacity*: Lagging private sector engagement in FP initiatives is traced in a number of instances to the capabilities of aid agencies and staff. Many agencies will need to consciously strive to build their capability through recruitment and training. Formal declarations of intent are rarely sufficient by themselves; otherwise, far more would have happened on this score in the past 10–15 years.

Most insights are relevant for health development assistance in general, not only FP programs.

## References

R. Batley and G. A. Larbi. (2004). *The Changing Role of Government: The Reform of Public Services in Developing Countries*. Palgrave Macmillan, Houndmills, Basingstoke, Hampshire; New York.

N. Bellows, B. Bellows and C. Warren. (2011). The use of vouchers for reproductive health services in developing countries: systematic review. *Tropical Medicine & International Health* **16**(1): 84–96.

D. Bishai and S. Madhavan. (2010). *Private Sector Engagement in Sexual and Reproductive Health and Maternal and Neonatal Health: A Review of the Evidence*. DFID, London.

D. Bishai, N. Shah, D. Walker, W. Brieger and D. Peters. (2008). Social franchising to improve quality and access in private health care in developing countries. *Harvard Health Policy Review* **9**: 184–197.

J. Bongaarts. (1995). *The Role of Family Planning Programs in Contemporary Fertility Transitions*. New York City. Population Council.

R. L. Ciszewski and P. D. Harvey. (1994). The effect of price increases on contraceptive sales in Bangladesh. *Journal of Biosocial Sciences* **26**: 25–35.

C. Cromer, T. Pandit, T. Robertson and A. Neiwijk. (2004). *The Family Planning Graduation Experience: Lessons for the Future*. LTG Associates, Washington, DC.

M. Das Gupta, J. Bongaarts and J. Cleland. (2011). Population, poverty, and sustainable development: A review of the evidence. World Bank Policy Research Working Paper, No. 5719. World Bank, Washington DC.

J. Esselman. (1994). Sustainability, sustainable development, and the health sector. Issue Paper Series. Washington, DC. USAID Accessed on January 29, 2024: https://pdf.usaid.gov/pdf_docs/PNABT155.PDF.

D. V. Glass. (1966). Family planning programmes and action in Western Europe. *Population Studies* **19**(3): 221–238.

D. A. Grimes, J. Benson, S. Singh, M. Romero, B. Ganatra, F. E. Okonofua and I. H. Shah. (2006). Unsafe abortion: The preventable pandemic. *The Lancet* **368**(9550): 1908–1919.

P. Harvey. (1999). Let Every Child Be Wanted: How Social Marketing is Revolutionizing Contraceptive Use Around the World. Westport, CT. Auburn House.

R. Levine (ed.). (2004). *Millions Saved: Proven Successes in Global Health.* Center for Global Development, Washington DC.

D. Montagu. (2002). Franchising of health services in low-income countries. *Health Policy Plan* **17**(2): 121–130.

N. Palmer (2006). An awkward threesome — Donors, governments and non-state providers of health in low income countries. *Public Administration and Development* **26**: 231–240.

B. Robey. (1987). Community-based contraceptive distribution: A Korean success story. *Asia Pac Pop Policy* (4): 1–4.

W. Robinson and J. Ross (eds.). (2007). *The Global Family Planning Revolution: Three Decades of Population Policies and Programs*. World Bank, Washington DC.

K. Schlein and D. Montagu. (2012). Clinical social franchising compendium: an annual survey of programs. San Francisco: University of California San Francisco.

J. Seltzer. (2002). The Origins and Evolution of Family Planning Programs in Developing Countries. ISBN: 0-8330-2928-2. Arlington VA. Rand.

J. Seltzer and F. Gomez. (1998). Family Planning and Population Programs in Colombia 1965 to 1997. POPTECH Report. Population Technical Assistance Project, Arlington, VA.

J. P. Skibiak. (1991). *Employment-Based Family Planning in the Private Sector: Lesson of Enterprise*. John Snow, Inc., Arlington, VA.

# Chapter 12
# Child Health

**Flavia Bustreo**

## Abstract

This chapter by Flavia Bustreo looks at the experience of programs and policy initiatives related to child health and tries to understand why these problems occur. In particular, it aims to understand why these programs tend to be implemented without engaging the private sector and what impact this has. Our research indicated that ignoring private provision is undermining program impact in many countries, and our analysis yielded some suggestions about program design and policy changes at the country level.

In this chapter, we examine how donor support is developed and implemented and how these processes influence the problems we observe. From this analysis, we suggest changes that donors can make in their development assistance for child health. We indicate where these changes are needed to improve program impact, especially where the context makes it likely that the private health sector will need to be brought into programs to help them achieve their goals.

Programs should, as a priority, scrutinize existing health system data from household, provider, and retailer surveys. They should aim to identify the most critical gaps between the populations they target to reach and the best available evidence on where those people are obtaining their services and products. Where private actors are playing a significant role, local consultation is necessary to identify where there is both capacity and willingness to engage in public–private collaborations. Program managers should seek opportunities for collaboration around the manufacture and distribution of products (e.g. fortified foods and oral rehydration salts). Where provider networks are substantially private, officials should consider contracting, either by public or social insurance agencies; "lighter touch" collaboration with private providers to expand coverage of priority interventions should also be considered (e.g. for immunization).

To achieve all of this, it is vital that political will and commitment exist at the global, national, and local levels to expand private sector participation, as well as coordination and communication among the multiple stakeholders.

### *The "cheap drug for the poor"*

*Sometimes, the person giving medical advice is just as important as the advice they give.*

*My name is Dr. Flavia Bustreo. In 1997, I was working as a medical officer for the child health program in Massalamia, a rural district of Sudan. In front of me stood a proud Sudanese grandmother, holding her baby granddaughter in her arms. The baby was drowsy, listless, and dehydrated, suffering the effects of diarrhea. If not cared for properly, this child would probably die. She had been seen in the dispensary by a health worker, recently trained through our program in the proper treatment of diarrhea. The worker had done everything right, reached the right conclusion, and correctly advised the grandmother to continue feeding the child and to give oral rehydration salts.*

*I was curious to understand how this advice had been received, so I asked the grandmother about the consultation and whether she would be able to provide the care the baby needed. Her answer stunned me. She clearly recognized me as a foreign doctor in this land of desolation and said: "The health worker explained this salt treatment for my grandchild, but it is a 'cheap drug for the poor', so I will not give it to her. I will take her to the village doctor [her word for the informal provider] who knows what she needs." I reflected that training this informal provider might have accomplished more to save this child because he had the trust of the grandmother.*

## The elephant in the room?

*Throughout the developing world, private practitioners treat sick children, while private pharmacies and drug sellers provide them with medicines. Private retailers sell mosquito nets, providing protection from malaria. In some countries, food companies fortify their foods to combat nutritional deficiencies that blight child health and development. Unfortunately, child health initiatives rarely deal with this reality: neither the potential of tapping into this capacity, nor the opportunity to ensure — through different policy strategies — that the private sector provides effective and responsible healthcare for children. And this omission has contributed to the disappointing results of many child health initiatives.*

*So, what's going on? If ignoring the private sector undermines program impact, why aren't private actors welcomed with open arms? The reasons relate to how health programs are designed and implemented. Programs are based on an out-of-date perception of developing countries' health systems, especially for frontline delivery of services and products. As a result, they usually follow a design "template" that relates exclusively to the public sector. And often, performance monitoring focuses on the number of staff trained or products distributed. These practices overlook the role of the private sector in child health and hinder the recognition of program strategies that aren't achieving meaningful improvements in coverage and quality.*

*The solution seems clear, if maddeningly elusive: initiatives should engage the private sector where they can contribute to child health objectives. At the same time, donors supporting these efforts should help this shift by altering their own templates for program design and monitoring. In many instances, closer scrutiny of population and "whole provider network" data can reveal the need to work with the private sector to achieve program goals; it can also help monitor efforts to mobilize private resources toward improving the health of children. Several strategies are emerging as powerful instruments to expand access (e.g. public and social insurance-based contracting and partnerships for food fortification) and to improve the quality of services and products critical for child health (e.g. accreditation and shifting private distribution channels with subsidies and demand promotion initiatives). For these strategies to work, engagement with the private sector needs to be complemented by investments in strengthening the stewardship capacity of ministries and public officials in developing countries.*

## 1. Introduction: Child Health and the Role of the Private Sector

Every day, more than 24,000 children die from illnesses that can be easily prevented or cheaply cured (UNICEF, 2009). Why is this tragedy happening? It can't be blamed on a lack of medical knowledge; most child deaths can be avoided by just 24 simple and cost-effective interventions (Bryce *et al.*, 2008). Nor is it simply a lack of resources since many of the interventions are inexpensive, and several poor countries have improved child health by getting them to children. Yet, a number of countries are making little headway in improving the health of their children.

Donors have long focused attention on improving the health of children in poor countries, and there have been some notable successes. For example, the establishment of the Global Alliance for Vaccines (GAVI) helped increase immunization rates in poor countries, leading to sustained reductions in some vaccine-preventable diseases, such as measles and polio. Nevertheless, donor-supported programs have had only a limited impact on the biggest killers of children: diarrhea, pneumonia, and malaria. The problem lies not in a lack of interventions or technologies, but rather in programs' inability to ensure that the children who need them most, namely the poor and marginalized, can access them. In many countries, donors have found it challenging to turn their support into successes, especially when working to extend programs' reach into communities and improve overall service quality.

This chapter looks at the experience of programs and policy initiatives related to child health and tries to understand why these problems occur. In particular, it aims to understand why these programs tend to be implemented without engaging the private sector and what impact this has. Our earlier research indicated that this tendency is undermining program impact in many countries, and our analysis yielded some suggestions about program design and policy changes at the country level (Bustreo *et al.*, 2003). In this chapter, we expand our examination to include how donor support is developed and implemented and how these processes influence the problems we observe. From this analysis, we suggest changes that donors can make in their development assistance for child health. We indicate where these changes are needed to improve program impact, especially where the context makes it likely that the private health sector will need to be brought into programs to help them achieve their goals.

Household surveys reveal that sick children in many developing countries are frequently taken to private providers, which range from clinics and doctors to drug sellers and traditional healers. The quality of care received varies from good to outright harmful; quality is a particular concern among the informal providers used so frequently by poor people. Extensive use of private providers even when public services are available is often linked to poor public service quality. Yet, similar private sector care-seeking occurs in OECD countries[1] with high-quality care (Montagu, 2021), and in LMIC[2]s, studies show that people persist in choosing these providers even when measurable improvements are made in public services.[3] For a range of reasons, people often don't trust their nearby public clinics (Olsen, 2009; Leonard, 2001), as Dr. Bustreo learned in Sudan. In these settings, it is necessary to improve the quality of private care on offer by engaging directly with private providers and to link these providers more closely with the public health system. While few child health programs have engaged private health actors, other related programs have (e.g. family planning and tuberculosis), and their experiences provide insight into engagement approaches. This chapter examines the few child health initiatives that have engaged the private sector. It sheds light on where private actors have most contributed to the health of children and why this often doesn't happen. It will also suggest actions that program managers and donor agencies can take to involve the private sector systematically in reaching more sick children with life-saving interventions.

---

[1]A group of the high-income countries around the world.

[2]Low- and middle-income countries.

[3]The highest documented proportion of population switching to improved services is in Bangladesh (9% increase in over five years), where it was a response to a fully implemented Integrated Management of Childhood Illness (IMCI) initiative and activities to increase referral by informal providers (see Arifeen *et al.*, 2009).

## 2. Making the Case: Why Engage the Private Sector in Child Health Programs?

### 2.1 *The nature of problems in child health and what is necessary to address them*

In developing countries, children die of health problems that are rare in most countries of the developed world. Among children under five, the most common causes of death are diarrhea, malaria, and pneumonia (Black *et al.*, 2010).[4] Newborn babies most commonly die of complications resulting from premature birth, low birth weight, birth asphyxia, or severe infections called sepsis. Most cases of diarrhea are contracted by drinking contaminated water, and most cases of pneumonia result from viral or bacterial transmission in overcrowded living areas. Underlying malnutrition problems frequently exacerbate their severity and mortality. In many countries, these health problems fall even more on poor people than on those with more resources. Globally, among the poor, on average, 135 of every 1,000 children die before their fifth birthday, which is almost double the number among the richest 20% (Figure 1).

Most of these child deaths result from the lack of basic services, knowledge, and nutrition that people in developed countries take for granted. These include robust and well-funded health systems, effective health promotion, and a plentiful supply of nutritious food. These things are largely absent in the poorest countries, where weak health systems lead to much worse health outcomes for children, who often receive poor-quality curative treatment. In the home, lack of knowledge or mistaken knowledge contributes to child illness when caregivers do the wrong things or don't take children for treatment when needed.

However, the problems lie deeper than the direct prevention and cure of illness. Nutrition problems, stemming from inadequate food and feeding practices, contribute to children's deaths. Micronutrient deficiencies contribute to other health problems, as well as undermining cognitive

[4]Children's deaths are linked to many factors beyond the health system (which is the focus of our discussion), including the country's and the household's economic strength, mothers' education, and the availability and quality of transport infrastructure and water and sanitation.

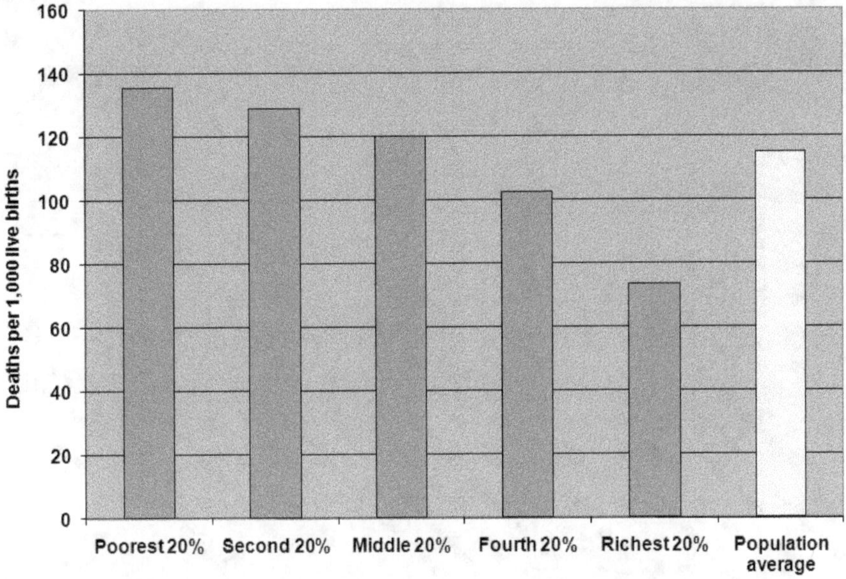


Figure 1. Poor children die more often: Under-five mortality rates by socioeconomic wealth quintiles.

*Source*: Gwatkin *et al.* (2007).

development and productive capacity later in life (Victora *et al.*, 2008; Walker *et al.*, 2007). Despite much progress, many countries still have low immunization coverage.

*The challenge for donor-supported programs*: Ideally, poor countries' health systems would quickly improve their frontline health services, including community outreach services. However, we do not live in an ideal world. These problems relate to the functionality of countries' basic provider networks, the adequacy of providers' curative and preventive services, and the adequacy of outreach services to communities and households. They can only be remedied through substantial systemic changes in frontline health services, both in terms of coverage and quality. Such changes have proven challenging for outsiders (e.g. donors) to support and implement.

Externally supported mass "campaigns" often deliver results, as shown by the coverage rates achieved for schedulable immunizations and

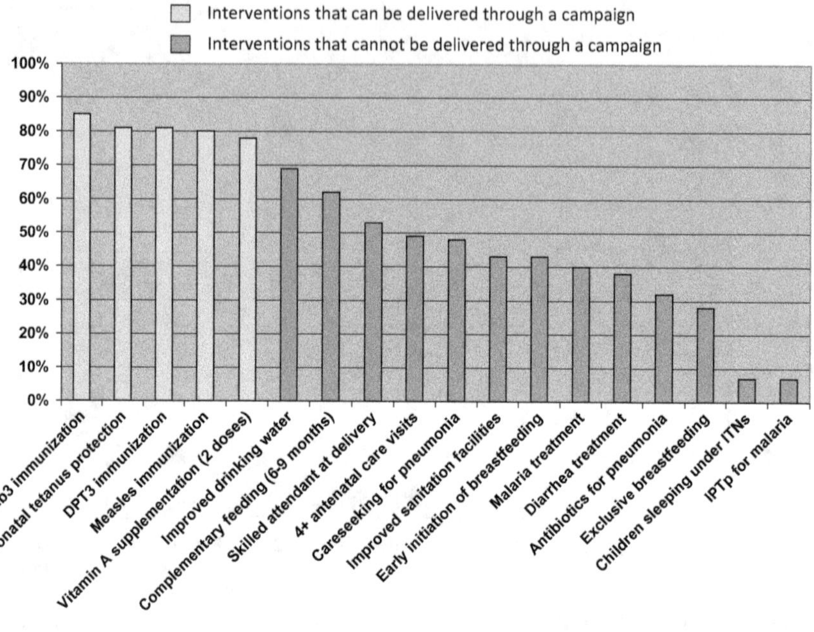


Figure 2. Success via campaigns, but not for other delivery platforms: Median coverage of key interventions in 68 countries.

*Source*: Bryce *et al.* (2008)

Vitamin A supplements. Figure 2 shows median coverage rates now exceed 70% across 68 countries that account for more than 95% of global maternal and child mortality. However, despite concerted efforts to expand coverage for other interventions, rates are much lower. In many countries, rates are stagnant, despite donor efforts. For example, coverage of treatment for diarrhea and acute respiratory infection, two of the leading killers of children under five, is 38% and 32%, respectively. Limited data on the coverage of neonatal interventions also indicate very low coverage. We have identified the interventions, but donors have found it extremely hard to get them *delivered*. In short, many developing country health systems, even with considerable donor support, have been unable to improve coverage of these interventions (Boerma *et al.*, 2008).

Some important child health problems are amenable to scheduled interventions, such as immunization and Vitamin A supplementation. That is, these interventions can safely and effectively be administered to all children within an age group. Health officials can deploy population-wide delivery activities for such interventions outside a country's existing service and product delivery platforms. Health officials often complement mainstream service and product delivery with mass campaign delivery activities to achieve rapid coverage increases. Exploiting the strategy's administrative separability, health officials have deployed it as a substitute for mainstream delivery in many countries with weak health systems (Restrepo, Trujillo, 2004). The delivery strategy can only work for certain interventions (see Box 1). By administratively separating implementation from the main service and product delivery system and deploying temporary delivery arrangements, such efforts have achieved notable coverage increases even in countries with weak health systems (see Figure 2, green bars).

Though simpler for donors to support, such implementation approaches rely on sustained external support to sustain coverage.

The other priority interventions depend on the availability and quality of routinely available services, delivered both in clinics and through outreach services to communities. Many, such as malaria treatment, rely on routine services that work and are accessible when children are ill. Some, such as the promotion of breastfeeding, require outreach services; that is,

## Box 1. Mass campaigns can increase coverage for certain interventions

Periodic campaigns are one platform that donors can predictably use to deliver interventions, though the strategy can be used for only a limited set of interventions which can be delivered at a pre-specified time to all people in a population category. This delivery modality also requires other conditions to work. First, the recipients are easily identifiable (e.g. they don't need to be sick). Second, delivery doesn't need to be linked to routine services to be effective. Third, delivery can be standardized (e.g. the same for every person, a red mosquito net for children and a blue mosquito net for mothers). Fourth, delivery doesn't require the deliverer to exercise discretion. Finally, the intervention can be delivered by one entity with broad responsibilities across a wide area (e.g. network externalities).

Table 1. Priority child health interventions by delivery platform and type.

| Delivery platform | Routine services | Outreach services | Government/ business collaboration | Campaigns |
|---|---|---|---|---|
| Type of intervention | Curative<br>Malaria treatment<br>Acute respiratory infection (ARI) treatment<br>Diarrhea treatment<br>Treatment of neonatal sepsis, asphyxia, and prematurity<br>Preventive<br>Antenatal care<br>Routine immunizations<br>Neonatal tetanus protection<br>Postnatal care<br>Prevention of mother-to-child HIV transmission | Promotive<br>Oral rehydration and continued feeding<br>Exclusive breastfeeding (<6 months)<br>Breastfeeding and complementary food (6–9 months)<br>Mosquito nets | Preventive<br>Food fortification<br>Pasteurization of milk<br>Guarding safety of food, drugs, and consumer products<br>Environmental sanitation<br>Clean water | Preventive/ schedulable<br>Measles, DPT3, HiB3 immunizations<br>Vitamin A supplement<br>Mosquito nets |

a health worker must go into communities and households to promote healthy caregiving behaviors. Food fortification requires an ongoing collaboration between health authorities and food production companies.

Table 1 presents the priority child health interventions and distinguishes them by type (e.g. curative, preventive, and promotive) and the mode or platform of service delivery most often used to get them delivered in developing countries.[5]

[5]Adequate mosquito net and immunization coverage cannot be achieved solely by campaigns, so mosquito nets and immunizations are listed under both routine services and campaigns. This takes into account the other activities outside of campaigns that must be undertaken to achieve coverage.

In the following section, we look at typical child health programs and where they have encountered barriers — focusing on those interventions and delivery modes that have presented programs with the biggest problems. For interventions that are not amenable to delivery via campaigns, we aim to shed light on the nature of the problems confronted by donors to achieve increased coverage.

We will see that the expansion of coverage often stalls at low levels because programs are unable to get routine services to work. Likewise, they have consistently had problems getting community outreach services working. The child health programs examined also did not include food fortification initiatives; instead, they focused more narrowly on curative and preventive health services. And many of these weaknesses were grounded in, or at least linked to, a failure to appreciate the existence, potential, and weaknesses of the private sector.

## 2.2 *How child health assistance and programs work: The example of IMCI*

The focus on increasing coverage is not new. Child health programs have long sought to improve coverage of the interventions referred to above, commonly using the IMCI program design to pursue improvements in child health in developing countries (Tulloch, 1999). Not all child health initiatives use IMCI as the main modality for improving health, but it is the most widely used and evaluated.[6,7] Hence, we have used it as an example of how child health assistance and programs work.

IMCI is based on the concept that treatment of common childhood illnesses should be provided in an integrated and holistic manner, maximizing the health benefits of each contact sick children have with public health facilities. IMCI was introduced between 1996 and 2001 in most

---

[6]Many programs include activities at the community level. However, we were not able to analyze these activities because they have never been characterized analytically (e.g. the core intervention elements have not been specified, nor have implementation mechanics); hence, it is not possible to draw insights from implementation assessments or evaluations across settings. In contrast, the IMCI approach has been extensively assessed through a multi-country evaluation.

[7]IMCI Multi-Country Evaluation (MCE), see http://www.who.int/imci-mce/.

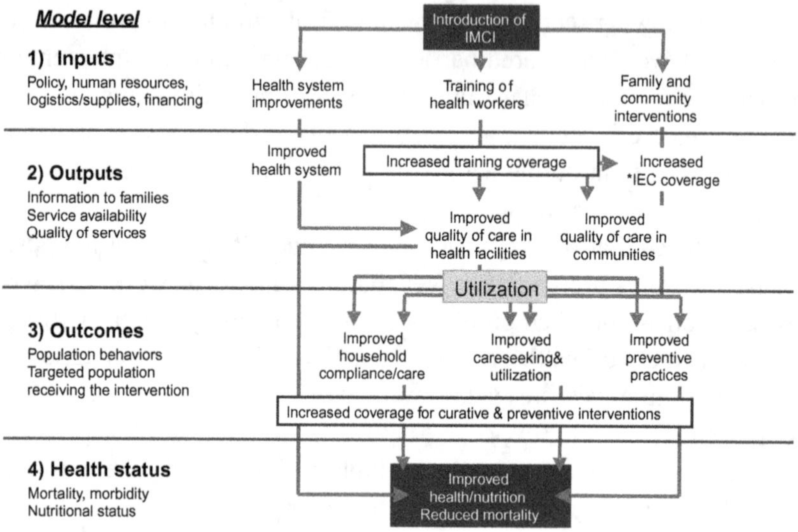


Figure 3. The IMCI impact model.

*Source*: Arifeen *et al.* (2009, adapted from Bryce *et al.*, 2005b).

*Note*: *IEC (Information, Education and Communication (IEC).

countries with moderate to high levels of child mortality. The program targets three areas: the quality of clinical care, the functionality of basic facilities, and effectiveness of outreach activities. Efforts to improve clinical quality typically involve training staff on how to treat the most common childhood illnesses. Public facility improvements, in particular staff supervision and drug availability, are also targeted. Outreach activities of some sort are usually included to educate caregivers in the community about good health practices in the home.[8]

IMCI implementation in a country starts with the adaptation of standard treatment guidelines to the country setting (taking into account the patterns of common illnesses and of antibiotic resistance). The guidelines are then translated into a standard training program for health workers. The IMCI model assumes that the training of health workers will improve the quality of care in health facilities, which in turn will increase the utilization of health facilities and improve health and nutrition outcomes (see Figure 3).

[8]The public facility improvement and community outreach activities are frequently not fully implemented, so in practice, most programs focus on quality improvements and training.

However, from the outset, problems emerged in the implementation of the IMCI strategy. No clear strategy for the strengthening of the public portion of countries' provider and product distribution networks emerged, so common systemic failings such as weak supervision of staff persisted. Few initiatives were able to remedy the systemic problems with public sector supply chains, so the availability of priority drugs did not increase. Likewise, problems occurred with the range of strategies applied to expand family and community interventions, which are critical to increasing caregiver knowledge about breastfeeding and the use of oral rehydration salts (ORS). As a result, implementation was inconsistent, and outreach services often deteriorated quickly. Four of the five countries where the implementation of IMCI strategies was rigorously evaluated had difficulty increasing population coverage with outreach services (Bryce *et al.*, 2005a. As a result, while treatment quality in frontline public clinics improved in some countries (Bryce *et al.*, 2005a; Victora *et al.*, 2006), attributable improvements in child health were found only in Tanzania (Schellenberg *et al.*, 2004a). The degree to which limitations within the public administrative and logistical systems reduce the effective implementation of IMCI was not appreciated when the program began.

Equally critically, the program generally did not explore the role and potential contribution of the private sector because the IMCI approach only included activities to improve services provided in public clinics.[9]

## 2.3 *How is the private sector relevant to improve child health?*

While policy discussions and program designs rarely reflect it, the private sector plays a substantial role in delivering healthcare and products to children, which means that it already influences children's health.

Countries' provision and distribution networks: For parents and caregivers, the practitioners, facilities, and retailers they encounter are the

[9]With the exception of sporadically involving some private providers in the IMCI training.

provider network. Examining this network reveals a different picture than the mental model of health officials and donor agencies. Household surveys reveal that in many developing countries, the private sector provides considerable treatment for diarrhea and respiratory illness in children (see survey analysis in the following). Household surveys, which are conducted regularly in many LMICs, collect data on the source of treatment for common childhood illnesses. We used data from these surveys from 51 countries to study the sources of treatment for respiratory illness and diarrhea (see Appendix Table A1 for a list of countries and survey years). The surveys show that, on average, the private sector provided treatment to 45% of children under five with respiratory symptoms and to 44% of those with diarrhea (Figure 4). The average masks significant differences between countries. For example, in Bangladesh, 81% of respiratory cases and 83% of diarrhea cases seen by a provider were treated in the private sector. By contrast, in Bolivia, the corresponding figures were 31% and 25%.

There are clear differences between regions in the significance of private providers as the source of treatment for ARI symptoms and diarrhea (Figure 5). In South Asia, East Asia and the Pacific, and the Middle East and North Africa, a significant majority of cases were treated in the private sector. By contrast, the overwhelming majority (about 90%) of cases in Europe and Central Asia were treated in the public sector. About 60% of cases in Latin America and the Caribbean were also treated by the public sector. In Sub-Saharan Africa, the public sector treated a somewhat larger proportion (about 50% vs. 45%) than the private sector.

It's not only the rich in developing countries who are treated by the private sector. The surveys show that the private sector also constitutes a significant source of treatment for poor people (Figure 6). However, there is a difference in the types of private sector providers used by the poor and the rich. The poor used informal providers and retail outlets more than the rich, who used formal providers to a greater extent (Figure 7). For example, as a proportion of all private providers, the richest 20% visited a private hospital, clinic, or private doctor for 51% of their ARI and diarrhea treatment, while the corresponding figure for the poorest was only 24%. The poorest also used traditional practitioners (12%) and vendors (24%) more often than the richest (4% and 11%, respectively).

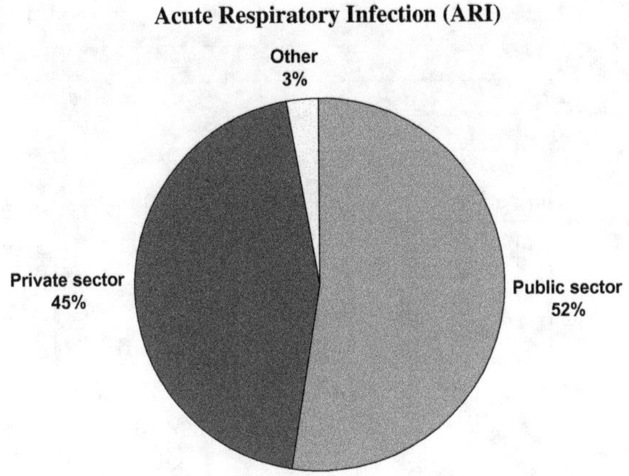


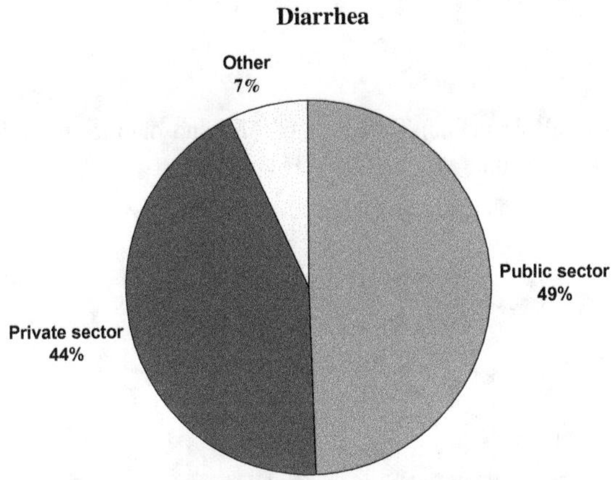


Figure 4. Where do they go? First source of treatment of ARI and diarrhea in children under five, by type of provider.

*Note*: The private sector includes hospitals, clinics, individual doctors, pharmacies, drug vendors, traditional practitioners, and NGOs.

*Source*: Demographic and Health Surveys.

The private distribution of medicines plays a significant role in the health systems of many developing countries. These private sector outlets provide much-needed access to medicines for many illnesses. For example, in Africa, private drug sellers are extensively utilized for fever and malaria treatment. It has been estimated that 89% of anti-malarial treatments were provided by the private sector in 2006, mainly by small and often informal drug sellers (Dalberg Global Development Advisors, 2007).

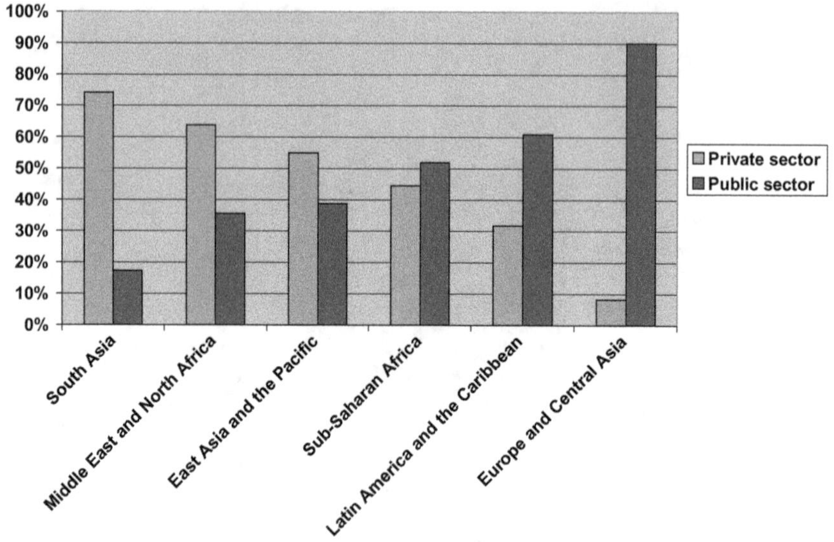


Figure 5. (Color available online) Treatment of ARI and diarrhea in children under five, by type of provider and region.

*Source*: Demographic and Health Surveys.

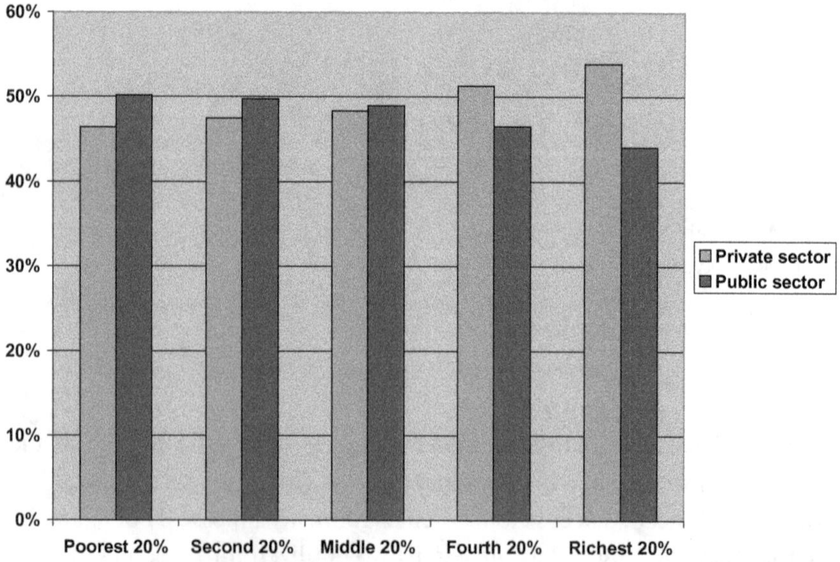


Figure 6. (Color available online) The private sector treats both poor and rich children: Treatment of ARI and diarrhea in children under five, by type of provider and socioeconomic status.

*Source*: Demographic and Health Surveys.

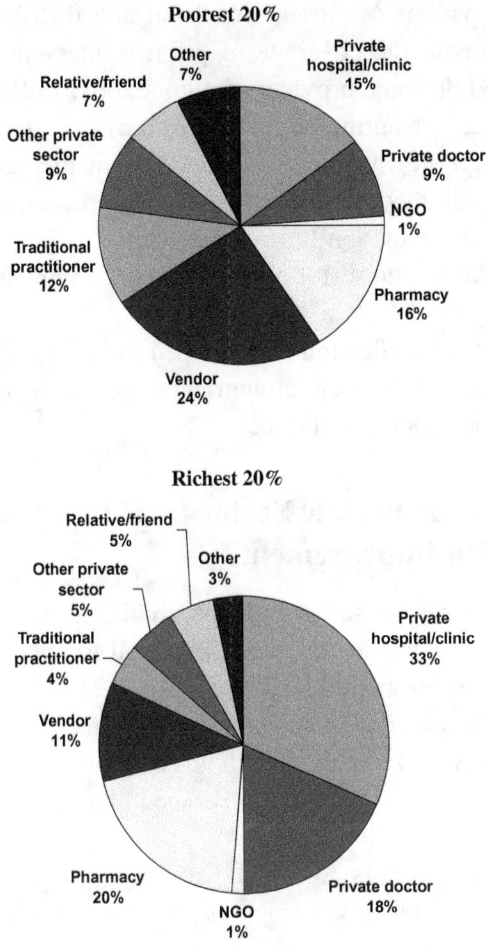


Figure 7. Across the spectrum: Types of private sector providers used by the poor and the rich for treatment of ARI and diarrhea in children under five.

*Source*: Demographic and Health Surveys.

People turn to the private portion of countries' provision and distribution networks for various reasons: convenience, trust, familiarity, predictability, and reliability. They are often located close by, open longer hours, have drugs in stock, see people more quickly, and treat them respectfully.

The private part of countries' provision and distribution networks clearly contributes to the coverage of priority interventions. However, issues remain. While some providers are good, others offer poor quality; they treat diarrhea with antibiotics and anti-diarrheals; they prescribe and dispense inappropriate malaria medicine. The quality of medicines is uneven. And though they do provide important preventive interventions (e.g. immunization), they don't provide enough (Levin *et al.*, 2011).

The role of the private sector extends beyond simply providing health services and drugs.

Food producers' fortification in developed and a few developing countries has significantly reduced micronutrient deficiencies. Yet, such fortification is rare in developing countries.

## 3. How Could the Private Sector be Harnessed Toward Child Health Improvement?

We know that the private sector influences child health significantly in developing countries. But is that enough in itself to open the flood gates to greater involvement in child health programs? The short answer is no. For that to happen, we need to be confident that greater involvement will contribute to achieving key child health goals by improving the care children are receiving and/or expanding coverage of the interventions that we know will save children's lives.

Evidence already exists for what happens when the private sector becomes more involved in health programs, and this can help us judge when and where greater engagement would be beneficial in child health programs. In this section, we discuss strategies that have been used primarily to expand coverage using private sector capacity, and in the subsequent section, we discuss strategies that have been used to promote access to products and then those aiming to improve the quality of care already being delivered.

### 3.1 *Strategies to expand coverage of services*

A range of strategies have been deployed to harness private sector capacity to increase the coverage of child health products and services. We review these in the following.

### 3.1.1 *Contracting NGOs to deliver health service packages*

Contracting with private organizations and individuals to deliver specific services has emerged as one of the most promising ways of enabling more people to access services, even in very challenging settings. This is significant because a key challenge for child health programs is to ensure that critical services and interventions reach more people.

A recent systematic review of studies in low-income countries identified eight cases that had measured impact in terms of quality and/or output and used a before and after and/or controlled design (Loevinsohn and Harding, 2005). We've applied the same inclusion criteria for studies since that review and found an additional study. Most of the cases involved contracting primary healthcare (PHC) packages, and a number of them specifically targeted coverage of preventive services (see Table 2).

The studies found that contracting did improve coverage, even in poor and remote areas. In the four studies of the review that had evaluated the intervention with controlled before-and-after designs, the median coverage increase in program areas versus control areas ranged from 3.4% to 26%. These four cases analyzed 31 main indicators, and all except one favored contracting. Larger improvements were found in relation to factors that are easier to change, such as immunization, Vitamin A, and antenatal care. Smaller improvements were found for factors that require more substantial changes in provider behavior and care-seeking, such as use of family planning and use of clinics and hospitals. Six of the studies compared the performance of contractors with government provision of the same services. Based on the measures of both coverage and quality of care, six studies found that contractors were more effective than government providers. While equity in coverage of services was only measured in one case (Cambodia), the evaluation found that, when equity targets were included in the contract, contractors were more effective in expanding coverage among low-income people.

There are a number of good examples where the contracting of PHC packages has achieved substantial increases in coverage of services. For example, contracting was introduced in Guatemala as part of a broader health reform that sought to introduce alternative management and organizational arrangements and make the service delivery system more

Table 2. Evidence from contracting service packages.

| Location & Type of Services | Type of Contract & Intervention | Scale (population coverage) | Contracting Arrangement | Evaluation Methodology | Main Results | Subsequent History |
|---|---|---|---|---|---|---|
| **1. Cambodia** Rural PHC & district hospital services | Service Delivery Contract (SDC) compared to Management Contract (MC) and Control (CC) i.e. government provision of services | 1.5 million | Competitively bid, formal contract, managed by special unit of MOH. Some problems with ensuring good relationships with provincial officials but NGOs were paid on time | Randomized controlled study with 12 districts as experimental units. Household and health facility surveys conducted before and after 2.5 years of implementation | SDC and MC much better than CC. Median double difference on 7 indicators for SDC vs. CC was 21.3%p for MC vs. CC double difference was 9.3%p | Expanded to twice as many districts |
| **2. Bangladesh** Urban PHC | SDC with NGOs compared to government provision of services, i.e. Chittagong City Corporation (CCC) | 4 million | Competitively bid formal contracts, managed by special unit of Local Government Division. Difficulties encountered with paying contractors on time and monitoring adequately | Controlled before and after study with 15 contracts compared to one large area implemented by CCC. Household & health facility survey by third party | Coverage data not yet published. Double difference for availability of specific services (e.g. immunization, family planning, etc.) was very large, 57–92%p | Contracts not yet completed. Planning for expansion of contracts far advanced and funding secured |

| Location & Type of Services | Type of Contract & Intervention | Scale (population coverage) | Contracting Arrangement | Evaluation Methodology | Main Results | Subsequent History |
|---|---|---|---|---|---|---|
| **3. Bolivia** Urban PHC | Limited MC in Phase 2. MC with expanded authority in Phase 3. Control area had continued public sector management | 250,000 | Single source contract with NGO. Contract management by committee including community representatives | Controlled, before and after design, but data from routine reporting system, only few indicators examined | Double difference for deliveries between MC and control was 21%p, 1%p for bed occupancy | Unknown |
| **4. Guatemala** Rural PHC in mountainous areas | MC in selected municipalities & SDC in more remote areas, compared to government provision (control) | 3.4 million | Competitively bid contracts with NGOs. Difficulties with financial management and supervision of contracts | Controlled design based on household survey conducted by third-party 3 years after contracting began | Median difference between MC and control on 5 indicators was 11%p (range 5–16%p) | Started as small pilot but expanded rapidly. Now covers 27% of country |
| **5. Haiti** NGOs delivering PHC in rural areas | NGOs with SDCs offered performance bonuses based on agreed targets | 534,000 | Input type of contract changed to one focused on outputs | Before and after (7 months later) design based on household surveys carried out by third-party | Average of follow-up minus baseline ranged from –3%p (antenatal care) to +32%p (immunization coverage) | Expanded to cover 1.5 million people, 19% of Haitian population |

(*Continued*)

Table 2. (*Continued*)

| Location & Type of Services | Type of Contract & Intervention | Scale (population coverage) | Contracting Arrangement | Evaluation Methodology | Main Results | Subsequent History |
|---|---|---|---|---|---|---|
| **6. Pakistan** Rural PHC | MC for the 104 basic health units in 1 district | 3.3 million | Sole source contract with NGO by local government. Received monthly tranche of funds regularly | Interrupted time series design based on routine recording and reporting system | Nearly a four-fold increase in the number of outpatient visits | Only started in May 2003 |
| **7. India** Improving quality of care by private practitioners | SDC for NGO working with private providers to improve MCH services | 54,000 | NGOs applied for grant from USAID and then informally contracted with private providers | Before and after (6 months later) design based on household surveys by community health workers | Rapid improvement in provider skills ranging from 25%p to 57%p compared to baseline | Unknown |
| **8. Nicaragua** Rural PHC | Combined with CCT; Performance-based contracting | 6,000 households | International competitive bidding to select providers (both private organizations and NGOs); Government provided vaccines | 2 evaluations, RCT (phase 1) and quasi-experimental (phase 2) | Phase 1 — contracted areas 16.4% more children <3 receiving preventive care compared to controls. Immunization coverage 9% higher in contracted vs. controls. 5.5% decline in stunting in contract areas | Government did not mainstream despite positive results |

Table 2. (*Continued*)

| Location & Type of Services | Type of Contract & Intervention | Scale (population coverage) | Contracting Arrangement | Evaluation Methodology | Main Results | Subsequent History |
|---|---|---|---|---|---|---|
| **9. Afghanistan** PHC nationwide | Performance based and non-performance based SDC with national and international NGOs | 23.9 million (82% of population) | Capitation | Household surveys for coverage, balanced score-card methodology for quality of care[a] | Reduction in the under-five mortality rate (from 257 deaths per 1,000 live births in 2000 to 161 in 2007), improvements on several coverage indicators; quality of care in contracted facilities increased by 32% from 2004 to 2007) | |

[a]See Peters *et al.* (2007) for a description of the scorecard methodology.

*Source*: Loevinsohn and Harding (2005), updated with Nicaragua evidence (Regalia and Castro, 2009).

responsive to clients. NGOs were contracted to deliver a PHC package, giving priority to prevention, maternal and child care, and basic curative care for 3.2 million people in mountainous areas. Two types of NGOs were contracted: health provider NGOs for delivery of the services and administrator NGOs that were responsible for administration and financial management. The provider NGOs received payment depending on the number of beneficiaries in their catchment area. The results of the contracting experience were evaluated in program versus control areas. The evaluation found that contracting led to more coverage per dollar spent and relatively more delivery of priority relative to other, less important, services (La Forgia, 2005).[10] In 1998, the cost per capita per year was US$6.25.

Contracting can be particularly effective if funding is linked to performance. In Haiti, the performance of healthcare NGOs was found to be extremely uneven, so performance-based contracting was introduced in 1999 (Eichler *et al.*, 2001). Three NGOs were contracted to deliver a PHC package, including maternal, child health, and family planning services, to 534,000 people in rural areas. The largest portion of the payment was still fixed, but a bonus of up to 10% of the fixed portion could be earned if targets were reached. Out of seven performance indicators, three were directly related to child health: use of Oral Rehydration Therapy (ORT) to treat diarrhea, immunization coverage, and average waiting time for attention to a child. A neutral third party was contracted to monitor performance. The most striking result of the contracting approach was the significant improvement in immunization coverage. The proportion of children aged 12–23 months who had received full immunization coverage increased from a baseline of 35–49% to 69–79%. Contracting has also been proven as a feasible and effective mechanism for delivering basic health services, including child health, in conflict and post-conflict situations (Box 2).

[10] The contracted areas faced considerably higher costs due to their remoteness and low population density. Compared to the public clinics, they were given additional resources to cover the extra costs. The evaluation developed a metric to compare efficiency which allocated costs to services and compared the costs for delivering the same service and achieving the same coverage rates to assess efficiency.

## Box 2. Contracting with NGOs to increase coverage of basic health services in Afghanistan

In Afghanistan, the government has contracted NGOs since 2002 to provide a basic package of health services.[a] Contracting in Afghanistan relies on capitation — payments made directly to healthcare providers for each individual enrolled with that provider by various national and international NGOs for a list of services included in the basic package. Evidence suggests that there have been significant improvements in coverage. Population coverage of basic health increased from 9% in 2002 to 82% in 2006. The rate of outpatient visits increased from 0.23 visits in 2003 to 0.94 in 2007 — nearly a fourfold increase. The contraceptive prevalence rate increased from 5.1% to 13.0%. The percentage of pregnant women receiving at least one prenatal visit increased from 8.0% in 2003 to 30% in 2007. Even the percentage of deliveries attended by a physician or midwife, which is an intervention for which coverage is typically slow to change, increased from 9.0% to 18.9% from 2003 to 2006. Increases have also occurred in routine immunization coverage: the percentage of children aged 12–23 months who had received three doses of DPT[b] vaccine increased from 21.2% in 2003 to 34.6% in 2006, although the absolute levels remain low by international standards.

Quality of care, as independently assessed by a score card, improved by 32% from 2004 to 2007, which represents an improvement larger than one standard deviation at baseline.[c] There were also sizable reductions in child mortality during this period. The under-five mortality rate decreased from 257 per 1,000 live births in 2000 to 161 in 2007, which is equal to a reduction of 37%. It seems likely to have been generated, at least in part, by the significant improvements in coverage and quality of services in contracted facilities. The quality of care in public facilities, which also received donor support, actually declined during the same period.

*Sources*: Loevinsohn and Sayed (2008), Loevinsohn and Harding (2005), Sabri *et al.* (2007), World Bank (2010).

[a]The initiative was supported by the World Bank, USAID, and the European Commission.

[b]Diphtheria, Pertussus, and Tetanus.

[c]The score card consists of data on indicators such as staffing; the knowledge of physicians, nurses, and midwives; the quality of observed patient — health worker interactions; and drug availability (Peters *et al.*, 2007).

### 3.1.2 *Expanding social health insurance to deliver health service packages*

Health insurance is another mechanism that can be used to increase access to Maternal and Child Health (MCH) services. Health insurance typically involves premiums, which can limit coverage of poor people. To enable population groups of less means, several health insurance programs have subsidized the insurance premiums for the poor. Colombia's program subsidized premiums for poor people, and it also enabled reimbursement of private providers and pharmacies.

In 1992, Colombians faced serious problems accessing healthcare services, particularly in poor and rural areas. Caregivers often did not take sick children for care. Caregivers sought care for children with diarrhea only 39% of the time and for children with fever only 49% of the time (Boerma *et al.*, 1991). To address this, the government established a basic insurance package and funded insurance premiums for poor people. People could choose their insurers and be reimbursed by them for all services included in the package, whether provided by a public or private provider. As a result, more people took sick children for treatment, and they sought care more promptly. Notable increases in care-seeking for children with coughs and diarrhea were achieved, especially in rural areas. Between 1995 and 2005, care-seeking for insured low-income children with cough increased by 35% and with diarrhea increased by 60%. Sizable increases were also achieved in antenatal care and attended deliveries. Subsequently, mortality rates fell sharply among infants whose mothers had access to antenatal care and the option of giving birth in a facility, compared with those whose mothers did not (Giedion and Uribe, 2009). Colombia illustrates the effectiveness of a mechanism that targets subsidies and taps into private suppliers to overcome health service and product access barriers for poor people.

### 3.1.3 *Contracting to expand outreach services*

It is one thing to make child health services more available for people seeking services; it is a distinct challenge to improve outreach services which are delivered in the community and people's homes. Public sector initiatives have often found it particularly difficult to expand coverage of these services, perhaps because it is so difficult to motivate and supervise public workers outside the clinic setting.[11] Private organizations and individuals have been contracted to increase the coverage and effectiveness of these important preventive and promotive services. Contracting with NGOs has been used to increase coverage of nutrition interventions (Marek *et al.*, 1999), immunization, and micronutrients (Bhat *et al.*, 2009), and to encourage more poor people to access services. Moreover, individual health workers have been contracted to undertake outreach activities, both generally and for specific behaviors, such as the promotion of exclusive breastfeeding (Tendler, 1997; Bhandari *et al.*, 2003; Quinn *et al.*, 2005).

NGOs were successfully contracted to undertake outreach services in Madagascar and Senegal. They were contracted to provide nutrition services to women and their children (Table 3). The projects targeted poor areas and covered more than 450,000 people in each country. NGOs were contracted to provide all aspects of the programs: management, delivery, training, operations research, and supervision. The services included monthly growth monitoring of children; weekly nutrition and health education sessions for women; referral to health services for unvaccinated children and pregnant women, severely malnourished children, and sick beneficiaries; home visits to follow up on beneficiaries who were referred or who did not come to the services; food supplementation for malnourished children; improved access to water standpipes (in Senegal); and referral to a social fund for income-generating activities (in Madagascar). An evaluation of the projects found that the program increased coverage significantly and that, as a result, severe malnutrition rates decreased by 6% while moderate malnutrition rates decreased by 4% (Marek *et al.*, 1999). Contracting NGOs for nutrition interventions has also been effective in Bangladesh (Table 3).

[11]Outreach services is a general term referring to all those activities which are primarily delivered outside the clinic setting, with regard to child health the activities aim to enable and persuade people to take better care of their children's health and to seek care promptly when necessary.

Table 3. Evidence on contracting for community nutrition services.

| Location & Type of Services | Type of Contract & Intervention | Scale | Contracting Arrangement | Evaluation Methodology | Main Results | Subsequent History |
|---|---|---|---|---|---|---|
| 1. Madagascar & Senegal community nutrition services | Madagascar: SDCs with 50 NGOs Senegal: SDCs with NGOs who worked through small groups of unemployed youth | 460,000 in Madagascar 490,000 in Senegal | Madagascar: Contract management done by unit in office of the president. In Senegal by para-statal. No serious problems encountered | Before and after (17 months) household survey of nutrition status in Senegal. 3rd party survey of participation in project and control areas | Severe and moderate malnutrition declined 6% and 4% respectively. Participation was 72% in project & 35% in control areas | Continued with NGOs in both countries, albeit in different format |
| 2. Bangladesh rural community nutrition services | SDC with NGOs compared to control areas with no organized nutrition services (i.e. normal government health services with no nutritional component) | 15 million population | Fixed price MOU. Initially sole source selection of NGOs, then competitive. Serious problems with payment & other aspects of contract management | Controlled, before and after study with 6 experimental and 2 control upazillas (sub-districts). Household surveys conducted by 3rd party | Malnutrition rates declined 18% points in SDC sub-districts compared to 13%p in controls (double difference = 5 %p. Double difference for Vitamin A was 27%p | Expanded to more than 30 million population |

In Ceará (Brazil), contracting outreach workers led to substantial increases in the reach and quality of community-based services, including educating mothers on oral rehydration therapy, vaccination, prenatal care, breastfeeding, and growth monitoring. The overall program led to a tripling of vaccination rates and a one-third reduction in the infant death rate (Tendler, 1997).[12] Comparable successes have been achieved by several large-scale programs that engaged private actors to promote appropriate breastfeeding practices (Parlato and Seidel, 1998). These programs have worked through actors such as health providers, village-based workers (Bhandari *et al.*, 2003), and peer counselors (Haider *et al.*, 2000; Morrow *et al.*, 1999).

### 3.1.4 *Strategies to promote demand for services*

In the examples discussed above, gains in coverage were achieved largely via contracted private services. However, in some places, demand for services is chronically low, so demand constraints are more important than supply constraints. In these settings, actions to increase demand are needed. The provision of health insurance coverage can reduce financial barriers. However, where insurance platforms don't exist, vouchers have also been used. In some cases, caregivers may undervalue services, such as vaccination or well-child checkups. Some countries have deployed conditional cash transfer programs to address these demand problems.

All three of these strategies share one important advantage over other instruments: they can be targeted at a group of individuals (unlike many strategies to expand coverage). For example, conditional cash transfers and insurance subsidies can be targeted at poor people. Vouchers can be used to get pregnant women to sleep under mosquito nets to protect them from malaria, which is so dangerous during pregnancy; they can be used to target the distribution of mosquito nets to households with children.

---

[12]The program utilized novel mechanisms of community participation in oversight of the contracted workers.

## 3.2 *Targeting subsidies and tapping private providers to overcome access barriers for the poor*

Targeting subsidies to the poor is one strategy to increase demand by addressing financial access barriers to care. Examples of such targeted subsidies include conditional cash transfers and health insurance. To be successful, these initiatives require an adequate supply of health services. If the public sector is not able to respond to the increased demand, the subsidies can be combined with contracting with private providers.

Conditional cash transfers are essentially welfare programs that pay cash benefits to participating families on condition that they undertake certain actions, such as keeping their children in school, making regular visits to the local health clinic, and participating in nutrition programs (Lagarde *et al.*, 2007). Conditional cash transfers have been used where ignorance of the value of, say, prevention services or "well-child" check-ups was leading to low use of services. Conditional cash transfers differ from traditional programs in that they focus on the demand for service provision with the dual objectives of providing short-term income assistance and motivating behaviors that will help poor people in the long term. In India, a conditional cash transfer program called Janani Suraksha Yojana has increased coverage of antenatal care and the proportion of births taking place in health facilities (Lim *et al.*, 2010).

While many conditional cash transfer programs have been implemented in developing countries (Lagarde *et al.*, 2007), particularly in Latin America, few have engaged private actors to deliver services. Conditional cash transfers usually require people to use public clinics. However, where these have been unable to meet the increased demand due to conditional cash transfers, some programs have brought in private providers, as occurred in Nicaragua (Regalia and Castro, 2009). In this case, many more poor people in rural areas began using services as a result of the conditional cash transfer program and the expanded availability of services from contracted private providers (Box 3).

To respond to inequities in immunization coverage, in 2001, the Government of Colombia implemented a conditional cash transfer program intended to stimulate demand for preventive healthcare which is provided by both public and private providers. The program reached over

**Box 3. Conditional cash transfers with private provision increased provision of priority children's health services**

A unique initiative in Nicaragua illustrates the effectiveness of mechanisms that target subsidies and tap into private suppliers to overcome health service access barriers for poor people.

In Nicaragua, the Social Protection Network program combined private sector contracting to expand the availability of services with a cash transfer to encourage poor people to use services. Payments were given to households provided they fulfilled certain conditions, such as increased school attendance and health service utilization, including antenatal and postnatal care, health check-ups, growth monitoring, nutrition education, and vaccinations.

The program contracted both for-profit and NGO providers through a competitive bidding process managed by the ministries of health and finance. Providers were compensated based on the achievement of service coverage targets. A randomized control evaluation found that the program led to substantial increases in service use. The percentage of children attending preventive health check-up sessions increased in the treatment group from 73.7% to 92.7% between 2000 and 2002, compared with an increase in the control group from 73.6% to 84.1%. Health outcomes were also improved. The number of stunted children in the treatment group decreased by 3.4%, while it increased by 2.2% in the control group.

*Source*: Regalía and Castro (2007).

700,000 extremely poor or displaced families. The program significantly increased the probability of adequate DPT vaccination for children less than 24 months of age (Attanasio *et al.*, 2005).

### 3.3 *Strategies to promote access to products*

The use of several products has proven critically important for child health, including ORS and micronutrients. As with other interventions, programs have turned most often to traditional public delivery channels to increase coverage of these products. While public distribution is often important, private sector engagement strategies are likewise valuable in many settings. We discuss here the experience with private sector engagement to increase use of important child health products.

### 3.3.1 *Promoting product use and distribution: ORS*

After acute respiratory illness, diarrhea is the leading killer of children under five. More than 1.5 million children die from the illness each year. ORS are an inexpensive and highly effective intervention to reduce the death toll from diarrhea (Jones *et al.*, 2003). Yet, parents often turn instead to anti-diarrheals or antibiotics.[13]

Health initiatives have sought to increase ORS use since the early 1980s;[14] they've worked to increase caregivers' understanding and to make ORS products widely and reliably available. Yet, as Figure 2 illustrates, coverage is disappointingly low. This average obscures considerable variation. Some countries have achieved notable and sustained increases in coverage. Wilson *et al.* (2013) compared better and worse performing programs and identified features of program strategies associated with success. The review identified several important features with respect to private sector engagement.[15]

*Demand*: Persuading caregivers that ORS is the treatment of choice is critical to success. Healthy behaviors involving product use can be promoted via commercial advertising-style marketing efforts.[16] Furthermore, the Wilson *et al.* (2013) review found that this kind of demand promotion has been an essential element of most successful ORS programs.[17]

*Supply*: Regardless of demand, high and sustained ORS use requires that the product be widely and continuously available and must be affordable. Additionally, prices must be low, as demand for ORS can be

[13]These are inappropriate for most instances of diarrheal and can be harmful.

[14]In 1982, ORS was a focus of UNICEF's "GOBI–FFF" selective primary healthcare strategy.

[15]The discussion in this section draws on Wilson *et al.* (2013) throughout.

[16]Such efforts involve consumer research and promoting behavior by "selling" a product (e.g. the attractiveness of its features).

[17]See Wilson *et al.* (2013, Table 4) for an explanation of program scoring.

sensitive to price. Programs have taken distinct strategies to achieve this. Most initiatives distributed program-provided ORS at low prices or for free through public clinics. The limited reach of the public portion of countries' provision and distribution networks has kept this approach, by itself, from achieving broad, reliable availability and use. Some programs with donor support, like Malawi's, deployed traditional social marketing initiatives. Traditional social marketing strategies for promoting product coverage promote demand using the commercial marketing techniques mentioned above. In addition, distribution is outsourced to private distributors and retailers who are reimbursed via product fees, and, typically, the management of both sets of activities is professionalized by outsourcing management or allocating management to an autonomous agency. In Malawi, starting in 1999, a donor-funded International NGO managed the demand promotion and distributed their branded ORS project via affiliated private distributors and retailers. By building demand and tapping into the capacity of vibrant private distribution networks, they helped increase ORS coverage from 48% to 69% in 2012 (Morris *et al.*, 2012). This coverage depends on donor support for management as well as external supplies, however (Morris *et al.*, 2012). Bangladesh, too, successfully deployed a traditional social marketing strategy and managed a transition to sustainable (e.g. not donor dependent) coverage. They "localized" the management organization, and they managed a transition from subsidized products to promote the development of local commercial production and distribution to achieve high and sustainable coverage with a market price of US$0.06 (Mosites *et al.*, 2012).[18] Several countries were likewise able to suppress anti-diarrheal use by prohibiting the import or manufacture of pediatric formulations of anti-diarrheal medicines.

In settings like Bangladesh or India, where public sector care-seeking is low and commercial pharmacy distribution networks are vibrant, working through private distribution channels is critical. Bangladesh managed to mobilize private distribution networks to contribute to ORS coverage. In India, on the other hand, anti-diarrheals and antibiotics are still widely used, especially in the private sector; India's failure to build a productive collaboration with private distributors and providers to promote ORS use

[18]ORS is also available for free in public clinics.

undoubtedly contributed to this (Wilson *et al.*, 2013). Both the Wilson review and a more recent review by Unger *et al.* (2014) confirmed that ORS initiatives which consciously develop private manufacturing, distribution, and retail are more successful and sustainable.

### 3.3.2 *Collaboration with commercial partners for food fortification*

Millions of people get sick each year because of micronutrient deficiencies. Many health programs have addressed this through the campaign delivery of micronutrient supplements, such as Vitamin A and, more recently, zinc. However, while this approach has managed to increase the uptake of essential micronutrients, food fortification is recognized as a better long-term measure for reducing some micronutrient deficiencies in developing countries, particularly in terms of sustainability (Horton, 2006; Darnton-Hill and Nalubola, 2002).

The cornerstone of any fortification initiative is the addition of a micronutrient to a widely consumed food, such as salt or bread, during production. Micronutrients that can be used to fortify food include Vitamin A, zinc, iron, iodine, folate, and calcium. A sufficient fortifier is added to ensure that consumption of the micronutrient rises to appropriate levels in the population. The delivery logic of food fortification is highly advantageous. Big changes in behavior aren't required with regard to either supply or demand. By fortifying the food that children eat, improved nutrition can be accomplished via the operation of the existing food distribution chain. It also requires less change in people's behavior than other strategies because they do not need to obtain and take a supplement or change their eating habits.

Food fortification is a very cost-effective intervention, at just a few cents per person per year, and reductions in disease and disability can be substantial. Although the exact costs and benefits depend on factors such as the extent and severity of the micronutrient deficiency in a country and how food is produced and consumed, they typically range from US$22 to US$60 per disability-adjusted life year (DALY) saved, depending on the micronutrient (Horton, 2006).

Successful food fortification initiatives usually involve government action to engage food producers to add micronutrients to their products, backed by a public information program to promote demand for fortified foods. Other important elements of a food fortification effort may be:

- funding food producers' investment costs and/or additional production costs to prevent retail prices from rising too sharply;[19]
- reduction in taxes and tariffs to reduce the cost to food producers of buying fortifiers;
- creation of regulatory standards for food fortification, backed by monitoring of compliance;

Box 4 describes China's successful efforts to reduce goiter due to iodine deficiency by working with the salt industry.

Despite broad consensus that harnessing private distribution networks is critical, child health and related programs rarely attempt to do so.

## 3.4 *Strategies to improve quality of care*

As discussed above, in many settings, private actors exist with whom governments can collaborate to achieve expansions in access and coverage of products and services. However, addressing quality problems in the private sector may be just as important for achieving child health goals, depending on the country setting. Where large numbers of sick children are taken to private providers with unsafe practices, we need to examine strategies to improve quality. We need to understand when such activities may contribute to the impact of child health programs. This is what we discuss in this section.

### 3.4.1 *Regulation to address product quality*

While typical standard-setting and penalties for non-compliance regulatory initiatives have rarely achieved quality improvements, there are a few

[19] Fortification can be implemented without subsidy, but this may require legislation or strong regulation. It can also be facilitated by government procurement of fortified food, e.g. Bishai and Nalubola (2002).

### Box 4. Improving child health by reducing iodine deficiency in China

Iodine is essential for the proper functioning of the thyroid, which regulates metabolism, growth, and development. A shortage of iodine leads to an overcompensating thyroid gland and a swollen neck, known as goiter. Iodine is also vital to the development of the brain, and iodine deficiency can reduce intellectual potential by as much as 15%.

In 1995, 20% of children aged eight to ten in China had goiter, and 400 million people were estimated to be at risk of iodine deficiency disorders. As a result, the Chinese government launched the National Iodine Deficiency Disorders Elimination Program, which received technical assistance from international organizations through the Iodine Deficiency Disorders Control Project. The donor-funded project focused on developing an initiative to produce and distribute iodized salt throughout the country. Existing salt factories were upgraded to increase production capacity, and new iodation centers were established. Other activities included regulation, monitoring, quality control, enforcement, and a public information campaign targeting provincial governments and the public.

The initiative cost US$152 million. To help cover these costs, the government allowed retail salt prices to increase by a small amount, but within limits considered affordable for most families. The World Bank, which financed the project with US$20 million, deemed the project extremely cost-effective, costing between four and five cents of external funding per beneficiary.

The joint efforts by the government and their development partners rapidly generated significant benefits. By 1999, iodized salt was reaching 94% of the country, compared with 80% in 1995. The quality of iodized salt also improved, with salt samples of high quality increasing from 30% in 1995 to 81% in 1999. This had a positive impact on health outcomes. The goiter rate for children aged eight to ten fell from 20.4% in 1995 to 8.8% in 1999. The success of China's iodation experience has made it a model for other fortification interventions.

*Source*: Vines (2007).

regulatory initiatives which have succeeded, in particular actions to use product market authorization. Control of breast-milk substitutes is one example. Breastfeeding is recognized as the ideal way of providing young infants with the nutrients they need for healthy growth and development (WHO and UNICEF, 2003). A 2003 study of child survival strategies identified exclusive breastfeeding in the first six months of life and continued breastfeeding from 6 to 12 months, as the single most effective way for mothers to give their babies the best chance of survival, with the potential of saving 1.2 million lives annually (Jones *et al.*, 2003).

Virtually all mothers can breastfeed, provided they have accurate information, the support of their families, and the healthcare system. However, like the other interventions we've discussed, strategies to increase breastfeeding have largely been ineffective, and rates have remained stubbornly low in developing countries.

One reason for low breastfeeding rates is that outreach services, designed to increase women's understanding of breastfeeding, often function poorly at the community level, which has been hard to fix. However, the problem has been exacerbated by aggressive marketing of breast-milk substitutes by private sector companies, which has persuaded many women who could breastfeed to use formula milk. To counter this, the World Health Assembly adopted the International Code of Marketing of Breast-milk Substitutes in 1981 (WHO, 1981). The code stipulates that there should be no promotion of breast-milk substitutes, bottles, or teats to the general public and that neither health facilities nor health professionals should have a role in promoting breast-milk substitutes. It also says that free samples should not be provided to pregnant women, new mothers, or families. Sixty-five countries have enacted legislation implementing all or many of the provisions of the code, with positive results. A recent study found an association between adoption of the code and exclusive breastfeeding rates, implying that it makes a difference when properly implemented (Cavagnero *et al.*, 2008). As noted above, some countries have reduced use of anti-diarrheals by prohibiting the import, production, and sale of pediatric formulations of such products.

## 4. Why Has Progress Been Slow?

To date, the full potential of the private sector to contribute to improving children's health has not been tapped into. The reasons are many and varied, but a major factor is the approach taken by international organizations, especially donors, to child health programs in developing countries.

Starting in the late 1990s, most support to improve child health applied to much or all of the IMCI program approach. IMCI's program logic derived from a tight focus on the priority health needs of children in developing countries (e.g. illnesses and preventable conditions generating the most ill-health and mortality). Countries' existing delivery networks for basic services and medicines did not figure into the logical framework (Gwatkin *et al.*, 2007). As Gwatkin points out, a strategy that targeted a less important illness, but more amenable to being delivered within the provision network utilized by caregivers and sick children, could very likely be more effective. Omitting the consideration of private provision and distribution was particularly pernicious in countries with high private sector utilization.

WHO and UNICEF, the leading technical agencies with regard to child health, worked through their regional and in-country advisors and support structures to advocate for and provide support for the implementation of IMCI in countries. The structure of program support was strongly influenced by the organizations' pre-existing relationships with member states, whose representatives were drawn from government bodies. This influence encouraged a mode of operation that focused on health ministries and public delivery channels.[20] While IMCI's preparatory work would examine household survey data to understand disease burden, they did not examine the data to understand the delivery system. Hence, even in countries where very few sick children are taken to public clinics, there was no opportunity to reflect on the need for additional or alternative approaches. The assumptions underlying the IMCI program design were that the public sector was reaching most children and that quality improvements resulting from IMCI would persuade those people using the private sector to switch. These assumptions proved unfounded and led to the omission of the private sector from programs, even in countries where private providers were actually seeing the large majority of sick children. Box 5 describes the IMCI experience in Bangladesh, where the program

[20]This point was made by interviewees, and also with regard to WHO, by Toonen *et al.* (2004).

implementation and evaluation provide compelling evidence about the tendency to overlook the private sector when designing child health programs. It also highlights how omitting the private sector in a country where the public sector reaches only a small proportion of sick children, severely limits the ability of improved public services to reduce mortality at the population level. Leaving out the private sector, and more importantly, those who seek care there, contributed to disappointing results in early experiences with IMCI, as discussed in the early part of this chapter. IMCI sometimes did improve public services, but people using the private sector didn't shift in large numbers to public services as a result.

WHO and UNICEF are the key technical agencies in child health. Both have a tendency to focus on government agencies and public networks. Some of the key financing agencies also focused their support on public delivery channels. For example, the World Bank's child health projects and project components tended to support the upgrading of facilities as well as training of public health workers. World Bank projects supported a few efforts to engage private providers (Axelson *et al.*, 2003).

IMCI and other child health-focused initiatives typically track "coverage," defined with reference to the proportion of health workers trained in how to identify and treat illness appropriately in a given geographical area. The actual coverage of the interventions (in terms of people using the services) was only measured through household surveys (Demographic Health Surveys (DHS) and later Multiple Indicator Cluster Surveys or MICS) every five years, with no direct link to program monitoring or management. Also, since baseline utilization patterns were rarely examined to gain a more accurate understanding of who was using the frontline public clinics which were to be strengthened, the actual reach of program efforts was not monitored; in many cases, programs that were failing to reach a majority of children were continued without proper review or much-needed adaptation.

Some agencies attempted to draw attention to the important role that private providers play in child health. Both USAID and the World Bank supported technical work and regional consultation in the early 2000s (Waters *et al.*, 2002). However, this did not generate much interest among international agencies more broadly to influence policy. A few small pilot projects were launched in countries, mostly with external financing,

### Box 5. IMCI in Bangladesh: A program that missed most children

In a cluster randomized trial, 20 first-level government health facilities in the Matlab sub-district of Bangladesh and their catchment areas (total population of about 350,000) were paired and randomly assigned to either IMCI (intervention; 10 facilities) or usual services (comparison; 10 facilities). The trial began in early 2002. All three components of IMCI were implemented in the intervention facilities — health worker training, health system improvements, and family and community activities — to give the strategy the best chance of demonstrating its effectiveness. Impact information was collected from household and health facility surveys. These tracked the intermediate outputs and outcomes as well as nutrition and mortality changes in both the intervention and comparison areas.

The IMCI program generated improvements in public clinics, including health workers' skills and health system support, in the intervention areas. It led to increased exclusive breastfeeding rates and reduced stunting rates. It also resulted in improved family and community practices that led people to seek healthcare from appropriate providers. For example, the proportion of children in IMCI areas who were sick in the two weeks preceding the survey and taken to an appropriate provider increased from 9% to 20%, while the rate in comparison areas remained below 10%.

However, despite the improved performance of health workers from the IMCI training and improved care-seeking behavior, this improvement was insufficient to reduce mortality at the population level because of the relatively small number of sick children taken to public facilities (even after quality improvements).

*Source*: Arifeen *et al.* (2009).

though these were not systematically evaluated (Bustreo *et al.*, 2003). Further progress in the policy debate has been hampered by the limited availability of evidence to show which policies most effectively influence the private sector to contribute to the reduction of child mortality and in which settings.

This lack of support from international agencies meant that there were few fora in which the issue of private sector involvement was discussed.

It also meant the international agencies did not provide systematic ongoing support to identify the most suitable policy measures for harnessing the private sector contribution to child health. Unlike some global programs, child health programs at the country and global levels receive no systematic help to analyze whether they need to engage the private sector and how to do so.

Finally, when comparing approaches to AIDS, TB, and malaria, no specific funder for IMCI has well-established mechanisms to link with the private sector. This contrasts with the Global Fund's mechanisms, which can fund implementation activities associated with private sector engagement relatively easily.

What drives child health-focused initiatives to so often overlook the private sector is not entirely clear. Wilson *et al.* (2013) noted that donor agencies supporting child health efforts appear not to recognize their importance.[21] Observing the heated opposition to testing strategies to distribute malaria medicines through private channels, some commenters suggest ideology and self-interest from involvement with implementing alternative strategies are likely at work as well.

Very few child health programs include metrics that help them change course if things are not working out. One that did was a program in Nicaragua set up to increase the coverage of services in underserved rural areas. At first, it applied a conditional cash transfer, believing that people didn't value the services enough but would use them more if welfare payments were tied to their use. However, after a year of implementation, metrics showed that use wasn't increasing and that the problem lay with a lack of services in the targeted areas. The program started contracting private providers to deliver services in those areas, and many more people began to use them. The program could only be adjusted to achieve its goals because utilization was being closely monitored, allowing the program team to discover they had initially misdiagnosed the problem: they had failed to recognize the supply constraints.

The most frequent constraints to engaging private providers for MCH services are summarized in Box 6.

---

[21] See page 11, Wilson *et al.* (2013).

### Box 6. Not dancing to the same tune? Constraints to private sector engagement

Efforts to involve the private sector in child health more systematically are hampered by constraints that involve the private sector, the public sector, and/or donor organizations.

1. **Private sector**
   - Lack of regulation or accreditation, which may lead to overcharging or poor-quality service.
   - The high-risk nature of public–private partnerships, which discourages private actors.
   - The fragmentation that arises from the unorganized and sometimes informal nature of the private actors in healthcare.
2. **Public sector**
   - Governments' view that the private sector is competing with them for funding and service provision.
   - Lack of skills to structure and manage private engagement.
   - Lack of external support for working with private providers.
   - Limited awareness of the ways in which the private sector can be engaged.
   - Poor regulation, corruption, and lack of transparency.
3. **Donors**
   - Operating constraints related to working with national governments as their main partners.
   - An ideological aversion to working with a profit-seeking private sector.
   - Familiarity with longstanding approaches that support public delivery and crowding out the private sector.
   - Donor support mechanisms are often better suited to supporting public sector activities.

## 5. Lessons Learned

In contrast with some health programs, in child health, there is no global agency or forum where active donors and country representatives can come together to review program effectiveness and adapt strategies.

Despite the collaboration of several major actors (WHO, UNICEF, and USAID) over a number of years to evaluate IMCI programs — and the problems revealed — there has yet to be any direct action to change child health program guidelines. The global child health effort is notable for this surprising lack of feedback and mechanisms to improve program effectiveness. The deficiency is particularly worrying since the IMCI evaluations found that the programs were not successful in reducing child mortality. The situation, therefore, warrants several changes, which we attempt to articulate in the following.

## 5.1 *Changes in approach*

First and foremost, the starting point for designing effective child health programs in developing countries must be the countries' existing provision and distribution networks, including private providers and product delivery channels. Without this information, programs cannot be designed to reach all segments of the population. Currently, the DHS surveys are the source of the most useful information in this regard. Yet, the reports of the DHS survey results do not consolidate the information about the composition of the provision and distribution networks. DHS sponsors should establish the practice of preparing a chapter on the countries' provision and distribution networks from the survey results (Meessen *et al.*, 2011).

Program design guidelines should be adapted to include the use of such information, further assessment of private provision, and the development of strategies to engage the private sector. Such adaptation of program guidelines has helped bring about changes in TB programs. In TB programs, continuous support, at the global and country levels, for the implementation of new strategies for private sector engagement has been available and has made a notable contribution to the improvements in program effectiveness. The establishment of similar support structures for child health would increase the chances of effective and sustainable collaboration with private providers.

In countries with substantial private sector utilization, the engagement of private sector actors should be considered where it is needed to reach large numbers of sick children. In addition, we must look specifically at where poor people go for their services and products. The strategies needed to reach them must be considered with special attention.

## 5.2 *Monitoring*

Second, programs which strive to harness the private part of countries' provider and distribution systems must develop and deploy different monitoring metrics. These should enable programs to maximize the effectiveness of their activities and reveal where and how private-sector actors are engaged and whether this engagement produces results. It is necessary to change program monitoring so that information from household surveys and information from independent provider and distributor surveys can be used to check program impact and inform changes where needed. A good step in this direction is the recent increase in the frequency of the MICS conducted by UNICEF in LMICs, from every five years to every three years. Program managers can and should use data directly from these surveys — and from DHS — for monitoring programs related to private sector utilization as well as impacts flowing from engagement efforts. Surveys of the availability, markups, and prices of medicine and other health products can be critically important for tracking whether markets are evolving in a desirable direction with respect to child health. (For example: Are ORS products more widely available? Have prices fallen? If so, by how much? Are market prices approaching broad affordability? If not, can they be further reduced? What about rural areas? Do special actions need to be taken?)

Child health programs also need to focus on reaching the poorest children. Tracking the operation of informal providers and retailers is especially important in this regard. Developing and deploying templates to collect information about these actors is critically important.

## 5.3 *Changes in strategies*

Third, and most importantly, based on experience to date, how can progress be achieved rapidly? Which strategies work, and for what? What is required to implement them and expand their application to achieve higher coverage of critical interventions among children? What is needed for child health is essentially what is needed for PHC — namely, strategic, evidence-based application of mechanisms to improve the care of sick children wherever they are taken. With this in mind, and recognizing that health systems' foundations, such as the government's stewardship function, are critical for success, the most promising strategies are as follows.

To increase the coverage of services where private providers are available, **contracting and performance-based contracting**, whether by public or social insurance agencies, should be expanded (along with the capacity to design and enforce contracts). Lighter-touch support, such as allowing private providers without access to a secure cold-chain to access publicly distributed vaccines, should also be considered.

To improve the coverage of product-based interventions, where private distribution channels are well developed, programs should take action to **promote and improve the private distribution of products**. This will likely involve demand promotion efforts as well as actions to expand, or shift, private provision in a positive direction (e.g. collaborating with food manufacturers and subsidizing preferred medicines).

For improving healthcare or dispensing quality, **accreditation** or **training**, combined with support for better practice and/or incentives, should be considered.

Alternatively, **conditional cash transfers** or **vouchers** should be considered where low demand for prevention-promotion services among the poor is a significant problem and adequate additional supply is available.

To build the evidence base, it is critical that all mechanisms are properly evaluated when they are applied in child health programs.

## 5.4 *Changes in donor support*

Finally, donors that focus solely on the public sector can help shift toward inclusive approaches where the setting makes it necessary to reach children. Global commitment to maternal and child health has increased at the political level, as shown by increased official development assistance for maternal and child health from 2003 to 2007 (Requejo and Bryce, 2010); therefore, now is the time to demand more health for the money. Donors can facilitate the implementation of the technical changes designed to increase private sector engagement, described above, by insisting on:

- analysis of service utilization before strategies are selected;
- supporting the revision of DHS results reports to consolidate information on countries' provider and distribution systems;

- consideration of alternative strategies involving the private sector for achieving child health goals;
- support for developing and deploying better, more inclusive monitoring templates;
- support for implementing needed adaptations based on data that emerge.

However, these improvements will not be achieved easily. Concerted, collaborative, and continuous action on the part of the key funders is required to change the existing, often ineffective, program approaches. The key actors must figure out how to do this. The Partnership for Maternal, Newborn & Child Health (PMNCH) offers a potential opportunity and platform. While other global health alliances, such as Roll Back Malaria and Stop TB, have explicitly worked to support countries in public–private collaboration, the PMNCH has yet to do so. However, a positive sign is that more than 50% of the board is composed of non-state actors, such as healthcare professional organizations, NGOs, academics, and research institutions. Experience from other similar alliances, such as the Stop TB Partnership (see Chapter 10) has shown that the creation of a specific private-sector working group — to generate ideas, innovation, evaluation, and plans for private sector engagement — can be very productive. PMNCH is uniquely positioned to lead the discussion about private sector engagement and the effectiveness of child health programs.

## 6. Conclusions

There is a growing recognition among donors and governments that effective PHC, including the delivery of critical child health interventions, often requires the engagement of the private sector. Child health initiatives' customary strategies based on a mental model of widely used public services and generally functioning public supply chains is unsuitable in many country settings.

Programs should, as a priority, scrutinize existing health system data from household, provider, and retailer surveys. They should aim to identify the most critical gaps between the populations they target to reach and the best available evidence on where those people are obtaining their services and products. Where private actors are playing a significant role, local consultation is necessary to identify where there is both capacity and willingness to engage in public–private collaborations. Program managers should seek opportunities for collaboration around the manufacture and distribution of products (e.g. fortified foods and ORS). Where provider networks are substantially private, officials should consider contracting, either by public or social insurance agencies; "lighter touch" collaboration with private providers to expand coverage of priority interventions should also be considered (e.g. immunization).

Donors and technical agencies should expand operational research on engagement strategies for working with fragmented, and often informal, providers and retailers, which are so often used by poor people. At the global, national, and local levels, it is vital that political will and commitment exist to expand private sector participation, as well as coordination and communication among the multiple stakeholders.

## Appendix

Table A1. List of countries and year of survey included in the analysis of demographic and health surveys.

| Country | Year |
|---|---|
| Armenia | 2005 |
| Bangladesh | 2004 |
| Benin | 2006 |
| Bolivia | 2003 |
| Brazil | 1996 |
| Burkina Faso | 2003 |
| Cambodia | 2005 |
| Cameroon | 2004 |
| Central African Republic | 1995 |
| Chad | 2004 |
| Colombia | 2005 |
| Comoros | 1996 |

*(Continued)*

Table A1. (*Continued*)

| Country | Year |
|---|---|
| Congo Brazzaville | 2005 |
| Cote d'Ivoire | 1999 |
| Dominican Republic | 2002 |
| Egypt | 2005 |
| Ethiopia | 2005 |
| Gabon | 2000 |
| Ghana | 2003 |
| Guatemala | 1995 |
| Guinea | 2005 |
| Haiti | 2005 |
| Honduras | 2005 |
| Indonesia | 2003 |
| Kazakhstan | 1995 |
| Kenya | 2003 |
| Kyrgyz Republic | 1997 |
| Lesotho | 2004 |
| Madagascar | 2004 |
| Malawi | 2004 |
| Mali | 2006 |
| Moldova | 2005 |
| Morocco | 2004 |
| Mozambique | 2003 |
| Namibia | 2000 |
| Nepal | 2006 |
| Nicaragua | 2001 |
| Niger | 2006 |
| Nigeria | 2003 |
| Peru | 2004 |
| The Philippines | 2003 |
| Rwanda | 2005 |
| Senegal | 2005 |

Table A1. *(Continued)*

| Country | Year |
|---|---|
| South Africa | 1998 |
| Tanzania | 2004 |
| Togo | 1998 |
| Uganda | 2006 |
| Uzbekistan | 1996 |
| Vietnam | 2002 |
| Zambia | 2002 |
| Zimbabwe | 2005 |

## References

S. E. Arifeen, D. M. Hoque, T. Akter, *et al.* (2009). Effect of the integrated management of childhood illness strategy on childhood mortality and nutrition in a rural area in Bangladesh: A cluster randomised trial. *Lancet* **374**: 393–403.

H. Axelson, F. Bustreo and A. Harding. (2003). *Private Section Participation in Child Health: A Review of World Bank Projects, 1993–2002.* World Bank, Washington, DC.

N. Bhandari, R. Bahl, S. Mazumdar, J. Martines, R. E. Black, M. K. Bhan and Infant Feeding Study Group. (2003). Effect of community-based promotion of exclusive breastfeeding on diarrhoeal illness and growth: A cluster randomised controlled trial. *Lancet* **361**: 1418–1423.

R. Bhat, D. V. Mavalankar, *et al.* (2009). Maternal healthcare financing: Gujarat's Chiranjeevi Scheme and its beneficiaries. *Journal of Health, Population and Nutrition* **27**: 249–58.

D. Bishai and R. Nalubola. (2002). The history of food fortification in the US and its relevance for developing countries. *Economic Development and Cultural Change* **51**: 37–53.

D. M. Bishai, N. M. Shah, D. G. Walker, W. R. Brieger and D. H. Peters. (2008). Social franchising to improve quality and access in private health care in developing countries. *Harvard Health Policy Review* **9**: 184–197.

R. E. Black, S. Cousens, H. L. Johnson, J. E. Lawn, I. Rudan, D. G. Bassani, P. Jha, H. Campbell, C. F. Walker, R. Cibulskis, T. Eisele, L. Liu and C. Mathers. (2010). Global, regional and national causes of child deaths, 2008. *Lancet* 375: 1969–1987.

T. Boerma, J. Bryce, Y. Kinfu, H. Axelson, C. G. Victora. (2008). Mind the gap: Equity and trends in coverage of maternal, newborn, and child health services in 54 Countdown countries. *Lancet* **371**: 1259–1267.

J. Bryce, R. E. Black, N. Walker, Z. A. Bhutta, J. E. Lawn and R. W. Steketee. (2005a). Can the world afford to save the lives of 6 million children each year? *Lancet* **365**: 2193–2200.

J. Bryce, C. G. Victora, J. P. Habicht, R. E. Black, R. W. Scherpbier and MCE-IMCI Technical Advisors. (2005b). Programmatic pathways to child survival: Results of a multi-country evaluation of integrated management of childhood illness. *Health Policy and Planning* **20**(Suppl 1): i5–i17.

J. Bryce, J. Requejo and The 2008 Countdown Working Group. (2008). *Tracking Progress in Maternal, Newborn, and Child Survival: The 2008 Report.* UNICEF, New York.

F. Bustreo, A. Harding and H. Axelson (2003) Can developing countries achieve adequate improvements in child health outcomes without engaging the private sector? *WHO Bulletin* **81**: 886–895.

E. Cavagnero, B. Daelmans, N. Gupta, R. Scherpbier, A. Shankar and The Countdown Working Group on Health Policy and Health Systems. (2008). Assessment of the health system and policy environment as a critical complement to tracking intervention coverage for maternal, newborn, and child health. *Lancet* **371**: 1284–1293.

Dalberg Global Development Advisors. (2007) *Biosynthetic Artemisinin Roll-Out Strategy.* Boston, MA. BCG/Institute for OneWorld Health.

I. Darnton-Hill and R. Nalubola. (2002). Food fortification as a public health strategy to meet micronutrient needs: Successes and failures. *Proceedings of the Nutrition Society* **61**: 231–241.

R. Eichler, P. Auxila and J. Pollock. (2001). Promoting preventive health care: Paying for performance in Haiti. In: P. J. Brooke and S. M. Smith (eds.), *Contracting for Public Services: Output Based Aid and Its Application.* World Bank, Washington, DC.

U. Giedion and M. V. Uribe. (2009). Colombia's universal health insurance system. *Health Affairs* **28**: 853–863.

D. R. Gwatkin, S. Rutstein, K. Johnson, E. A. Suliman, A. Wagstaff and A. Amouzou. (2007). *Socio-economic Differences in Health, Nutrition, and Population within Developing Countries — An Overview.* World Bank, Washington, DC.

R. Haider, A. Ashworth, I. Kabir, S. R. A. Huttly. (2000). Effects of community-based peer counselors on exclusive breastfeeding practices in Dhaka, Bangladesh: A randomized controlled trial. *Lancet* **356**: 1643–1647.

S. Horton. (2006). The economics of food fortification. *Journal of Nutrition* **136**: 1068–1071.

G. Jones, R. W. Steketee, R. E. Black, Z. A. Bhutta, S. S. Morris and Bellagio Child Survival Study Group. (2003). How many child deaths can we prevent this year? *Lancet* **362**: 65–71.

G. M. La Forgia. (2005). Basic healthcare in rural Guatemala: Comparison of performance of three different delivery models. In: G. M. La Forgia (ed.), *Health System Innovations in Central America: Lessons and Impact of New Approaches*. World Bank, Washington, DC.

M. Lagarde, A. Haines and N. Palmer. (2007). Conditional cash transfers for improving uptake of health interventions in low- and middle-income countries: A systematic review. *JAMA* **298**: 1900–1910.

S. S. Lim, L. Dandona, J. A. Hoisington, S. L. James, M. C. Hogan and E. Gakidou. (2010). India's Janani Suraksha Yojana, a conditional cash transfer programme to increase births in health facilities: An impact evaluation. *Lancet* **375**: 2009–2023.

B. Loevinsohn and A. Harding. (2005). Buying results? Contracting for health service delivery in developing countries. *Lancet* **366**: 676–681.

B. Loevinsohn and G. Sayed. (2008). Lessons from the health sector in Afghanistan: How progress can be made in challenging circumstances. *Journal of the American Medical Association* **300**: 724–726.

T. Marek, I. Diallo, B. Ndiaye and J. Rakotosalama. (1999). Successful contracting of prevention services: Fighting malnutrition in Senegal and Madagascar. *Health Policy and Planning* **14**: 382–389.

D. Montagu. (2021). The provision of private healthcare services in European Countries: Recent data and lessons for universal health coverage in other settings. *Frontiers in Public Health* **9**: 171.

A. L. Morrow, M. L. Guerrero, J. Shults, *et al.* (1999). Efficacy of home-based peer counseling to promote exclusive breastfeeding: A randomized controlled trial. *Lancet* **353**: 1226–1231.

M. Parlato and R. Seidel (eds.). (1998). *Large-Scale Application of Nutrition Behavior Change Approaches: Lessons from West Africa*. Basic Support for Institutionalizing Child Survival (BASICS) Project, Arlington, VA.

D. H. Peters, A. A. Noor, L. P. Singh, F. K. Kakar, P. M. Hansen and G. Burnham. (2007). A balanced score card for health services in Afghanistan. *WHO Bulletin* **85**: 146–151.

V. J. Quinn, A. B. Guyon, J. W. Schubert, M. Stone-Jiménez, M. D. Hainsworth, L. H. Martin. (2005). Improving breastfeeding practices on a broad scale at the community level: Success stories from Africa and Latin America. *Journal of Human Lactation* **21**: 345–354.

R. Regalia and L. Castro. (2009). Nicaragua: Combining demand- and supply-side incentives. In R. Eichler and R. Levine (eds.), *Performance Incentives for Health: Potential and Pitfalls*. Brookings Institution, Washington, DC.

B. Sabri, S. Siddiqi, A. M. Ahmed, F. K. Kakar and J. Perrot. (2007). Towards sustainable delivery of health services in Afghanistan: Options for the future. *WHO Bulletin* **85**: 712–718.

J. A. Schellenberg, T. Adam, H. Mshinda, H. Masanja, G. Kabadi, O. Mukasa, T. John, S. Charles, R. Nathan, K. Wilczynska, L. Mgalula, C. Mbuya, R. Mswia, F. Manzi, D. de Savigny, D. Schellenberg and C. Victora. (2004a). Effectiveness and cost of facility-based Integrated Management of Childhood Illness (IMCI) in Tanzania. *Lancet* **364**: 1583–1594.

J. A. Schellenberg, J. Bryce, D. de Savigny, T. Lambrechts, C. Mbuya, L. Mgalula, K. Wilczynska. (2004b). The effect of Integrated Management of Childhood Illness on observed quality of care of under-fives in rural Tanzania. *Health Policy and Planning* **19**: 1–10.

E. Smith, R. Brugha and A. Zwi. (2001). *Working with Private Sector Providers for Better Health Care: An Introductory Guide*. Options and LSHTM, London.

J. Tendler. (1997). Preventative health: The case of the unskilled meritocracy. In *Good Government in the Tropics*. Johns Hopkins University Press, Baltimore, MD.

J. Tulloch. (1999). Integrated approach to child health in developing countries. *Lancet* **354**: SII16–SII20.

UNICEF. (2009). *The State of the World's Children (Special Edition): Celebrating 20 Years of the Convention of the Rights of the Child*. UNICEF, New York.

C. G. Victora, L. Huicho, J. J. Amaral, J. Armstrong-Schellenberg, F. Manzi, E. Mason and R. Scherpbier. (2006). Are health interventions implemented where they are most needed? District uptake of the integrated management of childhood illness strategy in Brazil, Peru and the United Republic of Tanzania. *WHO Bulletin* **84**: 792–801.

C. G. Victora, L. Adair, C. Fall, P. C. Hallal, R. Martorell, L. Richter, H. S. Sachdev and For the Maternal and Child Undernutrition Study Group. (2008). Maternal and child undernutrition: Consequences for adult health and human capital. *Lancet* **371**: 340–357.

G. Vines. (2007). *Preventing Iodine Deficiency Disease in China*. Millions Saved Initiative, Case 15. Center for Global Development, Washington, DC.

S. P. Walker, T. D. Wachs, J. M. Gardner, *et al.* (2007). Child development: Risk factors for adverse outcomes in developing countries. *Lancet* **369**: 145–157.

H. Waters, L. Hatt and D. Peters. (2003). Working with the private sector for child health. *Health Policy and Planning* **18**: 127–137.

WHO. (1981). *The International Code of Marketing of Breast-milk Substitutes.* World Health Organization, Geneva.

WHO and UNICEF. (2003). *Global Strategy for Infant and Young Child Feeding.* World Health Organization, Geneva.

World Bank (2010). Implementation completion and results report: Health sector emergency reconstruction and development project. Report no ICR 00001294. World Bank, Washington, DC.

# Afterword

# The Institutional Economics and Organizational Theory of Mixed Healthcare Systems

**Alexander S. Preker and April L. Harding**

## Abstract

The authors review the institutional economics and the organizational underpinnings of mixed healthcare systems. They initially trace the historical context of healthcare systems as they have evolved over time. Then, they review the theoretical underpinnings of mixed healthcare systems from the perspective of both neo-classical microeconomics and organizational theory rooted in new institutional economics. This is followed by a detailed analysis of both market failure in private healthcare markets and government failure observed in large state-run national healthcare systems that are typical of government health services run by Ministries of Health at all country income levels. Following that the authors look at a range of instruments available to governments in addressing market failure — from least to most intrusive. These include doing nothing, requiring information disclosure, introducing regulations, contracting for services through prepayments, direct payments, subsidies through reimbursements, mandates, guaranteeing universal access, and public production. This is followed by a discussion on recent trends in the reform of mixed healthcare systems and what policymakers can do to take decisions about when to "make or buy" healthcare goods and services "in-house" or "contract out" to non-governmental and private funders and providers of healthcare. The final section of the chapter looks at how to get from "here to there" in terms of creating high-performing mixed healthcare systems. The authors conclude that policymakers could significantly improve the performance of their healthcare systems by empowering patients to get more involved in their own care by giving them a greater voice in their care and providing them an "exit" — "voting with their feet." Such reforms would require policymakers to depart from their historical dependence on loyalty and trust by patients in underperforming healthcare, which is seen in so many countries, and instead secure a strong policy framework and high performance of mixed health systems. These topics are central to understanding mixed health systems.

This chapter will provide a historical snap shop of the evolution of mixed health care systems. This will be followed by a review of the theoretical underpinnings in terms of microeconomic and institutional economic theory. Then there will be a discussion on market failure and government failure. This will be followed by a discussion on reform options and transformation process — "getting from here to there". The chapter will end with a brief conclusion and take-home messages.

## 1. Historical Snapshot

Advances in health during the past few decades are impressive. The increase in life expectancy accompanying the decrease in fertility and infant mortality throughout the world have been greater in the past 40 years than during the previous 4,000 years (see Figure 1). Life expectancy is over 25 years longer today than at similar income levels in 1900.[1]

These gains in health are partly the result of improvements in income and education, with accompanying improvements in nutrition, access to contraceptives, hygiene, housing, water supplies, and sanitation. As described by the World Health Organization (WHO, 2000, 2010) in its *2000 World Health Report* and *2010 World Health Report*, the

[1]The analysis presented in this chapter adds new insights to the earlier work on the institutional economics of healthcare developed by Preker and Harding (2000).

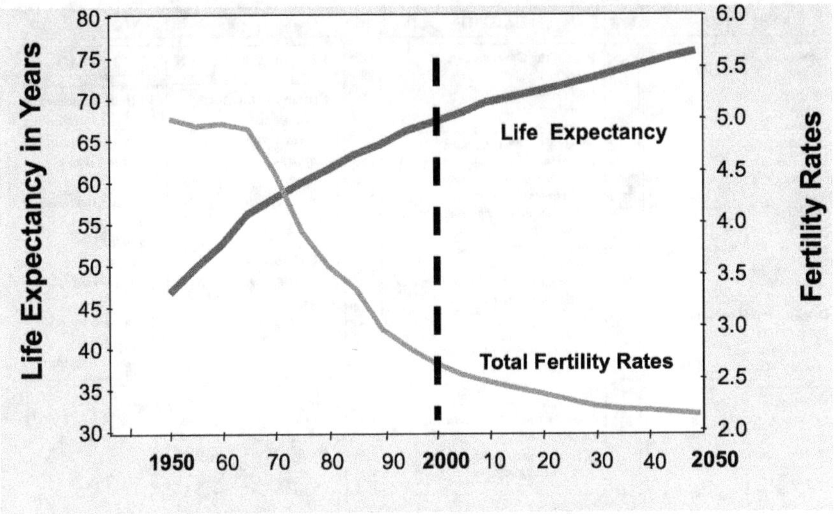


Figure 1. Unparalleled improvements.

achievements in health during the 20th and 21st centuries are also a result of new knowledge about the causes, prevention, and treatment of disease, and policies that make known interventions more accessible.

International experience indicates that the underlying cause of most threats to good health is well known today, and affordable drugs, surgeries and other interventions are often available even in low-income countries. But, because of dysfunction or weakness in the structure, function and performance of many healthcare systems, potentially effective policies and programs often fail to reach people who need care.

Health systems are deeply embedded in a country's political, economic, institutional, and social contexts. Without understanding that background, it is unlikely that the performance of a healthcare system can be maximized irrespective of its structural and functional components or changes in the public and private mix. Likewise, the historical evolution of a health system often predetermines the range of reforms that are possible (see Figure 2).

In the rest of the Afterword, reference will be made to elements of structure, function, and performance. Using a medical metaphor, a structure can be seen as the *anatomy* of a healthcare system — "what are its component parts" — without reference to "what it does" or "how well." This

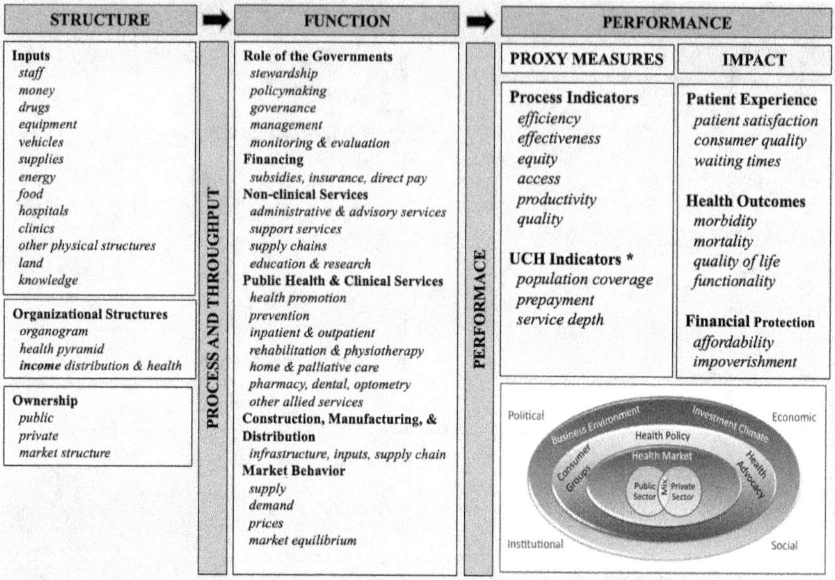


Figure 2. Performance of mixed health systems.

would include determining the level of inputs (both factor and product markets), how the inputs are organized, and the relative balance between public and private ownership. It might also include patterns of geographic distribution, etc. A function can be seen as the *physiology* of a healthcare system — "what do the different parts do." This would include the role of governments and markets and the role of the different parts, such as financing, delivery of public health, clinical services, and non-clinical services (including education and research) and the role of construction, manufacturing, and distribution. Finally, performance tries assessing outcome and impact — "how well the system does" — in achieving its desired goals. Since the impact in terms of health outcomes, financing, and patient experience is difficult to measure, most health systems use a range of intermediate proxy indicators (WHO, 2000, 2010; Preker, 2018).

We will revisit this framework and its component parts several times throughout the analysis of mixed health systems. Confusion about the difference between structure, function, and performance is one of the leading causes of misunderstanding and ideological bias in assessing healthcare systems.

## 1.1 *From centuries of minimalism …*

Ideological views on the roles of the state and the private sector belong to a long list of false antitheses in the field of medicine and healthcare (Black, 1984). Since the beginning of written history, the pendulum has swung back and forth between minimalist and heavy-handed state involvement in the health sector.

During antiquity, people used home remedies and private healers when they were ill. Yet, as early as the second millennium B.C., the *papyri* (ancient Egyptian clay tablets) provide fascinating evidence that Imhotep, an archetypal physician, priest, and court official in ancient Egypt, introduced a system of publicly provided healthcare with healers who were paid by the community (Mason and McCall Smith, 1987).

This early experiment in organized healthcare did not survive the test of time. The *Code of Hammurabi* (1792–50 B.C.) laid down a system of direct fee-for-service payment based on the nature of services rendered and the patient's ability to pay (Chapman, 1984). For the next 3,000 years, the state's involvement in healthcare revolved mainly around enforcing the rules of compensation for personal injury and protection of the self-governing medical guild. Control of membership and secrecy, reflected in the *Hippocratic Oath*, was characteristic of all trades (BMA, 1984).

At best, financing, organization, and provision of healthcare were limited to the royal courts of kings, emperors, and other nobility who might have a physician for their personal use and for their troops at the time of battle. The masses got by with local healers, midwives, natural remedies, apothecaries, and quacks.

## 1.2 *… to heavy-handed state involvement*

Unlike this early private participation in healthcare, during the 20th century, governments of most countries have become central to health policy, often both financing and delivering a wide range of care. Today, most industrial countries have achieved universal access to healthcare through a mix of public and private financing arrangements and providers. Today, the United States, Mexico, and Turkey are three exceptions in the Organization for Economic Cooperation and Development (OECD), where universal access has not yet been secured (Preker, 1989).

Proponents of such public sector involvement in healthcare have argued their case on both philosophical and technical grounds. In most societies, care for the sick and disabled is considered an expression of humanitarian and philosophical aspirations.

However, one does not have to resort to moral principles or arguments about the welfare state to warrant collective intervention in health. The past century is rich in examples of how the private sector and market forces alone failed to secure efficiency and equity in the health sector.

Economic theory provides ample justification for such an engagement on both theoretical and practical grounds to secure the following:

- **Efficiency:** Significant market failure exists in the health sector (information asymmetries; public goods; positive and negative externalities; distorting or monopolistic market power of many providers and producers; absence of functioning markets in some areas; frequent occurrence of high transaction costs). Several classic references are worth noting (Evans, 1984; Bator, 1958; Atkinson and Stiglitz, 1980; Musgrave and Musgrave, 1984).
- **Equity:** Individuals and families often fail to protect themselves adequately against the risks of illness and disability on a voluntary basis due to inability to pay, short-sightedness, free-riding, and/or characteristic shortcomings of private health insurance (moral hazard and adverse selection). Several classic references are worth noting (Barer and Getzen, 1998; van Doorslaer *et al.*, 1993; Arrow, 1963).

Largely inspired by the western welfare state experiences such as the British National Health Service (NHS) and the problems of market failure, during the past 50 years, many low- and middle-income countries established state-funded healthcare systems with services produced by a vertically integrated public bureaucracy.

## 1.3 *… and back to neoliberalism of the 1990s*

During the 1980s and 1990s, the pendulum began to swing back in the opposite direction. During the Reagan and Thatcher Era, the world witnessed a growing willingness to experiment with market approaches in the social sectors (health, education, and social protection). This was true even in countries such as Great Britain, New Zealand, and Australia — historical bastions of the welfare state (Young, 1986; Vickers and Yarrow, 1992).

As in the ascendancy of state involvement, the recent cooling toward state involvement in healthcare and enthusiasm for private solutions has been motivated by both ideological and technical arguments.

The political imperative that has accompanied liberalization in many former socialist states and the economic shocks in East Asia and Latin America certainly contributed to a global sense of urgency to reform inefficient and bloated bureaucracies and to establish smaller governments with greater accountability (World Bank, 1996; Barr, 1994, 2005)

Yet, it would be too easy to blame ideology and economic crisis for the recent surge in attempts to reform healthcare systems by exposing public services to competitive market forces, downsizing the public sector, and increasing private sector participation (Enthoven, 1978, 1988; Preker, 2018; Rice, 2023).

In reality, the welfare-state approach failed to address many of the health needs of populations across the world (WHO, 1996; World Bank, 1993, 1997b; UNICEF, 1999) as it did in other areas of the economy and social policy (Zubok, 2021). Hence, the dilemma of policymakers worldwide: although state involvement in the health sector is clearly needed, it is typically beset by public sector production failure (Barr, 1994; Preker and Feachem, 1996; Barr, 2005).

## 1.4 … *toward a new stewardship role of the state*

Today, governments everywhere are reassessing when, where, how, and how much to intervene or whether to leave things to the market forces of patients' demand.

The growing consensus is that addressing this problem requires a better balance between the roles of the state and the private sector, and their respective capabilities — getting the fundamentals right. Most health economists — even those favoring a more competitive marketplace — recognize that both the government and the private sector need to play a significant role in the health sector. In most countries, this means rebalancing an already complex mix of public and private roles in the health sector (Rice, 1998, 2023; Musgrove, 1996; Schieber, 1996).

To improve efficiency or equity, governments can choose from an extensive range of actions — from least to most intrusive. These include the following:

- providing information to encourage behavioral changes needed to improve health outcomes;
- developing and enforcing policies and regulations to influence public and private sector activities;
- issuing mandates or purchasing services from public and private providers;
- providing subsidies to pay for services directly or indirectly;
- producing (in-house) preventive and curative services.

In many countries, for reasons of both ideological views and weak public capacity to deal with information asymmetry, contracting, and regulatory problems, governments often try to do too much — especially in terms of in-house service delivery — with too few resources and little capability.

Parallel to such public production, the same well-intending governments often fail to achieve the following:

- develop effective policies and make available information about personal hygiene, healthy lifestyles, and appropriate use of healthcare regulate and contract with available private sector providers;
- ensure that adequate financing arrangements are available for the whole population;
- secure access to public goods with large externalities for the whole population.

## 2. Theoretical Underpinnings

This section describes the economic underpinnings of private and public roles in the economy more broadly and some of the specifics when applied to the health sector. It starts with a high-level review of the principles of microeconomics and institutional economics.

## 2.1 *From neo-classical micro-economics ...*

One of the central tenets of neoclassical economics is that, in an optimally functioning market, competitive forces will lead to a more efficient allocation of resources — *Pareto-optimal* efficiency and market equilibrium — than nonmarket solutions, see Figure 3.

According to the neoclassical model, when there are many firms and consumers — and prices are allowed to respond to the forces of supply and demand — competition will result in an equilibrium situation where it is impossible to make someone better off without making anyone else worse off. This will result in a welfare-maximizing situation called *Pareto-optimal* efficiency.

The underlying concept is that there is an "Invisible Hand" that guides *Pareto-optimal* efficiency. This was developed by Adam Smith who describes how free trade can benefit an economy (Smith, 1776), see Figure 4.

A free trade economy produces widespread benefits, for example, the benefits of being able to collect data to find what products and services are in high demand. Competition between businesses to bring products to market that consumers want, results in prices staying at a reasonable price.

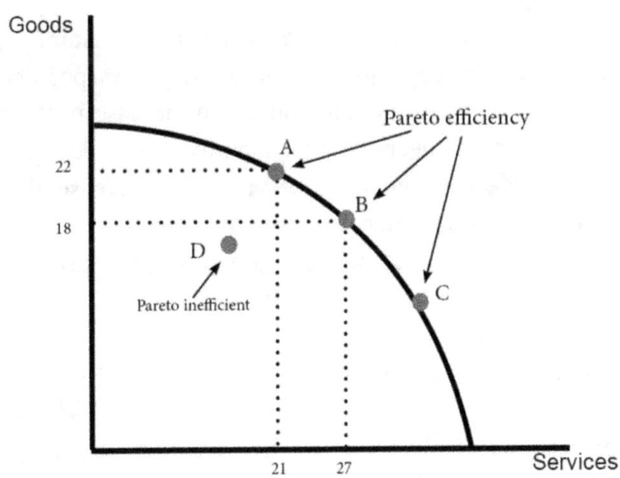


Figure 3. Pareto-optimal efficiency.

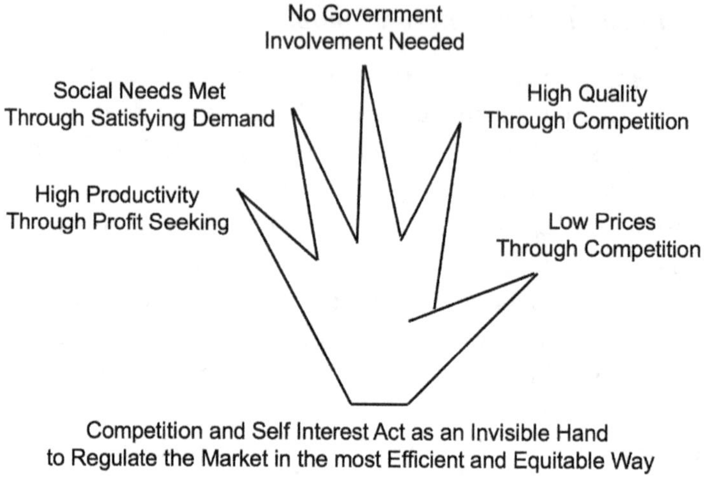


Figure 4. The invisible hand.

The benefits of a free trade economy are greater than those of a heavily regulated economy. The reason for this is that a planned economy doesn't allow consumers to acquire all of the products and services they want, and businesses aren't allowed to alter their production to meet the needs of consumers.

Demand is an economic concept that relates to a consumer's desire to purchase goods and services and willingness to pay a specific price for them. *Ceteris paribus* (all else being equal), an increase in the price of a good or service tends to decrease the quantity demanded. Likewise, a decrease in the price of a good or service will increase the quantity demanded. Changes in consumer preferences, such as taste, income, price expectations, market size, price of substitute goods, and price of complementary goods will shift the curve either to the right (more demand) or left (less demand), see Figure 5.

Supply is an economic concept that describes the total amount of a specific good or service that is available to consumers based on the willingness of producers to make them. *Ceteris paribus*, the supply provided by producers will increase if the price rises because all firms look to maximize profits and a decrease in the price will lead producers to decrease the supply of such goods or services. Changes in several factors will shift the demand curve either to the right (more supply) or left (less supply).

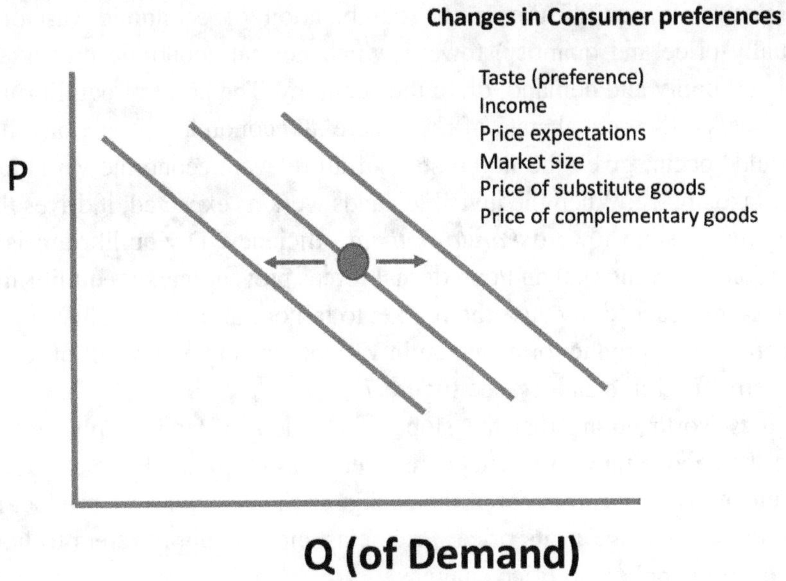


Figure 5. Demand and shifts in demand curve.

These factors include mostly things that impact on cost of production and profitability, such as cost of resources, productivity gains, new technology, taxes/subsidies, number of sellers, price expectation, and price of other goods, see Figure 6.

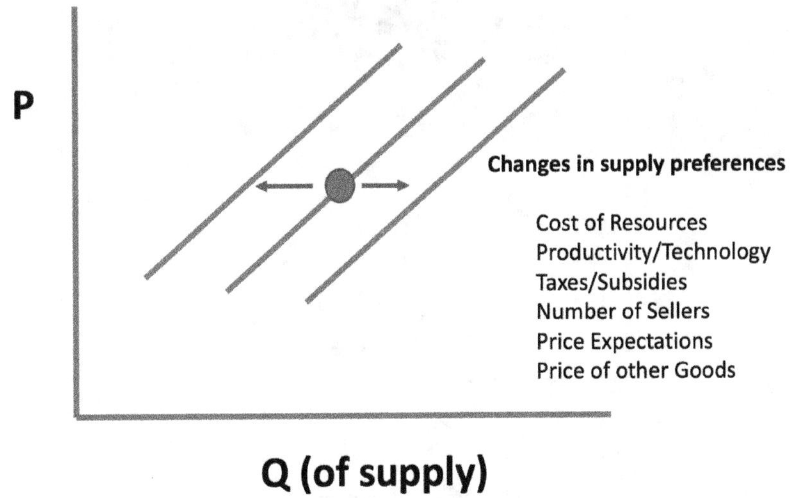


Figure 6. Supply and shift in the supply curve.

Economic equilibrium is the combination of economic variables (usually price and quantity) toward which normal economic processes, such as supply and demand, drive the economy. The point of equilibrium represents a theoretical state of rest where all economic transactions that "should" occur, given the initial state of all relevant economic variables, have taken place. When the invisible hands work as expected, it drives the economic system toward *Pareto-optimal* efficiency. Disequilibrium is a situation where internal and/or external forces prevent market equilibrium from being reached or cause the market to fall out of balance. This can be a short-term byproduct of a change in variable factors or a result of long-term structural imbalances, see Figure 7.

It is worth noting that the slope of the demand and supply curves described above may vary. This is referred to as elasticity. Price elasticity of demand is a measurement of the change in the demand for a product in relation to a change in its price. Price elasticity of supply refers to how responsive supply is to price changes.

Elastic demand is when the change in demand is large when there is a change in price. Inelastic demand is when the change in demand is small when there is a change in price. A similar situation can occur when there are changes in the slope of the supply curve. The slope of the curve may

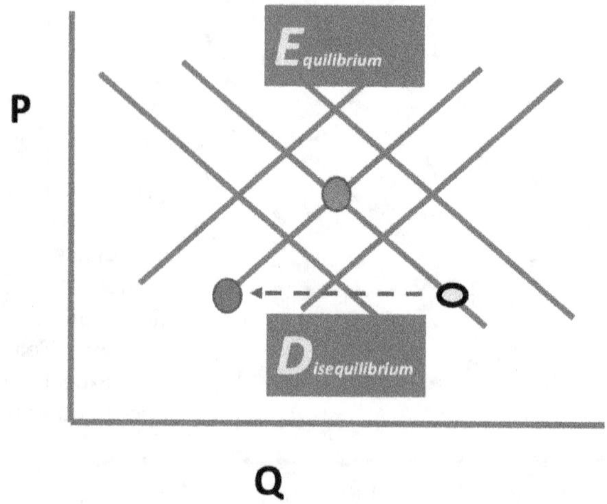


Figure 7. Market equilibrium and imbalances.

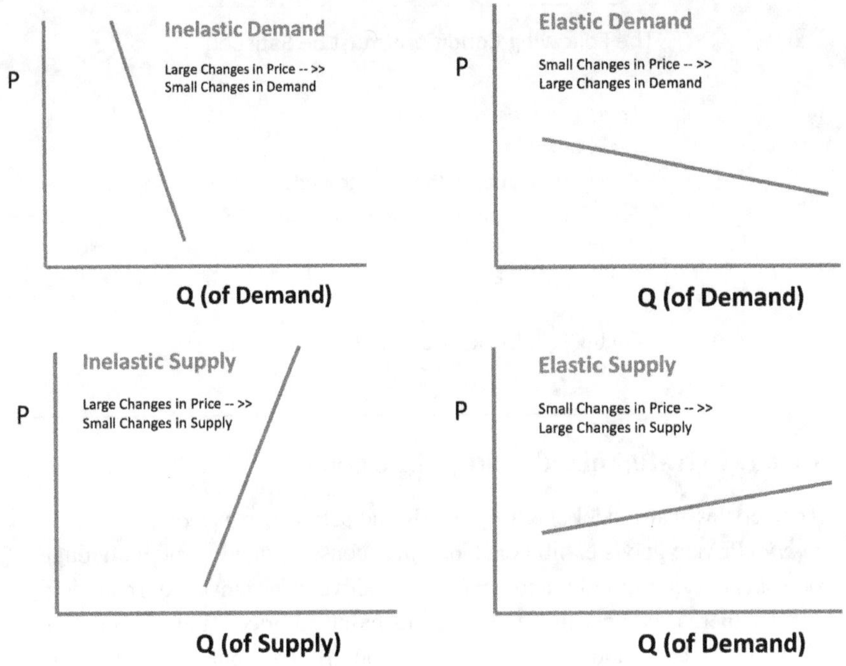


Figure 8. Price elasticity.

also vary related to other factors. The price elasticity of supply is related to producer behavior, where producers increase and decrease supply due to price. The price elasticity of demand is related to consumer behavior, see Figure 8.

The perfectly competitive *Walrasian* model, as it is sometimes called, requires several assumptions to be met: there must be free or low cost of entry and exit; there must be many buyers and sellers; there must be open competition with few distortions; prices must be set by an equilibrium between supply and demand, see Figure 9.

There are several underlying criteria that need to be satisfied before such a competitive market can achieve *Pareto-optimal* efficiency. These include the following:

- The goods involved behave like private goods, i.e. rivalry, excludability, and rejectability (see Box 1).
- Rights can be perfectly delineated.
- Transaction costs are zero.

**The Following Conditions must be Satisfied**

- Free or low cost of entry and exit
- Many buyers and sellers
- Open competition with few distortions
- Prices set by equilibrium between supply and demand

Figure 9. Neoclassical competitive market.

## Box 1. Private, mixed, and public goods

The neoclassical model classifies goods and services as *private*, *mixed,* or *public*. Private goods exhibit excludability (consumption by one individual prevents consumption by another — no positive or negative externalities); rivalry (there is competition among goods based on price); and rejectability (individuals can choose to forgo consumption). True public goods have significant elements of nonexcludability, nonrivalry, and nonrejectability. Mixed goods have some but not all the characteristics of private goods (see Figure 10).

| | Nature of Economic Good | | |
|---|---|---|---|
| **Properties** | *Public* | *Mixed* | *Private* |
| *Excludability* | -- | ± | + |
| *Rivalry* | -- | ± | + |
| *Rejectability* | -- | ± | + |

**Consumer Protection**

*Policymaking*
*Regulations*
*Setting Standards*
*Quality Control*

**Consumption Goods**

*Medical Clinics*
*Hospitals*
*Medical Suppliers*
*Pharmaceuticals*

Figure 10. Nature of goods and services.

According to neoclassical theory, a breakdown occurs in both efficiency and equity when public goods or services with significant market failure and externalities are allocated through competitive markets. Often, the market structure in the private sector does not meet the basic criteria set out in Figure 9. Likewise, as described earlier, significant problems occur in efficiency and equity when private goods are produced or provided by a public sector that disregards supply, demand, and market equilibrium.

Most healthcare goods and services do not behave like perfect private or public goods. Many are not perfectly excludable but are associated with complex externalities. Rights are often difficult to delineate, leaving residual claimants. Transaction costs are often high. Therefore, though in a *Pareto-optimal* state, it would be impossible to make someone better off without making someone else worse off, few situations meet such criteria in the health sector.

Although many public health activities (e.g. sanitation services, control and prevention of communicable diseases, and health promotion) generate significant externalities, they are not pure public goods. All have some element of excludability, rejectability, and rivalry. For example, a vaccine given to one patient cannot simultaneously be consumed by other patients. At will, patients can choose not to be vaccinated. Vaccination programs can, in principle, compete with each other for market share, see Box 1.

Likewise, even expensive diagnostic and therapeutic care — though often provided in publicly owned inpatient facilities at highly subsidized rates — is really a private good and hence marketable. The same is true for ambulatory and community-based care. Even when governments try to fully control the market for such services, preventing their sale in the informal economy is often difficult.

Therefore, although neoclassical theory is often invoked by mainstream economists to justify public and private roles in the health sector, consumption characteristics alone almost never indicate anything about the specific production processes needed to secure technical efficiency and equity. Neoclassical theory contributes little to the understanding of optimal organizational arrangements for service production. It is essentially "institution-free" (Robinson, 1997). Other theories are needed to fill this vacuum in understanding production characteristics.

## 2.2 … *to institutional economics of organizations*

Recently, much progress has been made in identifying the key factors causing wide variations in organizations' performance. The developments most relevant for understanding the advantages and disadvantages of different arrangements for service delivery come from *principal-agent theory, transaction cost economics, property rights, and public choice theory*. These fields are often grouped together under the title "institutional economics." Institutional economics directly addresses the issue of how best to structure organizations that consist of individuals pursuing multiple and often conflicting interests (OECD, 1992).

**Agency theory:** This framework highlights that social and political objectives may be more readily achieved through a series of explicit and transparent "contracts" for labor/services between an "agent" that undertakes to perform various tasks in an acceptable way on behalf of a "principal" in exchange for a mutually agreed award. Usually, the principal needs the agent's efforts and expertise but has only limited ability to monitor the agent's actions or evaluate whether the final outcome is satisfactory.

The agency literature surveys the range of contracts (e.g. payment and monitoring arrangements) observed in the economy as attempts to align incentives and reward cooperation between self-interested but interdependent individuals (Sappington, 1991). Several studies have generalized the agency insight from the employment context to the full range of relationships that make up the firm — now conceptualized as a nexus of many contracts (Fama, 1980; Jensen and Meckling, 1976) The need for incentive alignment is pervasive in the health sector: relations between patient and physician or governments and contracting agencies are classical examples of principal–agent structure.

**Transaction cost economics:** This field emphasizes the limitations of contracts and the need for flexible means of coordinating activities. Principals and agents are both opportunistic. Agents will seek to minimize the aggregate production and transaction costs and maximize the benefits (unless closely monitored, agents might be unreliable, engaging in behavior, such as rent-seeking, cheating, breach of contract, and incomplete disclosure). Principals will try to maximize their benefit to the extent that the relationship could become unviable for the agent.

The extent of such opportunism varies drastically from country to country and from one cultural setting to another. In some settings, such as monopolistic national health services, opportunism may be less apparent than in other settings where providers are more accustomed to competing with each other. Although opportunism may appear to be greater in countries such as Chile, India, and the United States, there is good evidence that principal–agent relationships within national health services such as Costa Rica, New Zealand, Scandinavia, Sri Lanka, and the United Kingdom are also vulnerable to opportunistic behavior.

This theory sheds most light on firm boundaries and the conditions under which activities are best arranged within a hierarchy instead of through market interactions with suppliers or other contractors. More generally, vertically integrated organizations, simple "spot" contracts, franchises, or joint ventures are interpreted as discrete structural alternatives — each offering different advantages and disadvantages for effective governance (Williamson, 1991). Governance arrangements are evaluated by comparing the patterns of costs generated for planning, adapting, and monitoring production and exchange (Williamson, 1985, 1989).

Despite these positive features, vertical integration suffers from characteristic weaknesses as a mechanism of governance. The two most prominent are the weakening of incentives for productivity and the proliferation of influence activities (Box 2). The weak incentives come as individuals capture less and less of the gains of their own efforts as rewards and their losses are spread throughout the organization. Despite its focus on the contracting problems that motivate internal organization, transaction cost economics views vertical integration as the governance mechanism of last resort.

Even in the many instances where policy objectives imply that spot market transactions are not desirable, contractual networks, virtual integration, franchising, or concessions will outperform unified ownership arrangements. See Box 3 for a discussion on high-powered incentives of ownership.

## Box 2. Influence activities

An important issue related to moral hazard and the structure of organizations is influence activities and the associated costs, known as *influence costs* (Milgrom and Roberts, 1990). Analysis has shed much light on the propensity of publicly owned service delivery organizations to capture inordinate portions of the sector budget as well as on their ability to influence sector policy to their benefit — often at the expense of the public interest.

In the health sector, provider organizations expend effort to affect decisions regarding the distribution of resources or other benefits among providers to their benefit. These *influence activities* occur in all organizations, but countervailing forces are particularly weak in public service delivery structures — and influence costs are one of the most important costs of centralized control. Evidence of influence activities is seen in public utilities where monopolies are often maintained to protect the low productivity of state-owned enterprises from competition from more efficient producers. In the health sector, the tendency to allocate resources to tertiary and curative care at the expense of primary, preventative, and public health is evidence of similar capture.

The cost of these activities includes both the losses associated with poor resource-allocation decisions as well as the loss associated with efforts to capture rents. These costs can be reduced when no decisionmaker has the authority to make decisions that service providers can easily influence. This condition can sometimes be brought about by creating legal or other boundaries between the policymaker, the funder, and the service provider unit. Many organizational reforms have attempted to diminish these activities. Examples include reforms that separate the policymaker from the payer and the payer from the provider in public service delivery. It also includes privatization of utilities.

**Property rights theory:** This field looks at the same incentive issues from a slightly different perspective. Since private ownership appears to have strong positive incentives for efficiency, property rights theorists have attempted to find out why. Explanations have focused on two issues: the possession of residual decision rights and the allocation of residual

### Box 3. High-powered incentives of ownership

Suppose a transaction involves several people supplying labor, physical inputs, and so on. If all but one party have contracted to receive fixed amounts, there is only one residual claimant. In that case, maximizing the value received by the residual claimant is the same as maximizing the total value received by all parties. If the residual claimant also has residual control, just by pursuing his own interests and maximizing his own returns the claimant will be led to make efficient decisions. The combination of residual control and residual claims provides strong incentives and capacity for an owner to maintain and increase an asset's value. Firms often attempt to reproduce these high-powered incentives by allocating residual claims in the form of bonuses or shares to key decision-makers in their firm.

Misalignment of residual rights and returns causes serious problems. The residual claimant to the returns from a state-owned enterprise is the public purse, but the residual decision-makers are effectively the enterprise manager, the workers, and the bureaucrats in the supervising ministry. None of these has any great personal stake in the value of the enterprise. The resulting low productivity is well documented. Another example of misalignment comes from the U.S. Savings and Loan (S&L) industry. Those who had the right to control the S&L's investment also had the right to keep any profits earned but were not obligated to make good on losses. That combination of rights and obligations created an incentive for risk-taking and fraud that was not effectively countered by other devices during most of the 1980s (Milgrom and Roberts, 1992).

These fields of analysis have led to a better understanding of the institutional sources of government failure. The framework has been used to design organizational reforms that seek to allocate to the holders of critical information the authority to make relevant decisions and the financial incentive to do so (in the form of residual claims on the outcome of the decision).

returns. Residual rights of control are the rights to make any decisions regarding an asset's use not explicitly contracted by law or assigned to another by contract. The owner of an asset usually holds these rights although they may be allocated to others (Milgrom and Roberts, 1992, Chapter 9).

The notion of ownership as residual control is relatively clear for a simple asset like a car. It gets much more complicated when applied to an organization such as a firm. Large organizations bundle together many assets, and who has which decision rights may be ambiguous. In addition to residual decision rights, an owner holds the rights to residual revenue flows from his assets. That is, the owner has the right to whatever revenue remains after all funds have been collected, and all debts, expenses, and other contractual obligations have been paid out.

**Political choice theory:** This field focuses on the self-interested behavior of politicians, interest groups, and bureaucrats, and studies its implications for effective government and the size of government. Individuals are viewed as rational utility maximizers. Bureaucrats, attempting to maximize their budgets, will acquire an increasing share of national income. As a result, the state will grow much bigger than necessary to deliver core functions. Powerful interest groups will capture increasing portions of resources. Institutional rigidities develop, reducing economic growth (Olson, 1982). This analysis has led public choice theorists to support conservative political agendas (minimizing the role of the state). Public choice is not neutral. There is a significant overlap between ideology and party politics, see Figure 11.

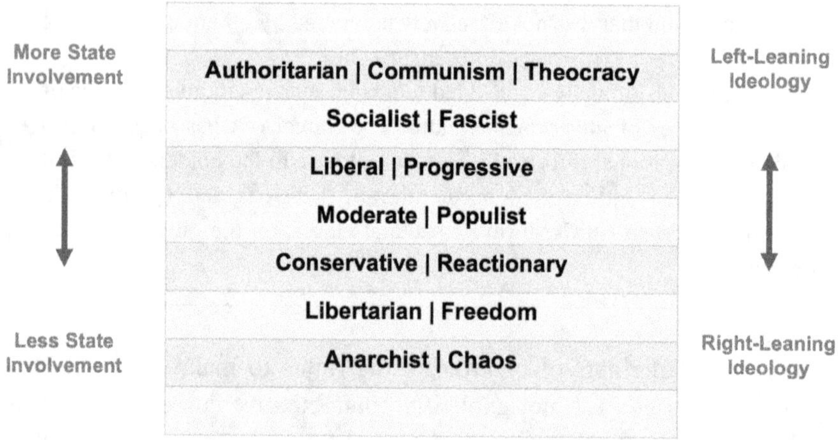


Figure 11. Political influence on public choice.

The following section will present a discussion of the most significant sources of government production failure to which market-based solutions are being applied and the market imperfections that must be addressed to optimize complementarity between the public and private sectors.

## 3. Market Failure

Unfortunately, in the real world, one or more of the four criteria described above for *Pareto-optional* efficiency is usually missing (see Figure 9). This is especially true in the health sector.

This leads to market failure, which refers to a situation where there is an inefficient or inequitable distribution of goods and services in the free market. As described earlier, in an efficient *Pareto-optimal* system, the forces of supply and demand balance each other out, with a change on one side of the equation leading to a change in price that maintains the market's equilibrium. In a market failure, this balance is disrupted. In such a system, the individual incentives for rational behavior do not lead to rational outcomes for the group. Everyone makes the correct decision for themselves, but those prove to be the wrong decisions for the group as a whole.

The following section will provide a brief description of eight major areas of market failure in the private sector which are particularly relevant to the health sector. These include the following: market failure in the nature of private goods and services; information asymmetry; agency problems; transaction costs; market power; profit maximization; corruption; and failure in policy formulation.

### 3.1 *Market failure in private goods and services*

As described earlier, goods and services can be characterized according to their *excludability*, *rivalry* and *rejectability*. When private goods or services are given away or when there is a charge for public goods or services that have large externalities, major problems occur in efficiency and equity. Application to the health sector and suggestions on how to address these problems will be described in the following sections.

The principles of institutional economics lead to a much more refined and useful understanding of the different kinds of institutional arrangements required for the efficient and effective production of goods and services. A model along these lines can be developed, based on two different and often ignored goods characteristics: *contestability and measurability* (Girishankar, 1999).

A market can be said to be perfectly contestable if firms can enter it freely (without any resistance from existing firms) and then exit without losing any of their investments while having equal access to technology (no asset specificity). Contestability allows competition *for* the market to substitute for competition *in* the market (Baumol *et al.*, 1982, 1984). But markets of course are not perfectly competitive (Shepherd, 1984, 1995).

Contestable goods are characterized by low barriers to entry and exit from the market, whereas non-contestable goods have high barriers such as sunk cost, monopoly market power, geographic advantages, and asset specificity. Investments in specific assets represent a "sunk cost" since their value cannot be recovered elsewhere (Klein *et al.*, 1978). An asset is specific if it makes a much larger contribution to the production of a good than its value in alternative uses.

Two specific assets that are especially relevant in the health sector are expertise and reputation. Once individuals or firms have invested in activities that result in expertise or generate trust, they create a significant barrier to entry for other potential suppliers, thereby lowering the degree of contestability. Opportunism, on the other hand, will lower such trust or barriers to entry. The degree of such opportunism will vary from one country to another and in different cultural settings.

These theoretical underpinnings are used in the following section to understand some recent reforms in the public sector.

## 3.2 *Information asymmetry*

Asymmetric information, also known as "information failure," occurs when one party to an economic transaction possesses greater material knowledge than the other party. This typically manifests itself when the seller of a good or service possesses greater knowledge than the buyer (about its value, availability, quality, etc.). The reverse is equally true.

Almost all economic transactions involve a range of information asymmetries.

As described above, measurability in the health sector, as in other sectors, is the precision with which inputs, processes, outputs, and outcomes of a good or service can be measured. Usually, however, it is difficult to measure with precision the output and outcome of health services characterized by a high degree of information asymmetry. This creates a special kind of information asymmetry about the performance. Without such information, it is difficult for users, beneficiaries, and contracting purchasing agencies to know what they are getting in return for their payments.

### 3.3 *Agency problems*

An agency problem is a conflict of interest inherent in any relationship where one party (agent) is expected to act on behalf of someone else (principal). Agents are supposed to act in the best interest of the principal, but often this does not happen, especially in the health sector. This will be discussed in much more detail in the following under application to the health sector.

### 3.4 *Transaction costs*

Transaction costs are expenses related to buying or selling a good or service, which are not intrinsic to their production costs. Examples include cost of financing, marketing, regulatory compliance, brokerage fees, legal fees, fines, taxes, patent protection, etc. Healthcare which is one of the most regulated sectors of the economy is heavily burdened by transaction costs. See the following for an application to the health sector.

### 3.5 *Market power*

Market power refers to a company's ability to manipulate the price of an item in the marketplace by influencing supply, demand, or both in an effort to maximize its market share and/or its profit. This allows companies to "extract rents" from consumers significantly above or below the market value that would result from an equilibrium between supply and demand. Firms that are successful in applying Porter's five forces to maximize profit usually end up abusing their market power.

Michael Porter's five-forces strategic analysis model, introduced in a 1979 article published in the *Harvard Business Review*, set out five forces at play in a given industry that offers them a competitive advantage over other firms. These were hailed by many business schools as a way for firms to succeed in the marketplace. These forces include the following: internal competition, the potential for new entrants, the negotiating power of suppliers, the negotiating power of customers, and the ability of customers to find substitutes. Following is a summary of each of Porter's five forces. Details are beyond the scope of this chapter but can be found in Porter (1979), see Figure 12.

When firms abuse their market power by exploiting Porter's five forces, it leads to a market structure that is not competitive. There is often a high cost of entry into the marketplace and exit from the marketplace. The number of buyers and sellers may be significantly restricted. There is a breakdown in competition, and it allows firms to fix prices and gouge consumers, see Figure 13.

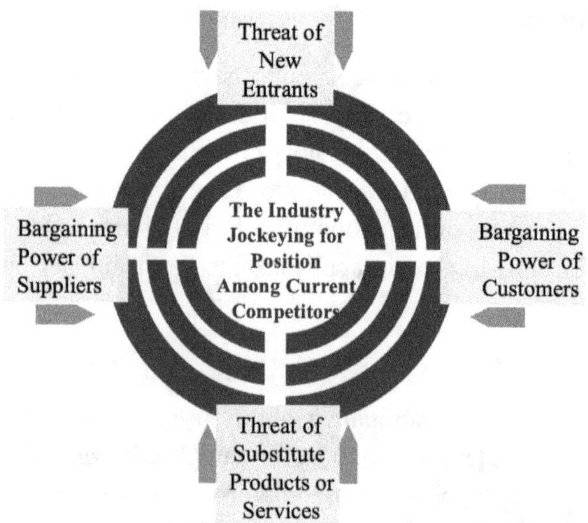


Figure 12. Porter's five forces.

Areas of Market Abuse

- High cost of entry and exit
- Limiting number of buyers or sellers
- Restricting competition
- Price fixing and gouging consumers

Figure 13. Failures in the competitive marketplace.

## 3.6 *Profit maximization*

In such a system, firms organize themselves to establish oligopolies, oligopsonies, monopolies, and monopsonies. The pressures for *Pareto-optimal efficiency* and prices set by an equilibrium between supply and demand are lost, see Figure 14.

In such a market environment, firms will try to exploit their market power to maximize profits instead of responding to the demands and expectations of consumers, reducing costs through efficiency gains, and expanding their product lines through innovation. Instead, wherever possible, they will seek to exploit market imperfections, such as information asymmetry and agency role.

## 3.7 *Corruption*

Although larger companies have a board and may even be supervised by external bodies like the Securities Exchange Commission (SEC), most small and medium-sized enterprises are single-owner companies or partnerships. There are few if any mechanisms for ensuring accountability.

Not surprisingly, dishonest behavior by those in positions of power can lead to corruption. Those who abuse their power may be individuals or they may be organizations, such as businesses and even governments. Corruption spans a wide range of activities such as giving or accepting bribes or inappropriate gifts, fraudulent claims, fake products, double-dealing, defrauding investors, and cheating customers.

**Quick Reference to Basic Market Structures**

| Market Structure | Seller Entry Barriers | Seller Number | Buyer Entry Barriers | Buyer Number |
|---|---|---|---|---|
| Perfect Competition | No | Many | No | Many |
| Oligopoly | Yes | Few | No | Many |
| Oligopsony | No | Many | Yes | Few |
| Monopoly | Yes | One | No | Many |
| Monopsony | No | Many | Yes | One |

Figure 14. Market structure.

### 3.8 *Failure in policy formulation*

Private markets are accountable to their owners and customers, not society more broadly. Although recently the notion of "corporate social responsibility" has become fashionable, when left to competitive forces and prices alone, due to market failure, the production and allocation of goods and services usually do not achieve a Pareto-optimal balance. This is usually left begrudgingly to the governments and non-profit organizations that may be driven by a mission, not their "bottom line."

These theoretical underpinnings of market failure in the private sector have parallels in healthcare and in the public sector which will be described in the following sections.

## 4. Government Failure

Discouraged by what they see as pervasive market failure in the private sector, many governments at all income levels, have tried to solve the efficiency and equity problems observed in the health sector by partially or completely eliminating competition and price signals determined by the equilibrium between supply and demand. Instead, they have reverted to Soviet-style command and control methods like what was done in the former Soviet Union during the Communist period (Preker and Feachem, 1996; Preker, 1998, 2018).

Not only has this not worked in solving the efficiency and equity problems in the health sector, but it has often made things even worse by introducing a new range of problems due to government failure.

Some notable examples of government failure that have parallels to market failure observed in the private sector are highlighted in the following: market failure in the nature of public goods and services; information asymmetry; agency problems; transaction costs; market power; profit maximization; corruption; failure in policy formulation.

## 4.1 *Market failure in the nature of public goods and services*

In private markets, problems are encountered when businesses try to sell goods or services that behave like public goods and services. Likewise in the public sector, serious problems are encountered when governments try to give away goods or services that behave like private goods. Black markets almost always emerge simply because private goods are marketable simply because people are willing to pay for them. The intention may be good, but the outcome is almost always bad.

## 4.2 *Information asymmetry*

Information asymmetry can occur in three major ways in the health sector: between patient (public) and healthcare professional; between patient and administrator of the healthcare system; and between healthcare professional and administrator of the healthcare system.

Patients know more about their symptoms than doctors but may — unwittingly or deliberately — not articulate this clearly. Doctors know more about the causes, prognosis, and effectiveness of available treatments but may not communicate this clearly to the patient. Or the patient may not understand the implications of what he/she is being told. For paternalistic reasons, the doctor may deliberately conceal information, based on a judgment that the patient will not be able to cope with the full knowledge of his/her ailment (e.g. terminal cancer). Through self-selection, these problems are typically worse in the public sector, which has to deal with large volumes of poorer and less educated patients.

When it comes to interactions between patients (the public) and healthcare administrators, patients may try to avoid being excluded or paying higher healthcare premiums by choosing to conceal pre-existing conditions. Similarly, there is often a lack of information and understanding of available public programs. The benefit of gathering useful data about such programs is usually undervalued compared with its cost. Some of these programs may be too complex to fully understand even if information were available. Frequently, the lack of transparency in the rationing of scarce resources is deliberate.

Finally, some serious information asymmetries exist between healthcare providers and the administrators for whom they work (or between administrators and owners). Healthcare providers — as advocates for patients — have a much better understanding of legitimate needs or demands. Administrators have a much better understanding of the supply and cost of available resources but know little about a selected intervention's appropriateness or effectiveness. The doctor's well-known information advantage over the patient is not solved by the existence of a public employer or administrator who knows even less about interactions between patients and providers.

### 4.3 *Agency problems*

Just as there are conflicting interests in private markets, so there are conflicting interests in the public sector. In the public sector, civil servants and others (agents) act on behalf of the population (principal). Like in the private sector, agents are supposed to act in the best interest of the principal, but often this does not happen. Both individual and political considerations often distort the behavior of the agent's behavior.

### 4.4 *Transaction costs*

Such information asymmetries add to agency costs in terms of structuring, monitoring, and bonding contracts among agents and principals with conflicting interests (Bennett *et al.*, 1997). Private firms, concerned about profits, have a strong incentive to limit agency costs related to information asymmetry (Fama and Jensen, 1983). Public agencies that are not held to a clear "bottom line" due to unspecified social functions and many complex sources of subsidies do not receive clear signals about the agency cost of such information asymmetry.

Not surprisingly, many public healthcare facilities in low- and middle-income countries do not keep detailed patient records, do not know throughput statistics, and do not know the unit costs of the procedures they are using or illnesses they treat. Hospitals are often not doing what policy-makers or administrators would like or what they think they should be doing. Doctors working in such public hospitals maintain an information advantage that gives them a great deal of latitude to pursue their own interests. Paradoxically, since public systems often give their beneficiaries less leverage than private systems give their clients, patients may be less able to use the information they *do* possess to influence their own treatment.

### 4.5 *Market power*

In most settings, the public sector does not compete with others. Although there have been attempts in Australia and New Zealand to force the public sector to compete with the private sector on a level playing field, most countries do that. Not surprisingly the monopolies, oligopolies, oligopsonies, monopolies, and monopsonies described above also exist in the public sector.

For example, monopoly power occurs for four reasons when the public sector gets involved in producing health services. This may be due to the following: (a) legal restrictions on competition; (b) access to subsidized capital and revenues, creating an uneven "playing field"; (c) below-cost distribution of goods and services to achieve equity goals; or (d) production of public goods or goods where markets are not viable.

When — in addition to the above accountability and information problems — the public sector enjoys monopoly power, people who work for it are given wide scope for abusing this power through the extraction of rents, the internal distribution of "slack" to employees, and the lowering of quality.

Public monopolies exhibit the usual negative features. First, monopoly suppliers often reduce output and quality, while raising prices. The excess in prices over and above what the market would normally bear — *rents* — leads to allocative inefficiency or a net deadweight welfare loss to consumers who have to forgo the consumption of other goods.

A manifestation of such rents is the informal user charges that are commonly levied on patients and their families in public health facilities. In many countries, these rents are not limited to doctors' accepting bribes or peddling influence (allowing privileged patients to circumvent the usual rules on resource allocation, receive preferential treatment, and cut waiting time). It also includes charges levied by other salaried workers for items ranging from toilet paper and clean linen to food, drugs, and medical supplies.

In a past study on corruption around the world, such abuses in publicly run health services ranked number one in terms of the burden placed on households (Kaufmann and Ryterman, 1998). Patients who can afford to pay formal charges in the private sector often prefer it to paying such rents in the public sector. Taxpayers charged twice for low-quality services and such abuses have little recourse but the blunt and often ineffective instrument of voting power.

Second, monopoly suppliers have strong incentives to lower expenditures through decreased output when staff members benefit from the financial residuals. Although public organizations cannot legally distribute such residuals outside the organization to shareholders, they can be internally consumed in several ways. First, executives often receive generous social benefits and travel allowances (perks). Second, time-keeping is often not enforced rigorously (doctors often work short hours in public institutions). Third, some of the residuals may be used to pursue personal agendas (discretionary spending on special projects and research).

## 4.6 *Profit maximization*

Although entities in the public sector, specifically speaking do not make a "profit" they nevertheless have to balance their budget. Often, there are many self-serving reasons that staff in the public sector actively pursue a "surplus" that allows them to get better salaries and use the surplus to develop new programs. The incentives built into Porter's five forces therefore equally exist in the public sector.

## 4.7 *Corruption*

Accountability in the public sector means that government action accords with the will of the people it represents. Yet, since people's values are never perfectly homogeneous in any society, accountability will always be based on some imperfect rule about the aggregation of individual values or respect for minority interests. Although there are no technical limits, few countries use plebiscites, and only for major issues of national interest. Even then, it is an imperfect instrument due to low voter turnout and other constraints.

This raises several intractable procedural issues relating to accountability in the electoral process, taxation policies, content of public spending programs, and vested bureaucratic interests.

The first set of problems relates to the difficult task of translating individuals' preferences into public policy and getting that policy implemented. As we know, all public interventions involve transfers of benefits to some people and costs to others, leaving both winners and losers. Much of this discussion is not new but firmly rooted in political and moral philosophy.

Ballots are blunt instruments that cannot capture the full range of issues that may be bundled together at election time. The intensity of views on any one issue cannot be reflected. Election promises are often not kept. So at best, public spending policies are an imprecise reflection of social values.

Majority rule can be a form of tyranny if applied strictly without constraints. Most democratic societies safeguard minority interests to some extent, but even with good intentions, there are limits to both practicality and desirability in this respect.

Finally, public servants may have strong conflicts between their own interests and their assigned responsibilities to execute the collective will of the society they represent. Their political *overseers* may also have strong vested interests that are different from those of the society that they represent.

Four interrelated causes have been identified that explain this observation (Vining and Weimer, 1990). First, direct democracy usually prevents the overseer from knowing the preferences of society. Second, overseers (representatives) typically pay more attention to constituencies and sensational issues that are most likely to be influential in their reelection. Third, public officials usually have more than one overseer, often leading to conflicting and unstable political demands. Finally, since overseers do not fully benefit themselves from the effectiveness of their oversight, they often devote inadequate time and effort to this task, leaving bureaucrats with a large range of independence.

In an ideal setting, good public accountability would be secured through a large intersection (*authorizing environment*) between fairly homogeneous social values, a political agenda that reflects such values, and vested bureaucratic interests (see Figure 15, left box). For example, there may be general social agreement that the population has to be protected against the financial consequences of illness through some sort of health insurance system. When the policies of the political party in power are consistent with such values and bureaucrats have the capacity to implement them, the intersection will be large (Moore, 1995).

In the health sector, further tension exists between the authorizing environment needed for good public accountability and most individuals' desire for some sovereignty over their own healthcare. This leads to difficult dilemmas during the rationing of care or design of compulsory programs, based on the application of some sort of majority rule that infringes on either perceived minority group rights or individual survival. This was discussed earlier in a later section under agency problems (Beauchamp and Childress, 1983; Lemmon, 1962). Normal rational individuals who may share social values about the need to ration healthcare resources often lose their commitment to such values

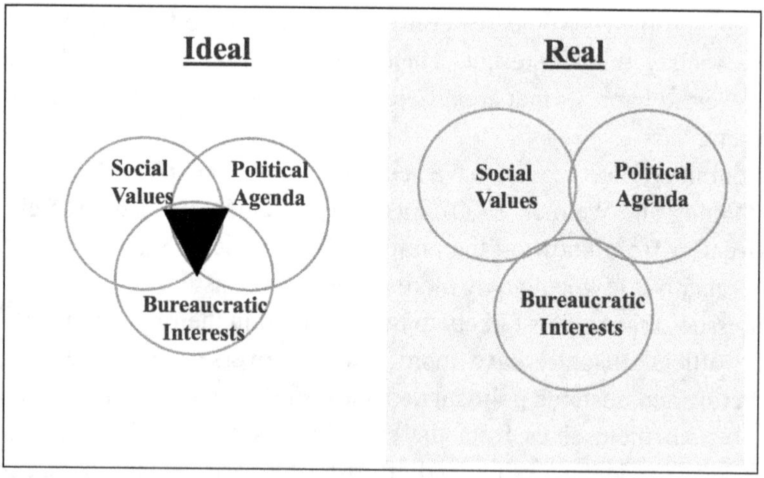


Figure 15. Authorizing environment.

when confronted by resource constraints in the face of serious illness or death.

Sometimes, corruption is difficult to detect due to information asymmetry, and lack of transparency by politicians, bureaucrats, organizations, and healthcare providers entrusted with public accountability.

Although deliberate deception and fiscal fraud are usually sanctioned severely, it is much harder to hold the public sector accountable for petty abuses, avoidance, and obfuscation. Such deception may take the form of hidden costs, subsidies, cost shifting, or inflation. Or it may occur as an amplification of benefits, exaggeration of the consequences of alternatives, or claiming credit for activities that originate elsewhere.

Given the complex nature of healthcare, it is not hard to imagine the considerable scope for misleading or defrauding patients and the public in the health sector.

## 4.8 *Failure in policy formulation*

The most frequently cited reason for greater government involvement in the health sector is that, when left to competitive forces and prices alone, in several other critical areas the market does not lead to welfare-enhancing production and allocation of a number of healthcare goods and services. These include the following:

- public goods (policymaking and information);
- goods with large externalities (disease prevention);
- goods with significant market failure (insurance).

It is therefore surprising that governments in the health sector often neglect the exact same three areas while they are busy producing curative services that the private sector could easily provide. Furthermore, when most public funds are spent on poorly targeted public production, few or no resources are left for strategic purchasing of services for the poor from nongovernmental providers.

The following section presents a discussion of some of the key theoretical underpinnings for a new approach to optimize complementarity between the public and private sectors.

# 5. Reforms Trends

## 5.1 *Policy levers to address market failure*

From the previous discussion, we can see that most goods and services have some degree of market imperfection in terms of achieving *Pareto-optimal efficiency*. Governments have at their disposal a variety of instruments that they can use to address these problems. A few of these instruments — from least to most intrusive — include doing nothing, requiring information disclosure, introducing regulations, contracting for services through prepayments, making direct payments, providing subsidies through reimbursements, issuing mandates, guaranteeing universal access, and resorting to public production, see Figure 16.

Most standard texts on health economics focus on market failure and provide various recommendations on how to address this problem across a range of topics, including health financing, health insurance, capital investments, service delivery, manufacturing of goods like pharmaceuticals, medical technology and IT, health administration and public health. The methods explored will not be part of this review. Readers are encouraged to refer to standard up-to-date sources (Evans, 1984; Rice, 1998; Lee, 2019; Unruh *et al.*, 2023).

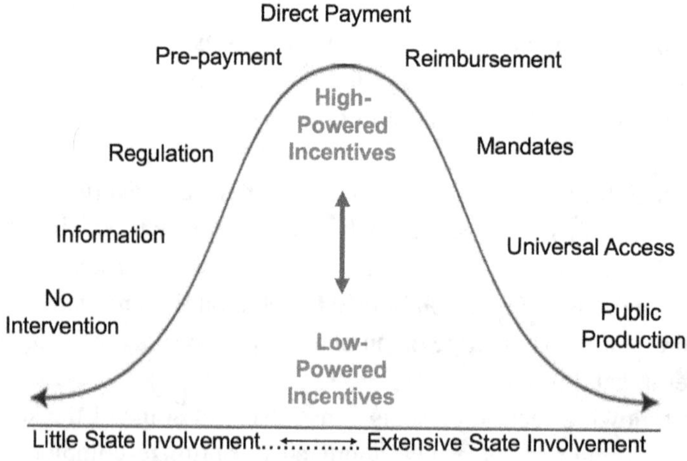


Figure 16. Incentives and instruments of state involvement.

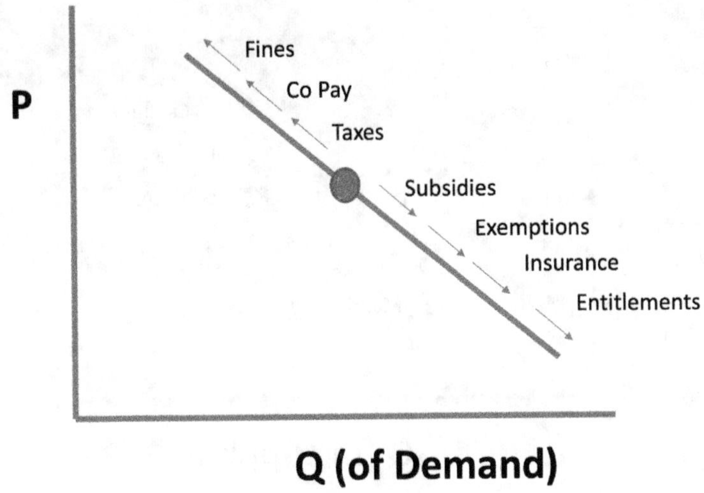


Figure 17. Demand-side financial levers.

On the demand side, several standard financial levers are often used to address market failure and influence consumption by consumers in desired areas. Taxes, co-payments, and fines all increase the effective price to consumers, thereby decreasing demand. Subsidies, exemptions, and insurance all reduce the effective price to consumers, thereby increasing demand. When universal entitlements are offered, consumers have no price signals at all. Other non-monetary factors will determine their demand. These financial levers also affect the slope of the demand curve and shifts in the curve. Such changes are not reflected in the graph in Figure 17.

On the supply side, several standard financial levers are also often used to address market failure and to influence production by providers in the desired ways. Taxes, fines, and mandates all decrease the profit of suppliers. Subsidies, exemptions, and free or reduced cost of capital all increase profit for suppliers. When universal entitlements are offered to the population at a fixed price, suppliers will either increase or decrease production according to their ability to balance their budget. Other non-monetary factors will determine supply. These financial levers also affect the slope of the supply curve and shifts in the curve. Such changes are not reflected in the graph in Figure 18.

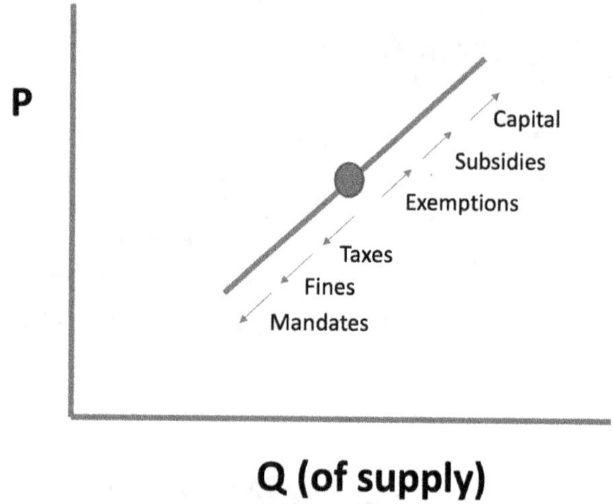


Figure 18. Supply-side financial levers.

## 5.2 *Policy levers to address government failure*

Many attempts have been made in recent years to reinvigorate the public sector through "best-practice" management and other techniques. Borrowed from the private sector and organizational reforms, these tools attempt to replicate the private incentive environment (Osborne and Gaebler, 1993).

These reforms have included efforts to strengthen the managerial expertise of health sector staff, both through training and recruitment policies (Preker *et al.*, 2019). Frequently, attempts are also made to use business process reengineering, patient-focused care, and quality-improvement techniques. Such efforts have also included setting up clinical directorates, introducing improved information systems to facilitate effective decision-making, and performance benchmarking (Saltman and Figueras, 1997).

Why has the public sector been so impervious to these types of management and organizational reforms? (Wilson, 1989; Donahue, 1989; World Bank, 1997a). A review of the origins of problems in government performance reveals profound parallels between the many areas of market failure observed in the private sector and similar problems in the public sector (Wolf, 1979; Peacock, 1980; Weimer and Vining, 1989; Vining and Weimer, 1990).

The current trend worldwide is to use three types of approaches to address the public sector failures in service delivery described above in descending order of importance (Hirschman, 1970; World Bank, 1997). These include the following:

- exit (consumer choice);
- voice (client participation);
- loyalty (unwavering trust/loyalty).

Although each health system is different, some common patterns have emerged. Most healthcare provided by Ministries of Health, especially in low- and middle-income countries, rely heavily on a centralized national health service model of public funding and delivery of health services. These health systems depend heavily on strategic planning, regulations, benchmarking, and management approaches to both funding and providing care. Policymakers, managers, and providers "tell" patients why they are sick and what to do, relying mostly on "low-powered" incentives like "trust" and "loyalty" to influence patient behavior. Patients either play the game and comply with the rules or are deprived of care with no alternatives. Increasingly, it is recognized that this model of care is bureaucratic and non-responsive to patients' perceived needs, disempowering them from involvement in their own care.

As a result, many health systems have tried giving patients a greater "voice" by allowing for feedback through client satisfaction surveys, complaint procedures and lawsuits to address grievances. Although there is a range of "medium-powered" incentives that make funding and healthcare delivery somewhat more responsive to patient needs and expectations, the resulting imbalances between supply and demand almost always lead to long waiting lists, poor quality of care and patient dissatisfaction.

Despite these efforts, such health systems remain bureaucratic and non-responsive, especially when organized in a national and centralized manner. As a result, over the past 30–40 years many policymakers have begun departing from the national health service model of care by introducing "high-powered" incentives, allowing patients to express their choice more directly through some form of "money-follow-the-patient" mechanism. This empowers patients to "vote with their feet" by "exiting" when they are not satisfied.

When patients have a choice and an opportunity to go elsewhere, funders and providers quickly learn that it hurts their "bottom line" when they are unresponsive to the needs of their patients. The funders and providers that survive are those that can deliver "patient-centered care."

This "organic" evolution and convergence toward "mixed" health systems, is in dynamic flux — not static — responding over time to political and ideological pressures on the one hand and market forces on the other hand.

Rarely does technical or systemic analysis alone influence the extent of public and private involvement in the health sector. In reality, both financing and service delivery arrangements are the product of complex economic, social, institutional, and political factors. This in turn affects the business and investment environment of the sector as well as the public/private mix in the health system. It is within this broader context that health policy emerges and exerts an influence on the health market in a mixed healthcare system, see Figure 19.

## 5.3 *Broad trends in public sector reform*

Extensive reforms of public sector organizations and state-owned enterprises, implemented over the past 30–40 years, addressed the same

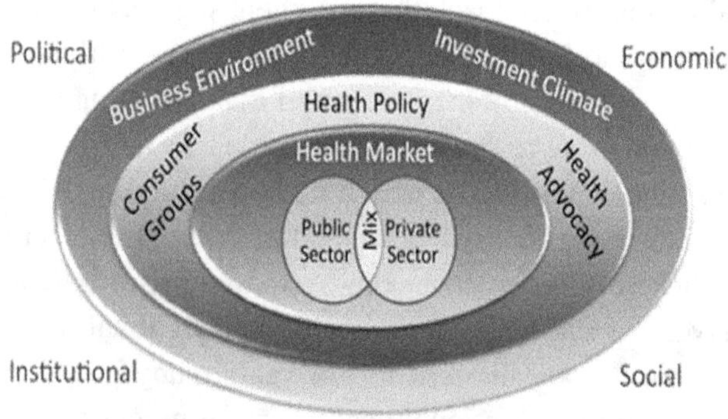


Figure 19. Comprehensive macro framework.

problems encountered in delivering public health services. In the realization that these organizational problems were structural in nature, using the analytical tools of organizational economics, these reforms have focused on altering the institutional arrangements for service. These developments shed light on similar problems in delivering public health services.

One way to understand organizational reforms in service delivery is to view the different incentive environments within which government's tasks can be performed. The civil or core public service lies at the center (usually constitutional control bodies, line ministries), and the activities of the staff are highly determined (Manning, 1998). Job tenure is also strong. Budgetary units (government departments), autonomous units, corporatized units, and privatized units are four common organizational modalities that straddle these incentive environments in the health sector (Preker and Harding, 2000).

In other parts of the public sector, such autonomous and corporatized units are also variously referred to as public or executive agencies, independent public organizations (IPOs), quasi-autonomous nongovernmental organizations (QUANGOs), and state-owned enterprises (SOEs). There is no standard functional distinction between these different organizational modalities, see Figure 20.

The broader public sector is distinguished by the relative flexibility of the financial management regime and managerial freedom in recruitment and promotion. This sector may include special-purpose agencies,

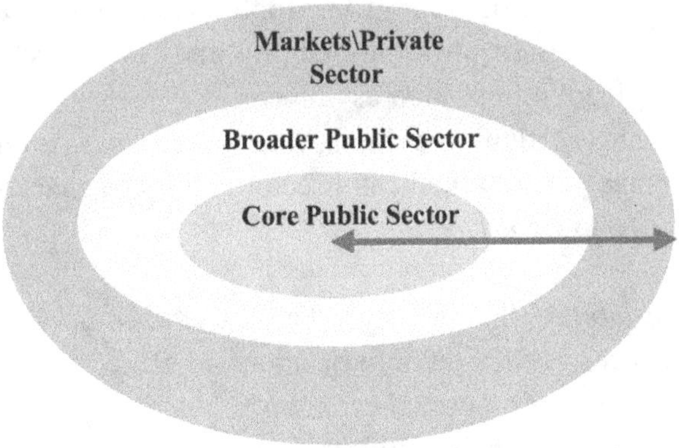


Figure 20. Incentive environments.

autonomous agencies, and on the outer limits, state-owned enterprises. Beyond the public sector lies the domain of the market and civil society. Services may be delivered by for-profit, nonprofit, or community organizations. The incentives for efficient production are higher moving toward the periphery, where service delivery is often better.

Many reforms throughout the world have sought to move delivery away from the center of the circle to more arm's-length contracts with public and private organizations. However, the nature of the outputs and the existence of mechanisms for public sector management of their delivery constrains moving delivery outward.

Increased autonomy or corporatization — moving from the center of the circle to the outer limits — requires accountability mechanisms not tied to direct control. These controls (e.g. contracts) take considerable capacity to write and enforce, especially for health services where outputs and outcomes are difficult to specify.

How far countries may go in pushing activities to incentive environments in the outer circles depends on the nature of the outputs (the services involved) and their capacity to create accountability for public objectives through indirect mechanisms, such as regulation and contracting.

## 5.4 *Application to the health sector*

Looking at the health sector, all healthcare goods and services can be categorized on a continuum from high-*contestability* and high--*measurability* services to low-contestability and low-measurability services, and significant information asymmetry.

The following sections provide a broad discussion on the range of activities that take place in the health sector and try to characterize them in terms of the following:

- their *contestability* (their ability to be subject to competitive forces as would be necessary for them to be allocated efficiently through market forces in a Pareto-optimal economy);
- their *measurability* (their ability to be monitored as would be necessary for them to be allocated efficiently through market forces in a Pareto-optimal economy).

In this respect, factor markets (inputs) and product markets (services) behave differently. They will therefore be discussed separately to highlight their unique characteristics. Although the following discussion refers mainly to activities in the health sector, the analysis could equally be extended to some of the broader intersectoral determinants of good health, such as water, sanitation, education, healthy lifestyle policies, and good nutrition.

**Factor markets:** For the production of inputs, this contestability and measurability matrix would look as follows, see Figure 21.

The production of consumable items and the retail of drugs, medical supplies, and other consumables would be the best examples of highly contestable goods where outputs are also easy to measure (Type I). Many companies usually jostle for a share of the market, and barriers to entry are few (the initial investment capital is modest and there are few requirements for specialized licensing or skills). Unskilled labor also belongs in this category.

As we move across the first row, a number of factors begin to contribute to raising the barriers to entry, thereby reducing the contestability of the goods or services in question (Type I). Investment cost (sunk cost) and increasing technical specifications create moderate barriers to entry in the

| | High Contestability | Medium Contestability | Low Contestability |
|---|---|---|---|
| High Measurability | Type I<br>• Production of Consumables<br>• Retail of<br>• Drugs & Equipment<br>• Other Consumables<br>• Unskilled Labor | Type II<br>• Production of Equipment<br>• Wholesale<br>• Drugs & Equipment<br>• Other Consumables<br>• Small Capital Stock | Type III<br>• Production<br>• Pharmaceuticals<br>• High Technology<br>• Large Capital Stock |
| Medium Measurability | Type IV<br>• | Type V<br>• Basic Training<br>• Skilled Labor | Type VI<br>• Research<br>• Knowledge<br>• Higher Education<br>• High Skilled Labor |
| Low Measurability | Type VII<br>• | Type VIII<br>• | Type IX<br>• |

Figure 21. Production characteristics of inputs.

manufacture of specialized equipment and supplies. Wholesale trade in drugs, medical supplies, and medical equipment has some entry barriers because of the larger investment requirements and more limited supply and distribution chains. The specialization and licensing of pharmacists contribute to these entry barriers. In the case of small capital stock (e.g. clinics and diagnostic centers), entry barriers are created mainly through certification and licensing.

Finally, as we move across to Type III activities, entry barriers are much higher, as in the manufacture of pharmaceuticals and high-technology medical equipment, due to large up-front investment costs that cannot be recovered later during the sale of the assets (sunk costs). These production activities are also associated with costly and long lead times for research, development, and registration of new products. Other barriers to entry under this category include product differentiation (specialized medical equipment) and copyright protection (brand-name drugs). Furthermore, because of the benefits conferred through economies of scope and scale, over time a significant global concentration of pharmaceutical and high-technology industries has occurred, giving them considerable monopoly power.

For all the activities in the first row (Types I–III), the measurability of outputs remains high. There is little information asymmetry.

As we move to the second row, the measurement of the outputs and outcomes becomes more problematic. Outputs and outcomes can be measured, but it is more difficult than in the case of activities in the first row.

Various barriers to entry reduce contestability. Training is almost always associated with special licensing and long lead times (Type V). The specialized labor market is usually associated with many professional barriers to entry as well as subsequent restrictions in the scope of practice and labor mobility. Contestability is even lower in the Type VI category. Most research and other knowledge-generating activities would fall under this category. So does the training of highly specialized staff in universities and other higher education centers.

There are no good examples of inputs for the health sector that would fit into the last row, with significant information asymmetry in addition to measurement problems.

**Product markets:** Interventions and services can also be categorized along a similar continuum from high contestability and high measurability to interventions and other outputs with low contestability, low measurability, and significant information asymmetry. Whereas reduced contestability due to market concentration is one of the main problems encountered in factor markets (production of inputs), a key problem with interventions and other outputs (product markets) has to do with difficulties in specifying and measuring outputs and outcomes, see Figure 22.

As we move to the second row (Type IV to Type VI), measurement of the outputs and outcomes becomes more problematic. Although routine diagnostics such as laboratory tests may be highly contestable (many players in a competitive market with few barriers to entry), monitoring their performance in terms of effectiveness and quality of the activities undertaken is much harder (Type IV). The same is true for various non-clinical hospital activities.

As we move across to the Type V category, contestability is reduced by various barriers to entry. High-tech diagnostics usually requires specialization, licensing, and large sunk costs, giving established players a

| | High Contestability | Medium Contestability | Low Contestability |
|---|---|---|---|
| High Measurability | Type I<br>• | Type II<br>• | Type III<br>• |
| Medium Measurability | Type IV<br>• Non Clinical Activities<br>• Management Support<br>• Laundry & Catering<br>• Routine Diagnostics | Type V<br>• Clinical Interventions<br>• High Tech Diagnostics | Type VI<br>• |
| Low Measurability | Type VII<br>• Ambulatory Care<br>• Medical<br>• Nursing<br>• Dental | Type VIII<br>• Public Health Interventions<br>• Intersectoral Action<br>• In-Patient Care | Type IX<br>• Policymaking<br>• Monitoring/Evaluation |

Figure 22. Production characteristics of outputs.

marked advantage over new entrants. A further barrier to entry for these activities would be government policies that control or restrict the introduction of some new technologies (CAT or NMR scanners). Clinical interventions are usually outsourced only to certified providers. In each of these cases, outputs and outcomes can be measured, but it is more difficult than in the case of activities in the first row.

In addition to difficulties in measuring output and outcomes, most clinical interventions are characterized by an additional constraint of information asymmetry. At times, information may be readily apparent to patients (e.g. the quality of "hotel services" such as courtesy of clinical staff, the length of waiting periods, the cleanliness of linens, the palatability of food, and privacy. Without survey techniques, however, such information may not be readily available to the contracting policymakers or administrative staff.

For these reasons, ambulatory clinical care would fall under the Type VI category (relatively low barriers to entry other than professional qualifications/certification of staff) but high information asymmetry and difficulties measuring outputs and outcomes. As we move across the third row, contestability diminishes due to specialization and cost, in addition to measurement problems. For these reasons, public health interventions, intersectoral action programs, and inpatient clinical care belong to Type VII activities.

This leaves a few clear-cut activities, such as policymaking, monitoring, and evaluation under the Type IX category. The contestability and measurability of these activities are extremely low. These activities are therefore usually retained as a core part of an integrated bureaucracy.

## 5.5 *"Make or Buy" decision grid*

The above framework can be used to guide policymakers in deciding when to "makein-house and when to "buy" services from non-governmental organizations (contract-in or contract-out).

Factor markets and product markets that have both high contestability and high measurability will be clustered in the left upper quadrant. Increasing information disclosure may be all that is needed to improve the performance of such goods and services. Those that have low contestability and measurability will be clustered in the right lower quadrant. Correcting the market failure of such goods and services may require much more aggressive policy interventions such as public financing and government production. Market failure in the goods and services between these extremes may respond well to regulations and contracting, see Figure 23.

**First set priorities:** In many countries, "make or buy" decisions are made before policymakers and providers have gone through an explicit priority-setting process. Priorities specified should include the range of interventions to finance through public resources (including preventive services) and should ensure that public subsidies are appropriately targeted (e.g. to the poor and other vulnerable groups). Countries often rush into "make or buy" decisions before setting priorities for needed and affordable interventions (Ham, 1997). Such prioritization is complicated by the fact that the cost of treating different illnesses varies greatly and often bears little relation to the effectiveness of available interventions (Musgrove, 1999). Furthermore, for a whole range of activities, information disclosure and coordination through a strong stewardship function may be sufficient.

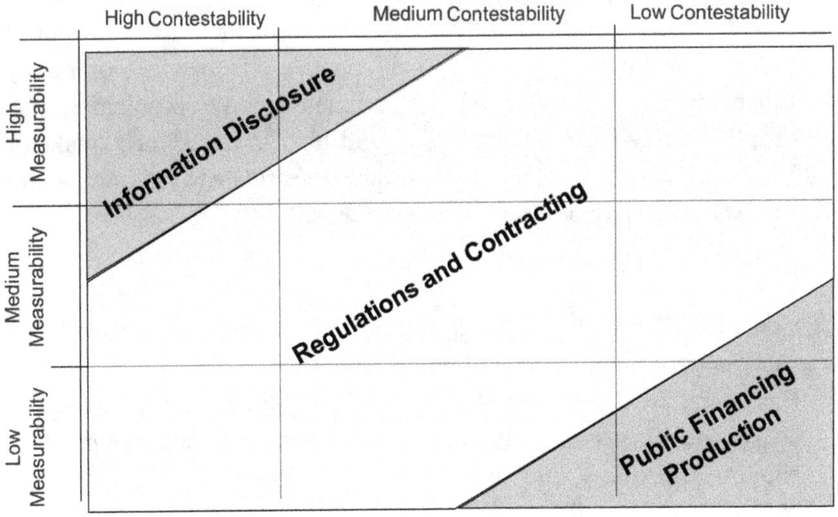


Figure 23. Policies and regulations to address market failure.

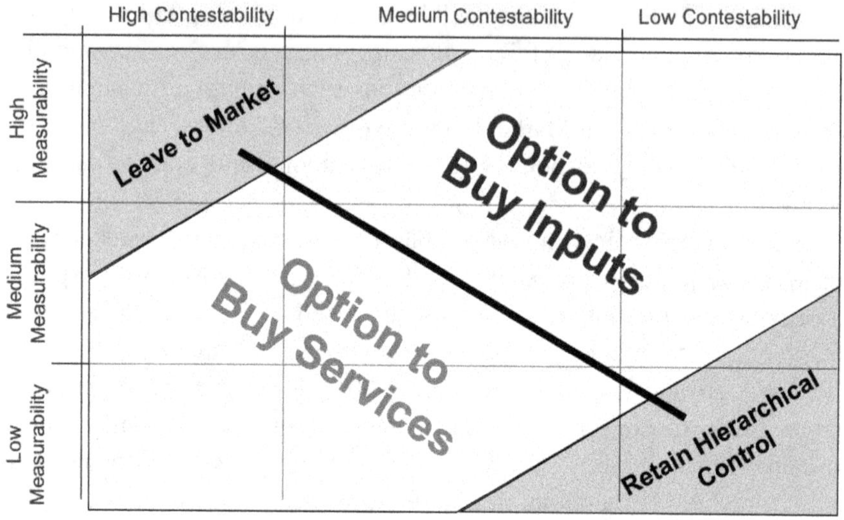


Figure 24. "Make or buy" decision grid.

**Then decide who can produce what:** Based on the above discussion, it is now easy to map the goods and services that can be bought, those where coordination is enough, and those that are better produced in-house by the public sector itself (Figure 24). The size of the "make" in-house production triangle will depend largely on the effectiveness of policy instruments to deal with contestability and measurability problems.

**Finally decide from whom to buy and how to pay:** Once "make or buy" options have been settled, the next questions relate to (b) from whom to buy; (c) how to pay or structure the purchase.

In deciding "*from whom to buy*":

- Consider all possible producers (public, nongovernmental and private-for-profit; domestic, and international).
- Base purchase decision on the best product at the lowest price responsive to specific needs — type of good, price, quantity, after-acquisition support, timeliness, and so forth (consider international competitive bidding when possible).
- If there is currently no market, consider stimulating demand rather than in-house production.

- If contestability is low and there is no competitive market, consider using benchmark purchasing (based on estimated reference costs) so that suppliers have to compete *for* rather than *in* the market.
- If there is a market, but it is dysfunctional, consider improving its function through appropriate incentives (strategic subsidies) or regulations (antitrust).

In deciding "*how to pay*":

- Choose the contractual arrangement most suitable for a given purchase (spot market for unpredictable items, medium-term supply contract for predictable items, franchise arrangements for standardized needs at multiple locations, and relational contract for difficult-to-monitor purchases).
- Once a buying decision has been made, all potential producers must be treated alike by creating a level playing field. This includes ensuring that there are no hidden competitive advantages such as tax concessions or access to subsidized capital. It means ensuring that no unfair competitive advantage is given to any producer through privileged access to information (Harding and Preker, 2000).

### 5.6 *Shift in degree of contestability and measurability*

**Factor markets:** For some inputs — the production of consumables, unskilled labor, and the retail of drugs, medical equipment, and consumables — there are a few serious market imperfections such as reduced contestability and low measurability (Figure, upper left corner of matrix). With minimal government intervention such as good information disclosure and some quality or safety standards, competitive markets are best at producing these inputs. Public production of these inputs usually leads to low quality, lack of innovation, and inefficient production modalities, see Figure 25.

The other extreme — training very specialized labor and generating knowledge about rare health conditions and their treatment — is characterized by considerable market imperfections due to reduced contestability and low measurability. A mix of strong regulation and in-house production is often needed to ensure adequate generation of these inputs.

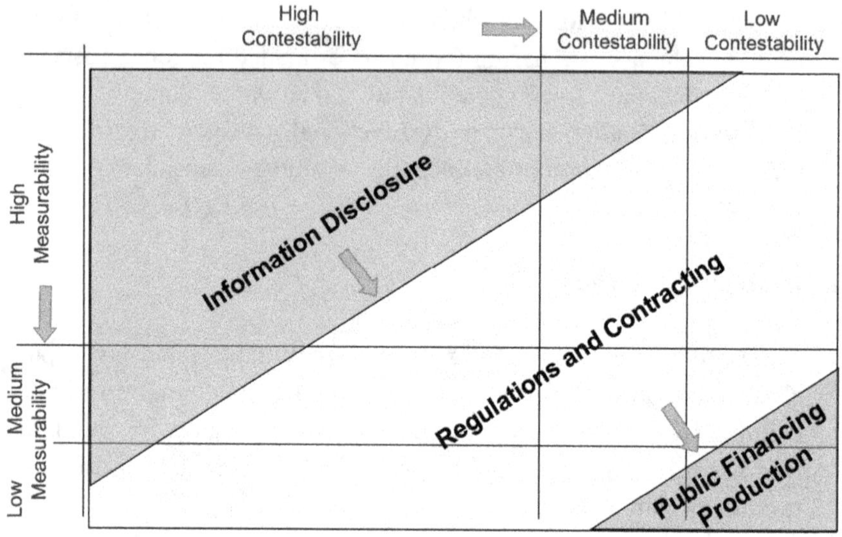


Figure 25. Improving contestability and measurability.

Most other inputs can be bought. However, markets often give the wrong signal about the level (surpluses and shortages), mix, and distribution of these inputs. This is especially true of human resources and the production of pharmaceuticals and medical equipment with a long development or training phase. Skilled use of regulations and contracting mechanisms is therefore needed when purchasing inputs that have moderate contestability and measurability problems.

Large producers may try to severely reduce contestability by erecting strong barriers to entry through protective policies (patents and licensing requirements), benchmarking (manufacturing standards), large sunk cost requirements, collusion, and a high degree of specialization (R&D). For these inputs, stronger policy measures may be needed such as monopsony purchasing power and long-term contracts.

Despite this complex landscape in goods characteristics, in many areas of reduced contestability and measurability, governments could achieve most equity, efficiency, and quality objectives through regulations and contracting (Herzlinger, 1997).

**Product markets:** As in the case of inputs, the production of interventions and other outputs can be "contracted out" (purchased) and do not in principle have to be produced in-house.

In practice, decisions about which interventions to make in-house and which to contract out are complicated by a number of factors. First, for some outputs (e.g. clinical interventions), what is to be delivered is much harder to specify than the inputs. This makes it difficult to manage the resulting contracts and prevent opportunistic behavior by providers (private health insurance is especially vulnerable to opportunistic behavior). Second, contestability is often reduced for the reasons described earlier in our discussion on inputs. Finally, complex health problems often require strategic coordination among different interventions and other outputs (integrated care, continuity of care, appropriate and timely referrals, and the like).

In the case of outputs, policymakers need to examine two critical questions in addition to the degree of contestability and measurability before arriving at good "make or buy" decisions. Is a strategic coordinated response needed? To what degree do the goods and services benefit from ongoing innovation and adaptability?

For example, nonclinical activities such as custodial services, catering, laundry, and management do not require special strategic coordination. They can usually be "unbundled" and "contracted out" as a standard service to firms that specialize in these activities without too much customization. In contrast, clinical and public health interventions often do need to be coordinated and tailored to the individuals and populations receiving them and the organizations providing them. Experience has shown that "unbundling" these activities often leads to many problems such as cost shifting, discontinuity of care, and poor quality (Manning, 1998; Bennett *et al.*, 1997).

## 5.7 *Other factors that influence organizational behavior*

The contestability and measurability of goods and services are not static but influenced by elements of the systemic environment. Government policies directly influence this environment and the "nature of the good," yielding alternative levers to take them closer to (or farther away from) the ability to use the indirect tools of contracting and regulation. These alternative levers include the following:

- **Governance:** The relationship between owner (governments) and healthcare organizations.
- **Market environment:** Competition in or for goods and services markets.
- **Purchasing mechanisms:** Funding or payment arrangements for the goods or services.

These three factors exert a powerful influence on the "nature of the goods" and hence on the ability to ensure delivery through indirect mechanisms. In the following three sections, we will see how these factors combine to determine the level of contestability in the market or measurability of a good. This will include a discussion of which instruments are effective in dealing with the related market and government failures.

**Governance and internal incentive regime:** Changes made in governance — the relationship between government and organizations — influence the characteristics of the healthcare goods and services in question. This relationship can be modified substantially in five different dimensions: (a) the *decision rights* given to managers; (b) the *residual claimant* status; (c) the degree of *market exposure*; (d) *accountability arrangements*; (e) adequacy of *subsidies* to cover social functions (Preker and Harding, 2000).

Contestability may be enhanced by the following:

- unbundling large bureaucratic structures (modification in governance);
- outsourcing other functions to specialized providers (modification in payment system);
- leveling the playing field by exposing all the actors to the same potential benefits and losses due to market exposure (modification in payment system);
- decreasing barriers to entry due to political interference or unwarranted trust in public production (modification in market structure);

- explicitly separating contestable commercial functions and noncommercial social objectives (modification in governance and stewardship).

Measurability may be enhanced by the following:

- relying on quantifiable results (output or outcome measures) for accountability and performance targets rather than process (inputs and bureaucratic procedures) (modification in governance and payment system);
- shifting from difficult-to-define, long-term relationships (employment or service arrangements) to shorter-term, more specific contractual arrangements (modification in payment system);
- using quantifiable monetary incentives instead of more difficult-to-track nonmonetary incentive payments, such as ethics, ethos, and status (modification in payment system);
- tightening reporting, monitoring, and accountability mechanisms (modification in governance and payment system).

For example, by removing restrictive government monopolies from vaccination services (governance/market), such programs could be shifted into a Type II or even Type I position. It is easy to measure the number of children vaccinated, who contract a given disease, and entry barriers for firms that want to provide vaccination services on behalf of the government. Similar action applied to other services could shift many away from the lower right corner of the grid toward the upper left corner.

In this way, goods and services that were of either low or medium contestability or measurability can be made more contestable and measurable. This would affect decisions on "make or buy" in a significant way (Preker *et al.*, 2000), see Figure 26.

Likewise, tertiary, and quaternary care provided in university hospitals could be shifted from a low-contestability/measurability grid to a medium-contestability/measurability position through better information on outcomes, policies that favor clearly defined contracts, performance benchmarks, and a tightening of reporting, monitoring, and accountability mechanisms. The same would be true for public health services and

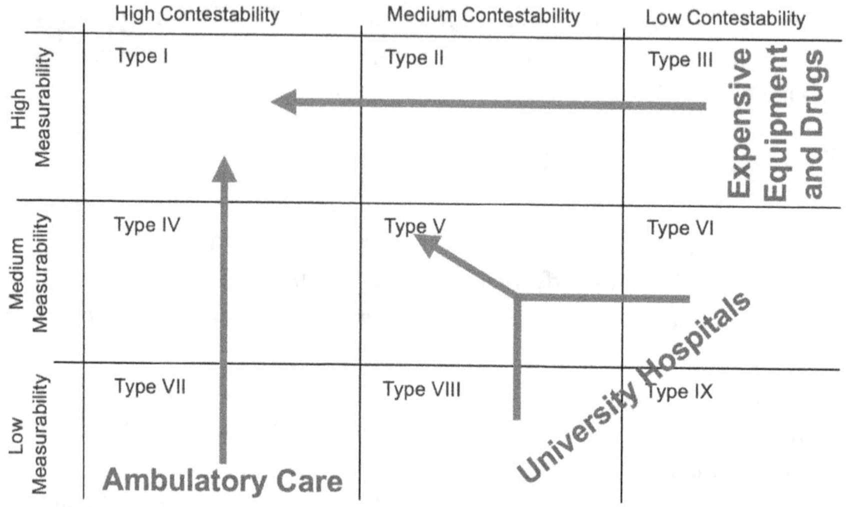


Figure 26. Influence on factor and product markets.

activities such as vaccination that are often part of the responsibilities of ambulatory care providers.

Several factors may also alter the goods characteristics of pharmaceuticals, medical equipment, and consumable supplies. As recently as 10 years ago, development costs, patent protection, and a small market share may have made highly specialized medical equipment or drugs (Type III goods) very expensive. Today, they may behave like ordinary goods (Type II or I). Examples include the quick production of generic drugs by many companies once patent protection expires or the rapid increase in the use of sigmoidoscopes and transcutaneous surgical instruments once the technology was no longer new and prices dropped.

This shift in goods characteristics is not a one-way street. The goods' properties can also become less contestable and more difficult to measure. Organizational reforms do not always lead to increased decision rights, residual claimant status, market exposure, accountability arrangements, and explicit subsidies to cover social functions. In fact, during the past 50 years, many national health systems deliberately shifted goods and services in the opposite direction by nationalizing ownership and production.

Market imperfections may contribute to entry barriers instead of lowering them. Doctors, dentists, and pharmacists can and do collude to restrict entry by potential competitors. Hospitals have a natural monopoly for their services for patients living nearby and can create monopoly power through relations with other hospitals and referring doctors. Medical equipment distributors with licensing agreements for the top international companies can easily monopolize a domestic market. Pharmaceutical retailers can control their markup by forming professional cartels. The public and nongovernmental sectors have a competitive advantage over the private sector due to their access to subsidized or free capital from domestic and foreign donors.

## 5.8 *Market environment*

A central argument in favor of exposing providers to market forces is that, in a functioning market, competitive forces will lead to a more efficient allocation of resources than a command economy or nonmarket solutions. The structure of the market to which organizations are exposed, therefore, has a critical influence on their behavior. It may directly determine what strategies make sense to generate more revenue.

Policies that influence the competitive environment through regulations or contracting can significantly alter the contestability of healthcare goods and services. Similarly, information asymmetry can be reduced by policies that increase the availability of good information on health services, enhance healthcare providers' institutional capacity to deal with such information, and improve patients' understanding of health problems.

Such policies not only address some of the underlying contestability and measurability problems but also shift both the contestability/measurability grid and the boundaries of needed government intervention to ensure favorable outcomes.

Conversely, in a less competitive environment with weak policies and data to overcome information asymmetry, the grid for services that fall into the upper left corner (Type I, II, and IV) may contract, with the grid in the lower right corner (VI, VIII, and IX) expanding.

**Addressing market imperfections in service delivery:** There are two related problems in the market structure of service delivery in most segments of the health sector. First, little or no competition may emerge, reducing the pressures on the provider to deliver "value for money" to maximize profits. Alternatively (or in addition), competition may emerge, but it may be dysfunctional. Both cases are discussed in this section.

Some health services, especially tertiary and quaternary, exhibit scale economies in production. This relieves incumbent hospitals from pressure from new entrants. Geographic monopoly over certain services may leave buyers very little leverage to negotiate with service providers. There are many examples of strong collusion among medical doctors that create a virtual monopoly, thereby shifting the grid for ambulatory medical care toward the left — and strengthening the need for direct provision or other policy intervention. Public monopolies and policies that prevent public funds from being used to contract services from the private sector have the same negative effect on contestability.

As seen earlier, even for services where monopoly power is not an issue, providers may still capture market share or maximize profits through various forms of distortionary behavior described by Porter's five forces.

Such distortionary features of health service markets often enable providers to the following: (a) counter the bargaining power of suppliers, patients, or purchasers; (b) ward off threats posed by new entrants and imitation products; (c) control a large share of the relevant market.

Information asymmetry in the health sector exacerbates these problems. For example, medical treatment is largely a "bundled" good where the seller (doctor) guides patients' consumption decisions: which hospital to go to for surgery, which lab to use for diagnostic services, and so on. Thus, providers can parley their information advantage into control over a rigid and lucrative referral chain. Doctors may "forward integrate" into diagnostic labs or pharmacies and steer their patients toward consumption where they have a financial stake. Hospitals may "backward integrate" by creating strong links with doctors, thereby cornering part of the market where they experience little or no competitive pressure. Medical professionals are frequently able to create cartels, limiting competitive pressures that strengthen the influence of patients and purchasers.

Since patients and payers know less than providers about the true value or cost of health services, providers can cream-skim, selecting patients who cost less to treat than other patients. Thus, providers can increase their profits, not by delivering better service to capture market share or cutting costs but by choosing more profitable patients.

Most of these market imperfections in service delivery can be corrected through appropriate regulations and contracting arrangements.

A few examples will illustrate this point. Equal access to capital and antitrust legislation, limiting the power of professional cartels, can significantly decrease the entry barriers for some segments of the healthcare market, especially for clinical services that fall in the middle band of the contestability/measurability grid. The same would be true for contracting practices that are open to both public and private providers and which leave open possibilities for choosing alternative providers or exercising "exit" strategies.

In other instances, supplier cartels, combined with low quality-control standards, shift activities such as retail sales and distribution of pharmaceuticals and medical equipment into the lower right corner, even though such activities belong in the upper left area of high contestability and measurability.

**Addressing market imperfections in private health insurance:** Even if private health insurance is contestable, due to severe information asymmetry, such services are often deliberately crowded out for strategic reasons by restrictive policies and public financing (Musgrove, 1996, 1999). As in the case of service delivery reforms, the default is often to nationalize and eliminate private health insurance completely.

This is shortsighted because it almost always leaves part of the population without adequate risk pooling. Instead, there are a number of economic and institutional reforms that could be used to address many of the market imperfections in private health insurance (Evans, 1984; Dror and Preker, 2002; Preker and Carrin, 2004; Pauly *et al.*, 2006; Preker *et al.*, 2006, 2010, 2013; Preker, 2018).

This topic is beyond the scope of discussion here, but is discussed in detail later and briefly in Box 4.

## 5.9 *Purchasing mechanisms*

Finally, provider payment systems also influence goods properties by interacting with three of the five key elements of the internal incentive regime of healthcare organizations: distribution of residual claims, market

**Box 4. The market imperfections of private health insurance**

Private voluntary health insurance is one area that is particularly prone to market imperfections, many of them related to information asymmetries.

Insurance may succeed in protecting some people against selected risks, but it usually fails to cover everyone who wants to subscribe to insurance plans and often excludes individuals who need health insurance the most or who are at the greatest risk of illness. This happens because insurers have a strong incentive to enroll only healthy or low-cost clients (risk selection or cream-skimming). Private insurers also have incentives to exclude costly conditions or minimize their financial risk by using benefit caps and exclusions. This limits protection against expensive/catastrophic illnesses.

Due to these factors, individuals who know they are at risk of illness have a strong incentive to conceal their underlying medical condition (adverse selection). Individuals who are — or think they are — healthy will often try to pay as low premiums as possible. This prevents insurers from raising the funds needed to cover the expenses incurred by sicker or riskier members. Worse, the healthy may even deliberately underinsure themselves in the hope that free or highly subsidized care will be available when they become ill (free-riding). When third-party insurers pay, both patients and providers have less incentive to be concerned about costs, and some may become careless about maintaining good health. This leads not only to more care being used (the reason for insurance) but also to less effective care or care that would not be needed if people maintained good health (moral hazard).

exposure, and provision for social functions (Preker and Langenbrunner, 2005; Preker *et al.*, 2007).

Service providers, in particular, respond differently to alternative funding and payment mechanisms. For example, collective purchasing by a strategic social health insurance fund in Germany sends a different set of signals to providers than the regulated competition in the United States, consumer-driven demand through out-of-pocket payments in India, medical savings accounts in Singapore, and monopsonistic purchasing in the United Kingdom.

Although reforms in governance may endow an organization with formal claims to residual revenue in different categories, the structure of the payments system will directly determine whether this claim has any real meaning or incentive effect. If, for example, services must be delivered at prices below cost, there will be no residual to claim. Thus, the relation of costs to the price-setting and capital-charging formula in the payments system is a critical determinant of the incentives of the model. The crucial factor is whether marginal cost-saving efforts by the provider can generate revenue flows that the provider can keep without deterioration in quality or effectiveness.

When reforms in organizations such as hospitals entail a shift in revenue earning by delivering services "in a market," what kind of market emerges becomes a crucial issue. Often, the government is the largest or only buyer. In this case, the process and terms on which the government purchaser engages the provider may well determine the degree of pressure on the provider to "deliver the goods."

To gain maximum benefits from reforms that expose the public sector to competition with the private sector, it is crucial that adequate steps are taken to secure competitive neutrality.

Two sets of policies must be built into provider payment systems to achieve competitive neutrality:

1. Monetization of social functions such as explicit subsidies that cover the cost plus a reasonable margin in delivering services to nonpaying or uninsured patients.
2. Leveling of the playing field through standardization of the fee structure and cost of capital for both the public and private sectors.

## 6. Getting from Here to There

As seen above, although there may be an argument for a continued and even an enhanced role for the state in providing strong sectoral *stewardship* and reform that mandate equitable and sustainable financing, the argument for strong state involvement in other areas of the health sector is much weaker.

Many countries today have large inefficient public sectors that produce goods and services which could be bought from non-governmental and private providers. Moving from one system to another will not be easy (Figure 27). Such a shift in the role of the state from direct control to oversight takes time and must be accompanied by capacity building in areas, such as contracting, regulation, and coordination of non-governmental providers.

A three-step process can be used to move gradually from one balance to another in the public–private mix in service delivery:

1. When there is already a large private sector, the public sector can begin by recognizing its existence and slowly increase the use of these resources through better coordination, contracts, and a positive regulatory environment.
2. Once some learning has taken place in coordinating and contracting with existing providers, the positive lessons from this experience can be transferred to other priority areas where nongovernmental providers may not yet be active.
3. In some cases where the public sector is clearly engaged in inefficient activities such as the public production of many inputs, these can be converted through outright privatization and subsequently bought from the private sector (Harding and Preker, 2000).

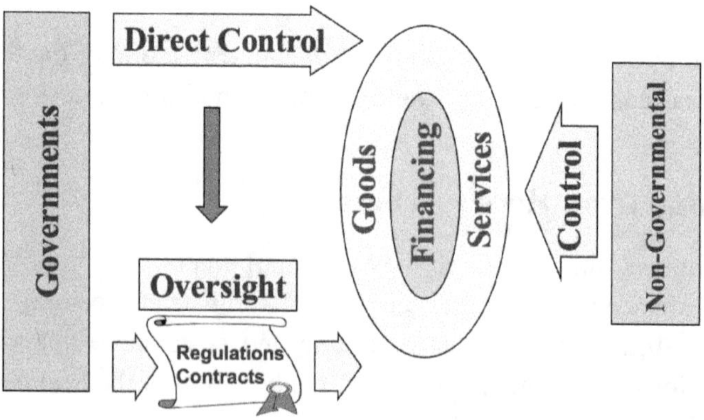


Figure 27. Shift from direct control to oversight.

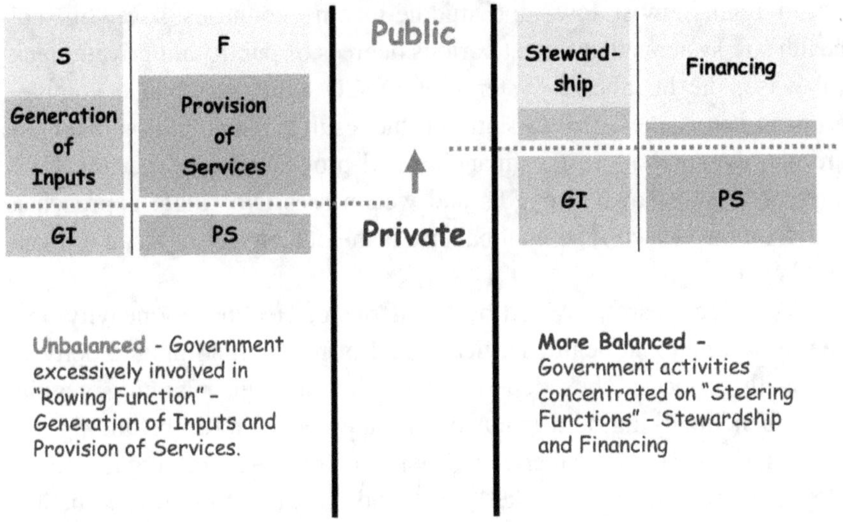


Figure 28. Adjusting balance in mixed health systems.

At the same time, the public sector may not currently be involved in strategic areas of importance where it should be. This would include activities such as ensuring that there are mechanisms to secure financial protection against the cost of illness and provide critical sectoral oversight in terms of its stewardship function. Parallel to moving out of the area of production of goods and services where the private sector can make a positive contribution, a strong argument can be made for a more integrated approach and greater public sector involvement in stewardship, policy-making, sectoral coordination, regulation, monitoring, and evaluation, see Figure 28.

## 7. Conclusion

Political debate about healthcare financing and delivery of care continues to present many "false dichotomies" between different approaches: public vs private ownership and service delivery; government vs non-governmental funding; civil service vs. contractual employment; planning vs competitive markets; public health vs patient-centered care, etc. The list is long.

In reality, most low- and middle-income countries have "mixed" healthcare systems that reflect various degrees of public and private roles. Likewise, the healthcare systems of OECD countries span a complex range of approaches. This evolution is the result of a recognition that there are no silver bullets in the financing and provision of healthcare. Each approach has its own strengths and weaknesses. No single approach is sufficient on its own. The final balance is the outcome of a "strife of interests" over time.

Most healthcare provided by Ministries of Health, rely heavily on a centralized national health service model of public funding and delivery of health services. They depend heavily on strategic planning, regulations, benchmarking, and management approaches to both funding and providing care. Policymakers, managers, and providers relying mostly on "low-powered" incentives like "trust" and "loyalty" to influence patient behavior. They tell why they are sick and what to do. Patients either play the game and comply with the rules or are deprived of care with no alternatives. This model of care is bureaucratic and non-responsive to patient's perceived needs. It disempowers them from involvement in their own care.

Recently, many of health systems give patients a "voice" by allowing for feedback through client satisfaction surveys, complaint procedures and lawsuits to address grievances. There is a range of "medium-powered" incentives that make funding and healthcare delivery somewhat more responsive to patient needs and expectations. But often this is not enough. Imbalances persist between supply and demand. This almost always lead to long waiting lists, poor quality of care and patient dissatisfaction.

Such health systems remain bureaucratic and non-responsive. This is even worse when they are organized as a national health services and in a centralized manner. As a result, in recent years, many policymakers have departed from the national health service model of care. Instead they have introduced "high-powered" incentives that allow patients to express their choice more directly through some form of "money-follow-the-patient" mechanism. This empowers patients to "vote with their feet" by "exiting" and chose other funders or providers when they are not satisfied.

Funders and providers quickly learn that it hurts their "bottom line" when they are unresponsive to their patients who end up going elsewhere for their care. The funders and providers that survive are those that can deliver "patient-centered care."

The opposite trend is equally true in countries that are at an earlier stage in the development of their health systems. In many low- and middle-income countries that have not yet introduced some form of risk-sharing mechanisms such as health insurance and where public subsidies for healthcare are so low that the range and quality of services provided through the state system is rudimentary and inadequate, patients must rely mostly on direct out-of-pocket payments to providers. Although these health systems rely mostly on "high-powered" incentives and patients can "vote with their feet," such systems leave individuals and families with no financial protection against the high cost of catastrophic illness or expensive care. They are also vulnerable to unscrupulous behavior, profit-seeking providers, and a wider range of known market failures. These healthcare systems are progressing toward more policy, regulatory or quality oversight.

There is no single perfect system. Not surprisingly, in recent decades, there has been a convergence across income levels and regions of the world toward mixed healthcare systems that combine all three incentive regimes: low-, medium- and high-powered.

The authors of this book paint a vivid picture of how, in many countries, the functions of policymaking, planning, monitoring, surveillance, and core medical education are dominated by the public sector, whereas activities in the manufacturing sectors, such as pharmaceuticals, medical technology, health IT and a wide range of other inputs to healthcare, are dominated by the private sector. Everything else is somewhere in between. This includes management, provision of services, diagnostics, financing, and allied healthcare activities that are needed to make the health system function.

This "organic" evolution and convergence toward "mixed" health systems, is in dynamic flux — not static — responding over time to political and ideological pressures on the one hand and market forces on the other hand. High-performing health systems focused on the needs of patients and outcomes rather than inputs and processes.

## References

K. W. Arrow. (1963). Uncertainty and the welfare economics of medical care. *American Economic Review* **53**(5): 940–973.

K. Arrow. (1980). *Arrow's Theorem: The Paradox of Social Choice*. Yale University Press, New Haven.

A. B. Atkinson and J. E. Stiglitz. (1980). *Lectures on Public Economics*. McGraw-Hill, Maidenhead.

L. M. Barer, T. E. Getzen, and G. L. Stoddart (eds.). (1998). *Health, Health Care and Health Economics: Perspectives on Distribution*. John Wiley & Sons, Chichester, West Sussex, England.

N. Barr (ed.). (1994). *Labor Markets and Social Policy in Central and Eastern Europe*. World Bank/Oxford University Press, Oxford.

N. Barr. (2005). *Labor Markets and Social Policy in Central and Eastern Europe: The Accession and Beyond*. World Bank, Washington, D.C.

F. Bator. (1958). The anatomy of market failure. *Quarterly Journal of Economics* **72**(3): 351–79.

W. J. Baumol. (1984). Towards a theory of public enterprise. *Atlantic Economic Journal* **12**(1): 3–20.

W. J. Baumol, J. C. Panzar, and R. D. Willing. (1982). *Contestable Markets and the Theory of Industrial Structure*. Harcourt Brace Jovanovich, New York.

T. L. Beauchamp and J. F. Childress. (1983). *Principles of Biomedical Ethics*, 2nd edn. Oxford University Press, Oxford, p. 4.

S. Bennett, B. McPake, and A. Mills (eds.). (1997). *Private Health Providers in Developing Countries: Serving the Public Interest?* Zed Books, London.

D. Black. (1984). *An Anthology of False Antitheses* Nuffield Provincial Hospital Trust, London.

British Medical Association (BMA). (1984). *Handbook of Medical Ethics* BMA, London, p. 6.

C. B. Chapman. (1984). *Physicians, Law, and Ethics* New York University Press, New York, pp. 4–5.

J. D. Donahue. (1989). *The Privatization Decision: Public Ends, Private Means*. Basic Books, New York.

D. Dror and A. S. Preker (eds.). (2002). *Social Re-Insurance: A New Approach to Sustainable Community Health Financing*. Health, Nutrition and Population Series World Bank/ILO, Washington.

A. Enthoven. (1978). Consumer choice health plan. *New England Journal of Medicine* **298**(12): 650–658; **298**(13): 709–720.

A. Enthoven. (1988). *Theory and Practice of Managed Competition in Health Care Finance*. North-Holland, New York.

R. G. Evans. (1984). *Strained Mercy*. Butterworth, Toronto.

E. F. Fama. (1980). Agency problems and the theory of the firm. *Journal of Political Economy* **88**(2): 288–307.

E. F. Fama and M. C. Jensen. (1983). Agency problems and residual claims. *Journal of Law and Economics* **26**(2): 327–349.

N. Girishankar. (1999). Reforming institutions for service delivery: A framework for development assistance with an application to the HNP portfolio, *World Bank Policy Research Working Paper 2039*. World Bank, Washington.

C. Ham. (1997). Priority setting in health care: Learning from international experience. *Health Policy* **42**(1): 49–66.

A. Harding and A. S. Preker (eds.). (2000). *Private Participation Toolkit*. World Bank, Washington.

R. Herzlinger. (1997). *Market Driven Health Care: Who Wins, Who Loses in the Transformation of America's Largest Service Industry*. Perseus Books, Reading, Massachusetts.

A. Hirschman. (1970). *Exit, Voice, and Loyalty: Responses to Decline in Firms, Organizations, and States*. Harvard University Press, Boston, Massachusetts.

M. C. Jensen and W. H. Meckling. (1976). Theory of the firm: Managerial behavior, agency costs and ownership structure. *Journal of Financial Economics* **3**: 305–360.

D. Kaufmann and R. Ryterman. (1998). Global corruption survey, *World Bank Working Paper*. World Bank, Washington.

B. Klein, R. G. Crawford, and A. A. Alchian. (1978). Vertical integration, appropriable rents and the competitive contracting process. *Journal of Law and Economics* **21**(2): 297–326.

R. Lee. (2019). *Economics for Healthcare Managers*, 5th edn. ACHE, Chicago.

E. J. Lemmon. (1962). Moral dilemmas. *Philosophical Review* **71**: 139–152.

N. Manning. (1998). Unbundling the state: Autonomous agencies and service delivery. *Draft World Bank Discussion Paper*.

J. K. Mason and R. A. M. Smith. (1987). *Law and Medical Ethics*, 2nd edn. Butterworths, London, p. 4, quoting Castiglioni, A. *A History of Medicine*, translated and edited by Krunbhaar, E.B. 2nd edn. 1947).

P. Milgrom and J. Roberts. (1990). Bargaining costs, influence costs, and the organization of economic activity. In Alt, J. and Shepsle, K. (eds.), *Perspectives on Positive Political Economy*. Cambridge University Press, New York, pp. 57–89.

P. Milgrom and J. Roberts. (1992). *Economics of Organization and Management*. Prentice-Hall, Englewood Cliffs, NJ, pp. 291–292.

M. Moore. (1995). *Creating Public Value: Strategic Value in Government*. Harvard University Press, Boston.

R. A. Musgrave and P. B. Musgrave. (1984). *Public Finance in Theory and Practice*, 4th edn. McGraw-Hill, New York.

P. Musgrove. (1996). *Public and Private Roles in Health: Theory and Financing Patterns*. World Bank, Washington.

P. Musgrove. (1999). Public spending on health care: How are different criteria related? *Health Policy* **47**: 207–223.

OECD. (1992). *Regulatory Reform, Privatisation and Competition Policy*. OECD, Paris, p. 17.

M. Olson. (1982). *The Rise and Decline of Nations: Economic Growth, Stagflation and Social Rigidities* Yale University Press, New Haven.

Osborne, D. and Gaebler, T. 1993. *Reinventing* Government. Plume, New York.

M. V. Pauly, P. Zweifel, R. M. Scheffler, A. S. Preker, and M. Bassett. (2006). Private health insurance in developing countries. *Health Affairs* **25**(2): 369–379.

A. Peacock. (1980). On the anatomy of collective failure. *Public Finance* **35**(1): 33–43.

M. Porter. (1979). How competitive forces shape strategy. *Harvard Business Review* (March–April), 137–145.

A. S. Preker. (1998). The introduction of universal access to health care in the OECD: Lessons for development countries. In Nitayarumphong S. and Mills, A. (eds.) *Achieving Universal Coverage of Health Care*. Ministry of Public Health, Bangkok, pp. 103–124.

A. S. Preker. (2018). *Universal Access to HealthCare: A Comparative Review of Landmark Legislative Health Reforms the OECD* World Scientific: New Jersey.

A. S. Preker, H. Beciu, and E. L. Keuffel. (2019). *Financing the Education of Health Workers: Gaining a Competitive Edge* World Scientific: New Jersey.

A. S. Preker and G. Carrin (eds.). (2004). *Health Financing for Poor People: Resource Mobilization and Risk Sharing*. Health, Nutrition and Population Series. World Bank/ILO/World Bank, Washington.

A. S. Preker and R. G. A. Feachem. (1996). Market mechanisms and the health sector in Central and Eastern Europe, Technical Paper Series No. 293 (Washington: World Bank); (translated into Czech, Hungarian, Polish, Romanian, and Russian).

A. S. Preker and A. Harding (eds.). (2000). *Innovations in Health Service Delivery: Corporatization in the Hospital Sector*. World Bank, Washington.

A. S. Preker, A. Harding, and P. Travis. (2000). "Make or buy" decisions in the production of health care goods and services: New insights from institutional economics and organizational theory. *Bulletin of the World Health Organization* **78**(6): 779–790.

A. S. Preker and J. C. Langenbrunner. (2005). The role of purchasing in hospital performance. *World Hospitals and Health Services Journal* **41**: 22–29.

A. S. Preker, M. E. Lindner, D. Chernichovsky, and O. P. Schellekens. (2013). *Scaling up Affordable Health Insurance: Staying the Course*. Health, Nutrition and Population Series. World Bank, Washington.

A. S. Preker, X. Liu, and E. V. Velenyi (eds.). (2007). *Public Ends, Private Means: Strategic Purchasing of Value for Money in Health Care*. Health, Nutrition and Population Series. World Bank, Washington.

A. S. Preker, R. Scheffler, and M. C. Bassett. (2006). *Friend or Foe: Private Health Insurance in Development.* Health, Nutrition and Population Series. World Bank, Washington.

A. S. Preker, P. Zweifel, and O. P. Schellekens. (2010). *Global Marketplace for Private Health Insurance: Strength in Numbers.* Health, Nutrition and Population Series. World Bank, Washington.

T. Rice. (1998). *The Economics of Health Reconsidered*. Health Administration Press, Chicago.

U. Unruh, A. J. Barnes, and T. Rice. (2023). *The Economics of Health Reconsidered,* 5th edn. AUPHA/HAP, Chicago.

J. Robinson. (1997). Physician-hospital integration and economic theory of the firm. *Medical Care Research and Review* **54**(1): 3–24.

R. Saltman and J. Figueras (eds.). (1997). *European Health Care Reform: Analysis of Current Strategies*. WHO, Copenhagen, pp. 213–214.

D. E. Sappington. (1991). Incentives in principal-agent relationships. *Journal of Economic Perspectives* **5**(2): 45–66.

G. Schieber (ed.). (1996). *Innovations in Health Financing*. World Bank, Washington.

W. G. Shepherd. (1984). Contestability vs. competition. *American Economic Review* **74**(4): 572–587.

W. G. Shepherd. (1995). Contestability vs. competition—once more. *Land Economics* **71**(3): 299–309.

A. Smith. (1776). *An Inquiry into the Nature and Causes of the Wealth of Nations*. W. Strahan and T. Cadell, London.

E. van Doorslaer, A. Wagstaff, and F. Rutten (eds.). (1993). *Equity in the Finance and Delivery of Health Care: An International Perspective*. Oxford Medical Publications, Oxford.

J. S. Vickers and G. K. Yarrow. (1992). *Privatization: An Economic Analysis.* MIT Press: Cambridge, Massachusetts.

A. R. Vining and D. L. Weimer. (1990). Government supply and government production failure: A framework based on contestability. *Journal of Public Policy* **10**(1): 1–22.

D. L. Weimer and A. R. Vining. (1989). *Policy Analysis: Concept and Practice*. Prentice Hall, Englewood Cliffs, NJ.

O. Williamson. (1985). *The Economic Institutions of Capitalism: Firms, Markets and Relational Contracting*. Free Press, New York.

O. Williamson. (1989). Chapter 3: Transaction cost economics. In Schmalensee, R. and Willig, R. (eds.) *Handbook of Industrial Organization*. North-Holland, New York.

O. Williamson. (1991). Comparative economic organization: The analysis of discrete structural alternatives. *Administrative Science Quarterly* **36**: 69–296.

J. Q. Wilson. (1989). *Bureaucracy* Basic Books, New York.

C. J. Wolf. (1979). A theory of non-market failure. *Journal of Law and Economics* **22**(1): 107–139.

WHO. (1996). European Health Care Reforms: Analysis of Current Strategies, Series No. 72. WHO Regional Office for Europe, Copenhagen.

WHO (World Health Organization). (2000). World Health Report 2000: Health Systems Performance. WHO, Geneva.

WHO (World Health Organization). (2010). World Health Report 2010: Health Systems Financing: The Path to Universal Coverage. WHO, Geneva.

World Bank. (1993). World Development Report 1993: Investing in Health. Oxford University Press, New York.

World Bank. (1994). World Development Report 1994: Infrastructure for Development, A World Bank Policy Research Report. World Bank, Washington, D.C.

World Bank. (1995). Bureaucrats in Business. The Economics and Politics of Government Ownership, A World Bank Policy Research Report. World Bank, Washington, D.C.

World Bank. (1996). Chapter 8: Investing in people and growth, *1996 World Development Report: From Plan to Market* Oxford University Press, New York, pp. 123–132.

World Bank. (1997a). World Development Report: The State in a Changing World. Oxford University Press, New York.

World Bank. (1997b). Sector Strategy: Health, Nutrition, and Population. World Bank, Washington, D.C.

World Bank. (2002). Building Institutions for Markets. World Development Report 2002. World Bank, Washington, D.C.

UNICEF. (1999). State of the World's Children UNICEF, New York.

P. Young. (1986). *Privatization around the Globe: Lessons from the Reagan Administration*. National Center for Policy Analysis, Houston, January.

V. M. Zubok. (2021). *Collapse: The Fall of the Soviet Union*. Yale University Press, Yale.

# Index

## World Scientific Series in Health Investment and Financing

*(Continued from page ii)*

---

Vol. 1 *Financing Universal Access to Healthcare: A Comparative Review of Landmark Legislative Health Reforms in the OECD*
by Alexander S. Preker

*Forthcoming*

*Financing Universal Access to Healthcare: A Comparative Review of Incremental Health Insurance Reforms in the OECD*
Alexander S. Preker

*Capital Finance in the Health Industry: A User Manual for Investors and Companies*
Alexander S. Preker and Les Funtleyder

*Internationalization of Medical Education: Investing in the Future of Health Around the World*
Anette Wu

www.ingramcontent.com/pod-product-compliance
Lightning Source LLC
LaVergne TN
LVHW011657200926
848484LV00004B/974